2ε

MORE
THAN
WORDS

Lou Block, MA, CAP, LMHC

CHICAGO SPECTRUM PRESS
LOUISVILLE, KENTUCKY 40207

This book is designed to provide you with accurate information about self-help so that you can deal more effectively with situations that concern you. However, your own situation may be different from the ones described in this book. In addition, circumstances are subject to change and varying interpretations. As a result, this book is sold with the understanding that the author nor the publisher is engaged in rendering specific professional services to any individual.

Copyright © 2004 by Lou Block

CHICAGO SPECTRUM PRESS
4824 BROWNSBORO CENTER
LOUISVILLE, KENTUCKY 40207
502-899-1919

All rights reserved. Except for appropriate use in critical reviews or works of scholarship, the reproduction or use of this work in any form or by any electronic, mechanical, or other means now known or hereafter invented, including photocopying and recording, and in any information storage and retrieval system, is forbidden without written permission of the author.

Printed in the U.S.A.

10 9 8 7 6 5 4 3 2 1

Library of Congress Control Number (LCCN): 2004108261

ISBN: 1-58374-100-3

To Bobby:

*Your Memory will be
with me forever*

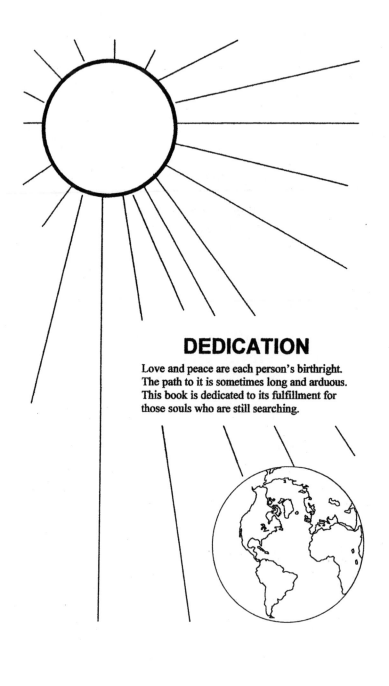

DEDICATION

Love and peace are each person's birthright.
The path to it is sometimes long and arduous.
This book is dedicated to its fulfillment for
those souls who are still searching.

PREFACE

The following pages outline this man's journey through discovery and recovery from the various wounds that were inflicted upon me and the pain I heaped upon those wounds as I reacted.

My transformation was accomplished as I gathered additional data to expand my cognitive process, worked to release long-frozen feelings, and practiced new behaviors to replace my old automatic self-defeating patterns.

Along this path, my Higher Power brought many teachers into my life. Out of their teachings came my process of recovery.

I have chosen to use an overall developmental approach to present what I have learned.

Hopefully, this book will be the catalyst to release you from your "bondage to self" (inability to change self-defeating behaviors) or the impetus to start you on your journey of self discovery.

MAY THE FORCE BE WITH YOU!

ACKNOWLEDGEMENTS

To all the great therapists in psychology who came before me and helped to open up my mind, expand my horizons, and clarify my thoughts. At times, the challenge was almost too great.

To my early teachers who wrote, lectured and taught about self-help. Without you, I wouldn't have the framework from which I operate today.

To all those in self-help who gave of themselves unselfishly when my need was the greatest. Without your unconditional love, support and continuous encouragement, I would not have made it.

To my writing team: Betty Lou B., Stephanie G., Peg W., Kathy L., and Judy M., who read, critiqued, typed, and proofed More Than Words into the finished product you are reading today. This was not an easy task for them and I am eternally grateful they joined my great adventure. Special thanks is given to Judy M. in demonstrating unconditional love to me when my son died....when so many were running away from me because of the intensity of my grief....she was able to hold me as I cried and healed. All should have friends like you Judy. Your demonstration of love will remain in my heart forever.

To Jay Mowery, who on a very bleak Saturday night, took two hours of his time, gave me the last piece to my puzzle, and changed my life profoundly. You were truly one of the angels my Higher Power has put into my life to guide me on my journey of self discovery and recovery.

To all the clinical supervisors I've had in the past who challenged me to be a good therapist. Thank you, thank you, thank you for making me live up to your high expectations.

To my psychodrama teacher, friend, and spiritual sister, Lori Naylor: Your openness, warmth, and talent, demonstrated to me how to be a gentler human being who could remain open to the intuition the universe was sending and use it in therapy for the client's highest good.

To my children, who have forced me to stay in life today and leave my antiquated thinking behind. I hope I've lived up to what your expectations of a Dad are. I've loved all of you from the moment you were conceived and will continue to do so until my last breath.

To my son, Bobby, whose death brought me to a depth of feelings that gave me only two options: One was to shut down and die: The other was to remain open, finish the work I had started, and live. I chose life! The ability to conceptualize and write this book is a by-product of his death. I love you Bobby, know you are at peace, and know Nana and Papa are watching over you.

To one of the most special women in my life, my sister Roberta, without whom I would never have made it out of early childhood nor endured as an adult. When I needed her, she was there. Everyone should have a sister like mine. The world would be a ten-times better place to live in. I love you very much Robi!

To my wife, my Soul Mate, who through her love, support and generosity, brings to my life a softness and quality that in the past I could only dream about. It was worth all the work that I've done, Jane. Without it, your soul would have passed me by in its journey. My love for you is forever.

CONTENTS

PREFACE 5
ACKNOWLEDGEMENTS 6
INTRODUCTION 16
ASSIGNMENTS 19
CASE STUDIES 20
ILLUSTRATIONS 21
AUTHOR'S INTENTION 24

AWARENESS

PART I: CONCEPTUAL OVERVIEW
CHAPTER ONE
    Overview 30
    Childhood trauma 31
    Impact of the problem 33
    Process 35
    The loop 36
    Energy system 37
    Transformation 39
    Life style 39
    Personal management system (pms) 40
    Summary 41
    Case studies 42

CHAPTER TWO
    Overview 45
    Consciousness 46
    The model 46
    Depth of the psyche 47
    Selective process 48
    Structure of cognition 49
    Conscious 50
    Preconscious 51
    Subconscious 54
    The Role Of Self-help 55
    Behavior As A Suppressant 55
    The Road 56
    Tasks Of The Journey 58
    Using The Program 61
    The Human Perceptual System 62
    Summary 63
    Case Study 65

CHAPTER THREE
    Overview 67
    Operating System 68
    Matrix Of The Operating System 70
    Surface Level Of Emotion 70
    Range Of Feelings 71
    Triggers 74

Impact 74
Process Of Change 75
Stress 78
Decision Tree 79
Summary 80
Case Study 81

PART II: PERSONALITY DEVELOPMENT
CHAPTER FOUR
Overview 85
Childhood 86
Impact 88
The Rules 88
Shame 89
Conclusion 90
Societal Determinants 90
Production-oriented Culture 90
Object-oriented Value System 91
Summary 92

CHAPTER FIVE
Overview 94
Adolescence 95
Impact 95
Process 97
Clinical Observation 98
Acting Out 99
Summary 100

CHAPTER SIX
Overview 102
Adulthood 103
Three-stage Process Of Adult Maturation 103
Impact 104
Childhood Tasks 105
Outcomes 107
Adolescent Tasks 108
Outcomes 110
Adult Competence 111
Summary 112
Case Study 114

ACCEPTANCE

PART III: INTEGRATION
CHAPTER SEVEN
Overview 120
Ego States 121
Filters 121
Example Of The Filtering Process 121
Internal Response Of The Filtering Process 124
Informed Consent 126
Structure 128

Analogy Between Physical And Psychological Development 129
Summary 131

CHAPTER EIGHT
Overview 132
Child Ego State 133
How The Child Ego State Presents 134
Reframing 135
The Power Of Shame 135
Developmental Deficits As Triggers 137
Stage One: Trust Vs. Mistrust 137
Stage Two: Autonomy Vs. Shame And Doubt 138
Stage Three: Initiative Vs. Guilt 139
Stage Four: Industry Vs. Inferiority 140
Summary 141
Case Study 142

CHAPTER NINE
Overview 144
Adolescent Ego State 145
How The Adolescent Ego State Presents 146
Reframing 148
Fear Of The Adolescent 148
The Power Of Shame 150
Developmental Deficits As Triggers 153
Stage Five: Identity Vs. Identity Confusion 153
Stage Six: Intimacy Vs. Isolation (Second Period) 155
Summary 158
Case Study 160

CHAPTER TEN
Overview 163
Adult Ego State 164
Tasks Of The Adult Ego State 164
The Power Of Shame 165
Developmental Deficits As Triggers 166
Early Adulthood 167
Stage Six: Intimacy Vs. Isolation (Second Period) 167
Age 30 Transitional Period 172
Middle Adulthood 172
Stage Seven:Generativity Vs. Self-absorption 172
Late Adulthood 177
Stage Eight:Integrity Vs. Despair 177
Summary 182
Case Study 184

PART IV: APPLICATION
CHAPTER ELEVEN
Overview 188
Internal Dialogue 189
Structure 191
Internal Dialogue Of The Child 192
Internal Dialogue Of The Adolescent 193

Internal Dialogue Of The Adult 194
Answer For Who Wrote The Child Section 205
Another Learning Experience 206
Summary 207
Case Study 208

CHAPTER TWELVE
Overview 211
The Grief Process 212
Grief As A Road In Life 213
Emotional Matrix Of The Grief Process 216
The Emotional Twilight Zone 217
Grief As A Therapeutic Framework 221
Factors Involved In The Process 222
Shock 225
Impact Of The Ego States 226
Potency Of The Five Factors 226
Denial 226
Spirituality In The Process 227
Impact Of The Ego States 228
Potency Of The Five Factors 229
Anger 231
Impact Of The Ego States 233
Potency Of The Five Factors 234
The Repertoire Of Problem-solving Skills And Strategies 235
Bargaining 236
Impact Of The Ego States 236
Potency Of The Five Factors 239
Emotional Twilight Zone 241
Depression 241
Acceptance 242
Summary 244
Case Study 245
Conclusion 248

CHAPTER THIRTEEN
Overview 250
Spirituality 251
What Is It? 251
Recognizing When You Have Spirituality 253
Application Of The Book 255
How Do You Keep It? 256
Roadblocks 257
The Impact Of The Ego States 259
The Child Ego State 260
The Adolescent Ego State 261
The Adult Ego State 261
Summary 267
Case Studies 268

ACTION

PART V: ADAPTATION
CHAPTER FOURTEEN
Overview 278
Addiction 279
Definition 279
Dsm-IV 279
Twelve-step Definition 279
Author's Definition 282
The Cycle Of Addiction 282
What Does It Look Like 283
Where Does It Come From 285
Pain Management Model 287
Structure 287
Culture 288
Assessment Of The Addiction's Spiral 290
Degree Of Use 291
Depth Of Damage Done 291
Effective Strategies To Combat Addiction 292
Gateway Drugs 292
Shame As A Gateway Drug 293
Summary 296
Case Study 298

CHAPTER FIFTEEN
Overview 301
Therapy 302
Psycho-dynamic/Developmental Paradigm 303
Process Of Therapy 305
Phase One 306
Phase Two 307
Phase Three 308
Borderline Personalities 308
Verbal Cues 309
Areas To Be Explored In Therapy 311
The Counseling Paradigm 312
The Model 312
The Counseling Process 313
The Ego States 313
The Consciousness 314
Counseling Goals And Tasks 315
The Process Of Resolution 318
The Grief Process 318
The Ego States 319
Cognitive And Affective Components 323
Diversity Of The Ego States 325
Journey Of The Ego States 327

The Completed Process 331
The Paradigm's Effectiveness.. 333
Effective Communication 334
Increased Learning... 334
Greater Productivity 335
Expanded Flexibility 335
Enhance The Developmental Process 335
Concise Probes 337
Relapse Prevention 338
Pain Management Construct 338
Relapse Prevention Training.. 340
Summary 344
Case Study 345

CHAPTER SIXTEEN
Overview 350
Twelve Step Program 351
Twelve Step Doctrine 351
A New Design For Living 352
A System Of Recovery 353
Clarity For Newcomers (And Also Long-timers) 355
Boundaries 355
Trust 360
Sponsorship.. 362
Support System 366
Outgrowing People — Not The Program 367
Summary 368

PART VI: SYNTHESIS
CHAPTER SEVENTEEN
Overview 370
Relationships 371
Part I : The Structure 371
Self Discovery 372
Definition 372
Problem And Solution 373
Needs 373
Maturation.. 377
Spirituality In Relationships 381
The Internal Structure 387
Central Personality 387
Executive System 388
Summary 395
Case Study 397

CHAPTER EIGHTEEN
Overview 401
Relationships — Part II 402
The Problem: Hidden Agenda 402

The Hidden Agenda In Relationships 402
Relationships = Confusion Multiplied By Two 404
Interactions Between Ego States 407
Structure Of The Ego States 408
Domination By The Child Ego State 410
Dysfunctional Reactions To The Domination 411
Domination By The Adolescent Ego State 411
Dysfunctional Reactions To The Domination 420
Domination By The Adult Ego State 429
Dysfunctional Reactions To The Domination 430
Summary 435

CHAPTER NINETEEN
Overview 438
Relationships - Part II 439
The Solution: Adult Domination 439
Adult Domination Of The Executive System 439
Adult Process 439
First Reaction 441
Second Reaction 442
Third Reaction 442
Adult Outcomes 443
Awareness 444
Reframing 444
Acceptance 448
Cognitive Restructuring 448
The Grief Process 449
Ethics 450
Integrity 452
Intimacy 454
Spirituality 458
Action 460
Change 461
First Order Change 462
Second Order Change 466
Process Of Change 468
Application 472
The Workplace 475
Your Boss Is Not Your Parents 476
Peers And Subordinates 479
Summary 479

CHAPTER TWENTY
Overview 483
Transformation 484
Life As A Problem 485
The Problem Loop 485
The Internal Structure 489

Life In The Solution 493
Life On Life's Terms 494
Multiple Stressors 499
Adaptive Process 501
The Perceptual System 501
The Language Path Of The Human Brain 503
Summary 508
Case Study 508

WHERE ARE THEY NOW 513
EPILOGUE 518
REFERENCES 524

INTRODUCTION

The most consistent statements and questions that I hear when people first enter recovery or therapy are: "Why do I do the same thing over and over expecting things to be different?" "Why can't I stop my current self-destructive behavior?" "I feel numb all the time." "I don't know what I'm feeling." "Why am I afraid all the time?" "Where do these feelings come from and what triggers them off?" "I was doing so well in my recovery, something happened, and I relapsed." "Why do I pick the same kind of person to have a relationship with and always end up hurt?" "Why do I hurt the ones I love?" "Why am I so alone?" "I feel like I'm on the outside looking in." "I feel like an alien and I'm waiting for them to come back to take me to a real world in which I belong."

Many people who ask these questions say they feel like they are crazy and afraid that someone will find them out and lock them up forever. They're not! They were brought up in a home that didn't meet their needs on a consistent basis WHEN THEY NEEDED IT. In the process of not getting these needs met, the developing youngster was wounded and had to devise a strategy in order not to feel its impact. The results of the following two combined: 1) Ineffective parenting and 2) Subsequent reaction by the developing person, sets the stage toward self-alienation as one learns to shut down, stuff and deny his feelings; thereby never getting in touch with his wants, needs or desires; and needs another person, place or thing to complete him. When one is out of touch with himself, he very rarely understands or gets his true needs met.

This concept is not about blame. Everyone, including parents, do the best they can with what they have. In fact, all the families I've had in therapy made it better for their children than they experienced themselves. Most thought they did a good job considering what parenting they received. And some, when given new parenting strategies and therapy to relieve the blocks from their past pain, were able to change. Unfortunately, not all were able to. Some came to a point in recovery and remained there. Some dropped out because the pain was too great. I personally feel, that in time, and a lot of patience with oneself, that all the changes one needs to make to have a healthy, happy, and productive life can be realized. This book is dedicated toward that goal.

It is this author's intention to give you a new framework for self awareness and personality development, in which you can lay a solid foundation or augment your existing one, and build a new life in which the following can occur:

1. Identify and label your feelings
2. Learn through patience what triggers your emotions
3. Know what issue is connected to them
4. Gain insight into what developmental age-stage they emanate from
5. Recognize the process of your internal responses
6. Know where you are on the road of your journey, with each of your issues
7. Experience relief from the guilt, shame, and impacted grief of past events that traumatized you
8. Have healthy choices to current self-defeating behavior that mires one in ongoing dysfunctional or problematic behavior of trying to change using the same old mind set

The overall strategy of the book will follow a developmental model in which the author will use an interactive approach with the reader in order to facilitate the best possible learning and assimilation of the new data. In this way, psycho babble and jargon will be kept to a minimum to eliminate as much confusion as possible when the new concept is being learned by the reader.

To insure that the author's intent of this book is realized by the readers, sound educational psychology practices of repetition, with a combination of seeing and doing, will enhance the learning process. The author will endeavor to tie the new paradigm (therapy or Personality Development) to current patterns of self-defeating behavior.

This book was not meant to be read once and put away. It is to be used over and over until one breaks the chains from the past that keep him in self-defeating behavior. Once the reader has the concepts of this book, the new information can be used repeatedly and applied to all areas of life to help gain a better understanding of one's self and their environment.

It is suggested by the author that the reader do two things: 1) Keep notes on what comes to your mind or is stirred up by the text, and 2) Write down your own personal information throughout the systems that are described. REMEMBER! Go easy on yourself. Life is a journey – not a destination.

Part One operationalizes my new paradigm. Within its pages, the human psyche is conceptualized as a system that enters, orders, and acts upon all external data that is relevant to the individual in order for him to survive, to build a life, and to complete his spiritual tasks.

Chapter One describes the circumstances in which the developing human being is sidetracked from his primary path toward self-actualization. Within its process, the growing individual develops what I call The Problem Loop, which is nothing more than a behavior sequence, designed to be used obsessively and compulsively in order to block, cover over, or medicate the rising feelings of past repressed trauma. The psychic pain originates from things that were done to him, not done for him, and what he did to himself as he reacted to the abuse or deprivation with dysfunctional behavior. Chapter Two conceptualizes the human cognitive system, demonstrates how external data is entered, interpreted, and acted upon. Chapter Three illustrates how feelings become the operating system of perception and how in its matrix, can alter the meaning of incoming data regardless of whatever it was meant to be.

Part Two is a theory of personality development which uses Erickson's Stages of Development as a framework to demonstrate how the evolving human being is sidetracked from actualizing and completing his spiritual task (the reason he was born). Chapter Four explores the impact of childhood, Chapter Five the role adolescence plays in human drama, and Chapter Six how early development effects all three stages of adult development.

Part Three is an integration of Parts One and Two into an operational model in which the therapist can better assess and treat his client, self-help members can understand themselves clearly and identify their issues sooner, and other earth people (non-program individuals) can have greater understanding of themselves, others, and the culture. Chapter Seven describes how the Ego States bring color to the tapestry we call life. Chapter Eight explores the basic data needed for living, Chapter Nine, the energy it takes to place the data into living, and Chapter Ten, how the data and energy are modified over the human life span to adjust to changing life events.

Part Four is the application of my new paradigm. Chapter Eleven shows it in relation to one's internal dialogue. Chapter Twelve adds a substructure to the model and demonstrates how the resolution of an issue occurs. Chapter Thirteen adds a spiritual component to the model's matrix and completes its architecture.

Part Five adapts the paradigm to the main thrust of this book: Chapter Fourteen to addiction, Chapter Fifteen to therapy and its process, and Chapter Sixteen to the workings of a Twelve-Step Program.

Part Six for most readers will be the nuts and bolts of this book as it takes the information from all the preceding chapters, applies it to relationships (Chapters Seventeen, Eighteen and Nineteen) and explains the human transformation process (Chapter Twenty).

ASSIGNMENTS

1. List of people who see and hear what they want to 49

2. List the situations when your reality was altered by others 49

3. How do you handle stress 62

4. How did your family model stress reduction? 71

5. List: a) Changed behavior b) Relapse type behavior. 77

6. List your current stressors. 79

7. Survey your cultural feelings about being productive 91

8. Identify your value system with people and possessions 92

9. Who do you know that disallows their internal cues? 124

10. Did you complete the tasks in your
    childhood development? 141

11. Are you codependent? 155

12. Do you recognize any adolescent developmental deficits? 158

13. How has your adult development progressed? 181

14. What voice dominates in your internal dialogue? 206

15. How do the stages of the Grief Process impact you? 243

16. What does spirituality mean to you? 265

17. What does addiction mean to you? 295

18. a) Therapists – Do you follow a model in therapy? 343

    b) Counselors – Does your therapist follow a model?

    c) Self Help Members – Did this chapter allow you to help
       yourself with more understanding?

19. What are your boundaries? 359

20. How do you trust? 362

21. Do you blame a present partner for a past hurt? 364

22. How were your needs met in your previous relationships? 372

23. How do you get your present needs fulfilled? 377

24. How is your spiritual maturation in relationships? 386

25. Which ego state is in charge of your Executive System
    when you are under stress? 395

26. Pretest to determine what is operating internally during
    relationships with others 407

27. Does your Child dominate your Internal Structure?............. 419
28. Does your Adolescent dominate your Executive System? 427
29. Which part of your Adult dominates your
     Executive System? 433
30. Identify your character traits that you feel are assets. 447
31. Identify behaviors you want to change and can't 465
32. Where are you on the road of transformation? 506

CASE STUDIES

1. Introduction of each case study 42-44
2. **Joe** in the Caribbean 54
3. **Dennis'** exploration of his ego states and the Grief Process ... 59
4. **Joe's** inability to use his awareness in the Caribbean 65
5. **Joe's** process in therapy 81
6. **Tanya's** two-stage process of losing childhood 97
7. Projecting **Tanya** into adulthood without recovery 114
8. **Joan's** inability to interpret her internal cues........................ 124
9. **Joan's** incomplete tasks of her childhood development 142
10. **Joan's** incomplete tasks of her adolescent development 160
11. **Mary's** entire process of recovery in treatment 184
12. **Brent & Sandy's** encounter with the critical parent............ 208
13. **Bill's** process of relapse when he entered the
     Emotional Twilight Zone 219
14. **Polly's** healing in therapy using the stages of
     the Grief Process 245
15. Example of spirituality for each case study 268-274
16. **John's** Gateway Drug and process in therapy 294
17. **Dennis'** process of recovery after his relapse...................... 298
18. **John's** self awareness using the Ego States 304
19. **John's** process of recovery 321
20. **John's** blocks in therapy broken down by each ego state 325
21. **Darlene's** process of recovery in therapy............................ 345
22. **Bill's** relapse when he didn't follow the program 352
23. **Joan's** adult process of changing codependent
     relationships 397
24. **Constance's** inability to take charge of her
     Child in treatment 419

25. **Stan's** inability to take charge of his Adolescent
     in treatment 427
26 **Brent & Sandy's** process through conflict 433
27. **Joe's** backward process to recovery 462
28. How **Joe** stopped reacting to his wife................................... 467
29. How **Joan's** problem loop medicated her past pain 487
39. **Joan's** internal process of how she skewed and acted upon
     tainted data 490
40. **Bill's** process of therapy 508

ILLUSTRATIONS

1.1 The Problem Loop 36
1.2 Energy System of the Problem Loop 37
1.3 Transformation Process 38
2.1 Operating Process of the Human Cognitive System 47
2.2 Visual Depiction of the Mind's Depth..................................... 48
2.3 Filters of the Conscious 51
2.4 Two-Stage Process of the Preconscious 53
2.5 How Behavior Becomes a Suppressant 56
2.6 The Path of Human Awareness 58
2.7 The Human Perceptual System and Cognitive Process 63
3.1 Operating System of Perception 68
3.2 Range of Feelings Scale.. 70
3.3 Linear Relationship Between Positive
     and Negative Feelings 72
3.4 Relationship as Positive Feelings are allowed in 74
3.5 Relationship when Positive Feelings are Sustained 74
3.6 How Triggers Operate in the Mind.. 75
3.7 Steps to Facilitate Change 76
3.8 Levels of Stress for Life Events 78
3.9 Decision Making Process 80
5.1 Two-Stage Process of Losing Childhood 97
7.1 Filtering Process of the Ego States 123
7.2 Three Level Process of Perception 126
7.3 Visualization of the Three Ego States...................................... 129
7.4 Parallels Between Physical and Psychological Development   130
8.1 Process of a Shame Attack.. 136

9.1 Developmental Process of Codependency 155
12.1 Detour From the Path of Life Due to a Life Event 214
12.2 The Grief Process as a Road 214
12.3 The Path of the Grief Process 215
12.4 Emotional Composition of the Grief Process 217
12.5 The Emotional Twilight Zone 219
12.6 Probable Outcomes Responding to Major Losses
     or Changes 224
12.7 Feelings Anger Suppresses 232
12.8 Process of Exposing Feelings 233
12.9 Combat Field of the Ego States in Early Recovery 237
12.10 Positions of the Ego States in Middle Recovery 238
12.11 Harmony of the Ego States in Late Recovery 239
13.1 The Road of Spirituality 253
13.2 Path of Connection With a Higher Power 255
13.3 Collaboration Between the Ego States 362
13.4 Consequences of Deviating From One's Spiritual Path 266
14.1 The Addiction Cycle 285
14.2 Remaining In the Problem Instead of the Solution 286
14.3 Connecting the Head with the Heart 290
14.4 Substance Abuse Indicators 291
15.1 Map of the Human Being's Internal Structure 317
15.2 Path of Resolution 319
15.3 The Path of Resolution Including the Ego States 321
15.4 Path of Resolution for an Integrated Personality 323
15.5 Possible Paths of the Ego States when Resolving Issues 329
15.6 Possible Nine Positions of the Ego States in
     the Grief Process 330
15.7 Complete Process to Work Through an Issue 333
15.8 The Relapse Cycle 339
15.9 Discovery Process of Relapse Antecedents 340
16.1 Process of the Twelve Steps 350
16.2 Visual Depiction of Boundaries 359
16.3 Trust Scale 361
17.1 Dysfunctional Process of Fulfilling Needs 376
17.2 The Executive System 389
17.3 Functional Development 391
17.4 Dysfunctional Development 392
18.1 Interactions of the Ego States 409
18.2 Spirituality in Relationships 414

18.3 Repeated Shifts of the Adolescent to Adolescent Mode 424
19.1 Re-balancing a Character Asset 446
19.2 Process of re-balancing a Character Trait............................ 447
19.3 The Process of Growing Apart in a Relationship 455
19.4 Backwards Process of Awareness 463
19.5 Process of Behavior Change 466
20.1 Path of the Problem Loop 487
20.2 Problem Loops 489
20.3 Influence Domain of the Ego States 493
20.4 Life Events Over the Human Life Span 495
20.5 Life's Path in "The Family Life Cycle" 496
20.6 Alteration of Life's Path in "The Family Life Cycle" 497
20.7 The Life Path of the Dysfunctional Family 499
20.8 Impact of Multiple Stressors on Resolving Issues 500
20.9 The Human Perceptual System and Cognitive Process 502
20.10 Initial Response to Negative External Stimuli 504
20.11 Internal Responses to Threatening External Stimuli 504
20.12 Interruption of Old Self Defeating Behavior Patterns 555

AUTHOR'S INTENTION

"More Than Words" is a powerful self-awareness tool. It was designed as:

1. A Do-it-yourself manual for those in a twelve-step program, or any other traveler on this Starship Earth, who wanted to gain greater insight into themselves, others, or human motivation in relationships.
2. An adjunct for the therapist's repertoire of skills to:
   a. Increase assessment skills
   b. Bond quicker with clients
   c. Decrease resistance in individual or group therapy sessions
   d. Increase the quality of communication in therapy sessions
   e. Enhance the therapist's skill-building abilities with clients in order to:
      1) Decrease the amount of therapy sessions or groups the client attends.
      2) Increase the client's ability to accomplish second-order behavior change

Included in the book's concepts is a new self-awareness paradigm which offers:

1. A visualization of the Human Cognitive Structure
2. A road map into the components of the mind's structure
3. Instructions on how to use the data generated by the new awareness in:
   a. What issue was triggered (if any) in any situation?
   b. Which part (ego state) of the human psyche was affected?
   c. The remaining distance, of the raised issue, for resolution or acceptance
4. A theory of personality development and the dysfunction that occurs when an individual's development is sidetracked or skewed due to:
   a. Addiction (alcohol, drugs, food, gambling, sex, work, criminality, etc.)
   b. Trauma (individual, family, cultural, etc.)
   c. Delayed or underdeveloped because of missing life skill data

Purpose of the Book

1. Reconnect one to his spiritual path by the following process:
   a)Stop his current self-defeating behavior through new information (education)
   b)Clean up the past obstacles to his current progress (therapy)
   c)Clear the mind (teach the new paradigm and its applications)
2. At the end of the process, one will recognize his spiritual goals,
   have better relationships with self, others and God, and have a
   greater potential to be happy if he allows himself to go through
   the process.
3. The book's primary spiritual purpose is to help quiet down the
   current noise level in one's head in order to receive spiritual
   guidance. When the spiritual voice is present, the individual is
   congruent within themselves (thoughts, feelings, and behaviors
   are the same), connected to God, and able to discover his "birth
   vision" or perform his spiritual tasks.

The Book's Strategy

The book is a developmental strategy, designed to increase a human
being's self-awareness by giving him a roadmap to his internal psychological structure. Within the book's process, the following can be
accomplished:

1. Lower resistance to change by using a common language
   (developmental terms)
2. Shorten up the process of recovery in therapy and self-help.
3. Create a greater understanding of one's thoughts, feelings and
   behavior.
4. Increase one's awareness of the internal motivation, which
   generates relationships, for him and others.
5. Expose the manner in which codependence or dysfunctional
   behaviors are spawned as a reaction to cover the overwhelming
   shame one feels when his developmental tasks of his various
   life-stages are not completed. In its process, the developing
   human being becomes wounded and:
   a)Shuts down instead of feeling
   b)Becomes dissociated from himself instead of acquiring the
   tools to develop greater self-knowledge

      c)Covers up the pain instead of developing emotional maturity by going through it

      d)Becomes enmeshed in relationships instead of remaining autonomous

      e)Doesn't feel whole within himself and usually needs another person (relationship), place (property or job), or thing (addiction, money, car, etc.) to complete him. Without an external device, he usually experiences a void in his life and is generally unsatisfied with himself.

6.   Reverse the codependent process and self-actualize through awareness, behavior, change and spirituality.

AWARENESS

Living is a risk!`

PART ONE

CONCEPTUAL OVERVIEW

FEAR OF THE
UNKNOWN

ANXIETY

LACK OF TRUST

The definition of insanity
is doing the same thing
over and over and
expecting something to be
different in your life.

CHAPTER ONE

Faith is the substance of things hoped for
And the evidence of things not seen

OVERVIEW

In Chapter One we will explore the following:

1. How unattended childhood grief sets the stage for later problems in all developmental areas over the life span
2. The dysfunctional process used to transform a childhood reaction into a lifestyle
3. Two major components of the transformation
    a)The Loop in which a behavioral set is exhibited each time the pain from the unresolved childhood grief begins to rise
    b)The Energy System that drives The Loop
4. The behavioral overview of the transformation
5. The subsequent created lifestyle
6. Impact on the Personal Management System

THE PROBLEM

CHILDHOOD TRAUMA

I'm watching a TV talk show. The topic is about kids controlling parents and being out of control. The girl speaking is 13 years old, angry, anorexic, and talking very belligerently. Adults in the audience scream, "She needs a good ass kicking." I think, "What's the secret that she is keeping?" The problem is so clear to me — so prevalent of what I see in therapy. "Why isn't it understood?" I ask myself, "Why do we keep shoving it back into the closet?"

The girl is so reminiscent of the adolescents that I've counseled in treatment. As I watch the program completing, I'm doing a psychological/sociological assessment in my mind, trying to pick up the little pieces that will put together my strategy to asses, unlock the secret, and free her from the prison of her pain.

Bits surface: trouble with gangs, verbalizing no hope, no body image, minimizing a vicious assault, and a well meaning but clueless mom.

There is a female therapist on the talk show. It's as if she is reading my mind. I see so clearly what has happened to the teen. The therapist goes with my lead. She validates the girl's anger, affirms her right to protect herself, and starts to give her information of what's under the anger.

The teen starts to change; foot starts jumping up and down, and looks like she's getting ready to run away. I start to cry and cheer her on – "Go girl! Get it out! Break the chain! Choose life, not bondage to a past event that cripples you for the rest of your life."

The teen's eyes soften as the therapist continues to encourage her to go on. The therapist's voice is soft, yet directional. The tears start to well up in the teen. Both the therapist and talk show host encourage the teen to bring up the secret. No words are spoken by the teen. Her eyes speak them for her. The tears are flowing like a river after a dam has broken. The talk show host says something about secrets, their need to come out or they will kill you, then gives more information on abuse and they go to a commercial break.

There are no commercial breaks in a therapy session when a major breakthrough occurs. The trauma or wound opens. The therapist goes to work helping the client talk about, feel, sort out, and process the pain of the injury and the subsequent impact it has had on the rest of his life. This is a natural unfolding which the person goes through and grows from: learning new skills to better facilitate his feelings and gaining emotional maturity by feeling them; participating in less destructive behavior; gaining new data for his personal information system, resulting in a more functional decision-making process — one in which the client will make healthy choices based on self love instead of choices necessitated because he is running from the past.

It doesn't make any difference what those past injurious events were, *from* the simplest abandonment of having two working parents, who had very little energy left over for the family once they got home from work; *to* having toxic parents who are overly critical, judgmental and/or emotionally distant; *to* greater dysfunction with enraged parents who fail to protect due to, alcoholism, drug addition, religious abuse, food addiction, gambling, adoption, workaholics, mental illness; *to* emotional, physical or sexual abuse, multi-generation incest, and ending at the deepest level which is ritual abuse. All have an impact on a child, with the depth of that impact determined by the extent of the event. (Children carry intense shame when their needs are not met on a consistent basis by their primary care givers.)

CHILDREN CARRY INTENSE SHAME
WHEN THEIR NEEDS ARE NOT MET
ON A CONSISTENT BASIS
BY THEIR PRIMARY CARE GIVERS

Not getting their needs met, set up the children to make poor personal decisions throughout their life spans because they never feel good enough about themselves to be entitled to have better things happen to them. Without help, most stay in self-destructive patterns of behavior the following ways: 1) becoming friends and having relationships with toxic people, 2) having unsatisfactory vocations, 3) using poor interpersonal skills, or 4) becoming alcoholics or addicts.

The self-destructive patterns also exacerbate the problems occurring during a Mid Life Crisis and retirement (when the person's developmental tasks begin to change because his energy and capacity is diminishing). In order to transcend those problems and maintain internal integrity, one has to draw from the past — the strokes given (positive reinforcement given by primary care givers), or the tasks accomplished. There is nothing to draw upon when all that is experienced or perceived is abuse and negativity. *One doesn't feel the joy of his accomplishments when he is shut down in order to avoid feeling the pain from his losses.*

Back to the TV program: The teen had no choice – except to behave in self-destructive patterns — until she exposed her shame to an insightful therapist. At age 10 she was gang raped. She was told that she would be killed if she "ratted" on them. All of this went unnoticed by an already overwhelmed mother. The girl was repeatedly abused by the gang over the next three years. As a reaction to the overwhelming abuse, she became angry, acted out, and was put down for it. Is this insane, when no one can see what's going on with her? Don't you think she feels insane because nobody noticed the changes in her or heard her cry for help?

Impact of the Problem

The process of building psychic pain is a simple one when it's envisioned. Once understood, it can be reversed and cleaned up. The work required to accomplish this relief is painful, and is a place where most people quit therapy or leave a "twelve step" program. What happens to frighten them is that they begin to take an honest, unvarnished look at what they did to survive, and begin to see *what roads they didn't have to take.* This is like being a Monday morning quarterback. Anyone can see the plays once the game is over. The trouble with life is that "the game" is always going on and **we do the best we can with what we have!** DON'T let the new information you learn today cause you to judge and beat yourself up for what you did in the past. Be gentle on yourself. **You deserve it.**

Some are also skeptics when it comes to the concept of how childhood trauma continues to impact them over their life span. Their statements are: "It's over and done with! I put it behind me! It doesn't bother me any more!" The following argument in logic is for those skeptics:

1. Look at feelings and emotions as energy
2. That emotional stress raises the individual's energy level
3. The body is a dynamic energy system
4. Energy doesn't dissipate — it's only transferred
5. **QUESTION: WHERE DOES THE RAISED ENERGY FROM CHILDHOOD TRAUMA GO IF IT'S NOT ATTENDED TO?**

The sole purpose of this book is to answer that question! Not only to explain the energy that drives the shame system, but to explain where the energy goes and how it gets there. It will also guide you on what course to take to correct any dysfunctional behavior.

Some will have difficulty with conceptualization of The Problem. The answer may be in looking at the problem as a mystery and asking the basic questions:

1. *What* is the question being asked?
   Answer: Where does childhood pain go after it has been experienced and left unattended?
2. *Where* does this happen?
   Answer: In the subconscious section of the brain.
3. *When* is the pain suppressed?
   Answer: In two developmental stages:
   a)Childhood — when the data is overwhelming.
   b)Adulthood — when the adult's internal structure (existing strategies to handle stress) is deficient or overwhelmed.
4. *How* is the process of shutting off overwhelming data accomplished?
   Answer: The child shuts down, stuffs, or denies his feelings and learns to focus externally on others. In this way he never has to look at himself.
5. *Why* is the process necessary?
   Answer: To protect the child and subsequent adult from being overwhelmed.

Some have felt uneasy about the words I use in conceptualizing the problem because they are so powerful. Words such as: transformation, lifestyle, shame as the energy, denial as a form of psychosis, and children managing their feelings. These **are** powerful words — even more powerful concepts, and **IF** true have far reaching consequences. The Problem is a powerful one. We need equally powerful countermeasures if we are to overcome and conquer it.

I'm very strong in my convictions about ending the dysfunctional behavior that is the result of the individual's strategy of dealing with The Problem. We can call this behavior a person's disease, reaction, or strategy; it makes no difference. Any toxic behavior, which can be done obsessively in spite of increasing consequences, over time, depletes all energy and resources and is the result of the problem.

The dysfunctional manner in which The Problem is handled becomes the facilitator of the painful feelings the evolving person experiences over the life span. This is intriguing and will be explored in the following sections.

PROCESS

The developing child's ability to handle overwhelming pain and the subsequent strategies devised by the adult to keep it hidden is a whole structure within itself. The process doesn't develop without trauma, or occur in a vacuum, and has a predictable cycle. The following is an example of that cycle.

A hurting child sets the stage, as he learns how to shut down, stuff, and deny his feelings when he experiences anything overwhelming. The child suppresses his feelings because he possesses no way to express them. The adolescent acts out the same feelings because he lacks the tools to facilitate them in a functional way. The adolescent's acting out is usually with dysfunctional behavior.

The adult's strategy of remaining in negative behavior is The Loop and becomes the subsequent Energy System which transforms the Child's reaction into a "Lifestyle." The Loop is a **behavioral set** that manifests each time the Child's pain is touched. An example is a drug addict who was abused as a child. Each time he remembers the abuse, he uses. Shame is the emotional fuel because it was the deepest, darkest feeling that the child experienced. When shame is felt in adulthood, it becomes the Energy System that drives The Loop. As all of the adult's energy is used to remain in The Loop, it transforms the Child's reaction into a Lifestyle. All resources are devoted toward maintaining the dysfunctional behavior as a diversion so as not to feel the childhood trauma, instead of developing adaptive coping skills to go through the pain.

**A CHILDHOOD REACTION IS TRANSFORMED
INTO A LIFESTYLE, WHEN ALL ADULT ENERGY
IS USED TO AVOID THE PAIN, INSTEAD OF
LEARNING COPING SKILLS TO DEAL WITH IT**

The Loop

The process that occurs when repressed data is triggered by current stimuli (persons, places, things, etc.) is best visualized as a loop or a road that one travels down to avoid the emerging pain.

In this loop, maladaptive behavior is the contrived response to the pain. Insight is never gained without change. The compulsive person remains in the Problem Loop by not learning from his past mistakes because he is preoccupied with starting or stopping the dysfunctional behavior and cleaning up the carnage left in its wake. He "leaves the problem and comes into the solution" when new stress-reducing strategies are devised by learning from his past situations instead of remaining in denial.

Figure 1.1 is a visual representation of the emotional Loop.

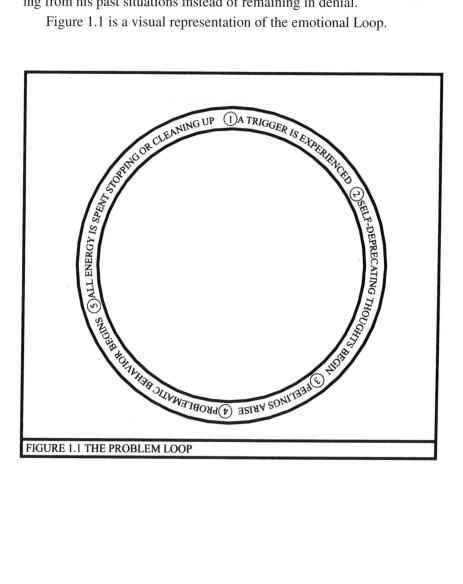

FIGURE 1.1 THE PROBLEM LOOP

Energy System

The Energy System (shame felt in adulthood) is the emotional fuel that drives the Problem Loop.

Remember, this Loop, which diverts repressed material, has been devised as a shield against emotional pain. The Loop's whole purpose is to allow the person to stay out of painful feelings that are perceived as overwhelming. It does the job perfectly.

REPRESSED MATERIAL IS TRIGGERED

CREATES CONFUSION IN THE MIND

INADEQUACY IS EXPERIENCED

SHAME RISES

SHAME IS BLOCKED BY SHUTTING DOWN

DYSFUNCTIONAL BEHAVIOR MANIFESTS AS A WAY OF
EXTENDING THE DIVERSION OF SHAME
UNTIL THE FEELINGS SUBSIDE

FIGURE 1.2 ENERGY SYSTEM OF THE PROBLEM LOOP

Both the Problem Loop and its Energy System will be used extensively in the next two parts as graphic explorations of how clients in the case studies:

1. Enter and remain in dysfunctional behavior
2. Can short circuit the process of entering the above
3. Use their maladaptive patterns as a "self awareness tool" to develop insight into current self-defeating behavior
4. Develop more adaptive coping skills

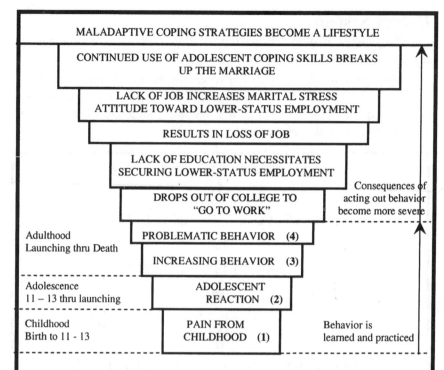

(1)   ORIGINAL PAIN:
What was done to the child: i.e., physical, emotional, or sexual abuse; emotional deprivation, or primary care givers who were not emotionally available on a consistent basis when the child needed them; what was not done for the child when no validation or affirmations were experienced.

(2)   ADOLESCENT REACTION:
Dropping out of school, grades dropping, avoiding higher educational opportunities as well as other opportunities, questionable life style, depression, anger or raging, smoking, defiance, criminality, jail or detention, sexual activity, promiscuity, pregnancy, drinking, drugging, gambling, over achievement, over involvement, overly responsible or parentification.

(3)   INCREASING BEHAVIOR:
The increase of incidents of using maladaptive coping skills (one of the problematic behaviors experimented with in adolescence) as a stress or management system in painful interpersonal or intra-personal situations.

(4)   PROBLEMATIC BEHAVIOR:
Behavior which causes college grades to drop or eliminates the seeking of higher educational opportunities.

FIGURE 1.3 TRANSFORMATION PROCESS

Transformation

The transformation of original pain into a lifestyle occurs in the following way. Pain is experienced in childhood. The developing child learns to shut down, minimize, stuff and deny his feelings, and then acts out in adolescence in order to relieve the pressure built up inside. The acting out is increased in adulthood instead of developing adaptive coping skills. During this time the behavior escalates. The consequences become more costly. All seems to be a vicious cycle, or like being on a runaway train: behavior increases, consequences heighten. Internally, one yells, "Stop the train — I want to get off!" Externally, the behavior continues in spite of what is felt inside.

The transformation is complete when all adult resources are used to maintain the negative behavior instead of looking for adaptive solutions, regardless of the increasing consequences. Figure 1.3 is a visual depiction of the transformation.

Life Style

The metamorphosis is complete in the last (adult) stage when maladaptive coping strategies transform into internalized norms. (This is the automatic response to the stressor.) The adult in this final stage now wanders through life continuing dysfunctional behavior which is exhibited as various addictions, unfulfilled vocations or relationships, generally experiencing low self-esteem and exhibiting a negative self-image. Behavioral reactions learned in adolescence increase (drinking, drugging, depression, gambling, etc.) because this is the person's automatic reaction to stress. When these behaviors are manifested as a coping strategy, the transformation is complete and it becomes the *lifestyle*! In the transformation process, all of the organism's energy is directed toward perpetuating problematic behavior, instead of devising adaptive coping strategies.

This book is meant to be a primer: first, to help the developmentally-impacted person to interrupt the transformation, and second, to transcend the losses of his past. This is accomplished by giving the appropriate information needed to understand the process and work through his wounds.

**THE BEHAVIOR EXHIBITED IN TIME OF STRESS
IS *ALWAYS* THE INTERNALIZED NORM
OR AUTOMATIC REACTION
UNLESS ONE IS AWARE OF
THE PROCESS AND HAS CHOICES**

In this healing process, the individual will be able to locate at what age the injury occurred, identify and experience the lost feelings, gain new intra-personal skills in which he can work with his wounded part, discover his position on the road of his journey, develop new skills, gain functional decision-making skills, and reduce problematic behavior by increasing his range of choices. Deep-rooted issues take skill and time to uncover and process. The novice does not possess the tools to accomplish this task. Having a skilled therapist and being actively involved in a twelve-step program is the perfect combination of resources. The actual work is done by the individual. This book is only meant to show you the process.

Personal Management System (PMS)

A word about individual competence is in order before this chapter closes. I believe that even though individuals have problems and they re-peat dysfunctional behaviors over and over trying to change, they are still highly competent. In fact, they are extremely bright, because they figured out, on their own, how to avoid pain so great, that the organism perceives death if it was actually experienced.

What we have is misinformation that was shaped into a stress reduc-tion system. All the energy of the system was used to keep it in The Loop of dysfunctional behavior instead of using the energy to learn from past experiences. What we have to do now is give the appropriate information (like this book) and divert the stress reduction system's energy to explore new strategies. This will be guided by the Personal Management System (PMS) of the organism (also known as the Executive System) which over-sees the decision-making process.

The information system the Executive System uses, in a healthy per-son, is envisioned as a page totally covered by writing. There are no blank spaces. All lines are filled. In the faulty system of the maladjusted person, there are words missing here and there, incomplete or missing sentences, and even paragraphs omitted, depending on the length and depth of the trauma. These missing pieces can be inserted in therapy or self-help meet-ings by working the steps of a 12-step program.

In order to develop this Management System (PMS) and input the correct data to run it, the evolving fledgling has to be guided. In times of pain, there is no guidance for the Child, only the desire for it to be over.

IN TIMES OF PAIN
THERE IS NO GUIDANCE
ONLY THE DESIRE FOR THE PAIN TO END

To enable the psychic pain to subside as quickly as possible, the organism has to *input faulty data to survive, "shut down" and dissociate so as "not to feel"* or not take in any data. Imagine if your computer did this. What type of finished product would you end up with? Now you get an idea of how bright and innovative these people are. When you work with this concept in therapy or self-help, the possibilities are endless instead of hopeless, as some of these clients present. The information given in this book will become the guidance to the developmentally-deprived person, and fill in the "missing gaps" in order to develop functional coping skills and become a healthy, adjusted individual.

SUMMARY

The problem is viewed as the person's inability to withstand ego-threatening situations. This emanates from being raised in a dysfunctional family, or one that wasn't child centered, whose members were never taught the life skills needed to facilitate or transcend life's occurrences. These can be natural problems occurring through living life as it unfolds, or trauma that happens while the developing child grows into adulthood.

Children carry intense shame when their primary care givers do not meet their needs on a consistent basis. These feelings are so intense that the child learns to shut down, stuff, and deny them in order not to feel. Remember, these feelings are perceived as death by the developing child because all of his cognitive systems are not fully developed and certainly not mature. This is all an internal process.

In adolescence the process becomes external and is acted out. During this time, various behaviors are experimented with which were introduced by the family, peers, or the social environment. Whatever works for the adolescent at this time is continued to early adulthood. Some of the behavioral manifestations are drinking, drugging, smoking, sexual activity, gambling, food addiction, criminality, over achieving, etc.

As the transformation of original pain into a lifestyle is completed, the overwhelming feelings are now externalized as behavior INSTEAD of emotions. In order to keep this repressed material from surfacing, the Problem Loop is unconsciously developed by the psyche. In The Loop, overwhelming feelings or events begin to rise, problematic behavior covers up the fear, and all energy is spent stopping the subsequent behavior and cleaning up its destruction. The emotional fuel for this process is shame.

CASE STUDIES

The following cases are typical. Clients come into therapy to find out what is going on and don't even know where to start – they only know that something is wrong. Some come in looking for the answer to their questions. Some don't even know the questions. These same case studies will be used throughout the book to demonstrate how the concepts being presented in the model, weave themselves throughout therapy and across the life span.

DARLENE is a 32-year-old working mom who enters therapy thinking she is going crazy, because a little over three months ago she started getting overly protective with her 7-year-old daughter. It started with low level thoughts that someone was going to hurt her, and progressed to a paranoid level of not wanting any males around her, including the father. Darlene is able to verbalize that, intellectually, she knows nothing is wrong. But her feelings present a different image. Darlene quit her job last week and now takes her daughter to school and picks her up, daily. Darlene states that she "has to do what she has to do" in order to protect her child, and will die if anything happens to her. Darlene wants to know what's wrong with her, why she thinks one way, feels another, behaves another, and wants to know when she will get over this.

JOAN is an executive in a large city firm and has just ended her fourth relationship in two years. She wonders why she seems to pick men who treat her badly, even though they look different at first.

BILL is a recovering addict, has just relapsed after two years of good, clean time, and states he doesn't know what happened because his life seemed to be going well.

JOHN, a computer programmer, has weight fluctuations of gaining and losing 25 to 70 pounds over the year. He doesn't know what causes the over and under eating, but states something happens to him when stress increases on the job, his parents come to visit, or the holidays come.

DENNIS is a recovering alcoholic. He has just relapsed after five years of sobriety, felt that he had had enough time in which the "drinking problem" was under control, and doesn't know why he drank. He claims that nothing major was going on in his life.

VALERIE is a 54-year-old housewife, feels lost and confused, and is experiencing low-grade depression. She has been married to the same man for 35 years, has all her children launched, except the last one that keeps moving in and out. She is doing fairly well in a vocation that she enjoys and doesn't know why she should feel the way she does.

JOE is a 42-year-old real estate broker who enters therapy stating, "There is something wrong with my marriage." When pressed for more clarity Joe continues, "I don't know." When asked to describe his marriage, Joe describes an emotionally distanced wife with a self-admitted inability to have the closeness that Joe desires in a marriage. Joe is unable to change things because he has always been "drawn" to this kind of woman. Joe was unable to put the above together until he came into therapy and began to explore his questions during the initial session.

MARY is a 78-year-old retired widow who came into treatment when she lost her desire to live because of aging problems, shut down, and went into a major depression.

CONSTANCE is a 67-year-old housewife who entered our group after she was Baker Acted when she refused to eat and reported she was going to kill herself.

STAN, a 71-year-old retired blue-collar worker who had shut down over the past year, is socially isolated – refusing to attend any family or outside functions, watches TV from morning 'til night, gets angry (sometimes enraged) when confronted, and states that he has paid his dues and nobody can tell him what to do. He also admits that the only pleasure he experiences in life is when he has his "few" drinks at night.

POLLY is a childless, 42-year-old divorcee who sought therapy when she discovered that she did not have the ability to be emotionally present for her current significant other, whom she reports is her soul mate, and wants to know why she thinks one way, feels another, and behaves contrary to the two.

BRENT, 45, AND SANDY, 42, are a married couple who came into counseling to check out their current strategy of raising children, and to work through some "tender" areas that seem to periodically come up between them.

TANYA, our TV teen, with some reframing, is a composite of the adolescents I've seen in treatment. Their situations were just different. In their stories, the gang became a metaphor that personified their abusers. Most were raped by people they trusted who took advantage of their precarious environment. For some, the rape was so brutal and prolonged that they were virtually socialized into the various dysfunctional behavior reactions. These Problem Loops were not only modeled by the abusers for the victims' use – they were encouraged. They helped the victims avoid the present pain of the rape and enabled their abusers to continue raping them. There are two aspects to this kind of rape. The first is a physical rape in which the victims are forced to have sex. The second is an emotional and spiritual rape in which their childhood is taken away and the emotion-ally-disturbed abusers' actions cause the victims to forget their "Birth Vision" (present and future spiritual tasks).

CHAPTER TWO

Man is only aware of what he can perceive
Nothing else is useful to him

OVERVIEW

In Chapter two we will explore the following concepts:

1. The consciousness or how we interpret perceived data
2. The inner architecture of the mind
3. The three-stage process of perception
    a)**Conscious** — Where all data is inputted, processed, filtered, and acted upon
    b)**Preconscious** — The two-stage process in which feelings begin to surface and are transformed into a behavioral response if the psyche does not possess the ability to withstand or facilitate the trauma
        1.Stage one — Where the repressed material breaks away from the unconscious and is experienced as uneasiness
        2. Stage two — Transforms the rising pain into a behavioral response to mask the overwhelming material
    c)**Subconscious** — Where all overwhelming thoughts, feelings, and emotions are repressed
4.How behavior becomes a suppressant
5.The role of self-help in the recovery or healing process
6.Suggestions to enhance a twelve-step program's effectiveness

CONSCIOUSNESS

Freud perceived the mind as a complex system and felt that it operated in three areas. The first was the part we are aware of; the second was the Id, or the area that was out of our reach; the third was a gray area -—one that we could feel every now and then, but not touch.

In working with clients, I've witnessed this to be true and have devised a model to give them a visual representation of the process. I started to do this with adolescent substance abusers, who needed a more concrete way to grasp the concepts that were being taught to them. The results were impressive. Trust was built more quickly and rapport established earlier. Concepts were grasped more easily. Issues were identified and explored earlier. Therapy time was shortened considerably. A by-product of the teens advancing at a faster rate was that the families did better because they were so impressed at their child's improvement that it became the motivator to move them into recovery as well.

THE MODEL

The process of perception occurs in two stages. The first is a physiological system that intakes data through the five senses. The second ia psychological system that orders, processes, and acts upon the environmental stimulus that's taken in by the senses. The following operations occur within the two-stage process:

1. The brain intakes stimuli from the environment through the senses
2. The raw data is ordered into concepts by the psyche within the mind (This is a mental process that gives the material meaning)
3. Awareness of the action to take on the data comes from the consciousness which is contained within the psyche
4. The internal structure of the consciousness is the Child, Adolescent, and Adult
5. From the internal structure develops the Executive System: A central personality that operates as the decision-making process

Figure 2.1 is a visual depiction of the operation of the human being's cognitive system.

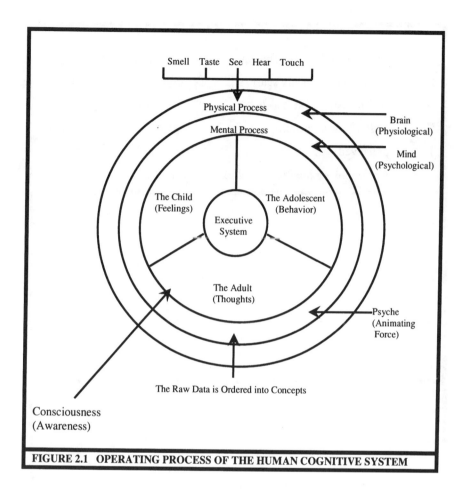

FIGURE 2.1   OPERATING PROCESS OF THE HUMAN COGNITIVE SYSTEM

Depth of the Psyche

When the raw data is absorbed into the brain, two processes occur:

1. The stimuli is ordered into concepts
2. How to respond to the data is determined

The depiction in Figure 2.2 is a representation of the mind's depth and the beginning of its operating system with the inclusion of **TRIGGERS**. The Range of Feelings Scale is only used as an indicator. It is not part of what drives the system.

L	Triggers in the Environment	High _____	
I	(Can come from any sense: sight,		Range
G	sound, taste, scent, touch,	Average _____ of	
H	and/or how something is		Feelings
T	perceived)	Low _____	
	Conscious or Surface Level of Emotion		

T	
W	
I	Stage 2
L	_____
I	
G	Stage 1
H	
T	**Preconscious**

B	
L	
A	
C	
K	**Subconscious or Unconscious**

FIGURE 2.2 VISUAL DEPICTION OF THE MIND'S DEPTH

Selective Process

It is said in the philosophy of perception, that the brain can handle only a small amount of the stimuli that is directed toward it at any given time. There is also a **SELECTIVE PROCESS** going on to determine what data is "most" necessary for the organism to continue. This is why some only hear and see what they want to.

When Selective Process is brought too far it can become problematic, at best, and self destructive, at its worst. Advanced further, it can lead to denial of one's external reality, repression of past events, or the alteration of one's current reality by avoiding positive things in life and focusing on the negative. Are there any people in your life that have done that or do it now?

**WITHOUT TOOLS MAN COULD NOT ADVANCE.
WITHOUT NEW SYSTEMS TO DEAL
WITH COMPLEX PROBLEMS —
MAN CANNOT CHANGE**

ASSIGNMENT 1: How many people in your life only see and hear what they want? Write a list of those people. If you remember! Write the situation in which it happened. Put this list aside for later use. It's probably a good idea to start a file folder or notebook at this time. This will keep you organized and avoid "lost" papers that you will need further along in the progression of this book. Remember, resistance is inevitable. It's only an indication of what you don't want to see. (Good assessing tool — isn't it?)

ASSIGNMENT 2: How many people in your life deny reality, repress, or minimize past events? These can be positive or negative situations. Who avoids good things and focuses on the negative, no matter how positive the situation is? Write a list and the situation in which it occurred, if you can remember. Do you do this? If yes, include yourself and the situations in which you do the same.

STRUCTURE OF COGNITION

The structure of the mind breaks into three distinct areas of what I call the consciousness. It's the way we *interpret* perceived data. Later on in therapy, these areas will be more overlapping along their edges.

The first area is the conscious or the surface level of emotion. It is an open area filled with light. We see all in our environment. Nothing is hidden or repressed. The unaffected person operates in the conscious state most of the time, does not deny the facts of his life, suppress his feelings, or repress prior events.

The second area is the preconscious — and it is murky. It is where things start becoming revealed. Feelings begin to surface. Anxiety starts to rise. This is the area that brings people back into problematic behavior or situations because they don't have an understanding of the psyche's process and/or lack insight into themselves. This is the area we'll do the most work with because it carries the keys which open the door of insight.

The third area is the unconscious or subconscious. It is dark and shrouded from us. It is the place where all the painful secrets are hidden and repressed from being revealed.

Do you think my structure is a dream? It's not. Millions of people live in these areas on a daily basis. The healthy ones remain in the light and handle life's vicissitudes on a daily basis without dysfunctional behavior or a problematic decision-making process. *People who live in the day and don't deny their external reality, have choices and adaptive coping strategies, based on learned experience from past situations. They learn and grow from the past because they REMEMBER IT!*

LIFE IS A SCHOOLROOM.
EXPERIENCE OUR GUIDE.
IT TEACHES US HOW TO ENJOY OUR MOMENT TODAY —
FROM WHAT WE EXPERIENCED IN THE PAST.
TO DENY OUR PAST IS TO GIVE UP OUR PRESENT.

Conscious

Everything that is initially perceived by any of the senses is processed in the conscious mind, or according to the model, at the surface level of awareness. This has to be understood as a concept, for the sake of clarity. After it is entered into the conscious, the data is ordered and acted upon.

During the process of prioritizing this material, the mind determines the level of importance, based on its perception of how threatening the data is. If it is task oriented or non-threatening, the process is a simple one and completed within the full view of the conscious mind. If the data is overwhelming or threatening, it takes a different track altogether. It becomes a trigger to the unconscious as the inputted data is suppressed.

This makes the conscious a filter for behavioral responses and is graphically described in Figure 2.3

DATA ENTERS THE CONSCIOUS THROUGH THE SENSES
⬇

THE MIND NOW FILTERS THE INFORMATION
⬇   ⬇

NON-THREATENING   THREATENING

Remains In The Conscious	1. Simple — Remains in the Conscious
Task Is Completed	2. Complex — Remains in the Preconscious and/or Stirs Low Level Fear
Decision Made	3. Overwhelming — Goes Directly to the Unconscious

FIGURE 2.3 FILTERS OF THE CONSCIOUS

Out of these Filters of the Conscious comes a decision-making process. The various paths that the internalized responses follow are based on how the conscious perceives the data. The person's subsequent behavior will emanate from these internalized responses.

Preconscious

The preconscious is where feelings and emotions are stirred up in a person. In early recovery, or healing, very little is known about this area. Feelings seem to come from nowhere, memories just materialize, and fear is suddenly present. Much is going on in this area and it is a backwards journey that opens it up. The work that is done is to look at what precipitated dysfunctional thinking or behavior. This can include any automatic behavioral responses you want to change.

The process of opening up the preconscious is really reconnecting the person to his own internal responses and making him more aware of the triggers that set off these thoughts, feelings, and emotions. It is the goal of this model to lower the threshold of the preconscious to allow the person to see his internal responses with more clarity, depth, and speed. This will allow a less problematic decision-making process, cut down negative automatic responses in perceived danger or fear, and allow the greatest possible range of choices.

The road the repressed information travels into the conscious, after it has been released from the unconscious, occurs in the two-stage process of the preconscious:

Stage 1: In Stage 1, anxiety begins as the repressed material breaks through the protective barrier of the subconscious. It is at this time that people begin to feel "uncomfortable," have "funny" feelings, and wonder what's wrong. They also begin to get jumpy and experience low-grade anxiety or agitation.

As the data continues to rise in this phase, anxiety becomes the leading edge of feelings. If they are given this framework, feelings become less confusing or traumatic. When used in conjunction with Stage 2, knowledge of the process becomes an incredible self-awareness tool into self-defeating behavior patterns.

Stage 2: As the anxiety travels into Stage 2, the transformation of the repressed material continues into behavior. This is the point where the confused person begins to act on those feelings and begins his automatic responses to stress. This is tantamount to a runaway freight train. Unless someone is there to put on the brakes, it will never stop. Awareness is the only brake and it's too early in recovery to have this insight.

Some of the ways one begins the behavioral changes are: stirring up the pot and becoming paranoid or neurotic over a job, events, or relationships; over reacting; becoming antagonistic; having cravings return; or starting the process of Building Up to a Drink (BUDing), Gorski (86). Anyone who lives with an alcoholic or an addicted person knows when this happens: They have *"that"* look on their face that you have seen so many times before they relapsed. They don't feel there is a problem. They wonder what's wrong with you for thinking that there is one. They ask, "Why don't you trust me?" They stop going to meetings. They say they have it all under control. Then they become crazy or use mood-altering substances. Sound familiar? It should.

This process is the same for those addicted to anything and it includes sex, gambling, food, religion, work, criminality, codependency, and any other behavior that can be used in an obsessive and compulsive way.

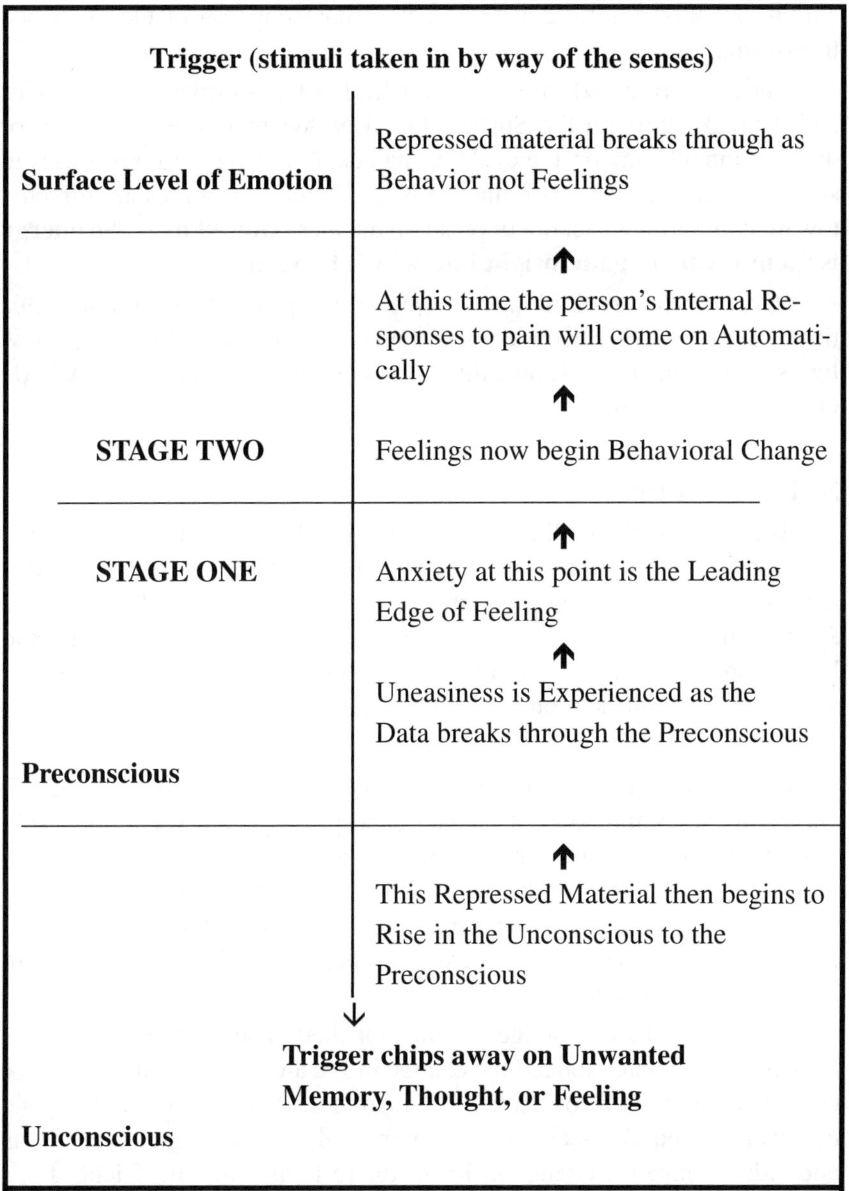

Trigger (stimuli taken in by way of the senses)	
Surface Level of Emotion	Repressed material breaks through as Behavior not Feelings
STAGE TWO	↑ At this time the person's Internal Responses to pain will come on Automatically ↑ Feelings now begin Behavioral Change
STAGE ONE **Preconscious**	↑ Anxiety at this point is the Leading Edge of Feeling ↑ Uneasiness is Experienced as the Data breaks through the Preconscious
Unconscious	↑ This Repressed Material then begins to Rise in the Unconscious to the Preconscious ↓ **Trigger chips away on Unwanted Memory, Thought, or Feeling**

FIGURE 2.4 TWO-STAGE PROCESS OF THE PRECONSCIOUS

The transformation of feelings into behavior is complete when repressed material breaks The Surface Level of Awareness as dysfunctional behavior. This is exhibited in relationships ending, getting a divorce, quitting a job, changing residences, committing a crime, having depression, a manic episode, psychosis, or relapse into any mood-altering substance including alcohol. Figure 2.4 is a graphic representation of the described transformation.

Once the triggered, repressed material is transformed into behavior and it breaks through the Surface Level of Awareness as acting out or dysfunctional behavior, the cycle of maladaptive behavioral responses to stress is complete. At this point the person's total resources are directed toward continuing to act out or clean up the mess **caused by it. No energy is spent trying to gain insight into why it happened.**

Many of you are thinking a couple of things about the author at this time: "Is he crazy?" "How does he know me so well?" To some, a few lights are coming on and some things are beginning to make sense. READ ON! It just gets better.

Subconscious

This area is where all unwanted thoughts, feelings, and emotions are repressed. Anything that is a threat to one's internal integrity is hidden here. Each one is locked away in its own compartment. I'll use a case study to illustrate the subconscious, how memories can be suppressed, and how its process is taught or reinforced by others. Its process is not a horror story, only the ramifications could be — and were.

CASE STUDY: Joe was on a Caribbean cruise with some friends. It was a mixed combination of business and pleasure. All was going well. The small group he was with had just disembarked and entered the stretch limo that was waiting for them. It was to take them to one of the island's better restaurants. As the limo left the dock area and traveled through the night in the Caribbean town, memories and powerful feelings started to surface and overwhelm him.

One of the other passengers, who happened to be his friend as well as a business associate, noticed the change in Joe and simply stated, "A door opened up didn't it?" Joe said, "Yes" then looked around to see if anyone else had noticed. All seemed to be engrossed in their own conversations and didn't notice the change in Joe or the response from his friend. Joe's friend continued in a very soft voice, "When that happens to me, I simply close the door shut." Joe answered, "I tried that and it didn't work." Joe's friend continued, "Sometimes you need some help." "Here's a two-by-four." "Put it up against the door." "Now put some nails in it." Joe followed the imagery and when his friend asked if it was working, Joe noticed that his feelings were starting to subside. When others in the limo started to comment on the conversation, Joe's friend played it off, stating that they were having some fun with an old door and proceeded to tell a funny story not related to the situation between them. When the story was over, everyone laughed, and Joe noticed the feelings and memories were gone. Joe was relieved to have the feelings over.

This seemingly triumphal situation and subsequent "help" from a friend, presents as benign enough, but only until we look at what came up later in therapy.

The Role of Self-Help

To those of you unfamiliar with the steps in a Twelve-Step Program or involved in Program and not using the steps, the following is for you. Like therapy, the Fourth Step helps you to take stock of who you are. For some it's probably the first time they will get a concrete view of their make up. This gives a person a firm foundation on which to build a fulfilling life.

In the Fifth Step, one learns trust because he has to share with another human being what he found in his Fourth Step. This, like therapy, begins to show him he is not as bad as he thinks he is, that he has developed many positive attributes, and that he did the best he could with what he was taught. Step Five paves the way for more positive relationships with people because of the trust it engenders in its process and is also looked for in non-program relationships. As one recovers, trust is not only expected, it's a prerequisite for any deepening relationship that one chooses to develop.

BEHAVIOR AS A SUPPRESSANT

Remember what was said earlier about awareness and insight being a backwards process? Joe's case study was a good example of this concept. When he first came into therapy, he did not have any insight into his problems. First he had to be aware of his caretaking, stop trying to fix his marriage, and then he would be able to identify the antecedents that predisposed him to unfulfilling relationships.

This is how the Tenth Step works: the recovering person completes a daily inventory and corrects the dysfunctional behavior in the process. Once the behavior is stopped, it no longer is a suppressant. If one remains out of the problematic behavior, the reason for it will surface. How one remains in the problem is described in Figure 2.5.

Initially Step Ten (or the counseling process) begins to work in Stage 3, when the individual sees the dysfunctional behavior and stops it. If the behavior continues to cover up, the recovering person would go back to Steps Four and Five to explore what is going on. In counseling, one would "dig deeper" with the therapist, to reveal what precipitated the need to perpetuate the maladaptive behavior.

Without this process, one would continuously go through the four Stages. It would be the internalized response to stress and would be repeated each time something breaks loose from the unconscious. This breaking away is a normal part of Program or therapy. The higher one's awareness, the more he will see.

STAGE 1	STAGE 2	STAGE 3	STAGE 4
Repressed, past events, thoughts, or feelings begin to surface	**CHOICE IS HERE** 1. Identify, feel, and process the emerging awareness **OR** 2. Go directly to acting out behavior	No choice is made. Problems of living increase due to the maladaptive behavior	All energy is spent cleaning up the problems caused by the dysfunctional behavior

FIGURE 2.5 HOW BEHAVIOR BECOMES A SUPPRESSANT

It is very special to watch the recovering person having a choice in Stage 2 instead of doing the same old behavior and ending with a mess to clean up. What if someone finds himself **stuck** at this point, wants to change, but remains in that same old pattern? Ask yourself, "Why is this behavior useful to me?" I will guarantee you that the behavior will change in time, or you will find out its benefits, if you keep asking the question and don't beat yourself up in the process.

THE ROAD

The road of life is the context in which the human perceptual system operates. In it, one has to take in, order, and act upon a multitude of stimuli.

During this process one is expected to have self knowledge, to interact with others, and to fulfill the demands of the larger culture by demonstrating socially-approved behavior. It's not an easy task.

The family is the social agency that has been delegated the responsibility of producing the finished product. This is called the Socialization Process. During this instruction period, the primary care givers were mandated to help the child know himself, learn about himself in relationship to others, and assimilate the rules of socially prescribed behavior demanded by the larger culture. This was a formidable job because the family existed in a dynamic environment with static rules. Some things were concrete to the culture (laws) although the social context the laws were written in, were fluid and changing. It wasn't until the human potential movement of the sixties that the family began to acquire the tools to fully complete its job. Up until then it was like digging a hole with your hands before shovels were invented.

There is another component to this process and it's called spirituality. In it, one also has a spiritual purpose, one greater than himself as an individual, which will contribute to man as a species. This contention states that we are not born accidentally. In fact — we are born with a purpose. The way to find this purpose is part of my paradigm. I don't debate it. I don't defend it. I only offer it to you as a possibility — one in which I found true and it profoundly changed my life. One of my mentors used to repeat over and over to me, "no defensible boundaries, Lou. Just allow the information in and let it take a course of its own. Let it rise or fall of its own weight. If you're defending you're blocking possibilities." He was right. It took time. Today I'm free and allow in the possibilities.

One of the major goals of my paradigm is to free one from the chaos of a noisy external reality and confusion of an internal battle when thoughts, feelings and behaviors are not congruent, in order to quiet the mind and enhance its receptiveness to a spiritual reality. The road I envision that one takes during his lifetime to discover his spirituality is depicted in Figure 2.6.

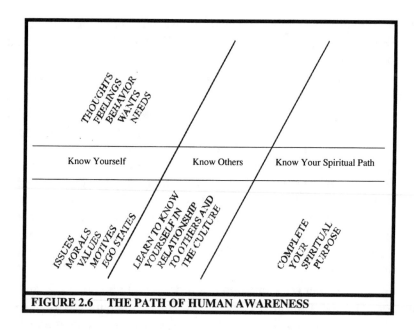

FIGURE 2.6   THE PATH OF HUMAN AWARENESS

Tasks of the Journey

The three tasks that need to be completed as the evolving human journeys along his path in life are:

1. Know yourself
2. Know yourself in relationship to others
3. Know your spiritual purpose

Each of these tasks has an additive value. If one stage is incomplete — the next one will not be finished. It is impossible to know yourself in relationship to others if you don't know yourself first. And one cannot complete his spiritual chore if the noise level in his head is traveling past the speed of sound because he is confused about himself or others.

The first half of this book was designed to help you know yourself intimately. The second half was structured to know you in relationship with others. Chapters 12 through 16 will spiritually enlighten you.

Structure

The path in life also has a structure which includes the ego states and the grief process. Remember, even though one is walking an external road in life, he is being guided by an internal path that allows him to interact in an external reality to complete his spiritual purpose.

The external path is usually clear. One can easily report what one is doing, e.g., walking, eating, going to work, driving, etc. It's one's internal path that one lacks direction in, e.g., motives, confusion, becoming lost, intentions, what one feels, why one can't change something, and why one thinks one way and acts another.

When we add the ego states and the grief process, we begin to solidify free-flowing feelings and quantify speculation. When the grief process is added to the human data bank and is configured as a road to a destination, one that includes mile markers, landmarks, signposts, and signals, it now becomes a tool to determine where the individual is, when trying to work on and resolve a problem.

As the ego states' contributions are included in a person's perceptual scan, he now has a workable understanding of his feelings, is able to sort out the confusion, and create adaptive solutions to situations that once confused him.

The road will be explored in depth throughout the last half of the book. I refer to it many times and try to tie it in where it's needed. I know once the concept is internalized, it becomes a valuable self-awareness tool and clears most internal confusion.

CASE STUDY: Dennis, our 45-year-old alcoholic, came into treatment to uncover why he relapsed after five years of sobriety. The obvious was pointed out to him — that he became complacent with the program and relapsed. He agreed with what I observed and added there was something more going on that he didn't understand and if he returned to the program without additional help — he would just relapse again. At this time he had an understanding of the Big Book, workable knowledge of the Steps, some experience with traditions and concepts, had fired his sponsor just prior to relapse because he felt he had outgrown him, and agreed to resume meetings. Without returning to AA, Dennis would not be allowed into our program, for this was a prerequisite to being allowed in.

During the initial assessment it became clear that Dennis had minimal awareness of his internal structure, made reference to a workshop he attended on his inner child, and admitted that he got very little out of it. He also had very little insight into what his issues were and stated that every time something came up with him at a meeting, he was told to keep the focus on himself, to stay in the day, and let "those things" take care of themselves. All he had to do was to stay sober.

This is true and it's Alcoholics Anonymous' primary purpose. The only problem is, "these things" would bring him back to drinking (as they did) or he could become a "dry drunk" if he didn't attend to what was trying to surface. I have no problem with AA — they do their job well. The rest gets taken care of in other twelve-step programs or therapy.

Dennis adapted to group well. He was able to understand the model, personalize the ego states in psychodrama, identify his issues with his parents, and work with the grief process as a road map of his internal journey.

While Dennis was working on assimilating the model as his new guide in recovery, he was able to personify his disease to gain a greater understanding of his triggers. This was a plus to him because the sharing by other alcoholics in our group, about why they drank, gave him deeper insight into himself and why he needed more help than AA had given.

The work Dennis did with The Child came in the backdoor one day when he was working on understanding the nature of his alcoholism. It was during a psychodrama that the following occurred. First there was a split as Dennis' personality changed from his Adult into his Adolescent and I quickly had him choose another group member to play his Adult. (Including another group member to play Dennis' Adult, allowed Dennis to remain in his Adolescent ego state, and explore the emotional baggage that was beginning to surface.) Then, from his Adolescent, Dennis berated his Adult in an emotional tirade. When the roles were reversed and the Adolescent alter mirrored back Dennis' Adolescent performance - Dennis started to cry. The tears came long and hard. It was as if a dam had broken and the floodgates could no longer contain the tears.

When he stopped crying, he was able to talk to his Adolescent. I knew he was in his Child Ego State. I had him quickly enroll another alter. In his Child state, Dennis was able to let his alter Adolescent know how much he was afraid of him because when the Adolescent was angry, he acted just like Dad.

Switching roles again, Dennis as the Adolescent softened when he talked to his Child's alter and apologized because he thought he was protecting and not scaring him. He even offered as evidence that he wasn't a womanizer like Dad. It was during this point that The Adult asked for help. In the Adult role, Dennis was able to look at the struggle that was going on internally and begin to identify issues he thought he resolved ages ago.

Later on in the group process, Dennis could use the grief process as a framework to understand why his issues with his dad were not resolved. During this time he was able to verbalize that, although his Adult had accepted his dad as an alcoholic who had hurt the family through his drinking and womanizing, his Adolescent was still angry, and his Child still intensely sad.

Further along in treatment he discovered that his drinking covered up the pain of his childhood as well as the shame he experienced while he was drunk when his behavior became bizarre.

The new framework gave Dennis the additional insight he needed to stay sober, identified his unresolved issues, increased awareness of his triggers, and decreased internal confusion. All of this was done because he had an image of the components of his internal structure (the three ego states) and a way to visualize where he was (along a path) with any issue in his life using the stages of the Grief Process as a roadmap.

USING THE PROGRAM

A word to self help members: Not everything has to be worked out with a therapist. Using this book as a framework, reading specialized literature pertaining to your particular issues, and working Steps Four, Five and Ten, will also help you overcome these problems. To me, toxic or unfulfilling relationships are only a symptom of the problem and one has to get to the root of the problem to overcome it.

In fairness to therapy, if one has a psychiatric problem, substance abuse, or has been abused, he will usually need therapy to help him stabilize, sort things out, and devise a plan for living. At this time a twelve-step program becomes a functional adjunct to therapy where the client can go out and try new behaviors in a safe environment.

During this time the client needs to make a commitment to a program in order for it to be effective. That includes:

1 Joining a group
2 Taking a job in group (doing service)
3 Being active in the group
4 Getting a sponsor
5 Reading the literature daily
6 Going to several meetings a week — they work the following way
   a) 1 per week — just holding on
   b) 2 per week — gets your attention
   c) 3 per week — starts to take in the new information
   d) 4 per week — ability to apply the new wisdom to your life

7   Developing a support system
8   Using the telephone in between meetings
9   Using the 24-hour plan

ASSIGNMENT 3:   Stop here. Don't gloss over this chapter's overview. Study The Model again and identify which area you operate from. Are you in the dark about things, shut down, or in depression? Are you a substance abuser? Do you use old problematic coping strategies to handle stress and wonder why your problems don't get resolved but come up another way? Do you handle stress in a non-problematic way? Do you learn from your past mistakes? Does life seem ongoing to you or are you stuck?

These are a few of the questions you can ask yourself to determine what area of the consciousness you operate in. This is not right or wrong. It's awareness only. Write your findings down. Don't go on a "Search and Destroy Mission" to find out "all" about yourself or "everything" you do. Instead, try just a couple problems you have experienced recently. They can be intra-personal (within yourself), family, school, work, etc. Take a simple and complete problem from each category you choose. In this way you will get a generalized view of your current coping strategies.

THE HUMAN PERCEPTUAL SYSTEM

The human perceptual system is a two stage process in which external data is: 1) taken in by a physical process and 2) ordered and given meaning by a psychological process. Figure 2.7 is a graphic illustration of both processes and in it we will look at the Psyche as a system:

1. **INTAKE** is accomplished through the senses
2. **INTERNAL FILTERS** come on line through the Child, Adolescent, and Adult
3. **THE DECISION MAKING PROCESS** occurs in the Executive System
4. **THE DEPTH OF THE PROCESS** is the Conscious, Preconscious and Subconscious

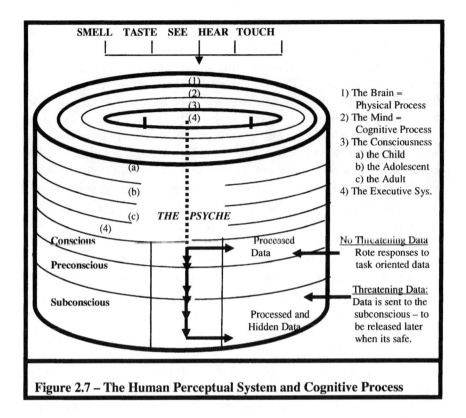

Figure 2.7 – The Human Perceptual System and Cognitive Process

SUMMARY

The individual's consciousness or perceptual system is a dynamic in-take mechanism in which data is funneled in through the senses and processed by the mind. The structure of the consciousness is broken down into three areas: the conscious, preconscious and the unconscious. The first area has been labeled 'The Surface Level of Awareness' because this is where the person is first cognizant of the data. The preconscious is fur-ther broken up into two stages for easier clarification.

As the data is being taken in and processed by the consciousness, it is also being filtered. This filtering is in two stages. The first is a Selective Process in which non-essential data is not ignored. The second stage is a priority assessment as to the level of impact the data will have on the individual. When the material is considered non-threatening or manage-able, it follows a logical path in which it remains in the conscious, evaluates past strategies used in similar situations, and the appropriate behavioral response is given. In task-oriented data (like opening a door), the internalized motor sequence is performed.

When the data is perceived as threatening and/or overwhelming, the material is suppressed in the subconscious. This can be seen as a shock absorber to prevent the individual from going on overload. It's also a good survival skill when it's the only tool available because "living skills" were not taught or modeled in the family of origin. This data will be released by the subconscious when it is no longer destructive to the individual. Emotional maturity occurs when one experiences life as it unfolds, doesn't deny its reality, and will be able to transcend more powerful situations.

As the data is released by the subconscious and enters the preconscious, it comes in as the original data or has become a trigger and has previous unresolved matter attached to it. If it starts this process clean, the events of the past will not be attached and it will be uncomplicated. The material will gradually enter the conscious to be acted upon.

If it comes up as a trigger, the process becomes very complicated and more sophisticated defense mechanisms have to be developed.

The subconscious releases the data into the preconscious, which releases the data into the conscious. As the material surfaces, it will come into awareness as a gradual release of the original circumstance or transformed into a behavior that is designed to cover up the overwhelming material. This is a two-stage process and is determined by how threatening the item is to the person.

When the rising, suppressed material is transformed into behavior, its primary purpose is to cover up or mask overwhelming facts or feelings because they are perceived as fatal. And if the person acknowledges the situation, and/or feels the feelings, *these emotions are so powerful that they can't be mediated by an internal process and they need to have a healthy external way of venting* (such as by talking or processing feelings). If they don't find a way to be released, the organism will explode (perhaps with psychosis or mental illness or extreme dysfunctional behavior such as drug abuse, alcohol abuse, food abuse or obsessive-compulsive behaviors).

POWERFUL FEELINGS "NEED" AN EXTERNAL WAY TO VENT — WHEN IT'S INTERNAL PROCESS CAN'T FACILITATE THEM "OR" THE SYSTEM BREAKS DOWN

Transformation is the basis for most dysfunctional behavior. It becomes the external manifestation of one's internal pain. Its roots are the dysfunctional behavior modeled in the family of origin as they tried to fix their pain and what was experimented with during their developing years. When the transformation of repressed material into behavior is complete, the act is now considered a suppressant because it **"medicates"** the feelings by covering them up. A "lifestyle" is developed when the individual has to repeat this behavior over and over in order to live in denial of his past trauma. Therapy, as well as self-help, can help to change these maladaptive coping strategies.

CASE STUDY

Joe's lack of insight is an excellent example for this chapter. Had the memories he experienced during the limousine ride in the Caribbean remained in the conscious, instead of being repressed, his life would have been profoundly impacted, and could have saved him from spending ten extra years in a toxic marriage.

The memories Joe remembered came back from a previous relationship. The feelings were good ones - memories and feelings of how two people can love one another and make life pleasant. The relationship didn't work out. That's not important to this point. What's important is that Joe experienced these wonderful feelings. Had he remembered them instead of repressing, he would have brought the experience forward to other relationships and probably wouldn't have married his present wife, who was not capable of having this kind of connection with him.

The feelings that almost overwhelmed him were triggered because he was having a good time and didn't have up his normal shields of busyness to block them from surfacing. Joe also experienced the very special times he spent with his ex-girlfriend in a tropical environment. The area he was in had reminded him of it. Everything that was going on with Joe was subconscious. He was oblivious to everything until the feelings surfaced and he became overwhelmed.

The other circumstances that were occurring during this time were that his marriage was continuously becoming more unsatisfactory and he was doing everything possible to make it work.

Joe had been taught to limit his range of feelings, avoid "too" happy situations, and remain "busy" with work and life. Joe couldn't understand why he wasn't happy and didn't know what he was doing wrong. He couldn't recognize he was in "Survival Mode," attempting to *internally* facilitate his wife's emotional unavailability — while at the same time *externally* doing everything he could to get her to respond to him in some unknown way, and fill the hole he's felt in his heart since being a little boy.

Had his insides matched his outside, he would have had to take action sooner, and he wasn't prepared at this time to take one that would profoundly change his life — divorce. Joe's story will be continued.

CHAPTER THREE

Emotions are the color of life
Without them
There is no living

OVERVIEW

In Chapter Three we will look at what drives the Operating System

1. Emotions as the fuel for the system
2. The three dynamics that encompass its process
   a) Range of Feelings — which act as a barometer
   b) Level of Feelings — to demonstrate the linear relationship between positive and negative feelings
   c) Triggers — memories of past events that surface
3. Steps needed to facilitate change
4. The role of stress in problematic behavior
5. The mind as a filter for traumatic experiences

OPERATING SYSTEM

The structure of the consciousness was described in the previous chapter. In Chapter Three we will explain the Operating System that drives and orders perception. This framework gives a unique perspective on how and why people react or respond in various situations. It also helps to build a repertoire of adaptive coping strategies by giving insight into repeated dysfunctional behavior and creating choices in the process. Figure 3.1 is a graphic representation of how the Operating System is started. It can also include multiple triggers because we have more than one sense that can each set off different issues, or come in a rapid sequence because the person is open and vulnerable.

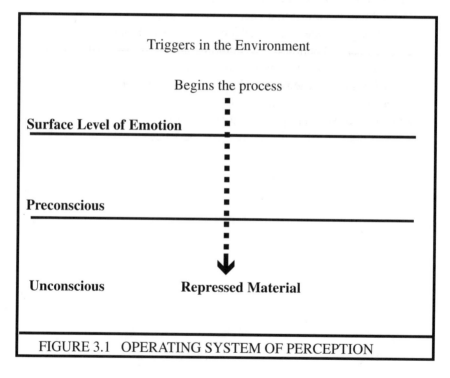

FIGURE 3.1   OPERATING SYSTEM OF PERCEPTION

The Operating System of The Consciousness is emotions. Without them, behavior would be nothing more than a rote performance of an internalized motor sequence as it responds to task-oriented data. The emotions are the color, that when added, bring life to behavior. And just as emotions add depth to an experience, they also bring complications.

This emotional tapestry drives the System and we will examine both its operating range and level of feelings. Added to this process will be triggers that stimulate prior unresolved issues or emotions and attach these triggers to presently occurring events. As this develops, the individual's normal operating parameters are breached, his level of feelings rise, and the subsequent stress from the event is geometrically doubled, tripled, or quadrupled, depending on which issues are attached.

As the above process occurs, the body responds both physically and emotionally. Stress is increased and the corresponding emotions also rise. If the threat is perceived as overwhelming, confusion begins, previous coping strategies are not retrieved, and the person starts to shut down. These reactions make it possible to deny the current overpowering reality until the threat subsides, because in order for the individual to maintain balance, his world has to be ordered, and internal integrity not compromised.

MATRIX OF THE OPERATING SYSTEM

The Matrix of the Operating System is comprised of the following components

1. Surface Level of Emotion where one begins to feel
2. Range of Feelings
3. Level of Feelings
4. Triggers

Each component adds a strand to our tapestry of living, how we interpret our environment, and the action we take on what is perceived.

Surface Level of Emotion

In my model of the consciousness or "how we order our perception," the conscious area is now relabeled Surface Level of Emotion because this is where the person begins to become aware of what he is feeling. It is very important that one knows this is only awareness of his feelings and NOT ALL THAT IS GOING ON INTERNALLY. There is a whole process going on continuously within the human brain and mind. We are only aware of a small part. Knowledge of this model and working it in your life will increase your awareness greatly.

Range of Feelings

The Range of Feelings Scale has been added because one has to be cognizant of the depth of his feelings, the reactions which occur because of those feelings, or what is perceived in his environment and his subsequent reaction(s). This range becomes one of the cornerstones of the model because most of the people I've seen in therapy, or heard in a twelve-step program, did not know what a normal range of feelings was. Some overreacted, some under-reacted — very rarely were they in balance. In fact, when in balance, most would say it was not a comfortable place for them to be.

People have to normalize their feelings — become concrete with them. If they don't, feelings become a puff of smoke so thin, they can be molded into whatever the person wants to perceive. Using this strategy as a survival skill, one can change his perception of reality at will, to avoid his painful feelings.

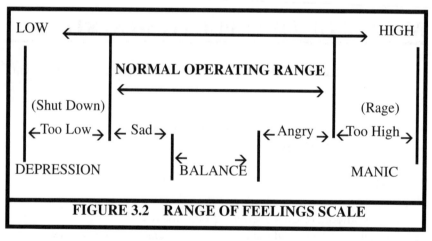

FIGURE 3.2   RANGE OF FEELINGS SCALE

When the recovering person applies the scale, it becomes a barometer for his feelings. He is now able to visualize where his feelings are along a continuum and will instinctively know if he is responding or over/under reacting. This is the beginning of having a choice about what behavior will follow a feeling. Most people do automatically what they were taught or learned in their family of origin.

WHEN A PERSON REACTS INSTINCTIVELY
MOST WILL DO AUTOMATICALLY
WHAT THEY WERE TAUGHT OR LEARNED
IN THEIR FAMILY OF ORIGIN.
THIS IS THE CONDITIONED RESPONSE
TO ANY SITUATION

ASSIGNMENT 4: How were you taught to handle stress in your family of origin? Did you react or respond with the same intensity no matter what the level of stress was? How did your father react to stress? How did your mother react? How did your primary care giver react? 'Primary care giver' is defined as the person(s) who took care of you the majority of the time. This could be biological parent(s), grandparents, babysitters, aunts, nurses, nannies, maids, adoptive parent(s), uncles, siblings or friends. Look at the stress levels in Figure 3.8 before you answer. Write about each area of stress that you have encountered in your present environment and your family of origin.

Level of Feelings

Most people manage their level of feelings through the following process because the relationship between positive and negative feelings is a linear one. As the positive feelings rise, so do the negative ones. To whatever level the positive feeling rises, the negative feeling will rise. Problems begin to manifest themselves because of the confusion created when two feelings surface at the same time or when negative feelings follow positive. More relationships are sabotaged and broken up because of this. I also believe it's one of the prominent factors that precipitates relapse in any addictive behavior.

One word of caution: Most will balk at this Linear Level of Feelings concept, stating, "How are these feelings controlled?" The answer is simple — avoidance, denial and confusion. Avoidance is an easy answer. One simply stays away from "too many" good times. One may do some fun things, but then stop abruptly and get busy in other areas. How many people do you know that are like this? Are you?

Denial is a tricky way to hold down the level of feelings. Used in combination with avoidance, denial can have one of the partners in the relationship confused and talking to themselves. An example is when the other partner doesn't "remember" the good times, or denies they happened and avoids any recurrence of a positive event. Minimization is just as devastating a tool in which the good times are played down as not being that good. Try to make sense out of that after one partner has witnessed the other partner having a fun time. Makes the grounded partner feel like he's crazy and he begins to doubt what he feels. Recognize anybody?

If one partner stirs the pot by adding antagonism, causing trouble, diverting the subject, getting angry, or shutting down when the subject comes up, the grounded partner feels dazed and confused — like he was hit with something. Or, if the grounded partner does react, he is asked, "What's your problem — you're always over reacting to nothing." When this goes on, the grounded partner is totally diverted from the subject. He walks away steaming or apologizing for his reaction. Keep track of this. The subject **never** goes back to having fun, only to putting the pieces back together. Sound familiar?

Figures 3.3 through 3.5 depict the process of the linear relationship between positive and negative feelings. This relationship is also progressive in that the higher the positive feelings rise, the further the negative ones are forced to the surface.

In Figure 3.3, the person's feelings are kept very low. Not feeling "too" many good ones and keeping the negative far below the surface. The more repressed, the lower a person's feeling level. If the history is too toxic or traumatic, a person can shut down or numb out and not have any feelings.

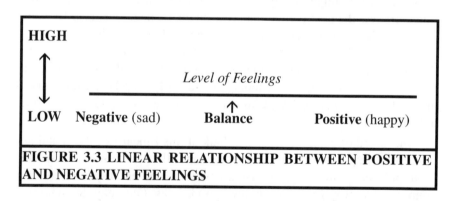

FIGURE 3.3 LINEAR RELATIONSHIP BETWEEN POSITIVE AND NEGATIVE FEELINGS

Feelings are allowed in, in Figure 3.4, and as the happy feelings bring up joy, negative ones begin to break through the previous barrier and begin to rise. In this process the negative feelings are one step behind the positive. This is when someone begins to experience the pain of past losses while feeling the joy of achieving goals.

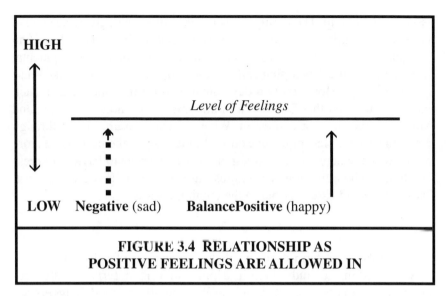

FIGURE 3.4 RELATIONSHIP AS POSITIVE FEELINGS ARE ALLOWED IN

Most people do not know the depth of the loss until they experience the joy of the gain. One denies joy as a way to cope, either because this is what was modeled in his family of origin, or to protect one's internal integrity which isn't mature enough to withstand the blow from the loss. These mixed feelings have confused most people and have reined havoc on many trying to deal with them

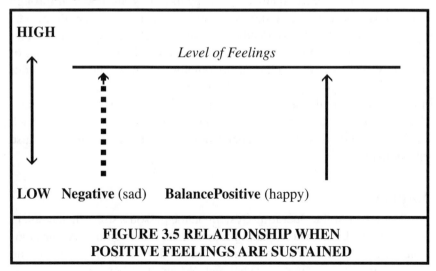

FIGURE 3.5 RELATIONSHIP WHEN POSITIVE FEELINGS ARE SUSTAINED

When the positive feelings are sustained (Figure 3.5) feelings will go on overload if there are a lot of secrets from the past being repressed in the unconscious. Most cannot maintain this level of feeling because of the issues they drag up. The family of origin or primary care givers seemed to have failed in this area when the person cannot mediate his feelings and emotions in a functional way. One of the family's main developmental tasks is to help the developing child sort out, identify, feel, and make sense of his feelings. Most adults today cannot claim this happened. In fact, most will tell you that Dad had a limited range of emotions, if any, and Mom was too busy or depressed. What the children are taught through modeling is not to feel or to have only a limited range of emotions. In more toxic homes, where abuse is going on, it is dangerous to have or express emotions. When emotions are expressed, someone is going to get hurt. This will be addressed further in the coming chapters.

Triggers

'Triggers' is a term used in relapse prevention of substance abuse. Anyone wishing to study them in depth should read Terry Gorsky's relapse prevention books. There are several and all are good. Triggers are not going to be used in this model to find out why the craving for a drug or the desire to drink returned. They are going to be used as a self-awareness tool to show how a particular feeling, emotion, or memory chooses to surface at a particular time, and give insight into a person's strategy in facilitating them.

Our environment is loaded with triggers. They are taken in through every sense: taste, sight, sound, scent and touch. They can be life events, holidays, birthdays, births, deaths, certain days of the week, a particular season, friends, lovers, spouses, children, bosses, loud voices, music, or **anything** that has an attachment to something that has gone on in your life. Not all triggers are negative. Some bring back strong pleasant feelings. These are not the ones we will look at. Pleasant triggers are not usually problematic. The triggers that we'll look at are the ones that bring back unpleasant memories or start to shake loose the repressed secrets that cause emotional pain.

Impact

The effect of the Operating System on the person's stress management strategies and his decision-making capabilities, are enormous. As the emotions percolate when repressed data is released by a triggering event, the System starts to become overwhelmed. When the Operating System becomes overwhelmed, confusion begins because of the unrecognized increased stress from the past that's imposed on the current situation. This is the main reason a person experiences a large emotional response in an innocuous situation. As all of this is whirling around in the person's head, there is little chance of adaptive decision making or of a person maturing through a growth-producing event, unless he is aware of the process and has acquired the skills to ameliorate the increased emotions.

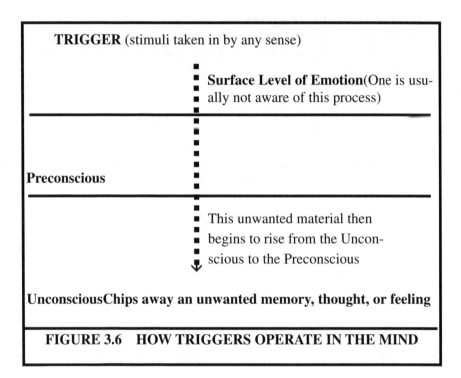

TRIGGER (stimuli taken in by any sense)

Surface Level of Emotion(One is usually not aware of this process)

Preconscious

This unwanted material then begins to rise from the Unconscious to the Preconscious

UnconsciousChips away an unwanted memory, thought, or feeling

FIGURE 3.6   HOW TRIGGERS OPERATE IN THE MIND

PROCESS OF CHANGE

Change is a process — it doesn't occur in a vacuum — or magically appears out of nowhere. For change to begin, it has to be beneficial to the individual. *"Without Benefits"* — *"Nothing Changes!"* The process also needs a new behavior to replace the old self-defeating strategy. It also requires lots of practice, until the adaptive change becomes the automatic response - when the situation repeats itself.

ALL BEHAVIOR IS USEFUL:
NO DISTINCTION IS MADE
BETWEEN POSITIVE OR NEGATIVE

We begin to see the complications of changing when it's acknowledged that:

1. **Change occurs in a process**
2. **Maturity requires remembering the adaptive responses or learning from the mistakes of previous self-defeating strategies**
3. **Emotions cloud this process**

Figure 3.7 is the course the process takes when behavior change is to occur.

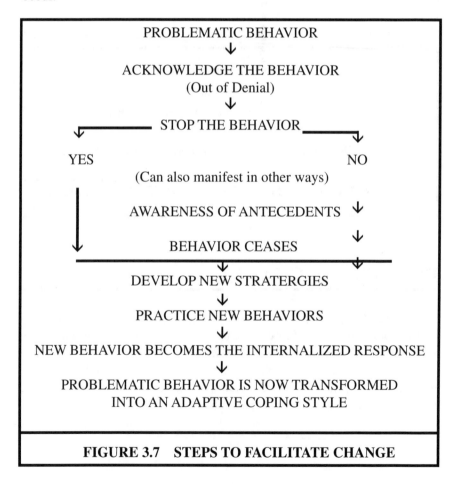

PROBLEMATIC BEHAVIOR
↓
ACKNOWLEDGE THE BEHAVIOR
(Out of Denial)
↓
STOP THE BEHAVIOR

YES   NO
(Can also manifest in other ways)

AWARENESS OF ANTECEDENTS ↓

↓

BEHAVIOR CEASES

DEVELOP NEW STRATERGIES
↓
PRACTICE NEW BEHAVIORS
↓
NEW BEHAVIOR BECOMES THE INTERNALIZED RESPONSE
↓
PROBLEMATIC BEHAVIOR IS NOW TRANSFORMED
INTO AN ADAPTIVE COPING STYLE

FIGURE 3.7   STEPS TO FACILITATE CHANGE

Alcoholism and drug abuse are excellent examples of problematic behavior. The first step is complete once the alcoholic or addict recognizes that his using has to stop — no matter what the reason. Some are able to stop with treatment and a twelve-step program (AA and NA). Some just use AA.

Others can't stop no matter what the consequences. Some switch addictions to gambling, sex, relationships, food, etc. For these people, a greater awareness of why they drink has to be developed. Without greater awareness, they will remain clean and sober for only a given amount of time — which varies greatly from person to person.

Relapse occurs and all energy is directed toward stopping the behavior and then cleaning up the carnage left in its wake. Clean time is experienced again. Relapse. The circle continues until the person is institutionalized, incarcerated or dead.

Once the drinking and drugging have been stopped (a day at a time), the alcoholic or addict can develop new coping strategies, in order to avoid returning to using mood-altering substances as stress reducers or pain killers.

The new behavior is then practiced. AA or NA will constantly reinforce the new behavior. Go to enough meetings, hear it over and over, and it eventually sinks in. Given enough practice, the drinking and drugging becomes extinct and the new behavior will become the automatic response to the stressor.

If the alcoholic drinks each time there is trouble on the job, he will drink each time in the future when there is trouble on the job. Simple — isn't it? (It takes forever for some to see this). When this is acknowledged by the drinker in AA, other members will suggest that, instead of drinking, he call someone in the program when trouble is experienced on the job. If he can accomplish this, problems on the job will no longer result in drinking. At this time, calling someone becomes the adaptive coping skill. This process can be applied to any and all problems.

ASSIGNMENT 5: Make two lists:
1. Behavior that was changed and strategies used to facilitate the change
2. Behavior you keep "relapsing into." In this list, write your relapse loop or the circumstances surrounding the behavior's return
    a)Write the behavior
    b)What happened before you "relapsed" — if you remember
    c)How you stopped the behavior again

d)What consequences were experienced

e)What happened in your life prior to your "relapse"

The relapse can be with smoking, swearing, buying items not needed, eating high calorie foods, over-exercising, being late, as well as drinking, drugging, etc.

What I am trying to show you is that relapse takes on many forms. I don't judge it. Just report it. To me it's a fact of life. If we keep a sense of humor and go gentle on ourselves and others, we can transcend *anything*. Be honest! Write the lists! Have fun with yourself!

STRESS

The role of stress in problematic behavior is paramount because of the synergistic effect of multiple problems. When one adds the residual impact of unresolved issues, it can become overwhelming. Although this sounds simple enough, a great deal of the population I've observed spends most of their time trying to avoid or deny the problem, instead of going through the feelings generated and developing adaptive coping skills.

OVERWHELMING
Loss of a child
Unexpected loss of a job
Premature death of a parent
The house burning to the ground
Unplanned pregnancy
Eviction from your home or apartment
Deteriorating health conditions (natural or premature)
Child's diagnosis of a chronic condition
Treatment of any family member
Incarceration of any family member
Relapse of any family member
Serious legal problems/divorce
Children or adolescent acting out
Purchasing a new home

HIGH
Child becomes sick
Car breaks down
House fire
Starting a new job (by choice or circumstances)
Pay cut or hours cut
Moving into a new home (by choice or circumstances)
Becoming ill (can be as simple as the flu)
Receiving a pay raise
Buying a new car
Child having difficulty in school
Bills are larger than expected
Planned pregnancy
Going to the doctor or dentist for annual check-up
Starting a new relationship or marriage

NORMAL
Everyday routine of raising a child
Keeping your job
Family
Intra-personal issues

FIGURE 3.8   LEVELS OF STRESS FOR LIFE EVENTS

Look at Figure 3.8. I've listed the stressors by how they progressively impact the individual experiencing them. The order has been determined by what I usually see in therapy. Each one, depending on which developmental stage it occurs, how it is perceived, and individual differences, can modify the position within the three categories of the scale.

ASSIGNMENT 6: List your current stressors. It doesn't make any difference at this point how you facilitate them — only what they are. Did any item(s) surprise you because they were positive events? Did you think all stressors were negative? Write your own personal stressors down. Include home, work, and personal stressors. Rate them according to the scale in Figure 3.8. You determine which category they fall under. Feel free to adjust the items on the scale to fit your individual interpretation of how a stressor effects you personally.

DECISION TREE

This decision tree is based on how the mind filters incoming data. Each stage in this process is a filter that enables the person from becoming overwhelmed when the inputted data is too threatening for his emotional processing system to handle.

The Decision Tree can also be viewed as a shock absorber. It is nature's way of stopping the organism from going on tilt and keeps it in balance by shielding it from overwhelming material. I believe when the emotional system is immature, it's like a child, if a child doesn't see something — it never existed.

Look at the stages of the grief process. The first two are shock and denial. Doesn't this protect the person when the impact from the loss is at its greatest? Why not apply this concept to **all changes**, good and bad, positive and negative? I'll do this later on in the book when I tie the grief process together with the model.

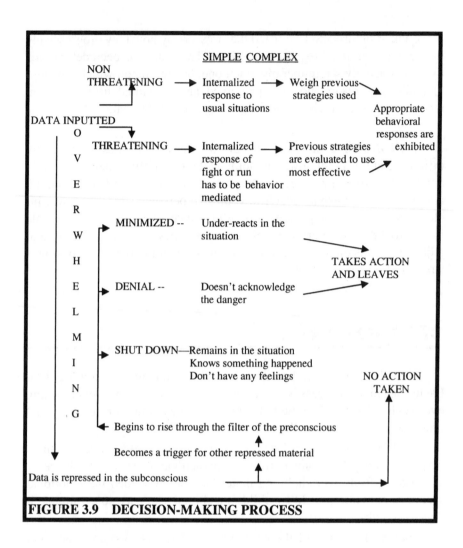

FIGURE 3.9   DECISION-MAKING PROCESS

SUMMARY

Rising emotions are the Operating System of the consciousness. Through them, a myriad of responding behaviors are created. To unweave this tapestry, or gain insight into its creation, one has to have an overview of how the System is driven.

Within this Operating System, there are three dynamics that encompass its process. The first is the "Range of Feelings" which acts as a barometer to let the individual know if he is in balance within his feelings. The second dynamic is the "Level of Feelings" that a person operates because of the linear relationship between positive and negative feelings. The third dynamic is a "Trigger" which occurs when a present situation attaches to an unresolved past event. This causes an over reaction to the current event and increases confusion within the person.

As this confusion breaks the "Surface Level of Awareness," the person facilitates the intense feelings with a dysfunctional behavioral response instead of responding by sorting it out and developing adaptive coping strategies. If we use this as a concept, we can see that **nothing occurs inside a vacuum and all behavior has a purpose.**

The first step needed to facilitate change is to identify and stop the undesired behavior. Therapy may be needed at this point if the behavior persists or manifests in another way. The second step is to develop new strategies and practice these behaviors until they become the internalized response. A recovering alcoholic or addict is a good example of how some can come into AA or NA and "a day at a time" not use mood altering substances. Others need extensive therapy to get to the same point.

Stress is a major factor as the individual becomes confused and shuts down when his normal coping strategies become overwhelmed. Shutting down occurs frequently when multiple stressors are experienced. In these cases, the present event triggers off an unresolved past issue, which creates a synergistic effect that multiplies the impact.

Effective coping strategies are based on the emotional maturity of the person as he experiences an ego-destructive situation and the ego remains intact. This manifests as adaptive coping skills, when the person is able to withstand the enormity of the feelings, goes through them, and remembers to do the adaptive coping skill when a similar circumstance arises at a later date.

CASE STUDY

In therapy, Joe was able to make the connections between how he repressed good memories, ended up in a toxic marriage, and what it cost him in life. This was not easy for Joe because as he experienced the new awareness, the pain from what he had to do to endure his marriage came flooding back. At this point in therapy, Joe had to hold on real tight in order not to run out of the room. This is when many people end therapy or leave a twelve-step program.

Joe was able to go through this wave of pain and make a further commitment to explore what set him up for this type of marriage. He felt that even if he got a divorce at this time that he would find another woman, just like his present wife, to take her place.

Briefly, what Joe was able to uncover, were the antecedents in his life that set him up. Joe was raised in a middle-class home in which both parents worked full time. Dad was absent most of the time with work and Mom was distant. Something always seemed more important than him. Throughout his childhood, Joe felt there was always something missing, but didn't know what. Joe's relationships with others throughout his life span were usually superficial. The one special relationship he had was described earlier. He remembers being very much in love, never wanting to be with anybody else — then he began to feel closed in. Joe became distant, his girlfriend complained, and when he was not able to maintain the previous intimacy, she broke off with him.

Exploring this in the first stage of therapy, Joe began to feel the abandonment from his childhood. Joe was able to feel, process, and forgive his parents because he felt, "they did the best they could with what they had."

In the second stage of therapy, Joe was able to see how blocking the pain from his childhood kept him in unfulfilling relationships. Joe avoided good relationships because of the "funny" feelings he experienced during this time. All he knew was that leaving people or situations made the feelings go away. As Joe worked this through in therapy, he was able to experience the feelings from the losses he encountered in his life due to his inability to be around healthy people. Joe saw that he avoided love because it brought up the pain of not having it from his family of origin.

In the final stages of therapy, Joe was able to sort out the past determinants from his present choices. He knew what he felt, responded appropriately, and had a good picture of the kind of woman he wanted in his life.

PART TWO

PERSONALITY DEVELOPMENT

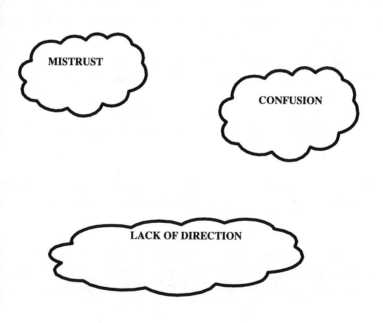

MISTRUST

CONFUSION

LACK OF DIRECTION

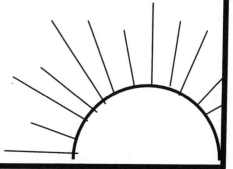

Children can be no more
than what is given to them.

PERSONALITY DEVELOPMENT

Personality development occurs in three stages:

1. Childhood
2. Adolescence
3. Adulthood

Each stage impacts the next when the deficiencies of the prior stage impede the forward progress of the following one. Some of the impediments are small and can be overcome by some rudimentary counseling or basic information designed to fill in the gaps of a person's knowledge base. Others are deep, painful, and in some areas need habilitation. Rehabilitation of some of the maladaptive strategies may not be possible because:

1. Adaptive stress-reducing skills were never acquired
2. The behavioral reaction was maintained over an extended period of time
3. The acting out became toxic and self-destructive
4. A large investment of time, energy, and resources were expended in the dysfunctional behavior

In cases such as the above, whole strategies have to be learned in order to acquire the ability to facilitate stress. They would include new stress-reduction strategies, increased problem-solving skills, awareness of intra-personal conflicts, and a new relationship construct. This will allow a person to have more meaningful relationships with self and others and thereby avoid the current self-defeating behavior that was designed to circumvent the loss or fill the gap of the broken relationship with self or others.

CHAPTER FOUR

Experiences in childhood
Set the stage
For all future behavior

OVERVIEW

In Chapter Four we will explore the following concepts:

1. Childhood as the preliminary information-gathering stage
2. How this information becomes skewed through:
    a)Mixed messages from primary care givers
    b)Ignoring physiological responses (like anxiety) when in conflict
       with the perception of all significant adults
3. Why the child perceives death when he is in conflict with his
    primary care givers
4. When learning "The Rules:" **Don't Talk, Trust, or Feel** becomes
    a conditioned response
5. Where shame becomes the motivating force to shut down
6. The social determinants to minimizing feelings in daily living
    a)"Production-Oriented Culture" — where production is valued
       higher than personal relationships
    b)"Object-Oriented Value System" — when possessions are
       regarded more highly than people

CHILDHOOD

Childhood is the stage that preliminary information needed to facilitate an intra-personal relationship with self and external relationships with others is gathered. It's as if the child is a computer being loaded with the necessary data for later use in adolescence and adulthood. When this data is faulty, it sets up the adolescent to practice a maladaptive coping strategy which later creates dysfunctional behavior in the adult.

This process of gathering skewed data begins when the child is given mixed messages and begins to disallow or deny his internal cues. In these situations the child has to ignore his physiological responses in order to make sense out of the things said by his primary care givers.

Children order their world according to the data conveyed to them by significant adults or older siblings. Through a child's eyes, these people are gods, for the child feels he could not exist without his care givers. He is right. To the child, the outside world is cold and scary.

If you ask any child what would happen to him if left alone by his parents — he would usually reply, "I will die." This is a powerful reason why the developing child **has** to order his world according to his care givers.

A CHILD PERCEIVES "DEATH"
IF LEFT ALONE BY
HIS PRIMARY CARE GIVERS

Physically, adults are bigger than children. The child has to look up at this god-like creature. At this point the child could not conceive of being on his own. During this time, cognitively, the child only possesses black and white thinking and does not possess the facilities of a combat soldier who can handle any number of stressors under adverse conditions.

Children have to order their world to survive. They don't have the ability to deal with abstractions. They take everything at face value. When they are given double messages — conflict, confusion, and anxiety arise. At this time they can choose to listen to those body messages or believe their primary care givers. In order to survive, they have to disallow their own physiological responses and believe the adults' message instead of the reality of what is actually occurring.

CHILDREN HAVE TO DISALLOW
THEIR PHYSIOLOGICAL RESPONSES
WHEN IN DISAGREEMENT WITH
THEIR PRIMARY CARE GIVERS

Some examples of messages that create these conflicts are:

1. "You didn't feel that" — after he is hit
2. "That doesn't hurt" — after he hurt himself
3. "It's not that bad" — when he is bleeding
4. "NOTHING HAPPENED!" — after witnessing something traumatic
5. "You didn't see anything" — when he asks about the event
6. "You didn't hear anything" — when he says something about the event
7. "You're not hungry" — when his stomach is growling
8. "You're not thirsty" — when he is parched
9. "You don't have to go to the bathroom" — when he has to go

Then, when the child can't hold it and goes on the floor, he gets slapped or punished. Imagine what that does to the child's perception. When forced to choose between his own perception of a situation, and what the primary care givers say, a child will do whatever it takes to ignore his bodily needs and disallow his internal cues (feelings).

CHILDREN BELIEVE ADULTS
EVEN WHEN THEY LIE

Not all of these messages are meant to hurt the child. Some are said with a lot of love in order to fix a situation that has just happened or minimize its impact. Most parents don't want their children to hurt and will do **anything** to take the pain away. This included the author. It's natural. It's what we were taught.

I look at it differently today. I believe that it's best to experience the pain of living. In this way one grows instead of running away and creating a dysfunctional lifestyle to avoid pain. Experiencing pain is how emotional maturity is developed and is the missing component with dysfunctional families. The dysfunctional family spends the bulk of its energy creating and facilitating crises, which are used as a smoke screen to mask the pain of stressful or threatening situations. Nowhere are feelings identified, labeled, felt or processed. In fact they are avoided like the plague.

THE DYSFUNCTIONAL FAMILY LACKS THE ABILITY
TO ORDER, MAKE SENSE OF,
OR PROCESS INTENSE FEELINGS

I don't judge the above. I only report it. The one constant I have found in therapy with these families is that **everyone did the best they could with what they had to work with and for where they were.** If the primary care givers had known how to do it differently, they would have. Hindsight is 20/20 vision. If we judge it, we perpetuate the maladaptive behavior and continue to stay in the problem (negative behavior) and don't see the solution (new adaptive strategies). This acceptance is not without a price tag. Once it's admitted, it will evoke much pain in the parents. They will later have to learn to transcend it. If this lack of knowledge is not addressed, the problem will only fester and block the healing the children will experience, once the parents change this maladaptive strategy into a living skill.

IMPACT

The developing child is impacted in two ways while all of this disorganization is going on. The first way is that he learns **"The Rules"** which are: **"Don't Talk, Don't Trust, Don't Feel."** The second way is **"shame,"** which is the predominant feeling he experiences as he disallows his perceptions and listens to someone else's interpretation.

The Rules

The rules growing up in a dysfunctional home are simple — DON'T, *under any circumstances,* acknowledge what is going on if someone says it didn't happen. This sets the child up not to talk, trust, or feel anything significant that is occurring in his life. The process can and usually does minimize the good, because to feel good, drags the bad up with it. Remember the "Range of Feelings Scale"? Here is where it applies. You never really think about children managing their feelings, do you? They do. More than we would like to admit.

THE *RULES*:
DON'T TALK
DON'T TRUST
DON'T FEEL

A child learning the rules is a classical case of a conditioned response. The conditioning starts very early when the child is told they are not "that" hungry because the care giver gets distracted with something else and puts off making supper. "You don't have to go to the bathroom" or "You're not thirsty" are two other examples.

Think about the child at this point. He perceives his environment through his senses and orders his world internally through his feelings. Imagine the chaos that transpires as he disallows his feelings and perceptions in order to remain in harmony with those "giant gods" who take care of him and protect him from being killed by someone in the outside world.

Take this conditioning and expand it to other areas of living. As one observes how it breeds abusive situations, he will no longer have difficulty acknowledging how the conditioning occurs or when it happens. Abuse is difficult to acknowledge because the child is told it's his fault it happened. When he is told this enough times, he begins to believe it. Even when there is an intervention, the child still believes it's his fault, and it becomes overwhelming for him to go against his primary care givers. The child still believes its worse in the outside world and the abuser will protect him from the waiting death that's out there.

All of the above is an "INTERNAL PROCESS." The child's thinking is black and white because he hasn't developed enough to perform abstractions. He does not have a support system to bounce it off of, or the resources to seek outside help. In fact, if he does seek outside help, he will be taken away from his parents. Remember, this is a death sentence to him. He can't survive without those big people. All of this confusion is mediated "inside" the child, and the prevailing feeling that is transpiring while he is "trying to figure it out" is **shame**.

Shame

Shame is the root of most dysfunctional behavior. Shame is the feeling that propels a person down the road to self-destruction so quickly that he arrives before he recognizes that he left.

Shame begins in childhood. It's the pervasive feeling the child experiences and becomes overwhelmed with as he tries to mediate between what he perceives in his environment and what the adult insists is happening.

When this child is grown and in his Adult Ego State, he will experience these exact same childhood feelings, when his adult world becomes confusing and overwhelming. Nothing changes with the emotions from the child to the adult because all of his energy and resources in childhood were used to avoid the feelings, instead of developing coping skills to experience the pain and go through them.

Shame is described in various ways:

Joan   Describes shame as something that keeps pecking away at her until there is nothing left — sort of like Pac Man who gobbles her up while she is becoming overwhelmed

Bill   Feels shame as a force that sends him into a deep hole which is so overwhelming that in order to live, experiences massive anxiety to propels him from it

John   Sees shame as a dark cloud over his head

Dennis Acknowledges that shame feels like something rising from the ground, covers him over, and he can't breathe

Valerie Describes shame as the force which transports her to a deep hole where it's dark and she feels lost and alone like a little girl

Joe   States that shame feels like slime which covers him up until he can no longer breathe

Conclusion

This dysfunctional family process is extremely overwhelming to the child. He has to shut down, stuff, and deny all feelings in order to survive in a conflicting world with his primary care givers. This survival skill will develop into dysfunctional behavior later on in the life span, when the Adult continues to use these childhood *survival skills* in adult situations, instead of developing mature *living skills*.

SOCIETAL DETERMINANTS

Production-Oriented Culture

Don't blame the primary care givers. We live in a production-oriented culture where a person's value is placed on what he does. There is no value placed on feelings in the production line. In fact, feelings are bad because they break concentration and slow production down. Feelings are being. Most of the time, a person is a human "doing" (producing), instead of a human "being" (feeling). Add to this the high cost of living, two parents working, breakdown of the extended family, changing domiciles, new demanding positions, the thousands of things that happen daily to keep you cognitively busy, and it's no wonder feelings take a second seat to producing.

**A PRODUCTION-ORIENTED CULTURE
VALUES A HUMAN "DOING" (PRODUCING)
NOT A HUMAN "BEING" (FEELING)**

ASSIGNMENT 7: Survey your own cultural feelings. How do you feel when you are doing nothing (being) instead of doing something (producing)? What are the messages you give yourself? What do others (friends, spouse, children, parents, etc.) say about you? What do you say about them when it's the reverse?

Don't judge yourself. Just be honest. This is awareness of a production-oriented culture only — not about right or wrong. When you are aware that you can "be," you have choices. When you're not aware you follow the culture's values and you are ignorant to and not free to develop your own personalized values.

Object-Oriented Value System

Much has changed over the last century. At one time people were looked at as a valuable commodity. Today, it's the system or machinery that is important, not the person.

**THE MODERN WORLD TODAY
IS A PRODUCTION-ORIENTED CULTURE AND
HAS AN OBJECT-ORIENTED VALUE SYSTEM**

In the past, things (possessions) were not as important as the family. Today it seems things are the object of desire. The bumper sticker on the new sports utility vehicle (worth about $40 grand) states, "He who dies with the most toys wins!"

It's the same with raising children. A large family was preferred in an agricultural society. There were more hands to do the chores. Children were an asset. As we went through industrialization and the rise of the cities, the family grew smaller. Today children are a liability because of the cost of living and the price of education. This adds a great deal of stress on the families and is not always the most nurturing environment in which to raise children.

Once again, I don't judge what is occurring, I only report it. If one is aware of it, it can be talked about, in the open, and not denied. **Remember! A child's perception is feelings — they will feel the dissension even if it's not expressed!**

ASSIGNMENT 8: Identify your value system. Do you value possessions over people? Don't answer too fast. Think! What do you work for today? Could you down scale your life and still be happy? Make a list of possessions you now own that you could do without. If you can do without them — why do you buy them? Would your life be simpler without them? Do you think children are as valued today as they were in the past? Why?

SUMMARY

Childhood is the developmental stage in which preliminary information to be used throughout the life span will be gathered. If the information is accurate, it will be used as the foundation to build a healthy, adaptive system. If the information is skewed, it will manifest in later stages as dysfunctional behavior. Unless something intervenes, the behavior will develop into a maladaptive life style.

Children gather this information in two ways. The first is by using their senses. The second is by messages that they are given by their primary care givers and authority figures. When children are given misinformation, it sets up a conflict between them and the adults. At this point the child will deny all his natural senses, and yield to the adult's interpretation, because the child fears dying if "abandoned" by the care givers.

Not all of the messages are meant to hurt the child. Some were given to spare him the pain by minimizing the hurt. The problem that arises is when the child doesn't acquire the necessary skills to facilitate emotional discomfort later on in life. It's no wonder we have so many emotionally immature adults.

We can't blame the parents because they did what was modeled by their parents and society. **The modern world is a production-oriented**

culture and has an object-oriented value system. This means there is no room for feelings because they get in the way of the production line and these systems are more important than people. It's hard to develop warm sensitive feelings in an environment where machinery is more coveted than people.

Shame is produced as the child disallows his own perception and physiological responses in order to believe the adult's interpretation of the situation. The fledgling at this point learns the "Don't Talk, Trust, or Feel Rules" which set up dysfunctional behavior further on in the life span, because the adult does not have the necessary tools to mediate his pain. The result of this process is the transformation of the reaction into a life style as the grownup uses all energy and resources to run from the pain, instead of developing adaptive strategies to cope with it.

All of the above is an internal process happening because the child is not capable of performing abstractions or of having the resources to develop a support system outside of the family (such as peers, therapy, or institutional help).

CHAPTER FIVE

Adolescence is
The rehearsal phase for adulthood.
It's the time for acting on
The information gathered in childhood

OVERVIEW

In Chapter Five we will explore some traits of adolescence:

1. How adolescence is a rehearsal phase for adulthood
2. Changes that are experienced during the transition from childhood
3. Why the child's internal process becomes externalized
4. The two-stage process of losing childhood
   a)Stage One:Early childhood — occurs as the novice shuts down
     to avoid the pain
   b)Stage Two:Adolescence — happens when the teen uses age-
     inappropriate behavior to mediate the pain
5. Clients' responses in therapy to self responsibility
6. Defining "acting out" and assessing its extent

ADOLESCENCE

Adolescence is a time of great change in the developing teen. The young person at this time has grown significantly. He is no longer intimidated by size. Some are as tall as their parents or close to it. Others have outgrown them. Their mental capabilities are much more sophisticated with their increased ability to handle abstractions. No more is there black-or-white thinking. Many shades of gray appear. A major change of thinking is that the primary care giver is not always right and can be wrong. They begin to challenge the information given to them.

The teens at this time also begin to develop an outside support group in their peers. No longer are they alone in their fight against confusing data given to them by adults. They also push boundaries and limits in their search to find themselves. All of this is normal during adolescence. (In functional, child-centered homes, adolescents stay within normal parameters. They push — but not too far. They very rarely get in trouble with the law and find more passive ways to act out.) Being raised in a dysfunctional family system is a different story.

In the dysfunctional family, misinformation is given frequently, important facts are denied, and acting out behavior is modeled by the care giver as a stress-reducing coping strategy. At this point the child learns how to manipulate his feelings in order to cut off the shame that arises when he is in perceived conflict with his primary care givers. In order to survive, the child has to shut down, stuff, and deny his feelings. This is an internal process in which he learns "The Rules": Don't Talk, Don't Trust, Don't Feel! The child lacks choices at this time because he has no outside support system and doesn't have the ability to verbalize his confusion.

IMPACT

During adolescence, the internal process of the child is switched to an external one and is acted out. At this time the adolescent feels the impact of being lied to and doesn't have the internal structure to deal with the pain. The greatest amount of the hurt is experienced through shame because his primary care givers, the ones he trusted, used him or did not fulfill their obligations as parents. This realization raises a great deal of shame because of the parental betrayal.

This is a crucial point. When the young person becomes aware of what was **done to him** (any kind of abuse) or **not done for him** (having a child-centered home), The "Don't Talk, Trust, Feel" Rules kick in. The Rules leave the young person alone and isolated **again! Just like childhood!** This no-win situation forces the adolescent to seek his own stress-reducing strategies and these coping strategies come from two places: 1) What was modeled in the family of origin and 2) What he sees his peers doing to mediate their pain.

**CHILDREN EXPERIENCE TWO TYPES OF PAIN
WHICH YIELD OVERWHELMING SHAME:
1) THINGS THAT WERE *DONE TO THEM*
(MENTAL, PHYSICAL, SEXUAL ABUSE)
2) THINGS THAT WERE *NOT DONE FOR THEM*
(VALIDATION AND AFFIRMATION)**

The adolescent at this time uses "adult" behavior as a form of pseudo maturity. This allows the young person to view himself as grown up and rationalize his maladaptive behavior as being OK. What he doesn't see is he has now stepped into the same role as his parents by giving himself misinformation.

**WHEN ADOLESCENTS PARTICIPATE
IN "ADULT" BEHAVIORS
THEY ARE NO DIFFERENT
THAN THEIR ADULT PERPETRATORS
THEY GIVE THEMSELVES MISINFORMATION
WHICH TAKES AWAY THE SECOND HALF OF CHILDHOOD**

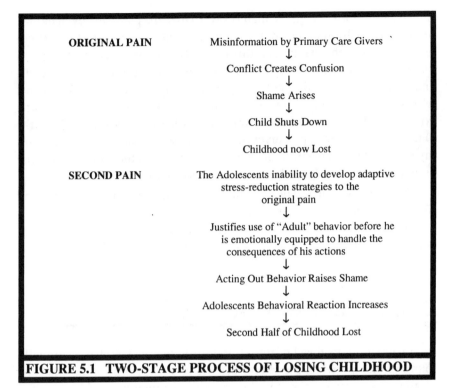

FIGURE 5.1 TWO-STAGE PROCESS OF LOSING CHILDHOOD

Process

The process of losing the innocence of childhood happens in two stages. *The first* is in the childhood stage where the youngster spends much of his time trying to mediate between how he perceives his world and the confusion created by the misinformation and double messages given to him by significant adults. *The second* is in adolescence when the teenager uses "adult" behavior to mediate his pain instead of completing his developmental tasks of exploring who he is. Figure 5.1 is a visual depiction of the process.

CASE STUDY: We can use the story in Chapter One to demonstrate how the two-stage process of losing childhood occurs:

In Stage One, the girl is raised in an inner city project by a poor, single mom. The child was gang raped at age 10 and her mom never noticed. The child takes on the shame of the violation and shuts down for two reasons. The first, that it happened, and the second, that it wasn't noticed by her mom or **any other adult!** At this point all innocence is taken away and the first half of childhood is gone.

In Stage Two, the girl is unable to verbalize the past pain, even though her childhood limitations are no longer present, because most of her energy is spent suppressing it. At this point, the teen goes external and acts out in the way other peers do by drinking, drugging, promiscuity, assaults, and defiance. This acting out to facilitate the pain raises its own shame, which increases the incidents of dysfunctional behavior. It's like chasing your tail or being on a runaway train. It never stops! **In fact — it can't!** Once it stops, the teen perceives death, because the pain is so overwhelming and she lacks the emotional maturity to facilitate the feelings. Without an intervention, the second half of childhood is lost.

This teen was lucky. For one thing, she appeared on a talk show, and for another, there was an insightful therapist who helped her to disclose her secret before adolescence was over. **Hopefully**, she will get the needed help to continue the healing process begun that day on TV.

CLINICAL OBSERVATION

I have to jump ahead of myself to inform the reader what is normally found in therapy when the client sees the two-stage process clearly. The awareness usually occurs in psychodrama or another kind of experiential intervention. Regular talk therapy very rarely opens up this profound insight into the adolescent's contribution to his dysfunction.

It's easy to do the Inner Child work. Many warm fuzzies are experienced. The perpetrators are brought out into the open. They now know "who did it to them." It doesn't make any difference how big or small the events or issues are… **All of the pain hurts! Like a thorn in the finger, it has to come out.** The problem begins when they realize how they perpetuated the pain by acting out in adolescence.

**IF THE PAIN OF WHAT THEY ARE GOING THROUGH
IS GREATER THAN THE PAIN THEY ARE HIDING
THEY WILL LOOK AT *ANYTHING!***

The roles change in adolescence and the young person perpetrates himself by continuing the dysfunctional behavior he learned from the caregiver. When the adult sees this in therapy, it's usually followed by functional changes. During this phase of recovery or healing, the Adult ego state begins to solidify and take charge.

The primary awareness usually takes place in psychodrama while The Adult is in his role of the Adolescent Ego State. This is when he acknowledges that his primary purpose was to protect the wounded Child from the original pain, and realizes that The Child was just as scared of The Adolescent as he was of the abusive care giver, because of the intensity and duration of the Adolescent's acting-out behavior.

The transformation happens as the Adult becomes the Executive System of The Psyche, curtails the acting out of The Adolescent by eliciting his help in exploring more functional strategies, and in the process protects The Child Ego State (Inner Child or feelings) from suffering more harm. When the Adult begins to take charge and the Adolescent is no longer able to act out on whim (the reparenting process), the Child can then disclose what happened to him because the Adult can now be considered a "safe" person to talk to. There is a whole set of dynamics that occurs while this is unraveling in therapy and we will explore them later on in the text.

Acting Out

Let's define "acting out" and separate some of the more common adolescent behaviors from the dysfunctional ones. It's not unusual for the adolescent to exhibit mood swings, to push boundaries, to experiment with his sexuality or a mood-altering substance, to be defiant, to question authority, and to want independence. In this way he learns about himself, becomes a separate person from his parents in the **individualization process**, has his own feelings, and begins the **separation process** which will eventually culminate when he is **launched** on his own.

When we look at the difference between these more common behaviors and dysfunctional behaviors, we begin to see that it's **the distance the adolescents push** that determines what end of the scale they're on. Healthy adolescents have boundaries as to how far they will go to get their own way. Their feelings tell them when to stop. Sometimes they don't know what the feelings are. They just know it's time to stop. These are internal cues that have not been shut off.

Dysfunctional adolescents have learned to ignore or disallow these internal cues, to push beyond limits, and then to suffer the consequences of their behavior. When I ask them in therapy, what was going on inside at these times, they reply, "I knew it was wrong. The little voice inside said to stop. I did it anyway." Some stated their behavior was automatic and weren't aware of anything going on internally.

Normal acting out goes over the line into dysfunctional behavior when the adolescent begins to use what he perceives as "adult" behavior. **At this time the process cannot remain internal.** That's how the child did it. The adolescent needs a tool or way to facilitate the pain externally. "Adult-type" behaviors are the vehicles. Subconsciously, the young person knows he is hurting himself, wants a way to stop, but fails when the pain is perceived as a death sentence if it's allowed to remain internal.

THE PROCESS HAS TO GO EXTERNAL
BECAUSE THE INSIDE PAIN IS TOO GREAT

At this point in time, the adolescent is not ready to look at the past pain because he doesn't have the emotional repertoire to deal with what will surface. He also knows subconsciously that what he is doing is wrong. This eats at him continuously, which causes further pain and continues to increase his dysfunctional behavior. This one-two punch is too much for the adolescent to facilitate internally and, like a rocket, he has to burst out of this huge hole he has placed himself in. At this point he uses pseudo maturity in the form of "adult" behaviors as the way to take the pain external. This manifests as drinking, drugging, overeating, pathological lying, spending, gambling, criminality, extreme defiance, promiscuity, dropping out of school, being overly responsible, over achieving, and parentification (when the child becomes the parent). Don't let the last three fool you. They are just other ways to lose oneself and they're more socially acceptable. The pain is the same. The Child and Adolescent get developmentally sidetracked because the focus is on others and not themselves. If there is an intervention at this time, the family as a system, and its history, has to be explored if effective therapy is to be given.

WHEN AN ADOLESCENT BECOMES THE I. P.
(IMPAIRED PERSON) IN FAMILY SYSTEM THERAPY
HE IS ONLY A "SYMPTOM" OF THE PROBLEM
NOT THE PROBLEM!!

SUMMARY

Adolescence is the rehearsal phase for adulthood. It's a time that witnesses changes in growth, intellectual ability, and development of outside resources for the evolving child. During this time it is normal to see the adolescent fight restrictions placed on him. This typical behavior becomes maladaptive when the teen shuts off his internal cues and pushes too far to get his own way.

Another major change that occurs in the dysfunctional teen is that he begins an external process of releasing his pain via acting-out behavior. This is usually in the form of "adult-type" behaviors. What he doesn't realize is that he is acting the same way his dysfunctional care giver did. *He becomes developmentally sidetracked when all energy is used to avoid the pain by participating in behavior that leads to consequences he is not emotionally prepared to deal with, instead of exploring who he is.* Sometimes this is the greatest abandonment of them all, because all that was missed during these developmental periods will have to be made up later on if the person is to mature.

Losing childhood is a two-stage process. The first stage occurs when he is little because he has little power over the adults. The second stage is where he reacts using "adult" behavior and loses himself in the process. When the adult realizes this in therapy, a profound change occurs as the adult re-parents himself and develops adaptive coping strategies.

CHAPTER SIX

Junk in !
Junk out !

OVERVIEW

In Chapter Six we will explore the following areas:

1. The three-stage process of adulthood
2. Impact of childhood tasks on adolescent development
   a)Ten generalized tasks of childhood development, and how they contribute to adolescent development
   b)The 10 tasks of childhood when not completed, and how their noncompletion detracts from the adolescent's ability to complete his development
   c)Outcomes when development is deficient
   d)Some assessing tools to determine germane issues in therapy
3. Contribution of adolescence on adult maturity
   a)Seven generalized tasks of adolescence and how their completion enables the adult to complete his tasks
   b)The tasks when they're not completed, and the deficiencies that brings to adult living skills
   c)Outcomes of the process
4. Depiction of adult competence

ADULTHOOD

Adulthood is the stage in which the developing individual uses the information gathered in childhood and the lessons learned in adolescence, to place him on a path to becoming the person he can be. During this stage he will work, have a family, self-actualize, make a contribution to mankind, retire and die. All of this occurs over the adult life span and can be viewed as a three-stage process.

THREE-STAGE PROCESS OF ADULT MATURATION

STAGE ONE — EARLY ADULTHOOD

Vocation —   A career is beginning as vocational choices are explored

Intra-personal —   Self concepts are firmed up

Interpersonal —   Relationships with others are more defined as the separation process from the family of origin is completed (the apron strings are cut)

Family —   A family is begun or a decision made to delay its inception

STAGE TWO — MIDDLE ADULTHOOD

Vocation —   A career is established and maintained

Intra-personal —   A deeper understanding of oneself, in which all areas of feelings are being explored. At the same time there is more time behind the individual than in front of him.

Interpersonal —   Further separation of self from others which allows one to be themselves in any relationship. One can empathize without taking on others' feelings.

Family —   Children reach adolescence and force the adults to look at their own values and goals. Those who delayed starting a family begin one, or make the decision not to have one.

STAGE THREE — LATE ADULTHOOD

Vocation —	Winding down of the career and the prospect of retirement
Intra-personal —	One is solid in his identity and comfortable with who he is
Interpersonal —	One is comfortable in his relationships with others and can have a variety of roles without losing his identity
Family —	Children are launched. Empty-nest syndrome is experienced. Downscale of life style in retirement. Power is transferred to the grown-up children.

The tasks described in this three-stage process of adulthood are the general ones. There are several good books available for those who want a more in-depth view. This three-stage process of adulthood covers a very large time span which is beyond the scope of this book to cover. It would take another publication to compare and contrast the differences between the numerous tasks and stages of the adult process, and to thoroughly examine the differences between healthy and unhealthy development.

1. In **Healthy** development, adaptive coping strategies are devised. These strategies develop creative solutions to life's vicissitudes that enable the evolving person to self-actualize and make a contribution to mankind.
2. In **Unhealthy** development, maladaptive behavior is used to cover up the feelings from the stressors. This behavioral response becomes the sole purpose for living as all resources, time, and energy are spent maintaining it.

Impact

In order for the adult to successfully carry out and complete the various tasks in the three adult developmental stages, he had to have successfully completed his childhood and adolescent tasks. I envision this as a foundation, (the same as a house) on which we build our adult lives. Without a firm, deep-rooted and reinforced concrete base, the foundation will be a shaky one — just as if it was built on shifting sand instead of firm soil. What is learned in childhood and experienced in adolescence, determines the type of foundation upon which we will build our adult lives.

CHILDHOOD TASKS

Development in many areas can be accomplished if these 10 tasks of childhood are completed.

1. Learn what our likes and dislikes are
2. Explore our needs
3. Begin to learn about what goes on inside of us
4. Identify our feelings
5. Experience feelings and emotions without becoming overwhelmed
6. Begin to develop strategies to facilitate stress
7. Learn how to get along with others
8. Learn socially acceptable behavior
9. Learn gender roles
10. Begin to develop self concepts

If the childhood tasks are not completed because of disengaged parents, an unsafe environment, unusual stressors in the home, substance abuse, mental illness, criminality, any type of dysfunctional acting out by the primary care givers, or abuse, the foundation will not be as strong and will have very weak points. This foundation is built on the shifting sand.

The above are significant tasks in an abbreviated form which are needed to sculpture a competent individual. In completing them, the evolving child is able to learn about **his or her own self.** *Internally*, the child will learn about his feelings, wants, needs, roles, talents, attributes; and *externally*, the child will learn to get along with others, social roles, and socially accepted behavior. This process is "supposed" to occur in a safe, warm, nurturing environment in which the child is encouraged to explore his potential, while being taught healthy limits at the same time. If a healthy balance is maintained in a child-centered home, all of these tasks will be accomplished.

To maintain this type of environment when raising children in today's world, is ideal, at best. There are too many factors that consistently bombard the family and inhibit the ideal environment. This is not an excuse, just reality. If, as parents, we know the facts and can admit our deficiencies, we can still prepare socially adept children who have insight into themselves, healthy self-esteem, a direction in life, and feel connected to others. **This isn't bad from an "imperfect" system!**

The truth is, as parents, we can never do a perfect job. We would need to be gods to accomplish perfection. At best, we can only do what we know and learn. It's on-the-job training. We need to have gentleness with ourselves and be honest, open, considerate and respectful when dealing with the children. Generally they turn out OK. It may not be according to our ideals. It doesn't have to be, as long as the child has become the adult he wants to be. Remember — it's his life — not ours! The following is an overview of the results if the 10 general developmental tasks are **not** completed:

1. The child doesn't have time to explore his preferences because no choices are given. He is not asked or considered. In some families it can be dangerous just to be different.
2. Needs are not considered because it is "selfish" to consider yourself first. (Usually everyone else is so needy that it's never your turn.) Great shame comes up later on when a person tries to get his needs met.
3. Personal insight is not achieved because the child is focused externally. This is the root of becoming "other directed." There are two reasons for this occurring:
   a.It is dangerous not to know what the adults are doing
   b.To avoid feeling the pain of "not getting their needs met"
4. Feelings cannot be identified because **all effort is being spent in avoiding them** by shutting down, stuffing, minimizing or denial
5. The rudiments to emotional maturity are not developed. This is because nothing is affectually experienced. In order for this to begin, the child would have to feel, process, and remember his experiences to build a repertoire of strategies to facilitate feelings and emotions as they surfaced. **Maturity cannot occur when the child is shut down.**
6. The only strategy designed to handle stress is avoidance. When it can't be avoided, then, shut it off
7. Submission or rebellion is the way the child learns to get along with others. There is no balance
8. In some cases the child learns to punch someone in the face when mad, puts holes in the wall or drinks or drugs when he can't get his way, steals, become a victim, wrecks a car, or hates authority (I can go on and on.).
9. Wrong opinions will be formed: that real men drink, hurt others, or have no feelings; that women have to be "nice," can't get angry, don't have any power.

10. Very few self concepts are developed except the names that they were called by significant adults in their family of origin. The names could be: jerk, loser, whore, thief, runt, slut, you will never amount to anything, you're just like your mother or father, delinquent, you're just like your hoodlum friends, you're bad, you will end up in jail, etc!

Outcomes

Some of the examples in the overview are extreme to some, and **everyday occurrences to others.** What most experience is somewhere in the middle. They get some of their needs met. Some needs are met partially. Some are not met at all. *All,* **and I mean** *all,* are affected in one way or another. *Nobody* had a perfect childhood. If they did, it wasn't on this planet. It's normal to have deficiencies in our upbringing, or in the way we raise our own children. It allows us to learn and grow later on as adults. For me, it's a freedom not to have to blame my parents for what they didn't know, or myself for what I lacked as a parent as I raised my children.

At this point, you, the reader, begin to get a feel for what the Child lacks in tools. It's hard to do this. Many feelings begin to surface for the reader, some overpowering, some disbelief. Yet, this is just the tip of the iceberg. The more dysfunctional the family, the greater the depth of the pain, as more abuse or deprivation is heaped upon the children.

In therapy listening to clients, or in a twelve-step meeting listening to members' stories, one thing became clear. It was like being raised in a war zone or concentration camp if the home was highly dysfunctional. Many of these children suffer from PTSD (Post Traumatic Stress Disorder) which manifests later on in adulthood as acting out, emotional problems, or lack of having a self identify because all that happened to them during childhood still lays unresolved.

The child's interpretation of an event is another area that is seldom explored, often judged, and mostly misunderstood. It takes a great deal of understanding on the therapist's part to work in this area without inadvertently invalidating someone because his childhood situation or event is not considered important.

**OUR INTERPRETATION OF A SITUATION
IS NOT IMPORTANT.
HOW THE PERSON FEELS WHO EXPERIENCED IT
IS WHAT'S IMPORTANT.**

Some situations therapists see as innocuous may be viewed as highly toxic by the child as he experienced it. Once therapists have this framework, it is possible to explore all that was felt by the wounded person, and because of the increased insight, the therapist can help with effective strategies. This also can be used to assess other impacted areas when the interpretation of a situation is explored. An under-reaction or over-reaction is an excellent indicator of what went on in childhood. An under-reaction suggests that the child learned to shut down. Why? An over-reaction indicates that the reaction is attached to something else from the past. What was the event, feeling, or situation? The guidelines I use in therapy to explore these reactions are:

1. Is the situation getting resolved or is the person stuck?
2. Are the feelings passing or remaining overwhelming?
3. Is the client objective or obsessive?
4. Is his life moving forward or regressing?
5. Is his behavior appropriate or acting out?

These five filters have worked very effectively for me and have opened up many germane issues in therapy.

Before we look at adolescence, I want to remind the reader that completing the tasks of childhood begins the foundation on which we will build a life. If they are accomplished, the framework for the foundation will be set, footers will be dug deep, and the adolescent will be ready to practice what was learned. When the tasks are not accomplished, the soil isn't firm. The framework can shift and the footers are shallow. This will later create deficiencies in the adolescent because of what the child didn't learn.

ADOLESCENT TASKS

When adolescent tasks are accomplished, the adult will have a healthy framework for living:

1. Develops an outside support system with peers
2. Develops self concepts

3. Can go outside the family for resources
4. Explores vocational interests
5. Has educational choices
6. Completes the individualization process by:
   a)Becoming a person separate from the family
   b)Having his own feelings
   c)Exploring his own value system
   d)Having ideas different from the family
   e)Developing his own boundaries (physical, emotional, and
      spiritual)
7. Complete the separation process from the family of origin by
   leaving and starting a life of his own

As all of the above are being completed, the individual still feels like he is a member of his family of origin. This is one of the joys of functional or adaptive development. The individual can be separate from the family and still be whole within himself, while feeling and being a viable member that belongs in his family of origin.

The completion of the adolescent's developmental tasks adds to the firm foundation on which the adult life will be built. The cement of this foundation is how much of the differentiation process the evolving adolescent completes and how far he gets in separation. The further along he gets in becoming his own person, the easier it is to handle the problems of daily living.

Within this deep, reinforced foundation will be positive self concepts, stress-reducing skills, ability to facilitate feelings and emotions, vocational goals, healthy self-esteem, functional and adaptive behavior, social ability, a sense of belonging and realistic boundaries and limits. All of this is developed as the adolescent tries out new behaviors and experiments with new strategies. This all occurs in an environment that supports the adolescent's struggle to be independent, and at the same time maintains appropriate boundaries and limits. In this way, the adolescent is allowed to grow as a person and at the same time learn self-discipline.

This delivers to the adult a multitude of benefits in stress-reducing skills, adaptive behaviors, functional relationships with others, increased intra-personal skills, heightened awareness, and stronger self concepts. All of these skills increase the probability of successful outcomes when used by the adult in interactions at work, in relationships, or in intra-personal situations.

The following are the deficiencies which occur when the adolescent tries to use the skewed information from childhood to develop adaptive behavior:

1. The adolescent develops a support system with other acting-out teenagers instead of with adaptive teens.
2. The self concepts are negative: bad boy, troublemaker, doper, alcoholic, thief, whore, etc. Acts on impulses instead of sublimating one's desires.
3. Doesn't go outside the family. Doesn't break the "Don't Talk, Don't Trust, Don't Feel" rules. Keeps everything inside.
4. Doesn't explore a vocational future. Instant gratification is the only value. This can begin a sub-rosa or criminal life style. Also magical thinking occurs when they say, "I'll hit the lottery."
5. Doesn't see the need for higher education or doesn't feel it can be attained. Feels street learning is the best.
6. Doesn't complete the individualization process in the following ways:
   a) Remains enmeshed in the family system by perpetuating its dysfunctional behavior.
   b) Is emotionally intertwined with the family and acts out or becomes shut down according to what the family feels.
   c) Maintains the family's skewed, self-seeking, value system or moves to its opposite. Too much or too little, but never in balance.
   d) Mindsets are maintained from one generation to the next. Black and white thinking is the norm. Rigid rules are enforced.
   e) Boundaries are not developed. Physical boundaries are mostly violated. Emotional boundaries are non-existent because the teen acts out what the family feels. Spiritual boundaries are never explored because the mind is so actively staying ahead of the impending danger that it's never quiet enough to make a spiritual connection.
7. Doesn't separate from the family because no matter how far he travels away, he's still connected and being impacted by the family of origin.

Outcomes

Adolescents who do not complete their developmental tasks try to become mature by using "adult" behavior. They drink, drug, become sexual, smoke, quit school, have babies, go to work, get married, run away, do criminal acts, etc., long before they are able to make a mature decision or realize the consequences of their actions.

Adolescents who do complete their developmental tasks try out new behavior and push the boundaries, but don't break them; they move slowly enough to feel the ramifications of the behavior, to determine if they want to continue with the behavior(s). From this process, the adolescent does the footwork for what is to be the adult's wants, needs, and desires. Through the process, the adolescent gains greater insight into himself, has positive peer interactions, fewer problematic behaviors, more adaptive living skills, and a wider range of educational and vocational choices.

These tasks are a big job, and many times they are not completed for the adult. It's the result of the child not being allowed to grow and the adolescent having too much or too little freedom to experiment with behavior. The resulting deficiencies are carried into adulthood as the individual tries to navigate through the trials of living.

ADULT COMPETENCE

Adult competence doesn't happen in a vacuum. They just don't wake up one day and have the ability to handle everything. It is a process of trial and error. Each event that occurs is experienced, remembered, and the results become another piece of the tapestry we call living skills. This is an ongoing process, one that is modified over time due to the changing needs during the three adult stages.

The adult needs a firm foundation in order to accomplish this. He needs all of the information gathered in childhood and experiences of adolescence in order to build an adaptive life in adulthood - one in which the following will occur:

1. Attain a vocation, maintain employment, and retire.
2. Begin a family, have children, and launch them.
3. Gain intra-personal skills and develop strong self concepts with positive self-esteem.
4. Self-actualize to reach full potential.
5. Make a contribution to mankind.

From this process will emanate an **emotionally mature, responsible adult** who will be able to facilitate life on a daily basis without retreating to dysfunctional behavior.

**THE TRAITS OF A COMPETENT ADULT
ARE ONES IN WHICH
ADAPTIVE COPING STRATEGIES ARE DEVISED
TO DEVELOP CREATIVE SOLUTIONS
TO LIFE'S VICISSITUDES
WHICH ENABLE THE EVOLVING PERSON
TO SELF-ACTUALIZE AND MAKE A CONTRIBUTION
TO MANKIND**

The successful accomplishment of the childhood, adolescent, and adult tasks contributes to the completion of a competent adult. Any deficiencies will manifest as a problem. Some of them will cause difficulties only. Some will take a lot of work to overcome. Some problems will not be transcended until the deficiency is corrected. These will be explored in the next chapter as the three developmental stages are examined as ego states.

SUMMARY

Adulthood is the stage that uses the information gathered in childhood and the experience of adolescence as the foundation on which one's life will be built. During adulthood one will work, have a family, self-actualize, contribute to mankind, retire and die. All of this happens in a three-stage process.

In stage one, everything begins for the individual. A career is started, self concepts are firmed, relationships with others become more defined, and a family is started or a decision made to delay its inception.

In stage two, a career is established and maintained, a deeper understanding of one's self is achieved, further separation from others is accomplished, children reach adolescence and, if delayed earlier, a family is started. At this time there is more time behind than in front of the individual.

Stage three brings retirement, the person is comfortable with his identity, has a variety of roles without losing himself, children are launched, and power is transferred to the grown children.

In order for the adult to mature in a changing world, he has to use adaptive coping strategies to develop creative solutions to life's vicissitudes, which allows the growing person to self-actualize and make a contribution to mankind. This does not happen in a vacuum and takes the completion of the developmental tasks in the two previous stages of child-hood and adolescence to make it happen.

Any missing information from the childhood stage will leave gaps in the adult's intra-personal skills and social ability, feelings, wants, needs, talents, roles or accepted behavior. In order to gather the appropriate information, the child has to experience a safe, warm, nurturing environment in which he is encouraged to explore his potential and is taught healthy limits.

There are many ways to derail a child-centered home. Some of them include having disengaged parents, an unsafe environment, unusual stressors in the home, mental illness, substance abuse, or **any other behavior that diverts the parents from their primary tasks.** At this time the foundation will not be strong. It will be built on shifting sands and have large deficiencies.

With skewed childhood development comes the following problems: The adolescent lacks choices, feels selfish when taking care of himself, becomes "other directed" to avoid feelings, learns to maintain a safe distance from inconsistent adults, shuts down to avoid feelings, begins to tolerate unequal relationships, uses inappropriate behavioral responses to feelings and situations, learns negative gender roles and develops poor self concepts.

Adolescence is the stage that the information gathered in childhood is acted upon. If it is healthy, the adolescent develops self concepts and explores educational and vocational choices. He completes the individualization process which culminates in healthy separation when launched. At this time, he is separate from the family of origin, yet still feels he is a member and belongs.

When the tasks are not completed, the following deficiencies ensue and are brought into adulthood. Self concepts are negative and educational choices are not explored. Vocational interests are apathetic; enmeshment remains in the family of origin and is always there even if he physically leaves. He uses "adult" behavior to feel grown up long before he is mature enough to make the decision or realize its consequences.

Adult competence is a process. In this process the adult learns and grows from each experience. If he has a firm foundation, the rudiments of appropriate behavioral responses, the results will be adaptive, and the adult will complete all of the tasks of the three stages of adulthood. This will allow the adult to attain vocational goals and retire; begin a family, have children, and launch them; develop strong self concepts with positive self-esteem; self-actualize to reach full potential; and make a contribution to mankind.

Problems will manifest later if the foundation is weak and life experiences negative. At this time, maladaptive behavior will be used to mask the feelings arising from life's problems. This reaction can be any type of obsessive/compulsive behavior that can be used to take the focus off themselves. It would include drinking, drugging, eating, gambling, sex, relationships, work or over achievement. At this time normal development is sidetracked while all resources, time, and energy are spent maintaining the dysfunctional behavior. The above is not a description of an emotionally mature adult who can facilitate the problems of daily living in an adaptive way.

NOTE: I've deliberately not given out any formal assignments for Chapters Four through Six. You will be referred back to those chapters after Chapter Seven. I wanted the reader to have all of the information before he started to work on the material.

CASE STUDY

Remember the teen in the TV show? Let's call her Tanya and project her into adulthood without any treatment. First, some more background information.

Tanya is born into a poor inner city family. Dad is a functional alcoholic who works during the week and drinks on the weekends. Mom works and always seems preoccupied. On the weekends, Dad is usually drunk or going out, and Mom is angry. The fights never seem to end.

They get divorced when Tanya is seven. Dad moves to another state and she and Mom move into a project because of poor economics. The projects are a fearful place in which to live. There are gangs, disrespectful teenagers, and drug use is prevalent. There always seems to be "weird" men hanging around the area. For the first three years, Mom is able to adjust her schedule to walk Tanya to school and pick her up. Tanya is never allowed to go anyplace by herself because the area is too "dangerous."

Mom's schedule changes when Tanya is 10. She has to walk home from school by herself and prepare supper because Mom doesn't get home until 6:00 p.m. Mom is tired, distant, and always seems mad. Tanya's only friends are a couple of girls in school who don't live in the project, TV, and her dreams. Her life is changed forever when she is raped and it goes unnoticed by her mom or any other significant adult. Tanya is "socialized" into the gang through repeated rapes, coercion, her own lack of power, and her need for protection because of her fear of being killed by one of those "weird" men who hang around the project.

Tanya's foundation for life is shallow, weak, and deficient at best. It will not be one in which **higher order** goals, needs, or desires will be fulfilled. Hope will be minimal. She will view herself as a victim throughout life.

During childhood, Tanya was preoccupied with surviving the mental trauma of being raised in a dysfunctional (alcoholic) home with a preoccupied or distant mother. Tanya felt love during the times her father didn't drink and Mom looked happy. At this time, she would do everything perfectly, and everyone was pleased with her. Tanya would try to repeat the same behavior when her dad was drinking, but couldn't please anyone or make them happy. It didn't make any difference how hard she tried. Tanya was very confused by this and never really understood what she did wrong to make her parents unhappy. Tanya never got in touch with her own feelings because she was preoccupied worrying about how Dad would come home from work, act on weekends, or how Mom would react to him. Tanya was further confused because Mom would say things like, "Dad's not drunk," or "I'm happy" when her face showed otherwise, or "We're not fighting" when they were yelling at each other. And one night after watching them physically fight and throw things all around the house she was told, "You must be imaging it — nothing happened last night!"

When we add up the impact of preoccupied parents and being in perpetual conflict with them, with the rape and the subsequent invalidations, there is an enormous investment made in not feeling, and denying the present reality. The world is a very unsafe place to live in and too dangerous to explore. This fear limits the child's ability to demonstrate competence, or expand her horizons. All she has is a very limited view of the world through the experiences at the "project" or what she perceived from the sitcoms on TV. When you compare Tanya's environment to the one in a child-centered home, it becomes clear how the developmental tasks of childhood fail to be completed. This lack of information or misinformation is taken into adolescence to be acted upon.

We now pick up Tanya in adolescence on the TV show. She is angry, anorexic, ungovernable, and beginning to use serious drugs. What she learned in childhood was: she was not safe in her family, she would die without the gang, and feelings only got in her way.

There is no room here for experimenting with new behaviors unless they are drug involved or a new scam to make money. The individualization process is not complete because life without the gang's protection cannot be visualized. The separation process of becoming one's own person only occurs while acting out. At this time the adolescent feels power because she is using "adult" behavior and is blind to the fact that she is not emotionally prepared for the adult consequences to her acting-out behavior.

The adolescent at this time is socialized into street values. Later on this will manifest as problematic at best, when she tries to respond to problems of daily living. It is almost impossible to develop adaptive coping strategies out of a violent background.

As an adult, Tanya will *try* to accomplish her goals in the socially prescribed way: start or delay a family; begin, maintain and retire vocationally; explore educational opportunities; learn about herself; self-actualize; and make a contribution to mankind. But, Tanya is mostly clueless to the facts or process of what normal development is because she has spent most of her young life surviving in a very limited environment.

These deficiencies play themselves out for Tanya in the following ways. In the project, the socially accepted way of attaining one's goals was to be a thief, drug dealer, or prostitute herself, which can be done in many ways by both boys and girls. Starting a family was determined when the teen became pregnant and had to decide whether or not she wanted an abortion. Jobs were for suckers. There would always be money to be made in the street. Education was for nerds (and yet she had been an "A" student). All of her values were learned in the street. There was nothing to learn about herself. She was a victim and she would do "anything" not to be hurt. The goal was to survive and "what is that crap" about making a contribution toward mankind? No wonder we have so many 30, 40, 50-year-old adolescents out there today.

None of this case study is made up. It is a generalization of the ramifications of being raised in a dysfunctional home. I've actually toned down what I usually see in therapy. The population I treat is dual diagnosed with substance abuse and a psychiatric illness, and usually experienced multiple relapses. My observations are simple: the more dysfunction an individual is subjected to — the greater will be the manifestations of acting out or problematic strategies occurring later in adulthood.

ACCEPTANCE

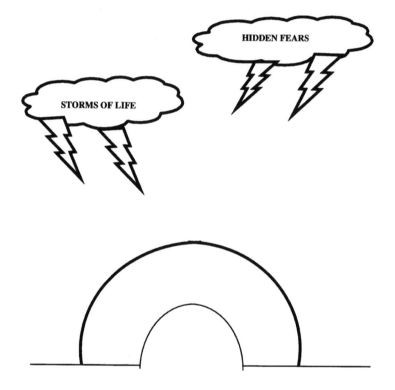

It's hard to distinguish
if the light ahead is freedom
or the headlight from an
oncoming train!

SHAME

ADDICTION

PART THREE

INTEGRATION

DEPRESSION

DENIAL

If you do what you did
You get what you got.

CHAPTER SEVEN

Man is complex
The description of the complexity
Is just as complex

OVERVIEW

In Chapter Seven we will begin to explore the ego states' Matrix.

1. How the filters of the ego states determine a behavioral response
2. Examine how the filtering process of the conscious operates and why the course of action it takes depends on the mental, physical and spiritual balance of the individual.
3. Negative consequences that occur if the paradigm is misused
4. Look at the components of the structure of the ego states
5. Explore the parallels between physical and psychological development

EGO STATES

Ego states are ways of being. In them is determined how we:
1. **Interact with others**
2. **Interpret a situation**
3. **Decide the course of action or inaction that we will follow in any situation**

These states of being are fluid and change as the environment (or one's perception of it) and the current psychological condition of the individual changes. No two interactions are alike, although there are many generalizations made by the psyche. The role response in an everyday situation is a good example. This is when one says hello to a friend that he meets on the street. The only thing that changes is the enthusiasm given with the greeting. On a bad day there is very little enthusiasm. On a good day it is, "Hi!" This book cannot detail all of the normal responses. What it will do is:
1. **Identify the responses that are off center**
2. **Help you to gain insight into their causes**
3. **Offer another response or different possibilities**

FILTERS

These ego states, or states of being, are also ways of acting **human**. Ego states act as filters, interpreting our environment. A situation that is being filtered can take any type of course. I know the average person's appreciation for his internal process is minimal and taken for granted. I can't blame him because there is usually so much going on in his everyday struggle. Also, I don't feel much energy has to be expended in this area unless there is **problematic behavior, confusion, recurring issues** that can't seem to be resolved, or come up another way — **vocational impasses, dysfunctional or toxic relationships,** or **ANY INTERNAL CONFUSION.** Did I leave anything out? You can see how encompassing the filtering process can be, and I feel everyone can use a little more insight into himself in order to be in harmony with self and others.

Example of the Filtering Process

The following is an example of how two different endings can result from the same situation: there are five men talking on a city street. As the conversation progresses, one of the voices begins to rise. How the situation is perceived through the filters will determine the type of action the individual will take.

In scenario A, the environment is a calm one in an upper scale neighborhood where not much street crime is experienced and a raised voice will be perceived as less threatening. Someone might ask why a voice was raised or dismiss it as just being excited with the conversation. Each one of the men is in good physical condition with no chronic ailments. Because of this, no one feels in danger, and if a skirmish broke out, each man could physically handle it. This lowers a person's defense mechanism and enables the men to ignore the raised voice. All of these men are also in good mental health as well. None are experiencing depression, rage, paranoia or any other major psychiatric symptom. This results in an accurate assessment of the situation with no action taken, and everything remaining manageable. There are no hard feelings. All feel good about the meeting and leave with no harm done to the friendships.

In scenario B, the environment is an inner-city housing project with strange men hanging around in doorways. It is perceived as hostile because of its high rate of street crime. All the men talking are keenly aware of their environment because the area is so threatening. Immediately, as someone's voice begins to rise, paranoia begins to rise. "What do you mean by that?" one of the men snaps back. Another one of the men shouts at someone in a doorway, "What are YOU looking at!" Tensions are now high. All are defensive and waiting to make a move. The physical condition of these men is good to fair. The ones in fair shape know they can't handle being physical for too long. They have to act more quickly and with more force than others in good shape. This usually guarantees that an aggressive action will be taken before all the options are weighed. The psychological condition of people in this environment is mostly unbalanced because they have to be partially paranoid in order to survive. Figure 7.1 is a graphic representation of the filters' process.

The filtering process of the ego states and the resulting action described in the above scenario B can happen in any dysfunctional or maladaptive environment. Sometimes it happens in healthy homes when multiple stressors overcome the family's usual coping strategies. Its members become overwhelmed and as things get ugly, the Adolescent rises to help the individual survive. At this point, the situational responses originate from column B because the environment becomes unstable.

TWO TYPES OF SITUATIONAL RESPONSES

A	B

FILTER ONE: ENVIRONMENT

1)*Stable* —upper scale neighborhood with little or no street crime; child-centered, adaptive home.

2)*Unstable* — inner-city housing project with high rate of street crime; dysfunctional, abusive, maladaptive home.

FILTER TWO: PERCEPTION OF THE SITUATION

1)*Non-Threatening* — No, or very little, action is taken

2)*Threatening* — some form of action is usually taken

FILTER THREE: PHYSIOLOGICAL CONDITION

1)*Healthy* — less defense mechanisms are present because the person is secure

2)*Sick* — one has a distorted view; more defense mechanisms will be present because the person is vulnerable when resistance is low

FILTER FOUR: PSYCHOLOGICAL CONDITION

1)*Balanced* — one can accurately assess the situation

2)*Unbalanced* — one can be depressed, manic, anxious, or fearful; they are off-center; one has a distorted view; and a response will be more volatile.

RESULTING ACTION FROM THE FILTERING PROCESS

1)*De-escalation* — the situation remains manageable; all are content with its ending

2)*Escalation* — the situation becomes unmanageable, tempers are high, and mostare left with negative feelings

FIGURE 7.1 FILTERING PROCESS OF THE EGO STATES

Most clients that went through therapy related to the fact that a negative change in their environment had caused them to change their coping style from using adaptive strategies to using ones that maintained survival only.

CASE STUDY: Joan had a clear recollection of the downward path her survival skills brought her to when she was able to visualize the process in Figure 7.1. At this time she exclaimed, "It was like 'The War of the Roses.' Each time it started to go downhill, it was like a rocket sled ride. One moment I was in love with my 'Soul Mate' and the next moment I was asking, who is this person I am married to or in a relationship with." At this point Joan is describing her environment as *unstable* or *threatening* because she is perceiving a rapidly changing life and feels out of control.

During this time she also reports experiencing physical deterioration with headaches, backaches, diminished energy, loss of appetite, and a negative attitude. It was generally during those times of stress that she caught the flu — or should I say that it caught her. The reason is that stress reduces the human immune system's ability to ward off disease, like the flu, and she would become physically *sick*.

Psychologically, Joan was *unbalanced* because she was experiencing paranoia, fear, depression, mood swings and anxiety. The instability distorted her view of the situation, made her reactions more volatile, and decisions exaggerated and arbitrary. The situation *escalated* until the breakup.

ASSIGNMENT 9: Do you know anyone that has had Joan's experience? If yes — write out their process. It's okay not to remember all that happened. You will remember enough. The rest will fill itself in. Did this ever happen to you? If yes — what happened? What was your process, based on Figure 7.1? Did you learn anything from the experience prior to reading this book? What do you see now?

Internal Response of the Filtering Process

None of the perception in scenario A or B occurs in a vacuum. Internally, several processes go on simultaneously, which interpret, order, and decide which course of action to take on the incoming data. Most of this occurs automatically due to the conditioning the person encountered over his life span and the resulting action determined by prior experience (what he remembers) or the internalized behavioral response (what he does without thinking).

Remember the basics to perception at this time
1. Everything we perceive is brought in through the senses
2. The new information is then processed through the consciousness or the conscious mind
3. The data is first ordered into concepts to allow effective processing by the Executive System. This is also a selective process because the mind could not handle all of the stimuli it is being bombarded with, and extraneous material is ignored or eliminated.
4. The material is now filtered to determine if it's non-threatening, simple threatening, complex threatening, or overwhelming.
   a) Non-threatening and simple-threatening material remains in the conscious and the appropriate behavioral response to the person's conditioning is exhibited.
   b) Complex-threatening material is sent to the preconscious.
   c) If the data is overwhelming or is **perceived** as similar to a past experience, it is sent to the subconscious. At this point it makes no difference if the experience is real or imagined — **it's real to the conscious mind and that's what it takes action on!**
5. The suppressed data then attaches to and/or is triggered by a past event.
6. As this energy (past event) is released, it travels through the first stage of preconscious and is experienced first as uneasiness and then as anxiety.
7. During the second stage of the preconscious, the triggered repressed material is transformed into a behavioral response. At this time, the person's internal responses to pain will engage automatically, when dysfunctional behavior is exhibited as it breaks through the person's surface level of awareness. Figure 7.2 will serve as a reminder.
8. The behavioral response will have two determinants:
   a) The energy system's strength that is proportionate to the amount of shame the situation evokes
   b) What type of behavior is used in the individual's problem loop?

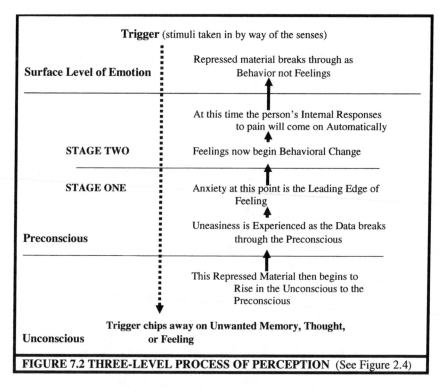

FIGURE 7.2 THREE-LEVEL PROCESS OF PERCEPTION (See Figure 2.4)

The entire system described above is an internal process. It is driven by feelings, emotions, past experience, and interpretation. The internal structure that mediates this conglomerate of data is the individual's ego states which are comprised of all three developmental age stages: child, adolescent, and adult — with the adult having two modes. One side is very critical and the other side is nurturing. The three ego states all have a voice in the resulting action of any situation. Figure 7.2 (2.4 repeat) is a graphic illustration of the internal filtering process that all information entering the human perceptual system is subjected to. It is repeated from Chapter Two for the reader's convenience.

Informed Consent

Before I get into the issues, I have to give you a warning. I do this because I believe in the concept of **Informed Consent**. I believe all should have choices through being given all the available information. When this is accomplished and the intent of this book is fulfilled, a person **"fore-warned is forearmed!"** The warning is this: *NONE OF THE MATERIAL*

IN THIS BOOK CAN BE USED TO HURT OTHER PEOPLE WITHOUT THE PAIN COMING BACK TO INJURE YOU!

I've actually seen others use this to stay "one up" in various relationships, and it always came back to haunt them. It usually returns when the other person retaliates after he uncovers the manipulation. As one grows and loses the need to control other people, he maintains his spiritual connection to a higher power, because he is focused on helping others instead of self-seeking by no longer being self-absorbed in the fear of being abandoned.

As you progress through this book, it is postulated that a part of you (The Adult Ego State) sees all that you do and knows your intention even though it is hidden from your present awareness. This will no longer be true. This book opens up the past behavior to scrutiny and makes it difficult to deny previous controlling or manipulative behavior. These behaviors were internalized responses, learned as a child, in order to survive a traumatic childhood experience or life. Now they **get in the way of living!**

PREVIOUS BEHAVIOR WAS INTERNALIZED RESPONSES LEARNED AS A CHILD IN ORDER TO SURVIVE TRAUMATIC CHILDHOOD EXPERIENCES OR LIFE

Through this book you may find what traumas were hidden in your past. However, **discovery takes away the ability to have freedom of behavior with a relatively clear conscience.** This is why they say in Alcoholics Anonymous, "all the fun is taken out of drinking." The person's "disease" is ruined. He can't drink the way he did and enjoy it. At this point, if the drinking is not stopped, it increases as the new knowledge turns into a two-edged sword: freedom when the alcoholic can stop drinking, pain when he continues — for he now knows the consequences his drinking brings to himself and others. At this point, he drinks to get drunk to cover up his pain — can't suppress the memories — drinks more to cover up the inability to forget and enters a never-ending loop until death or recovery. The same principles apply to any twelve-step program. I use AA as an example because drinking can be clearly observed. Some of the other addictions cannot be readily seen, are easily denied, or "minimized out" as not being that bad. Can anyone name the part of me that included the warning during Informed Consent about using the new paradigm for selfish reasons?

STRUCTURE

Webster defines the following two words:

PERSONALITY . . . is the quality or state of being personal, or of being a person . . . an integrated group of emotional trends, behavior tendencies, etc.

EGO . . . is the self, whether considered as an organization or system of mental states . . .

The internal structure of a human being's personality is comprised of three ego states. These ego states, or ways of being, are spawned and refined as the individual traverses through the developmental stages of childhood, adolescence, and adulthood. Each stage carries certain traits. When all three stages combine, the traits embodied within its structure, produce the whole person with its distinct personality. Just as the genes determine physical traits — the three ego states determine the person's psychological traits. This matrix includes the **resulting behavior** that is generated because of how an **interaction is interpreted** by the individual's conscious or ego states.

BEHAVIOR IS DETERMINED BY HOW THE EGO STATES INTERPRET A SITUATION NOT BY AN OBJECTIVE REALITY

The designation for these ego states is:

1. **The Child**
2. **The Adolescent**
3. **The Adult**

They are composed of the traits from each developmental stage and carry all the memories, information and experience from what transpired during its particular period. The information gathered is not a selective process. It is taken in whether we want it or not. If an event happened during a child's development, it's recorded in one of the ego states. **It doesn't make any difference if he remembers it — it's still stored within the memory.** This is why we can't put something behind us. The event or memory is only placed on hold and will only come up again or find another way to manifest. The only way out of the trauma is to go through the feelings that were left buried in the psyche, when they are triggered today in a new situation.

Acceptance 129

**THE ONLY WAY OUT
OF A PAINFUL SITUATION
IS TO GO THROUGH THE PAIN**

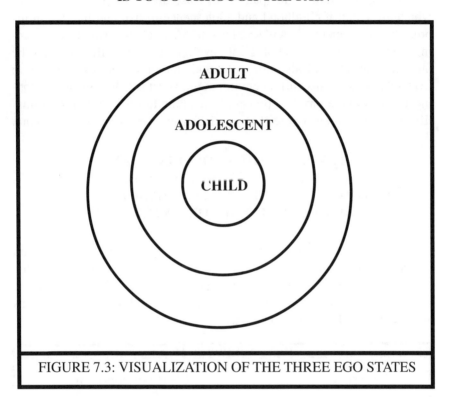

FIGURE 7.3: VISUALIZATION OF THE THREE EGO STATES

Analogy Between Physical and Psychological Development

A visual depiction of how the personality of a matured adult is produced is seen in Figure 7.3. The broad outside line is the fully developed adult. Inside of this shell are the three segments of its makeup. Just as in physical development, the child grows outward from a seed — so grows the personality as it expands outward from all childhood experiences.

In physical adolescent development, the evolving teen continues to grow outward. He becomes heavier and taller, adding to the child. Most of this growth is dependent on the type of health care and nutrition the child received. These are necessary if the adolescent and subsequent adult is to reach his full physical potential. The same is true in personality development. The adolescent emerges out of the child's experience and begins to practice behavior he will use in later life as an adult. He will accomplish this based on the information entered during childhood.

During the adult's life span he will use all of his physical systems which grew out of childhood and adolescence to live and interact in his present environment. He will see, hear, taste, touch, and smell the incoming data. The adult's psychological development is no different than the physical one. He will also use childhood and adolescent experiences to live and interact in his current environment. What psychological development brings to the physical process is meaning to life. Without meaning, life would be a series of rote physiological responses to task-oriented data.

PSYCHOLOGICAL DEVELOPMENT BRINGS MEANING TO LIFE. WITHOUT IT, EXISTENCE IS A PHYSIOLOGICAL RESPONSE TO TASK-ORIENTED DATA

Figure 7.4 is a visual depiction of the analogy between physical and psychological development. In it, one may glean the overall intent of the developmental process. It's fascinating to see these parallels between the systems — to watch maturing - the forming of a mind/body experience, as an integrated, whole, human being.

HUMAN DEVELOPMENT	
PHYSICAL	**PSYCHOLOGICAL**
CHILDHOOD	
A child grows outward from a seed.	Personality development grows out of childhood experiences.
ADOLESCENCE	
The adolescent continues to grow outward based on the nutritional and healthcare needs that were provided during childhood.	Personality continues to grow as the child experiences physical and cognitive enhancements. The adolescent begins to practice adult behavior based on information gathered during childhood.
ADULTHOOD	
The adult will use all physical attributes that developed during childhood and adolescence to live and interact in his present environment.	The adult also uses the experiences of childhood and adolescence to continue his personality development. This process will bring meaning to life.

FIGURE 7.4 PARALLELS BETWEEN PHYSICAL AND PSYCHOLOGICAL DEVELOPMENT

SUMMARY

The ego states are ways of being human. In them is determined how we interact with others, interpret a situation, and decide a course of action. When the individual is healthy in body, mind, and spirit, the action based on the filters of the ego states will be adaptive, functional, and balanced. If the person is unhealthy or out of balance in any or all of these areas, the reaction will be skewed and possibly volatile or inadequate to facilitate an adaptive response.

The internal response of the ego states' filtering process follows a specific course. In it, the raw data is taken in by the senses, ordered into concepts by the psyche, and filtered by the ego states to determine what kind of action, if any, needs to be taken on the new material. During the data's journey through the consciousness, overwhelming items are transferred to the unconscious for storage until such time that it's safe to acknowledge, or until something triggers its release.

When the ascending previously suppressed event remains toxic to the human's emotional integrity, its rising feelings and emotions will be transformed into a behavioral set. This covert reactionary response, will dissipate the energy of the rising emotions, and mask the true reasons for the reaction....to hide the suppressed data from the individual's awareness.

The internal structure of the human's personality is made up of three ego states: the Child, Adolescent, and Adult. Each one brings its own filter into the process and is spawned from the memories, the information gathered and assimilated, and experiences that occurred during his developmental time span.

There appears to be a parallel between physical and psychological development. Each one grows outward from a seed, develops over time, and is dependent on the success of the previous stage in order to flourish.

CHAPTER EIGHT

In childhood lies
The motive behind
All adult behavior

OVERVIEW

When you have completed Chapter Eight, you will be able to recognize:

1. When you or others are in their Child Ego State
2. What a Shame Attack is:
    a)How it feels when you or someone else has one
    b)How it looks when it occurs
    c)What behavior usually follows the attack
3. How developmental tasks are essential to development
4. When and how uncompleted tasks skew the developing individual's maturation process regarding: self awareness, boundaries, trust, emotional availability to self and others, ability to risk and facilitate making a mistake, being competent, validating self without having to receive external rewards, and learning how to be a "human *being*" instead of a "human *doing*" (it's not always important to be productive)

CHILD EGO STATE

The Child Ego State can best be visualized in the adult as a part of them that's still a child. Its age is birth to 11 or 13 depending on how fast they matured. My particular scan in therapy observes them at age two and up. Other colleagues have noticed preverbal expressions. I haven't. This ego state houses a large amount of the softer feelings and stores all of the basic data that has been entered as the child learned and grew. The Child Ego State is also a place that gets confusing because the adult regresses to black and white thinking and becomes egocentric. This confusion results as the adult inputs raw data through their senses and hasn't got the ability to manipulate it because they become overwhelmed and act as a child. In this process they take responsibility for all that happens to themselves and those around them.

The adult slips into the Child Ego State when he becomes:

1. Overwhelmed during a current crisis
2. A past event is triggered by a present situation
3. A present situation is *perceived* as overwhelming
4. It can occur during the following times:
    a)At work with co-workers or your boss
    b)While talking to your spouse
    c)Being challenged by your teenage child
    d)Having sex (Stop getting mad! I'll explain it later.)
    e)Being stopped by a police officer
    f)Going to court
    g)In school with a teacher or dean
    h)*With your parents!* (Oh God! He knows.)
    i)Going to the doctor
    j)Talking to any church or religious figure that has authority
       (When was the last time you said no when asked to do some-
       thing for the church?)
    k)Being in conflict with *"ANY perceived authority figure"*
    l)*ANYTIME SHAME IS INVOKED!*

HOW THE CHILD EGO STATE PRESENTS

When the adult is in this ego state, he manifests all of the characteristics of a child and his:

1. Thinking becomes black and white and egocentric
2. Emotions are highly charged or diminished
3. Behavior is childlike — determined to get his own way. Nothing changes his mind no matter how much something is explained.
4. Body language becomes childlike with the following:
   a) Eyes will close or eye contact will be avoided
   b) Covering of ears or stating he won't listen
   c) Crossing of arms and displaying an angry, childlike face
   d) Voice usually lowers and in some cases disappears
   e) The body is actually pulled in and appears smaller and in some instances the legs are tucked under him
   f) Legs are animated and he has to go to the bathroom
   g) Thumbs can be sucked
   h) Fingers play with hair
   i) Face or mouth is stroked with hands
   j) Stuffed animals are held like a child and cuddled
   k) In extreme cases the person can shut down, go into a fetal position or become catatonic
5. Sometimes he will even display a temper tantrum. It will be less exaggerated than a child's, but it will still be a tantrum. This, you really have to look for. Once it's in your scan, you will see how it takes its many forms.

The preceding descriptions have been given for three reasons:

1. To see it in clients
2. To see it in others for all non-clinician readers
3. To see it **in yourself!**

This side is not always negative. It's also the part of the individual that allows them to be playful, enjoyable, loveable, and spontaneous. These are wonderful qualities for an adult who can still display them. These traits only become problematic when the adult has a fear-based reaction, shuts down, or manifests the immature behavior of a child and is no longer available to participate in the give and take of adult relationships.

This ego state is also a major determinant of the depth experienced in an intimate relationship. Relationships do not begin if the Child part doesn't connect or feel attracted to the other person. There is also a danger when the ego state is too domineering. This is when someone "looks for love in all the wrong places." (More on this later.)

Reframing

To anyone having difficulty with the concept of a Child Ego State or Inner Child, I offer a reframed version in which it's relabeled "the adult's Feeling State." In this state is contained most of the adult's feelings. You can still use all the material given for the Child as an assessment tool by adding one step to the process of reframing — look at the client's (friend or self) presentation as being mature or immature. For clarification in this section, maturity will be defined as the person's ability to manifest the appropriate feelings and level of intensity warranted by the situation. Immaturity will be demonstrated as the individual displays inappropriate feelings which were not warranted by the situation, displays no feelings at all, or displays too much or too little intensity in his behavior. The appropriate, mature response to a situation will be referred to as "normal" behavior.

The Power of Shame

Shame was the primary motivator of the child. It's the predominate feeling experienced by the child when anything negative occurred in his environment. Shame arises for the adult **anytime or any situation** in which he feels dominated or overpowered by an authority figure. A list of situations that can cause the adult to slip into this ego state was listed earlier in this chapter.

This is an important concept to understand because it transforms a perfectly competent adult into a child who becomes helpless and hopeless. How many times have you felt "little" when your boss wanted to talk to you or said, "Be in my office at 4 p.m."? When was the last time one of your parents gave you "the look" and remained silent when they didn't approve of your actions? How do you feel when this happens? Just like a little person. This is your Child Ego State, Inner Child, Feeling State, or whatever name you want to place on it. Rename it "The Child" now that you've identified what's occurring internally. Also label the feeling you experience during these interactions as *shame*. Using this as a framework, you can identify issues that arise for you and identify them in others as they appear. This is a great freedom, not to have to remain in the Child Ego

State or feel responsible for anyone else's feelings, as they experience them during your interactions.

SHAME ATTACK — The shame attack is provoked through the authority figure's actions. During the attack: you think you made a mistake, think or subconsciously feel you are an incompetent adult, shame rises, you begin to shut down, and then feel you are the mistake. You have just had a shame attack in your Child Ego State. Figure 8.1 is a visual depiction of the process.

ACTION OF THE AUTHORITY FIGURE

1. "The Look" is given by one of your parents
2. The boss says, "Come to my office"
↓

RESPONSE INVOKED BY THE ACTION

1. You feel "little"
2. You think, "What did I do wrong?"
↓

RESPONSE PROVOKED BY THE THOUGHTS AND FEELINGS

↓   ↓

<u>With</u> the internal Adult's input: <u>Without</u> the internal Adult's input:
1. Feeling "little" diminishes   1. You continue to feel "small" and
2. Being an adult is affirmed   wonder if you will ever be able
   and positive reasons are   to break off parental control
   concluded as to why the   2. You think about how many things
   boss wants to see you   you've done wrong and wonder
                                                 when the boss will find out you
                                                 are a fraud and fire you
↓

THE ADULT REMAINS IN   **THE ADULT IS NOW IN THE**
THE ADULT EGO STATE   **CHILD EGO STATE**

                                              The reaction is a full-blown shame
                                              attack in which the adult is reduced
                                              to being helpless and hopeless with-
                                              out any options.

FIGURE 8.1 PROCESS OF A SHAME ATTACK

Not all that's engendered in a shame attack has to be as drastic as the preceding described, unless you experienced a highly dysfunctional childhood. If this is the case, most of your severe reactions, will usually render you ineffective within the situation. This will continue to perpetuate your subordinate position with authority figures. It can cost you a better job, force you to play catch-up in relationships, keep you a child when around your parents, lower self-esteem, and diminish self concepts.

THE DIFFERENCE BETWEEN GUILT AND SHAME: GUILT SAYS YOU MADE A MISTAKE; SHAME SAYS YOU ARE THE MISTAKE

DEVELOPMENTAL DEFICITS AS TRIGGERS

Any uncompleted childhood tasks will induce great shame within the adult. This occurs when the lack of maturity in a present situation has its roots in a developmental goal that was unfinished or never attempted.

According to Erik Erikson, there are several stages of development that need to be completed during childhood to deliver a competent individual into adolescence. Each stage has its own conflict to resolve or task to complete. Unfinished stages will effect the next ones because development is cumulative. During these stages, the child will learn to trust, become autonomous, gain initiative, and become competent. If any are incomplete, they will show up later as deficiencies in the adult's maturity, decision-making process, self-esteem, social skills, and stress-reduction strategies.

STAGE ONE: Trust vs. Mistrust

During this stage the child is **forced** to trust his primary care givers because he lacks the resources or ability to survive without them. This is replicated in adulthood when the individual is **"forced," by convention,** to trust in different degrees, friends, spouse, parents, bosses, fellow workers, institutions, and the culture. The issue of mistrust is spawned in childhood when significant adults violate the infant's trust through abuse, neglect, or inconsistency in meeting his needs. The depth of this issue is determined by the intensity of the offences committed against him and how long it prevailed. This is a birth to age one stage issue that prevails through the life span until it's resolved. The trigger for the mistrust arising occurs when the adult's trust is violated by one of the significant persons listed above, and the present situation mimics or duplicates a past event. At that point, great feelings (usually shame) or energy is released into the person's unconsciousness. This sudden flood of feelings is released as the present situation attaches itself to an unresolved childhood issue. (This process is unknown to the adult.) At this point he becomes confused, overwhelmed, and shuts down. The person is now in his Child Ego State and ineffective in adult situations. This reaction by the adult, as in all others, will vary over time, issues, and circumstances. This is always dynamic and fun to work with for a clinician that enjoys this type of introspective work.

STAGE TWO: Autonomy vs. Shame and Doubt

In this stage the toddler explores his world under the watchful eye of the care giver. During this time he learns about himself and his environment. If successful, he will gain self-control, and a sense of self-worth and self-confidence. When a child is smothered, controlled, ridiculed or punished for trying to explore this natural independence or autonomy, the resulting consequences are that he will feel shame and doubt. This stage includes ages two and three, and like all unresolved developmental issues, will prevail over the life span when the issue or task remains unfinished.

These issues emerge in adulthood with family and friends, at work, or in social situations, when the individual is trying to maintain his physical, emotional, and/or spiritual boundaries and is berated for it. The intensity of the reaction will come from its attachment to a previous experience, if, at the time, he is being controlled.

The adult experiences shame during these encounters because the message being conveyed is that he is not competent. Boundaries are essential for autonomy. They maintain one's integrity and keep out intrusions on the psyche. The intrusions I'm referring to are the ones that invalidate a person's self concepts for the sake of another person's self-seeking. This is when the first person wants the second person to give themselves up so the first person can get ahead at the expense of the second person.

EXAMPLE: The following is a work situation in which the employer would not grant time off for an essential family function. He wanted the employee to work additional hours that were allotted for child care, because the firm was understaffed and didn't want to hire another employee. The employee feels a deep obligation toward his family, is doing his job 110%, and feels it's not fair. If this stage's tasks are completed, the employee will state the boundary to his employer (hours he can work), negotiate what time off he needs, and maintain his self concepts. If not, the employee will work, feel shame because he was badgered or coerced into working, lose his sense of independence, and shut down. During this process he will relive the failures of his childhood when he tried to stretch his world and was controlled or ridiculed by primary care givers. This coercion will come back later and bite the employer on the rear end because the employee will aggressively act it out with verbal dissent, quitting or passively demonstrating it by reduced production, becoming ill, pilferage, sabotage or being involved in a work-related accident.

This process will occur anytime someone is taken advantage of. Payback is an eye opener! It happens in families between siblings, children and parents, in marriages between spouses, with friends, acquaintances, lovers, neighbors, and employers. It happens anytime there is injustice. Being a therapist, I become very inquisitive when someone's behavior seemingly comes from nowhere. Sometimes the responses are automatic ones and the motive inaccessible. With slight probing the answers are easily exposed. Most of the times the behavior is a deliberate retaliation for a past hurt. When it occurs, it's usually the Child getting back at his perpetrator through the Adolescent.

STAGE THREE: Initiative vs. Guilt

In this stage, children begin to risk by exploring beyond their comfort zone. They try new things. They become more assertive and aggressive. If they are successful, they will learn to deal with people and situations in an adaptive manner. The child learns about roles through play and fantasy by imitating his primary care givers. If the fledgling is successful and encouraged by significant adults, he begins to develop self worth and initiative. If he is ridiculed or shown disinterest, guilt feelings will prevail. Guilt will turn into shame if the child is deeply wounded during this stage. The initial feelings of the child is that he can never do anything right. This is guilt. The subsequent feelings are that the child is not right. There is something wrong with him that can't be fixed. This is shame.

This issue manifests in adulthood when the individual risks doing something new and is ridiculed or no interest is shown. This can happen in any area of life where the individual takes the initiative to attempt a new task, behavior or idea. It's also an area that impacts one's behavior today when it returns (in memory), or is triggered, and wipes out a person's forward momentum.

Have you ever seen someone start a project — doing a wonderful job, then someone special or significant makes a negative comment, and it looks like the person has just been stabbed in the heart and all the wind is taken out of his sails? From this time forward, momentum is negligible and sometimes the project will be abandoned.

If the individual has good self-concepts, the project will be completed after he facilitates the pain that surfaced from the negative comment. When this task is completed, the adult will be able to take in any appropriate comments, weigh them for validity, modify the project (if it's indicated), and even appreciate what was said. This is a mature process and it signifies solid self concepts and high self-esteem. I'm not saying that some things won't hurt. I feel that we will always maintain a modicum of sensitivity when someone we love or highly respect makes a personal comment about us. Our ability to feel is our human birthright.

Our Inner Child lives on forever!

STAGE FOUR: Industry vs. Inferiority

This is the stage the child learns to "do." (Remember — a human doing instead of a human being.) In it the child further develops his self concepts and self worth through learning to become more competent in the various skills society demands. If the novice is successful during this period (age 6 to 11 years old), he will develop the required skills needed to fulfill a productive life. Also during this time, the young person will develop a balance between working and living. When out of balance, a person's identity and self-esteem is based upon production goals only. Very little value is placed upon interpersonal relationships or endeavors. All or most energy is placed on producing and the person becomes a workaholic in later life.

Lack of completing this goal is felt throughout the life span when the only sense of accomplishment the adult feels is when he is productive. All else is placed on hold or takes second position to it. This includes family, marriage, spouse, children, friends, and social situations. Nothing is ever as important as the job. Know anybody like that? The list is probably endless. How about you! Where are your priorities?

If this issue isn't resolved prior to, or going through, adulthood, the adult has very few, if any, meaningful relationships. It's very lonely waiting for these people to come home from work.

Retirement becomes a nightmare for the workaholic. Developmentally, the aging human adjusts to diminishing capacity by slowing down. This becomes "a fate worse than death," as developmental tasks begin to conflict when the retiring person can't slow down because all of his self concepts and self-esteem is based on being productive. This looks like another instance in which one chases his tail. (How's that for a key issue for the Problem Loop? Turn back to those pages and try it.)

ASSIGNMENT 10: How was your childhood developmentally? Did you miss or not complete any developmental tasks because your primary care givers (usually parents) were too rigid, fearful, overly religious, emotionally distant, non-existent, or abusive (mentally, physically, emotionally, spiritually, or sexually)? What do you recognize in the chapter that you have to do for yourself to complete them? Do you recognize any of these developmental shortcomings in your parents, spouse, significant other, or children? If yes — how can you help them? Do you have to help them? You will gain more insight into what your role is in another person's life, during the last half of this book.

SUMMARY

Childhood is an age stage in which the developing personality of the human host is gathering the basic data needed for living. During this time period the Child Ego State takes in the necessary data in order for the individual to learn the basic rudiments of his feelings, start to form a self identity, learn about himself in relation to his primary care givers, explore his environment, and define his boundaries. If all developmental tasks of the Child are completed, the forth-coming adolescent will be equipped to increase his development outside the bounds of the family. If the tasks are not completed, the Child will experience shame and carry these feelings throughout his life span as inadequacy.

The feelings of shame experienced when one makes a "normal" mistake in life, can reduce the most competent individual into a "little person." The process of the adult regressing to a child is called a *"SHAME AT-TACK."*

Shame attaches itself to unfinished developmental tasks and is carried throughout one's life span until they are completed, or until death. Each developmental stage of childhood has its own tasks, triggers, and consequences.

CASE STUDY

Joan's story is a clear example of skewed childhood development, which reveals itself in her failed relationships. At first she was confused with the concept because she was vocationally successful and automatically thought that vocational maturity indicated that she was emotionally mature as well. It's one thing to be cognitively adept with task-oriented data that work situations dictate — it's another when trying to deal with the fluid state of one's internal process or the dynamic nature of relationships with love objects or family members.

Joan could not please or impress her parents no matter how well she did in school, in sports, or with tasks. They were always looking for her to do it better or in another way, although they would state she could be anything she wanted to be. This double message confused her. On one hand she knew she could do anything. On the other, she felt that she never did "anything" good enough to succeed.

The mixed messages Joan was given were shame-based and created an internal void, or, as others have described it — a hole in their heart. The internalized response to these messages was the shame attack in which the adult Joan would regress to a child when the feelings from the rising shame overwhelmed her. In the process, she would "shut down" and hide from the overpowering feelings. When the episode would subside, the adult Joan would reappear. As Joan hid, she never emotionally experienced the event, and without it being a valid learning experience, she was doomed to repeat the cycle over and over until the event was felt and remembered. The shame attack usually occurred when she was in conflict with one of her parents, a love object, or a powerful member of the hierarchy in the corporation she worked for.

As Joan began to unravel her childhood memories, it became clear to her why she experienced the overwhelming feelings of being a helpless and hopeless child and shutting down because of it. What she didn't understand was why she needed to *work* with her Child because the Adult could "handle" it. Joan at this point had to be *connected* to her childhood feelings and was assigned to a psychodrama group, where she was given several assignments designed to accomplish this reconnection.

Joan's maladaptive reaction was identified in the following issues: when aware of the possibility of losing a love object, being incorrect or less than perfect on the job, or during conflict with one of her parents. In these situations, her process, or "Problem Loop" she entered, was mapped out as a sequence of behavioral responses to overwhelming or unidentified feelings in which her "Inner Child" or Child Ego State thought it was going to die, if she didn't do "something" to stop the rising feelings.

During this stage of therapy, Joan was taught parenting skills in order to re-parent herself. At first it was very uncomfortable for her and she appeared awkward while she was completing the exercises. It was the group that really helped her overcome the fear as they loved, validated, and affirmed her until she could do it for herself. The group became the change agent, modeling parenting skills, and allowing her to complete her "unfinished" childhood tasks:

STAGE ONE: Trust vs. Mistrust
1. Learned that trust was a process and not to trust because someone was familiar
2. Became emotionally available to her "Inner Child" (who began to trust the Adult) and gained access to her feelings

STAGE TWO: Autonomy vs. Shame and Doubt
1. Learned that she had boundaries and not to allow anyone to violate them
2. It was OK to be a separate person from her love object
3. That enmeshment was smothering and disengagement was cruel

STAGE THREE: Initiative vs. Guilt
1. Learned that it was OK to risk
2. It was normal to make mistakes and she wasn't a mistake
3. It was permissible to try out new things
4. That she didn't have to be perfect

STAGE FOUR: Industry vs. Inferiority
1. Learned that it was OK to be competent
2. There was an internal reward for being competent when she felt good about herself, and more importantly, didn't need external agreement for it to be valid
3. Discovered she needed to learn how to be a "human *being*" instead of a "human *doing*." It meant that working wasn't everything and she needed a balance between work, leisure, and relationships.

CHAPTER NINE

The adult's power is generated in adolescence.
Without it, the adolescent is compelled to:
Be victimized by the lack of choices or become
The victimizer for fear of being controlled.

OVERVIEW

When you have completed Chapter Nine, you will be able to:

1. Recognize when you or others are in their Adolescent Ego State
2. Understand how codependency develops when childhood and adolescent tasks remain incomplete, or were completely missed because of past trauma or the skewed parenting practices of dysfunctional or clueless care givers.
3. See how a Problem Loop impedes emotional maturity
4. Determine when the Adolescent's fear blocks adaptive behavior strategies from being developed
5. Identify shame when it rises in the Adolescent
6. Be able to connect the head (thoughts), with the heart (feelings), so that the action taken (behaviors) is congruent with one's inner harmony
7. Discover the internal damage that is created by an over-reactive adolescent when he tries to "protect" himself from real or imagined danger
8. Learn how incomplete adolescent developmental tasks impede the maturation of the individual as he tries to complete his adult goals in relationship to self, others, work, family, and society

ADOLESCENT EGO STATE

The Adolescent Ego State is a segment of the adult's personality structure that remains in adolescence. Its chronological time frame begins at ages 11 to 13, depending on maturation level, and can last up to 28 due to advanced schooling which delays launching.

What I usually observe in the client during therapy is ages 13 through 17. This is the most profound area of the stage. At 13, hormone levels are changing rapidly, mood swings are common and physical growth is bringing new power that surpasses the young person's intellectual capacity to handle it. Through the next four or five years, the teen will continuously push boundaries and limits, develop a support group outside the family, further solidify his self concepts, and become a person separate from his family of origin, via the individualization process. In these feats, he will begin a healthy separation process in which he can be launched from his family of origin without losing membership, even though he no longer resides at home after launch.

During high or overwhelming stress, the central personality of the adult can be observed regressing back to any phase or task of adolescent development that wasn't fully completed. The regression occurs because a deficiency in his stress reduction system is created with the incompletion. When I assess during these periods, I can recognize the reaction and identify the skills that are needed for better facilitation of the problem area.

The Adolescent Ego State is the energy system of the adult. It is very powerful and in its own mind is "ten feet tall and bullet proof." This is also the part that stopped the childhood abuse from continuing. To those of you who were unable to stop the abuse and it continued through adolescence, you have one very angry Adolescent inside. This angry Adolescent can turn self destructive through depression, self mutilation, substance abuse, toxic relationships or marriages, dead-end vocational attempts, or remaining in the victim role throughout life without any adaptive or creative solution-oriented choices.

The energy of the Adolescent has to be released somehow. If it's not, the Adolescent perceives death, and he has too many survival instincts to die. The usual way the Adolescent activates these survival skills is to act them out. Unfortunately, up until a few years ago, this was predominantly a male trait. Today things are different. Women can now get angry instead of turning it inward. This reaction of turning the anger inward is now an **"equal opportunity destroyer"** because both do it as well. I guess that's twentieth century progress.

The adult regresses back into the Adolescent Ego State when he becomes:

1. Overwhelmed during a current event
2. Over-reactive in a present situation because it triggered unresolved issues or feelings from a past event
3. Afraid he is going to be taken advantage of
4. Insecure when his power is diminished
5. Violated when his boundaries are crossed
6. Intimidated when being disrespected and talked down to
7. Inadequate when unfair standards are imposed
8. Depreciated when unequal relationships are occurring
9. Inferior when he is threatened
10. Abused when **"ANY" perceived authority figure** attempts to use his power in an unjust manner against him
11. Betrayed, *anytime* **the adult is shamed,** because he is experiencing healthy development and completing his prescribed tasks

HOW THE ADOLESCENT
EGO STATE PRESENTS

The adult manifests all the characteristics of a teenager when he is in the Adolescent Ego State when he:

1. Uses force or control in order to take charge of a situation
2. Uses too much power
3. Thinks in a highly directional and egocentric way
4. Is highly charged emotionally
5. Has rapid or recurring mood swings
6. Is unable to use reason when threatened
7. Acts and reacts swiftly and without thought
8. Becomes highly verbal and loud
9. Uses acting out, "adult" behavior without the maturity to handle the consequences of his actions. This includes anything that can be used addictively, i.e.: drinking, drugging, food, sex, relationships, gambling, criminality, *ACTION*, work, overachieving, etc.
10. Uses self-destructive behavior that is turned inward. This includes depression, self-mutilation, anorexia, bulimia, isolation, prostitution, and somatization of psychiatric symptoms, also physical ailments which are directly or indirectly produced by internalizing stress.

11. Uses very threatening body language
    a. Behaves in a highly aggressive manner
    b. Stares and his eyes look hard
    c. Tries to over-talk you or isn't listening and drifts off
    d. Uses many gestures and arms are animated
    e. Pushes his body out, muscles tense, and appears larger
    f. Has legs that can be highly animated
12. Escalates to the point of blowing up, which happens in extreme cases. At this time the person is out of control and can be highly dangerous. If you let him vent, (some call this throwing up on you), he will de-escalate by himself. Some at the end start to cry and become childlike. When HE blows up it is nothing but an adult temper tantrum. The only thing you have to remember is that a fearful adult is doing it and not a little child.

As in the Child, this state is not always negative. There is an important function to the Adolescent Ego State. It's the segment of the individual that maintains power, integrity, and boundaries. It's also the part that protects The "Inner Child." In other words when the Child (the person's feelings) is hurt, the Adolescent (the power or energy) comes to its aid. Did you ever wonder what happens to turn a seemingly meek person into a raging bull? It's the Adolescent, which somehow was activated, and came to life to protect the threatened Child.

Without the Adolescent, an individual would be void of power. Anyone could hurt him. The Adolescent's retaliation can be swift or planned and with such exactness that the person targeted doesn't have a chance to defend himself. To wait or not is immaterial to the Adolescent. He only knows **payback!**

The Adult's internal integrity is also protected by the Adolescent. Check out when someone tries to invalidate one of the Adolescent's important self concepts and the Adolescent bows up like a snake and almost takes his head off. That's the Adolescent. The same reaction is experienced when the Adult's boundaries are crossed. The energy of the Adolescent only becomes problematic when the Adolescent **reacts** in these situations, instead of using thought out, mature, adaptive strategies as **responses.**

This ego state is also responsible for bringing the energy, sexuality, intensity, games, or excitement to a relationship with someone a person is attracted to. As in the Child, if this part is not attracted to the person, they "kick them to the curb" or don't even begin a relationship. This is also the part of the human personality that's responsible for **continuing** to "look for love in all the wrong places."

Reframing

To those of you who are still skeptical about the thought of having a full-blown Adolescent as part of your internal structure, I offer the following. Reframe the Adolescent to the energy or power that maintains the adult's life. In life, this energy is ever vigilant to boundaries, safety, and the person's internal integrity. This is also the part that wards off all threats — real or imagined — and protects the segment of the individual, who at the time is vulnerable. It's usually when the individual regresses into his Child that it happens and is generally the result of the insecure feelings one experiences when he is vulnerable.

Whatever framework is appropriate for you is okay. The added benefit of using the original framework is that it personifies the energy by placing the Adolescent's face on it. It's then easier to work with the concept during experiential therapy, especially when issues are deeply impacted, and the individual doesn't trust anyone. In therapy I bond with the Adolescent quickly because he is the key to ending maladaptive behavior.

Fear of The Adolescent

Establishing trust with the Adolescent is easy to do if the therapist is competent and sincere. If not, the Adolescent senses it and keeps the therapist out by becoming resistant. I make a simple statement to someone new to therapy, "Don't trust me until you think I'm trustworthy. Watch me work. See if I deserve your trust." The Adolescent is going to do this anyway, no matter how much they say they trust me. I bring it into the open. Adolescents watch a person's behavior because most of their lives someone repeatedly told them, "It won't happen again," "I'm sorry," "I'll change," or "things will be different next time." At first they believed them. After a while, they learned how to ignore the words, observe, and see if the change was made before they let down their guard. It's hard to go against years of conditioning. It's easier to move with the resistance. In that way, you can lead them anywhere you want them to go.

Another intervention I use is to address the Adolescent when someone begins to escalate during therapy. I inquire why he is present, check to see if I inadvertently violated an internal boundary or opened up too much without allowing the client enough time to develop significant resources to handle it. I assure him that his boundaries are as important to me as they are to him, and apologize for the transgression. I then restate (remember informed consent) my therapeutic strategy or intentions — that I do push a client a little beyond his comfort zone each time we work together, because I feel the bulk of the problem in dealing with painful feelings or situations is his lack of emotional maturity. I also inform him that the immaturity comes from childhood when he shut down in order to survive a painful or traumatic event. I validate this skillful development of survival techniques and demonstrate how they become toxic as the adaptation to living skills is attempted and continues to impede his development. The Adolescent needs this information if he is going to be able to change. My clinical task at this stage of therapy is to:

1. Educate about the antecedents to their present problematic behavior
2. Validate their choices
3. Increase their cognitive ability to facilitate their feelings during painful or overwhelming events

This process of bonding with the Adolescent actually works. In it, resistance is minimized and forward progress is enhanced. I know when we talk about therapeutic style, that each of us has one and I'm not trying to force mine on you. I only want you to grasp the concept. What you do with it is up to you.

To the skeptics: see what I did here? I confronted your resistance because I know this concept, to some, can be a hard one to grasp. I also validated your skill and style. Hopefully, I've done my teaching and opened you up to possibilities. It's an important concept. Try it!

There is also a fear of non-clinicians to work with this part of themselves introspectively because they are afraid of what they'll see, afraid of what behavior may manifest when the Adolescent is stirred, or afraid to admit previous behavior or capability of shameful behavior that has been suppressed for years. Some clients have told me it was like they had a dark side, a stranger inside, and if they let him out he would do awful or vile things. This is a great deal of internal fear. It will have to be acknowledged and confronted emotionally **after** the person's cognitive ability has been developed. This book is one of those cognitive tools. With issues stemming from deep wounding during childhood, substance abuse, or mental illness, it will take a trained therapist to confront and work with the Adolescent.

Much fear is raised within the person who tries to confront another's Adolescent. This is healthy. There is usually a degree of danger when trying to interact with someone who is in his or her Adolescent state. The Adolescent usually materializes out of fear or seduction. In seduction, he is looking to get his needs met, and it can happen in families, work situations, with friends, or lovers.

This part can be fun to play with. The only trouble that occurs is if the therapist goes over the Adolescent's imaginary line — whatever that is — depending on a million fluctuating factors. The Adolescent can violate one's boundaries quickly. An example would be interacting in a playful way that was mistaken by the client as flirting, and finding yourself being coerced sexually. This can be male or female. Adolescents are not gender specific anymore. We now have sexually aggressive people in both genders. In the past men were the aggressors and women were passive and shut down. No more. I guess it's another example of twentieth century progress.

To those readers who are with aggressive partners, in toxic relationships or marriages, battered or abused in any way — **GET HELP!** *You can't do it alone!* There are many 12-step programs, counselors, agencies, and treatment programs that can give you help. You deserve a better way of life. It is your birthright to live free of disharmony, dissension, and pain. This book can't give you all your answers. It can only give you a rudimentary framework to base your changes on. It won't get to the underlying issues of why you entered into and remained in an abusive situation. This will have to be explored with someone who has the ability to help you through it. Remember, you can't work with another person's deficiencies until you have recognized and corrected your own. After you have corrected your own skewed framework, you can decide *if* you want to continue working through your partner's "stuff", because you're the trigger for your partner's volatile reactions. Most that experience toxic relationships choose not to continue. They usually exclaim, "It's the first time I've had choices. In the past I felt it was what I deserved."

The Power of Shame

Shame is also the chief antagonist to the Adolescent. The road it travels is through the contribution from the Child. How it traverses its path is as follows:

1. The Adolescent will attempt or complete a strategy, process, or task, and will get ridiculed or ignored
2. These negative feelings will stir within the Child Ego State and provoke the Adolescent:
   a. *Into action* with an **exaggerated** behavioral response
   b. Out of action by remaining internal and shutting down

This process of acting out or going internal is designed with **one objective** in mind, *to protect the child from being hurt!* This is maladaptive in a functional world although extremely adaptive in a dysfunctional world. (Remember, "One Flew Over the Cuckoo's Nest"?)

THE SHAME FOR THE CHILD WAS SO GREAT THAT HE WOULD HAVE DIED — HAD HE ACTUALLY EXPERIENCED THE FULL PAIN OF THE INVALIDATION.

The over-reaction by the Adolescent has a two-fold purpose:
1. To dissipate the energy released from:
   a)The feelings themselves
   b.)The effort expended to ensure suppression
2. To create a diversion that helps to:
   a)Remain focused externally
   b)Create something else to look at or blame
   c)Keep the person in the situation (his head), instead of his
      feelings (his heart)

To insure the Adult's ability to maintain congruence between thoughts, feelings, and behavior, one has to have his head and his heart connected. During a shame attack, it is virtually impossible for the Adult to make this connection, as he lacks the ability (emotional maturity) to facilitate the stressful event. This situation usually engenders overwhelming anxiety that exacerbates the current feelings which are being experienced. The pressure builds up, and is interpreted as impending death, unless some action is taken to make the feelings stop. At this juncture, the Adult casts himself into the Adolescent Ego State where all of the defense mechanisms are stored. The Adolescent then facilitates the situation. Remember this is a **survival skill.** Emotional living skills cannot be developed unless one has:

1. **A cognitive framework** to intellectually facilitate the pain that will surface
2. **The emotional maturity** that occurs as one repeatedly experiences the feelings and emotions instead of deflecting or running from them

I refer to the process of emotional maturity as the ability to connect the head (thoughts) and the heart (feelings). There are 18 inches between them physically: During the periods of shame that the adult in the Adolescent Ego State experiences — it might just as well be eighteen miles.

Do you ever wonder why you think one way, feel another way, and don't behave according to either one of them? The following is the reason for it! When a person's thoughts and feelings are alienated from each other, either because (a) the Child has shut down or (b) the thoughts and feelings are conflicting and brawling with each other when the Adolescent stirs the pot — the individual lacks a highly developed internal Adult. This maturity is necessary to facilitate between the two conflicting parts, and thereby be congruent in thoughts and feelings on any action the Adult has to take.

> **ALIENATION FROM SELF IS WHEN THE
> HEAD AND HEART ARE DISCONNECTED.
> DURING THIS TIME, ONE DOES NOT
> *FEEL, THINK, OR ACT* CONGRUENTLY.**

A noteworthy fact at this time . . . Even though the Adolescent has finely honed survival skills to protect the Child from feeling extremely painful emotions, he also heaps pain upon the Child due to the intensity of his reactions. This ramification of the Adolescent's behavior is extremely poignant to the client when it's revealed in therapy. Many times the Adult has significant growth after the revelation. The Adolescent also experiences a profound transformation because his *intent* was never to hurt the Child, only to protect him. What he usually exclaims is, *"I'm no better than my perpetrator! I hurt me like they did and caused my own pain!" How right the Adolescents are! They did hurt themselves by their reaction to the trauma and in order to get past it, have to admit it, and go through the pain the revelation triggers.* This is not a moral issue. They didn't know how to do it any differently. Without additional strategies, The Adolescent would have been crazy to attempt it differently. All do the best they can with what they have. This includes the adolescent. The only problem with the acknowledgement is that the Adolescent can't continue with the old behavior without causing himself a great deal of pain. It ruins his ability to act out in ignorance, and some still find it hard to stop the behavior. It's the same way AA ruins the alcoholic's drinking.

Whatever questions the revelation raises in you will have to be worked through. With help, the Adult Ego State is solidified, as thoughts and feelings are integrated. At this point, The Adult will be able to skillfully facilitate the thoughts, feelings or reactions that emerge out of a shame attack instead of: shutting down, becoming helpless and hopeless to the process, and creating a crisis he will have to clean up when the episode is over. In time, the Adult will be able to facilitate the shame when the attack begins and dissipate its destructive nature, long before it becomes a problem. Now that's progress!

DEVELOPMENTAL DEFICITS AS TRIGGERS

Failure to complete adolescent tasks or stages exacerbates problems previously created by the developmental deficiencies of childhood. In adolescence, the evolving novice will put into action (behavior) the lessons learned in the previous stage. If he has learned to trust, has become autonomous, gained initiative, and become competent, he will have a firm foundation to build upon. If he hasn't accomplished these tasks and mastered the previous four childhood stages, he will build his world upon "shifting sands." It's like trying to run a program in a computer without an operating system. **It just won't compute!** What happens when the adult tries to solve problems without adaptive solutions, mediate stress with dysfunctional behavior, develop equality based relationships, enhance self concepts, and increase self-esteem or vocational skills? *It just doesn't work!* Without the basic knowledge and completion of developmental tasks and stages — non-problematic, functional, adaptive, and creative adult solutions cannot be developed. As in childhood, unfinished adolescent stages will impact adulthood because all development is cumulative.

STAGE FIVE: Identity vs. Identity Confusion

This is an early adolescent task, ages 12 — 15, and in it, the neophyte has to integrate a main identity within all the various roles he experienced or witnessed during childhood. When the modeling in the roles is skewed or dysfunctional, the central personality will lack the basic skills it needs to facilitate life events. It's impossible to develop a well-balanced personality from skewed data. The reverse is true when the tainted data from the misconceptions is corrected.

Skewed data is also the root of workaholism and occurs when one is out of balance. In the lack of balance, he values work. It becomes his highest priority and personal relationships suffer. Employment uses all of the individual's energy and very little is left over for anything or anybody. Balance is now gone as the individual slights his personal and spiritual needs.

Another factor in the Adolescent's inability to complete his developmental tasks is also embedded in childhood. It occurred when survival skills were produced instead of living skills. These dysfunctional strategies spawned a child, who in order to survive, learned how to manage his feelings by shutting down, stuffing, minimizing, denying and dissociation.

In the process, wants, needs, and desires are rarely, if ever, explored. This creates a clueless adolescent, who through others, tries to find out who he is. Adolescence is difficult under "normal" circumstances. This lack of self-awareness only increases confusion at an inopportune time and further impedes the completion of his developmental tasks.

Needless to say, the Adolescent also suffers low self-esteem, exhibits little self-confidence (except when reacting and acting out blindly), easily becomes fragmented in his individuality, and is insecure. This constitutes a weak foundation for further personality development and brings an inadequate internal structure into adulthood.

CODEPENDENCY — What occurs in Stage Five becomes the mire in which the roots of codependency can be anchored to. It occurs when a central personality is not developed because the child was not able to manage his feelings and through the process learned to focus externally and became "other directed."

**THE EMERGING PERSONALITY BECOMES
"OTHER DIRECTED"
WHEN HE LEARNS HOW TO FOCUS EXTERNALLY
TO AVOID FEELING HIS OWN PAIN**

As feelings are avoided, wants, needs, or desires are never identified because the focus was outside the child. At this time the central personality becomes fragmented with an inconsistent identity. This causes the adolescent and subsequent adult to need another person, place, or thing to complete them because their **internal structure has not solidified.**

**CODEPENDENCY IS DEFINED AS SOMEONE NEEDING
ANOTHER PERSON, PLACE, OR THING TO COMPLETE
THEM BECAUSE THEY ARE NOT
WHOLE *WITHIN* THEMSELVES**

The process of becoming "other directed" throughout the life span begins in childhood and breeds codependency in adolescence when a consistent central personality is not developed. The lack of balance moving into adulthood further generates dysfunctional behavior, maladaptive coping strategies, poor decision-making skills, low self-esteem, and unacceptable social skills. Figure 9.1 is a visual depiction of this process.

ASSIGNMENT 11: Based on this chapter's criteria for codependency, are you codependent? Were you socialized to be that way by unknowing care givers? What do you need to change in yourself today to no longer be codependent? Do you recognize it in your spouse or significant other, friends (intimate or otherwise), co-workers, your children or parents? If so — what can you do for them according to the chapter?

THE CHILD EGO STATE (THE CHILD)

↓

Shuts down, stuffs and denies his feelings

↓

Self-abandonment is spawned when wants, needs, and desires remain unexplored

↓

The child becomes "other directed" by learning to focus outside himself

↓

Self alienation is produced by the process

THE ADOLESCENT EGO STATE (THE ADOLESCENT)

↓

Tries to develop a central personality

↓

Draws from his resources and comes up empty

↓

Develops a dominant personality that is based on emulating the behavior
of others or the perception of how he should act

↓

This leads to acting out (aggressive behavior) or acting in (depression)

THE ADULT EGO STATE (THE ADULT)

The adult is never whole within himself and needs another person,

place or thing to complete himself

FIGURE 9.1   DEVELOPMENTAL PROCESS OF CODEPENDENCY

STAGE SIX: Intimacy vs. Isolation (Second Period)

This is a late adolescent and early adulthood stage. Ages range from 16 to 23-28, depending on the age they finished school and were subsequently launched. During this stage the Adolescent develops the ability to share himself with another person without losing his identity in the process. This is the place that manifests all of the deficiencies of previous stages that were not completed. The following is briefly what occurs:

STAGE ONE: When this stage is completed, the young adult has an internalized process of trust which allows him to identify and engage with trustworthy people. If he fails to do this, he will not trust and will look for people he can control. He also will gravitate toward what's familiar. What he has usually seen under these circumstances is his parents or primary care givers participating in dysfunctional relationships that are toxic, abusive, inadequate, unequal, or unfulfilling.

STAGE TWO: As this stage is fulfilled, the evolving youngster develops boundaries to maintain his individual integrity, and avoids enmeshment with others. Having this sense of autonomy allows one to be vulnerable and spawns intimacy. When this stage is unfinished, relationships become hostage situations. During the power struggle one becomes a hostage taker, or, victimized by his own lack of confidence and self-esteem, becomes the hostage. One of the prime reasons some cannot establish intimate relationships is because they are afraid of being swallowed up by another person.

STAGE THREE: Its purpose is consummated when the novice learns to risk beyond his comfort zone and out of its process is derived the competency to deal with people and situations in an adaptive manner. *Developing risk allows a person to get close to another, "or" to leave when the relationship is at a dead end or toxic.* With competency, the young adult will acquire negotiation skills in order to get his needs met. If this stage is incomplete, the risk will not be taken to enter into an intimate relationship, nor will he be able to leave a toxic or unfulfilling one. Most needs usually remain unmet because the ability to bargain was impeded, skewed or not developed.

STAGE FOUR: This stage is attained when the young adult is able to maintain a balance between working and living. At this point, self-esteem is derived in many ways. One of these hallmarks is the success of personal relationships that leads to intimacy. In this way, intimate relationships are as highly regarded as vocational success. If this stage's goals are not met, most of the energy is expended on vocational endeavors, with little left over for relationships. This void is problematic at best, because over the life span, it will impact all levels of adult development.

When there isn't a balance between work and living, all roles that the adult plays are shortchanged. As partners in marriage, all priorities are placed on the job and not in the marriage. Time is not allotted to the couple-ship. Normal events are missed frequently. There is little, if any, social life. Parental duties and obligations are minimized or completely left out. A climate for intimacy is stifled or never developed, when the individual's self-esteem and identity is based on production goals or vocational successes.

STAGE FIVE: This stage is wrapped up when a consistent central identity is formulated within the evolving personality. When completed, the maturing teen can actively become involved in intimate relationships, without fear of losing his identity in the process or having the need to control. One who has completed this task will *not* demand conformity from others. He will celebrate their differences and recognize the uniqueness in others. When this stage is left unfinished, the Adolescent creates a fragmented and insecure central identity. This causes him to remain in unsatisfactory relationships, or provokes the need to control. Either way, there is a lack of intimacy because the fear of being abandoned is so great that the anxious youngster will "do anything" to preserve the relationship. At this juncture, we can use intimacy as an acronym for "In to me see." As you can imagine, there is no room for looking inside of someone, when fear has closed him off as he channeled all his energy into controlling (external) or being controlled (internal). Lack of a central identity is also a factor in producing codependency because the novice is not whole within him and needs another person, place, or thing to complete himself.

STAGE SIX: This stage can be broken up into two sections. The first is late adolescence — early adult stage in which the novice gains experience in life outside the family of origin's limits. It's the beginning of forming adult committed relationships, entering a vocational career, and socially interacting without the protection of the family. It is a time in which self concepts begin to solidify against the pressure to conform to external standards in relationships, work, and society. During this period, one learns who he is in relation to a myriad of roles that are presented for examination, approval, and action.

In the second half of stage six, self concepts are solidified as the person begins and maintains a family, raises children, manages a home, and establishes a career. During this period the individual is happy, on task, and secure within himself. It is a time when one feels right about what he is doing with his life.

As in the previous five stages, when development is skewed or incomplete, stage six will mirror negative results: poor self concepts, low self-esteem, inadequate social skills, maladaptive relationship strategies, ineffective parenting skills, and underemployment in entry level jobs or frequent unemployment.

ASSIGNMENT 12: How was your adolescence developmentally? Were you able to "spread your wings" and allowed to develop? Were you able to do "anything you wanted" without boundaries and limits being placed on you by your primary care givers? Were you able to start becoming an individual, separate from the family, and at the same time still remaining a member? Did you start or attain healthy separation from your family of origin by moving out or making a plan to be on your own? If you were subjected to abuse during childhood — did you stop it somehow in adolescence? If yes, how? Do you recognize any adolescent developmental incompletions in yourself? In others? If yes, who? What does the chapter indicate that you have to do to complete them? The second half of the book will give you greater insight on how to take care of yourself first, and also, how to keep out of your partner's way when he is having the same problem.

SUMMARY

Adolescence is the stage in which the data collected in childhood is transformed into behaviors as the developing individual applies the learning to the various roles he is experimenting with such as: defining his individuality, separating from his family of origin, developing vocational goals, and building relationships with self and others.

In the process, one both completes his development tasks and brings a competent individual into adulthood, or fails, which results in skewed development. When the process fails, one does not become an emotionally mature, responsible adult with a repertoire of strategies to facilitate the vicissitudes of life (problems that happen during daily living in a changing world). He is unable to use functional and adaptive solutions in an effective and non-problematic manner. When this failure occurred: the developing child shut down, minimized, stuffed, or denied his feelings. He never identified his wants, needs, and desires, and subsequently needed another person, place, or thing to complete himself. *As a result, he was never whole within himself.* This failure in the process is called a "soul sickness" and breeds codependency instead of the capable individual a completed developmental process would produce.

Codependency occurring as a byproduct of human trauma is a process that can be reversed by education, self-awareness, therapy and/or a 12-step program. In it, one puts the focus on himself to see who he is and what he needs, and devises an adaptive and functional strategy to attain them. This is a *"Human Birthright"* instead of needing an external object to define himself (which is *"Bondage to Self"*), and a fear-based reaction to trauma.

When an emotionally mature, responsible individual enters into adulthood, he is a fully-empowered grownup who can facilitate life's problems in an adaptive manner without regressing and using childlike responses of manipulation, emotional blackmail, and instant gratification.

To anyone experiencing problems with the concept of the Adolescent, all you have to do is reframe it to energy or power that enables you to enforce boundaries, ward off threats, attain goals, and maintain internal integrity.

Shame is also an antagonist to the Adolescent. In his response to shame's devastating feelings, he can *act in* (depression, anxiety, or self-deprecation) or *act out* (substance abuse, gambling, food, sex). Without a new type of framework, the Adolescent will continue to hone his survival skills instead of developing living ones. As he fails to acquire living skills, his thoughts, feelings, and behaviors will remain incongruent, and the Adult will not be connected to himself. In fact, he will remain alienated when he is unable to connect internally. This dysfunctional process is also a component to shame's matrix and has to be explored.

When the Adolescent recognizes the contribution he makes to dysfunctional behavior, a profound change occurs within him as the energy he used to kindle the flames of the "Problem Loop" is transformed into the energy needed to develop or remain in solution-oriented strategies.

Each of the two stages of adolescent development has its own tasks to fulfill. When completed, these stages will deliver a competent individual into adulthood who can handle life as it unfolds and doesn't allow himself to get involved in situations he doesn't belong in, or that will take him off his spiritual path.

Stage Five is where the process of codependency occurs when the growing individual can't differentiate himself from others and becomes afraid of intimacy. In Stage Six, one risks further by expanding his world outside of the family's safety when he enters college, begins employment, or initiates and maintains intimate relationships with non-family people.

CASE STUDY

Joan, our executive from a major city, continued to work in group after she completed her "Inner Child" work, and switched the focus to her Adolescent. Initially, she had to identify what "Problem Loops" or behavioral sequences she used to cover up the recurring feelings of shame she experienced in childhood that were being triggered and attached to today's situations. She was also incurring additional losses today because her past childhood needs were not being met in her present relationships.

Joan's behavior during adolescence turned inward as depression, low self-esteem, usually feeling there was something missing inside of her, under eating, and inconsistent sleep — until she found out that hard work and overachievement could change her mood. It was during her first school project that she was validated because of the great job she did — and was hooked. In this situation, she experienced her mood swing *from* the depths of depression *to* heaven with joy. From this point there was no stopping her — anything that anyone wanted done — all they had to do was ask. Later on in life the same pattern prevailed in work and she became a workaholic.

The problems didn't begin until she started going with boys. It seems she usually picked the ones who were emotionally unavailable to her or distant. At first she thought the distance was sexy in a man. Later on, after several disastrous relationships, she would change her mind about the characteristic, but didn't know what to replace it with.

Her pattern with males was simple: First, she would fall "head over heals" in love with a "soul mate", one whom she thought would spend eternity with her. Second, she would not get the same acknowledgement from her "soul mate" after the initial intensity of the relationship began to diminish. Third, she began to see flaws in her *perfect* "soul mate" and internalized the awareness as shame because she didn't learn from her past mistakes, thereby, she was the mistake. Fourth, she waited for the "other shoe to drop" which would end her now flawed, "perfect" relationship. Fifth, when it didn't come, she broke up with him, BEFORE HE DID IT TO HER!

What she uncovered in therapy was the emotional devastation her reactions caused. Let me remind the reader at this point — if she didn't accomplish completion of her "Inner Child" work, which subsequently connected her back to her feelings (the Child), she could not have attached the emotional contribution her feelings made to her behavior when a relationship started to break up. This would have left her clueless to her triggers, kept her experiencing the same type of breakups over and over, and unable to achieve another ending.

As Joan's emotional pattern emerged, she was able to identify how trivial problems in the relationship would trigger her shame, and how, when she felt insecure, she would try to fill the void through the validation from her newest love object — and failed. At this time her Child would become afraid, get shamed by the rebuke, and start to shut down. It would last until the depression affected her work performance and her Adolescent would take over and bail her out of the hole she had placed herself in.

This mood swing would come as a jolt to her love object, and usually triggered off their stuff (past unresolved issues). This, in turn, would trigger off more of Joan's issues. Her Adolescent would "dig her heals in," or take the change as evidence of the accuracy of her assumptions. At this point, she would now be experiencing "the Two Step Dance of Codependency" — each one making their moves on what they think they see, not what's accurately occurring, and further reacting to their partner's reaction to their reaction. Sort of like the tail chasing the dog. Nobody wins. Everybody loses. All wake up the next day alone trying to figure out what happened.

Emotionally, Joan had much to learn. She needed to understand that feelings were visitors and not facts. That good situations as well as bad events would trigger off past unresolved issues. She had to learn when she was out of her day, reacting to old tapes when the present situation mimicked a past one, and was causing her to over react to the present event because of the cumulative value of both situations together. She also needed to identify when she was bouncing off his stuff by separating her issues out from his. Joan was able to accomplish what she needed to learn, and in doing so completed the following developmental tasks:

STAGE FIVE: Identity vs. Identity Confusion

1. Defined her self concepts
2. Identified her adult needs and learned to acquire them herself (reparenting) or ask for them to be met instead of manipulating for them or expecting her partner to be a mind reader (risk and mature behavior)
3. Learned how to identify and correct a "Problem Loop," which would send her back into codependent behavior (relapse) if it was left unchecked

4. Acquired emotional maturity each time she went through her feelings instead of creating another "Problem Loop" to deflect them

5. Opened up her boundaries to emotionally safe people and began to have intimate relationships based on self-love and service, instead of taking hostages or becoming one in a self-seeking relationship spawned in the fear from her Child's abandonment issues

STAGE SIX: Intimacy vs. Isolation (First Period)

1. Acquired a better balance between work, leisure, and relationships based on her redefined self concepts

2. Initiated and maintained intimate relationships with emotionally available people — based on Adult needs instead of her Child's fear

3. Was able to internally identify, process, and take action on, previous feelings or memories that overwhelmed her when they attached themselves to a present situation

4. Stopped the recurring "Problem Loops" from starting up again.

CHAPTER TEN

Adulthood is the space over the life span in which the data inputed during childhood and behaviorally experimented with in adolescence, becomes the foundation to facilitate everyday life. If the data and behaviors are functional and adaptive — the corresponding adult strategies will reflect it.

OVERVIEW

In Chapter Ten we will examine:

1. The three stages of adult development and the contribution they make to adult adaptation
   a)Generalized tasks of adult motivation
   b)Developmental conflicts that arise in the process
   c)The power of shame on the process and the deficiencies left in one's internal structure as a result of it
2. How developmental incompletions become triggers that increase stress, cloud issues, confuse situations, and hinder further development
3. How to:
   a)Recognize when someone is developmentally stuck
   b)Break the impasse by learning the tasks of the three stages
   c)Identify an incomplete stage through the self-defeating behavior manifested
4. Explore how the "Mid Life Crisis" impacts development because of the concept of "more time behind than in front"
5. How the "Empty Nest Syndrome" precipitates the renegotiating of marital roles

ADULT EGO STATE

In adulthood there are four components interacting throughout the life span, and together, determine what course human development will take. They include the person's internal structure or personality, family, work, and society or the predominant culture. Each section helps to weave the tapestry that we call life. The influence they exert is always fluid depending on which task is highlighted or what particular stage the developing human being is traversing.

The following theories will be utilized as a supplement to Erickson's "Stages of Development" ("Childhood and Society," 1963) and Maslow's (1954) "Hierarchy of Needs." They will include the family, work, and society as influences, motivators, or determinants in a life span approach to human development and how they impact the Adult Ego State's evolution. These are the stages of "The Family Life Cycle" (Carter & McGoldrick, 1980), Havighurst's (1953) "Developmental Tasks over the Life Span," Levinson's "Seasons of Man" (1978) and "Super Stages of Vocational Life" (1957). All of these writers' works have validated my observations of clients in therapy and what I personally experienced across my life span.

TASKS OF THE ADULT EGO STATE

The adult ego-state is the Executive branch of the personality structure. It's the section that's responsible for the mature and adaptive facilitation of anything that transpires throughout the adult's life span.

The following are its responsibilities:

1. Applies creative solutions to problems
2. Devises adaptive strategies to stress
3. Ameliorates any difficulty emanating from interpersonal relationships
4. Facilitates intra-personal conflicts with self
5. Investigates and follows through in vocational attainment
6. Begins and maintains a family
7. Negotiates the struggle between society's demands and the self's fulfillment
8 .Learns from past mistakes and grows from the process
9. Engages in life

10. Attains self actualization
11. Makes a contribution to mankind

All of the above processes are firing simultaneously during the three stages of the adult's life span, as the following major developmental conflicts arise with self, others, family, work, and society:

1. The personality changes which occur as the person traverses life and grows through the experience
2. Responding to changing needs which manifest over the life span
3. Facilitating age thirty when adult roles concretize and complete graduation from adolescence has been achieved
4. Re-evaluating self at age forty, through "Mid Life Crisis", by accepting there is "more time behind -than ahead" and all goals will not be accomplished
5. Adjusting to family life cycle changes
6. Renegotiating roles with children, parents, and significant adults
7. Transformation of marital roles with spouse
8. Changing stages of the vocational life cycle
9. Adjusting to retirement with fewer resources and society's low expectations of seniors
10. Adjusting to diminished capacity, loss of friends and spouses through death, and coming to an understanding about death

If the previous tasks and stages of development have been accomplished, the Adult will respond to the developmental crisis with creative, adaptive and functional solutions and deliver them as an emotionally mature, responsible adult. In this way, the Adult grows through all the adversities by using them as *opportunities* to grow. *If the tasks and stages of development have not been completed*, the Adult will react to adversities as a child and not have available, a repertoire of adaptive responses, or, will become aggressive as an adolescent and use dysfunctional behavior as a subterfuge to avoid addressing the problem.

The Power of Shame

The power shame continues to wield during adulthood is just as debilitating as the previous two stages. In childhood it mandated the child to shut down in order to survive. This reaction produces an immature emotional system which enters tainted data into the child's developing internal structure. The resulting self-abandonment left a void inside of the fledgling that has been described as "feeling like they have a hole inside their heart." During this time the only system produced to facilitate adversity is avoidance.

This process leaves the subsequent adolescent clueless when trying to develop adaptive and functional skills to handle stress. As shame is exacerbated in the adolescent stage, the teen generates two strategies to work it out. The first is to react internally and shut down through depression. The second is to act it out externally with dysfunctional behavior.

The two preceding developmental stages leave the evolving adult with the following deficient characteristics in his internal structure:

1. No emotional maturity
2. No system devised to facilitate painful feelings and emotions
3. No adaptive problem-solving skills
4. No functional stress-reducing strategies
5. No or few choices to stop or reduce self-defeating behavioral reactions
6. Little ability, if any, to develop creative solutions to life's vicissitudes

For the above listed reasons, any attempt by the adult to problem solve will deliver strategies that will be skewed, deficient, or problematic. The odds of promulgating creative or adaptive solutions, which are balanced and fair, will be negligble. This leaves the adult ineffective, at best, when it comes to negotiating in relationships, family, work, or society. The resulting shame inundates the adult and further hinders his effectiveness.

DEVELOPMENTAL DEFICITS AS TRIGGERS

It is in the three stages of adulthood that the deficiencies of earlier uncompleted tasks and stages come to fruition. Here, as the apprentice tries to grow and learn, roadblocks emerge that seem insurmountable. Answers are searched for like a soldier on a search-and-destroy mission. The intent to find them is there. The answers always seem illusive. Always out of reach. Just around the corner. Never seeming to materialize when they are needed. The following are illustrations of how these inadequacies create confusion, instead of resolution, throughout the life span.

Early Adulthood
STAGE SIX: Intimacy vs. Isolation (Second Period)

During this segment the evolving executive system increases its maturity level and solidifies concepts in relation to self, others, family, work, and the culture. In this process the individual is able to experience committed intimate relationships without losing his identity in the process. This self-confidence enables him to marry, begin and maintain a family with children, establish a career, define his social responsibility, be able to abide by the law for the sake of social order, and respect individual rights in democratically accepted law. The following areas of human interaction will illustrate how the adult matures or fails during the next three stages.

*Intra-personal:*During this stage the expanding individual solidifies his self-concepts and graduates from the uncertainty of adolescence to the realm of adulthood. In this process the person is no longer unsure or insecure of his person-hood. He feels like a whole person who can take on the responsibilities of life and he does.

When tasks are not completed in previous stages the following occurs. The personality is fragmented. The executive system is underdeveloped. Self-concepts are frail. The individual's person-hood is tenuous at best. This creates conflict within the individual and usually leads to dysfunctional behavior because the pressure of living becomes too great. What is usually seen during this period of uncertainty is adolescent behavior. This process inhibits the ability to further personality development and exhibited when the individual remains self centered, egotistical and aloof or shut down into depression.

During this stage, the internally stuck young person can exhibit maturity in task-oriented skills, and use it as evidence that he is developing. The larger culture can also validate this trait as being valuable and indeed it is. The only problem that arises is the seeds of workaholism that are germinated during this time when the apprentice develops work skills as a replacement for intra-personal skills. This leaves the evolving individual with a life full of purpose - by getting the job done - although adds no meaning when it comes to intrinsic value. Look around. It seems like everyone is scurrying to acquire more things. Has it made them happy? No! Has it brought meaning to their lives? No! Has it sent them on a search for answers? Yes! This book and its concepts, philosophy, psychology and sociology are part of the answer. With the right information entered into the individual's data bank, all of these questions are answered internally, for to succeed in *living* — *NOT DOING* — one has to learn about oneself first. All else takes care of itself.

TO BE A SUCCESS IN LIVING
ONE HAS TO LEARN ABOUT ONESELF

Developing intra-personal skills will also occur in an environment that will exert pressure on the individual, as he tries to define and fulfill his evolving needs, in contrast to the expectations (sometimes contradicting) of family, work, and society. These conflicts will become opportunities for a mature person to grow. They will also continuously test the individual's mettle, and how they're resolved will determine the adult's maturity, values, character, integrity, and strength. With balanced strategies, one's internal structure continues to mature as ego strength is increased and self-concepts become further defined.

Interpersonal: When affiliation needs are met in this segment, the maturing adult is able to maintain committed and functional relationships with others without fear of losing his self-identity. The foundation for a healthy relationship is poured in self-knowledge. This knowledge is what forged our self-concepts, which in turn maintains our self-integrity (internal), and our boundaries (external). This is what keeps you separate from others physically and emotionally, and avoids enmeshment mentally and spiritually.

In this process, one is always separate, still feels he belongs in the relationship, and spiritually does not become diverted from his life path.

I personally believe we were born with a purpose, a job to do that will add to mankind: A contribution to help further man's growth. The fulfillment of my spiritual purpose is to write this book, the ones that follow, and to teach man to live for a higher purpose based on self-knowledge. I've known that I was going to do something wonderful and special with my life since I was a little boy. I even had a hint that it would happen during my present age. What I didn't know was which life experiences would contribute toward this end. I know today that all of them counted.

When this area of the personality development is impotent, it breeds poor relationships with little or no intimacy because the person is afraid of losing himself or of not being worthy of a good partner. Under these circumstances, the individual gives himself up because of poor self-concepts, or takes control to avoid abandonment and maintain his power.

The control this power struggle generates is created to quiet the fear an emotionally immature person feels as he enters into a committed relationship. It is also designed to cut his losses by preserving his frail self-concepts and avoid losing the love object. In actuality it provokes the opposite reaction from others as they back away from being controlled or withdraw into submission. The resulting feelings are shame and abandonment: shame because there is something wrong with them when the relationship didn't work; abandonment when the person physically, emotionally, or spiritually left, AND self-abandonment as principles and ideals are sacrificed for control.

THE POWER STRUGGLE IN A RELATIONSHIP
IS GENERATED TO QUIET THE FEAR
IN AN EMOTIONALLY IMMATURE PERSON

Self-abandonment is the greatest pain because it's self inflicted. It occurs as the person continuously gives himself up in a myriad of circumstances. Nobody, but the self, can get as close to the person to perpetrate this atrocity. This concept really gives you something to think about if you participate in this type of lifestyle.

This scenario manifests in all relationships. No one is spared; it happens with spouses, children, parents, lovers, friends, neighbors, co-workers, or bosses. It has no territorial bounds; it breeds in urban, suburban or rural areas. Economics does not control it; all suffer equally whether rich, poor, or somewhere in the middle. It makes no difference: What your vocation is (being a worker, supervisor, or owner does not determine it); What color you are (black, white, brown, yellow or red - all are exploited); What religion you are (being Catholic, Protestant, Buddhist, or Jew does not alter its course); What nation you live in (Eastern or Western Europe, the Mediterranean, Middle East, Asia, Africa, or any of the Americas) . . . *THE PROCESS IS AN EQUAL OPPORTUNITY DESTROYER!* Nobody benefits except the disease of fear.

Family: There are two areas that the evolving adult has to master with his family. The first is healthy separation from his family of origin. One in which membership is maintained, antiquated intergenerational belief systems are discarded for functional ones, and the young adult is whole within himself. In other words, "the apron strings have been cut." The second area is beginning his own family, having children if desired, and maintaining his family of procreation. If the preceding developmental tasks have been completed, the maturing adult will be able to complete both areas. If not, the following hindrances will occur.

Healthy separation and full launch from the family of origin will not prevail. The evolving adult will be drawn back to an enmeshed family system. No matter how hard he tries, he will not be able to detach without disengaging from the family altogether. This is a two-edged sword because the child loves the family and doesn't want to lose it. The adult doesn't know how to accomplish healthy separation. The adolescent takes charge and says "screw them" and leaves, or turns the anger inward and shuts down into depression. The internal pain is still there and the unresolved conflict from the family of origin will be played out in the rearing of their children when it comes time to launch them into adulthood.

All unresolved conflicts from the family of origin will recycle in the next generation. They are brought forward when the children become the age their parents were when they had their original conflict. Don't forget the young adult is the center span that bridges three generations. This period is the hardest for him because he is leaving one family to start another, and is a beginner in both processes.

Vocation: Vocational needs during this period mandate that the adult take decisive action. It's the time that energy is readily available, intrapersonal needs have to be fulfilled, for most school or training is over, family necessities dictate a dependable income, and society demands the individual be gainfully employed or it labels him a "bum."

It is a time, according to "Vocational Developmental Theory" (Super, 1957), that the individual establishes his career. In it, the evolving adult takes what was learned in past job or training experiences and applies the knowledge to start a career. If all has gone well through the previous vocational and life stages - the adult will be prepared to establish a satisfactory career based on:

- Intrinsic values of what he wants to accomplish
- Current needs
- How he can best serve mankind

He will also choose a supportive environment that will nurture his growth and enhance self-esteem.

- If there are deficiencies within the person's character, they will manifest as menial jobs, under employment, low pay, lower status, dead-end endeavors, being undervalued, or, a critical environment that depreciates the self-concept, stifles ambition, and lowers self-esteem.

A person suffering from the negativity of a critical vocational environment is stuck in the Child and/or Adolescent Ego State. In the Child Ego State, the Adult's self-esteem is low, self-concepts underdeveloped, self-image poor, and blind to behavioral alternatives. He feels helpless and hopeless, victimized by society or God, and demonstrates no hope. The Adolescent acts it out differently and more aggressively. He quits jobs, fights with bosses, ruins or destroys equipment, drinks or drugs on the job, steals, or turns inward and creates his own internal pain (depression, anxiety).

Another way the Adolescent and Child work together is in workaholism. The Child wants to do the best job possible, be a good boy or girl (good worker), and harnesses all the energy from the Adolescent to accomplish it. All energy is diverted to the job and away from personal growth or committed relationships. What the individual's Child ego-state is trying to accomplish, is to win approval from his bosses who really personify his parents, instead of looking for self-approval. This dynamic is a constant throughout the entire life span for the underdeveloped or developmentally sidetracked individual. It permeates his entire decision-making efforts and becomes the chief motivation in life. It has caused competent people to give themselves up to meaningless, unsatisfactory, and dead end jobs. It is also the underlying factor when they sabotage themselves in vocational endeavors.

Society or the Dominant Culture: The social structure one lives in extracts a price for membership. It has norms, values, mores, folkways and culturally prescribed ways to attain one's goals. Deviate too far from center and one will be sanctioned. Follow the prescribed ways and one will be socially competent.

If the family has done its job in the socialization of its young, it will launch socially adept young adults, who will fulfill the expectations of the culture. If not, the developing individual will create a lifestyle in conflict with the social structure. Success will enable the developing individual to evolve with the culture throughout his life span.

Look at what's happened to the American culture over the past century as we went from an agrarian society, through the industrial revolution, and into a growing technological society. Note the changes in the family structure as it downsized *from* a large extended family with plenty of children to help with the chores, *through* the small nuclear family in which children had a moratorium from adult responsibility until they finished school, *to* the latch-key kids of today being raised by a single parent. Observe the value placed on children today as compared to one hundred years ago. During that time they were an asset. Today they are a liability - and a big one at that. Check out the hostile environment bombarding the family today, which didn't exist a century ago. You now get an idea of how the culture affects the socialization process of the individual as he responds to changing social demands over the life span.

The expectations of the culture during the early adulthood stage are to begin and maintain a family and to become gainfully employed. The completion of these goals is to be attained in the socially approved manner. No criminality is tolerated. Deviant lifestyles are frowned upon. The fulfillment of these goals in the socially prescribed way is important because the culture's approval of us is one of the ways our self-concepts are developed and validated.

Inability to complete these goals will label the initiate a failure and will trigger off the Child's shame because enough ego strength hasn't been developed. This, in turn, produces an adolescent response of acting out and creating a deviant lifestyle or turning it inward (acting in) with depression and giving up on life. At this point, the young adult will conceive a dysfunctional family or not begin one. At the same time he can be under employed or generating sub-rosa income.

Age 30 Transitional Period

At thirty, one seems to let go of the bonds from childhood and finally become an adult. It's as if he suddenly grows up, is no longer the "ten feet tall and bullet proof" adolescent, and becomes a responsible adult.

To me, it's the culmination of the practical experience of living, trying new things, risking, learning and growing. For those who have completed their developmental tasks, it can be a joyous time to finally feel grown up. For those who haven't, it can be the opposite with the Adolescent or Child in charge, and never quite mature enough to feel like a grown up.

Middle Adulthood
STAGE SEVEN:Generativity vs. Self-Absorption

As this stage is transitioned, several tasks will be accomplished, which will help the growing person to change his frame of reference from self to others. The hallmark of the ego at this time is to transcend self-centered interests in favor of future generations. Middle adulthood is also a reflective stage in which one looks back and assesses the progress made attaining his projected goals with self, others, family, work, and society.

If the goals of this stage were completed, or, a respectable amount accomplished, ego strength is further developed. This helps the mature adult to transcend diminishing physical attributes, and the integrity of the individual's internal structure remains intact. Stage seven, like adolescence, is a rehearsal for the next stage. If the tasks are completed, it will deliver an emotionally mature adult, able to facilitate some of the adversities that befall an aging human, and becoming a senior adult will be accomplished with dignity.

Incompletion of this stage's tasks will bring an immature adult, in his Adolescent Ego State, covering up the inadequacies of his inner child. In this state the Adult will either shutdown, go into depression, and become the victim, or experience anxiety, pump up with anger and become a crotchety person. Either way he will lose because the energy he needs to go on will be used to maintain the anger or keep him in the pit of depression.

Intra-personal: During this stage there are profound changes transpiring within the evolving human's person-hood as his temporal time line is changed from *time ahead* to *time behind*. During this period the aging human knows what life goals have been achieved and also has a realistic idea of the goals that won't. This re-framing of more time already spent living - than time left to live - is the catalyst for the "Mid Life Crisis" that occurs during a person's forties.

In this segment of Stage Seven, one assesses his performance, takes credit for goals accomplished, accepts his human limitations, and the integrity of the adult internal structure remains intact. The acceptance of one's frailties and retention of the experiences gained, delivers an empowered, competent adult to the next stage of life. If all of this is accomplished the "Mid Life Crisis" will be transcended and self-concepts will be further solidified.

Failure to successfully mitigate this stage and resolve its "Mid Life Crisis" will generate an individual who will be self-absorbed with fear. In this fear, the person's self-esteem, confidence, and self-concepts will be diminished. At this point, negative internal dialogue will dominate the person's thoughts and become self-depreciating. From this self-talk will emerge a defeated Child who is helpless, hopeless, and unable to take care of himself or his advancing limitations. This deterioration of his ego strength will stir up the Adolescent Ego State. As this power emerges, it will drain the remaining energy that is needed to successfully negotiate one's diminishing life. This maladaptive strategy will create depression and anxiety and predispose the aging adult to further psychiatric difficulties in the following stages.

Interpersonal: Relationships grow during this period or they begin to diminish. If a person transcends the lowered esteem felt from his diminished capacities or attributes, he will be able to maintain his self identify in any relationship. This includes work, friends, society, as well as family relationships with spouse, children and parents. The framework for relationships is also transformed from self-seeking interests to helping the common good or future generations.

Relationships will fail or not materialize during this segment if the person cannot adjust to the changes, becomes fearful of the intimacy which is generated by being honest about one's limitations, reacts by trying to control, or disengages emotionally with depression and shuts down. When the other person is shut out in *any type of relationship,* there is no relationship. Relationships fail emotionally and spiritually long before the physical one ends. How many aging couples that you know only exist because of convenience? Look at how many thirty- forty- fifty-year marriages are ending because there is no communication or it's an unsatisfactory relationship? How many aging couples do not talk or are highly antagonistic or demeaning toward one another?

Family: During stage seven the family experiences many changes and successful fulfillment of its tasks impacts the developing human. At this time children are launched and the "Empty Nest Syndrome" is experienced. Roles also change between the spouses. Men become more nurturing. Women become wage earners. In younger marriages today, with two wage earners, this is an easier task, although today women still get the brunt of household responsibilities. Both spouses have to learn to relate to each other as people because of the role changes in diminished capacities (physical, financial, social), developing an adult relationship with grown children, adjusting to aging or death of parents, and adjustment needed because there is "more time behind than in front" of them. When these tasks are completed the individual is able to fulfill his roles in the family. Children are successfully launched and an adult relationship is established with them, power is passed on to the next generation, spouses become people and the dyad relationship is re-established, adjustments are made for aging parents, and emerging limitations are adjusted to.

If these family tasks are not completed, the following reactions will occur. The established role between spouses will not change. The dominating spouse will insist on roles remaining unchanged, try to control the other partner, and may use coercion if necessary.

Another reaction is that children will not be successfully launched. Hooks will remain in them as they are emotionally blackmailed (any reason can be used) and drawn back into the family's dysfunctional system. In this family, the adult children never grow up in their own feelings, are viewed by the family as children, and an adult to adult relationship is never formed. This also extends from the parents to their parents: the cord was never cut, emotional enmeshment exists, and power is not transferred because the parents remain children in their parents' eyes. They don't adjust to their aging or possible death, their own mortality, nor do they set a good example to their grown children about death.

During this time, the Child Ego State is in fear of the changes that have to occur within the family. Instead of letting go to examine the fear and get on with his life, the Adolescent emerges and through power (real or implied), tries to control everything, everybody, and only ends up in the way of growth. The Adult Ego State during this time is nowhere to be found or impotent at best.

Vocation: This is the "Establishment Stage" of vocational life (Super, 1978). In it the developing worker will establish and maintain his career. If he is successful, career goals will be accomplished and a balance struck between work, leisure, and family harmony. Also during this stage, an additional balance will be achieved when the individual does not forsake personal development for vocational success. Balance has to be maintained in all areas if the person expects to evolve and prepare for his next stage. If not, all esteem, worth, and self-concepts are determined by the individual's job and salary. When both begin to diminish in the next stage - the person's self-concept will shrink as well.

"Mid Life Crisis" impacts the vocational cycle when the worker reflects on vocational goals attained and the price paid in lost opportunities in other areas of his life. If he has achieved balance, the resources gained by investing in all areas of existence will be returned when work ends in the next stage, as all of the worker's person-hood does not hinge on his vocational success.

If this stage is not completed, most self-concepts will be determined by production-oriented vocational goals. All other areas of his life were neglected when only work was valued and everything else was secondary.

This out-of-balance is created by insecurity, on the adult's part, when he failed to develop a complete identify.

This fear will also be exacerbated by the "Mid Life Crisis" when vocational goal attainment is acknowledged and the price paid for success in other areas of life is determined. This success-to-cost ratio can be devastating when it's too great.

Once again the fear of the child will cause the adolescent to rear his powerful head and take over. Instead of using the energy, generated by the fear, to develop balance, it will be used to "dig in" at the vocational level and ignore all other areas of life. Even if it's confronted, the adolescent will use the energy to defend his position instead of changing his behavior. *I can tell you that it takes more energy to defend than it does to change. It's the fear that keeps one in the problem loop.* As all energy is expended on the job, the needed skills to transcend the next stage's limitations will not be developed. This deficiency will produce a limited adult who is not capable of adjusting to vocational wind down and retirement.

Society: The shift from egocentric goal attainment to a broader base occurs during this period. The evolving adult shifts from focusing on self-centered interests and uses that energy in favor of the needs of future generations. This shift is also brought on by the "Mid Life Crisis" in which the individual reflects on his social performance. If the tasks have been completed, his focus will be placed upon civic and social responsibilities. This begins at a time when family and vocational responsibilities are winding down. It's also a time when one enjoys the intimacy of interpersonal relationships because he is solid in his self-concepts and doesn't have to fear losing his identity as he is being vulnerable with another human being.

When this stage is not completed, the frail ego enters into a fear-based mode, remains egocentric, and ignores his civic and social responsibilities. All effort is expended on personal goals because this is what his value system deems important. "Anything else is for fools" is what the Adolescent Ego State verbalizes. "Take care of yourself," they say, "nobody ever took care of you when you needed it." This is true in many cases, but it doesn't have to take the individual off his spiritual track by not completing what the "Celestine Prophecy" (Redfield, 1993) calls "the birth vision," or why a person was born. I believe that everyone has a spiritual job to do; that is why we were born. Many times, this is the stage that it's revealed, because the noise of the worlds demands quiets down during this period. What seems to happen during this time frame is that a curtain is opened during that quiet, and something is revealed to us that will lead us to a path to fulfill our destiny. When one is in the fear of his Child Ego State, or in the action of his Adolescent scurrying around at a frantic pace, (after all there's more time behind than in front, and I have to hurry to get my toys), the noise level remains at a deafening volume and the curtain remains closed. Even if the curtain were open, its rustle would not be heard, nor would its opening be noticed because the Adolescent is so intently focused on accumulating material goods. This process generates a socially inept individual who will isolate during the next phase instead of enjoying the social interaction.

Late Adulthood
STAGE EIGHT: Integrity vs. Despair

Late adulthood is the stage that witnesses the human's decline. It is the last stage in the life span and can encompass four decades. During this time one becomes retired and adjusts to: the aging of self and parents, death of parents and the possibility of one's own death, death of spouse, loss of friends, and loss of power, increased illness, and being helped instead of being the helper. It is also a reflective stage in which one looks at what he has accomplished. If he is satisfied with these achievements, a major task of this stage will be completed, and the aging person will acquire a sense of integrity. If not, the senior adult will view his life as a series of missed opportunities, and feel despair because it's too late to accomplish them.

This stage is the finale in ego state development, when the emotionally mature responsible adult becomes able to facilitate his own decline from this earthly plane. As this occurs, the healthy Adult Ego State is able to use what was learned from the seven past developmental periods. This knowledge and experience is used to generate adaptive strategies to transcend the losses of this stage and the certainty of one's impending death.

If the previous tasks and developmental stages were not completed, we will observe the Adult unable to remain mature, and he will regress to an earlier state. In the first state, the Adult will be a helpless and hopeless child who enters depression or anxiety and withdraws from the world. In the second state, the Adult turns into an adolescent who presents as an angry old person. Either way spells doom for the senior adult, for the energy needed to overcome the losses and still maintain ego strength and self-concepts is depleted through acting out (anger) or acting in (depression).

Intra-personal: The maturing adult traverses this stage with a solid identity, integrity, and a healthy ego structure when he is able to reflect back on life's accomplishments and is satisfied with his achievements. This enables him to transcend his waning physical, social, and financial attributes. It also helps him to overcome the death of a spouse, parents, and friends, and to add meaning to his life in spite of having to face his own mortality.

When an immature adult has to negotiate this phase, he lacks emotional maturity, personal integrity, and ego strength. In this process he becomes victim to the "poor me's," can't take the credit for past accomplishments, and lacks the ability to offset his present deficiencies with previous gains. This attitude usually drives him into depression and social isolation.

Interpersonal: During this stage, a shift has to be experienced in personal relationships. The aging person cannot always be the care giver, and in declining years has to be the care receiver. This realignment has to be completed without destroying the ego. If one is now able to assess his performance in earlier stages of life and is satisfied with his accomplishments, the individual's internal structure will be enhanced, self-concepts will remain intact, and intimate relationships will take a deeper meaning as the aging person declines and becomes more vulnerable. The more one's attributes diminish, the more help he needs, the more growth it produces as he is able to adjust. All of this happens as the aging person retains his identity and adjusts to secondary roles.

Also, during this time, the aging individual has to adjust to death. Friends, acquaintances, and neighbors die. An era is coming to an end and these deaths also foreshadow one's own demise. How one adjusts to one's own mortality via the deaths of significant others is one of the hallmarks of this stage.

Failure to adjust to the realignment of self-concepts in relationship to others and to deaths that occur through aging, and not being satisfied with past accomplishments, usually creates or engenders a propensity to form a psychiatric illness in which the senior becomes socially isolated. In this form of isolation, most, if not all, family and social relationships usually wane and this spawns a lonely and suffering senior adult instead of an evolving person enjoying the fruits of his labor.

Family: This segment of the family life cycle is the hardest to complete. The family is going through major adjustments: generations are dying, power is being transferred, and another generation is aging. Roles are being renegotiated as the breadwinner retires and looks for some kind of meaning in his life. The other spouse has to adjust to the change in routine. Young adults grow, marry, and bring outsiders into the family. The family has to adjust to the new entries. All of this also occurs in a changing societal climate.

All of the above tasks can be successfully resolved when the individual is in his adult ego-state, maintains his personal integrity, and has ego strength to draw upon. When this happens, power will be transferred to the next generation. Aging grandparents will be cared for with dignity and their death processed with the family. Parents will retire, adjust to aging as a couple, and mourn the passing of one of them. The family will open a place for outsiders as new marriages are formed.

These natural transactions will not take place if the family is dysfunctional or the individuals have developed maladaptive coping strategies throughout their life span. Everyone will react; all energy will be expended on cleaning up problems instead of developing creative solutions. The death process will be avoided. Denial will remain high even in the face of overwhelming facts. Alcohol and drug addiction can prevail as an older person drinks too much or younger persons act out. Emotional cutoffs will prevail as family members try to keep balance in the family. This maladaptive behavior is one of the strategies used to facilitate the stress of remaining emotionally shut down. It's too overwhelming to feel the reality of this stage for emotionally immature people.

Vocation: All tasks of this stage are centered on adjusting to retirement. In this stage, the evolving adult will facilitate the losses derived from reduced income, status, and choices. Successful completion will encompass changing one's life style in response to less income, shifting the way status is viewed from being work oriented to adjusting to retirement (after all, this is the retiring adult's primary job, just nobody told him), and exploring less expensive choices for leisure time activities.

The previously endowed adult will maintain his self-concepts, esteem, and internal structure when his life has been realigned from being work oriented to leisure directed. It is just as important to be able to facilitate the stress that comes from leisure as it was to learn to deal with the stress from work.

Sometimes leisure is harder because there are no distractions. In time off one is alone with oneself. For some, this is possibly the first time in their lives that the struggle of living is gone. It is a difficult time if there are any unresolved issues from the past. This stage, amongst them all, is extremely dependent on the successful completion of the tasks from the previous stages, because it is the one stage, without specific therapy, where the adult can't go back and fix loose ends.

The combination of unresolved grief and adjusting to retirement is like the one-two punch in boxing. The first one sets you up - the second one knocks you out. The fact of having any deep unresolved grief signifies the lack of ability to facilitate these issues. During retirement there is much grief: loss of job, money, status, esteem, friends, distractions, *AND A PART OF LIFE SOMEONE EXPERIENCED FOR AS MUCH AS FIFTY YEARS! THIS IS A GREAT LOSS! ONE THAT HAS TO BE EXPERIENCED IN ORDER TO CONTINUE LIVING IN AN ADAPTIVE STYLE!*

**WHEN RETIREMENT OCCURS,
IT'S THE END OF AN ERA.
THE LOSS OF A WAY OF LIFE —
HAS TO BE EXPERIENCED!**

The culture doesn't prepare you for retirement nor help you through the grief process to mourn the passing of a way of life. The culture says: "Celebrate!" "You've earned it." This is true — although it's also the end of a way of life that has to be grieved.

Those who have left too many unresolved issues in the past will have great difficulty being able to enjoy this final stage of life. With the loss of vocation will come the loss of self. When all past energy was spent on the job at the expense of relationships, it's no wonder that the individual in retirement experiences shallow connections with others or, none at all. The results of this imbalance are depression, anxiety, social isolation, and despair instead of joy, peace, happiness, and integrity.

Society: During this portion the retiree will probably experience his greatest and smallest contribution toward society. This is mainly due to the fact that he will have the most time and energy to give of himself. At the onset of retirement, much of the struggle and distractions of daily living are lifted and this energy has to be diverted somewhere. Along with the released energy, comes the drive to fulfill one's civic and social responsibility and to create meaningful activity in one's life. This also helps to transition the gap between work and retirement and to realize one's external primary purpose from vocational pursuit to leisure activities.

Also during this time, society demands very little from the senior adult. Less and less is expected of him as expectations are shifted to or maintained by its younger members. This is a major blow to the ego as power, authority, and influence are stripped from the aging adult. This is not because he is incapable or unable to perform his duties. It occurs because he is getting older. This is really a perceptual problem by the culture, as it is mesmerized by youth, and ignores the assets of it's more experienced members. This is changing slowly. My age group is the largest segment of the population; as we are aging, so will the concept of social aging change. This subject usually stirs up my adolescent. He goes off in my head and wants to rock and roll to prove how young we are. I have to keep reassuring him by channeling my energies in constructive ways, appropriate to our time frame, that we will be young forever. He likes that and doesn't give me too much trouble.

The well adjusted person will be able to make the various shifts throughout this last stage of his life, remain productive, maintain his ego strength, solidify his self-concepts, transcend major losses, as well as diminishing capacity and health, and at the same time be happy, joyous, and free. Those who are not well adjusted and lack the strategies to facilitate this stage's joys and losses, will remain in self-centered fear, become paralyzed, and experience depression, anxiety, and social isolation.

ASSIGNMENT 13: How has your adult development progressed? Are you solidifying your self concepts? Learning from your past mistakes? Adjusting to life changes? Maintaining personal integrity in relationships? Have you completed healthy separation from your family of origin? Can you adjust to changing marital roles? Begin and maintain a vocational career? Maintain a balance between work and leisure? Remain within the norms and values of the predominant culture? How are you adjusting to the "more time behind than in front" concept? Are you preparing for retirement? Are you having a "Mid Life Crisis"? Why? How are you dealing with the "Empty Nest Syndrome"? How are you dealing with the aging process? How are you doing in retirement? How are you adjusting to your own and others' mortality?

SUMMARY

The growth of the Adult Ego State occurs through three phases: Early, Middle and Late Adulthood. Each stage has its own tasks and when completed, produces an emotionally mature responsible adult who is able to:

1. **INTRA-PERSONAL** - Solidify his self-concepts, learn from his past mistakes, increase his decision-making capabilities and stress-reduction strategies, facilitate internally the various changes that occur in his life, and later adjust to the concept of diminishing capacity

2. **INTERPERSONAL - Maintain his self-concept and integrity while he interacts and forms intimate relationships with family, friends and co-**workers

3. **FAMILY** — Complete healthy separation from his family of origin by becoming an individual separate from it, and still maintain membership in it. Begin a family of creation - marry, raise and launch children, and adjust to changing marital roles

4. **VOCATION** - Begin, maintain and retire from an acceptable position and maintain a balance between the needs of work, family and leisure

5. **SOCIETY** - Transact all the above tasks in the culturally prescribed way without violating its norms, values, mores or folkways, and without deviating too far from center - staying within the undulating flux of an evolving social order

When the adult fails during these stages due to the inability to complete child and adolescent tasks, the Child Ego State dominates and shame underlies most transactions. When the Adult reacts by "acting in" with depression and being the victim — the Child is in charge. When he "acts out" with substance abuse, any kind of obsessive/compulsive behavior, anger, or by victimizing people — the Adolescent is the boss.

STAGE SIX: Intimacy vs. Isolation (Second period)

Problems the developing Adult can encounter in Early Adulthood when tasks are not completed are a fragmented personality structure; an underdeveloped executive system; substance abuse or another kind of acting out behavior; fear of losing himself when entering into intimate relationships; enmeshment or emotional cutoffs in his family of origin; beginning a family before one is emotionally and financially able to fulfill his responsibility; have menial, low paying or lower-status jobs or be underemployed; have difficulty adjusting to the changing culture; and use sub-rosa means or criminality to attain his goals.

STAGE SEVEN: Generativity vs. Self-Absorption

During Middle Adulthood, the Adult's primary task is to adjust to the "more time behind than in front" concept and shift from the egocentric thinking of one gathering his toys, to one making a contribution to man. If he cannot successfully facilitate the goals that will never be, take the credit for what he did do, prepare himself for retirement, and become more culturally oriented - he will lack the foundation to successfully transition into and adaptively traverse his next and last stage of life. It's sad to watch this happen to individuals because they lack the necessary training.

When Middle Adulthood is not successfully transitioned, the following manifestations usually occur. One may experience massive changes when he goes through his "Mid Life Crisis," exacerbating low self-esteem, depleting ego strength, and ending relationships due to self absorption when fear dominates his inability to be honest about diminished capacity. He may fail to launch children because of the "Empty Nest Syndrome." He may be unable to renegotiate the changing roles of the spouses and will maintain enmeshment with his parents or children, thereby never having power so he cannot transfer it to his children. He may not attain a balance between work, family and leisure, and may experience problems with self-esteem when the job ends. He may be unable to adjust to family relationships as work was always more important. He also may not make a societal contribution because he is too wrapped up in himself.

STAGE EIGHT: Integrity vs. Despair

In late Adulthood, the benefits of successfully completing tasks in earlier stages are exhibited by maintaining one's dignity through the aging process — otherwise one becomes an angry, soured, disillusioned old person. If he is not successful, we may witness the following: an inability to offset his present deficiencies with previous gains; depression, anxiety, substance abuse, addiction to gambling and prescribed medications; a waning of personal relationships where he withdraws through fear and isolation; lack   of adjusting to death of family members and friends and denying his own mortality; not adjusting to diminishing resources in a changing culture.

CASE STUDY

Mary was a 78-year-old retired widow who entered treatment as a result of the depression she experienced after she fell several times and temporarily had to go into an ALF (Adult Living Facility) because she couldn't take care of herself due to the injuries she sustained during the falls.

While she was being assessed for the program, it was determined she was over medicated for her age, and seemed to be acquiring a dependence on her pain medication (Vicodin). During the treatment plan the doctor agreed to adjust the doses of her medications to best suit her age and to get her off the current pain pills. She did experience some withdrawal while being titrated off the Vicodin, although no more than we anticipated. She was also given a complete physical and blood work was completed (which included salt, sugar, and potassium levels) to determine any deficiencies in her system. After she was physically balanced, she was able to work in the program.

Mary was raised by two dominating parents who culturally believed in "pulling yourself up by your own boot straps." They were judgmental, critical, and upwardly mobile. Mary was married, had children, a career (which was good in those days) and became a taskmaster herself. She was successful by all cultural standards, followed the prescribed route to goal attainment, and could brag about her laurels. The only fly in the ointment was when she wouldn't adjust to her changing physical condition; when she had a problem.

While working in group with Mary, she was given my developmental framework personalized to her through her current situation's thoughts and feelings, in order to demonstrate how they impacted her present self-defeating behavior.

She was able to identify her inner child first as she talked about a fearful experience. It was during this time she expressed that it was the first time in her adult life that she could talk about it without feeling like a sissy. Giving her the concept gave her permission and the ability to "break the rules" and talk. It was during this time that her children and her care givers began reporting that there was something softening within her and she wasn't as abrupt or demanding as before.

The concept of the adolescent was next. She loved the empowering part of the concept but hated the accountability when she was confronted about using it as a shield when she was antagonistic toward others and used this energy to stay out of her feelings.

This reaction is only one side of the coin. The flip side is "acting in" when one becomes depressed, suicidal, or gives up the desire to live. The reaction is different - the results the same! Both strategies cover up feelings.

Working with Mary directly was hard. I knew she had to learn to feel, see the damage she did to herself, and resolve the missed opportunities she experienced in life.

Her awakening came through the back door as so much does in group work. It was when she helped others in the group that she began to feel vicariously and I could start to personalize it to her. When she helped others she remained open. When she was singled out she acted up by becoming defiant or shut down with the "poor me's" saying that she was too sick, old, or tired to continue. I normally go with the resistance, push a little, back off, and recognize it as a boundary that the clients cannot go any further. I also give them "informed consent" about my strategy so they know the strategy, feel empowered, and even expect it.

My strategy is to increase their threshold to endure emotions. The only way I know how to do this is to give them needed information, set an example, and push a little to increase their tolerance to it.

Mary was two months in treatment before she had any major breakthroughs. She opened up while we were processing another female group member's loss of an old boyfriend that her parents didn't approve of. At first Mary was confused, became angry, and then started to cry. She confessed she loved this man who raised unlimited passion in her, but broke it off because of her parents' disapproval. Later she married a man who loved her and the children, was cold, and left her unfulfilled. She thought she had dealt with it by forgetting and "putting it behind her" and all she did was put it on hold.

The next gain she made was when she realized that she had never cut the apron strings; she had become like her mother in order to please her, and never came to think of herself as an adult. It was during this time that she accomplished separation from her parents, and healthy individualization based on her needs and not on what her parents thought was good for her.

This was a major step because her parents were so rigid, would never take any help, brought Mary up the same way, and when she needed help, could not admit it because the parental message about self sufficiency was so imbedded in her mind that it superseded the present need.

The next hurdle for Mary to overcome was to see how she had mistreated her children when she began to have physical problems at retirement. This was painful for Mary and she shed many tears over it.

At the end of treatment Mary could identify her feelings through her inner child, recognize when she was using her adolescent to set self-defeating boundaries or to hide from her feelings, and do an accurate assessment of her current needs based on today and not on misguided parental messages from the past.

Mary could also forgive her parents for their limitations and love them for who they were. She could also forgive herself for any mistakes she had made. She had a greater appreciation for accomplishments she had made in her life. She was able to make amends to her children for how she treated them after she became sick. She stopped her unpleasant behaviors toward them.

Is Mary a miracle? Yes. We had lots of them, both men and women. The therapy may seem simple....it's not....it is. It's simple in nature and profound in results. The therapy we did in treatment was designed to bring a person through all eight stages of development, increase his skill level in many areas, and have him gain an increased understanding, awareness, and appreciation of himself.

Could we do this for everyone? No. Some couldn't make the trip back in their memories. They just tuned out and shut down. There was no reaching them. I suspect that more went on in their lives than they wanted to reveal and they had a vested interest in it remaining that way. Most were shut down for several years before they came into treatment. Some were substance abusers and the family was in denial. Others were mean people whom the family wasn't willing to risk and change the status quo. Usually they left Against Medical Advise (AMA) at the beginning of treatment. Some died after they left because they couldn't go on living.

167

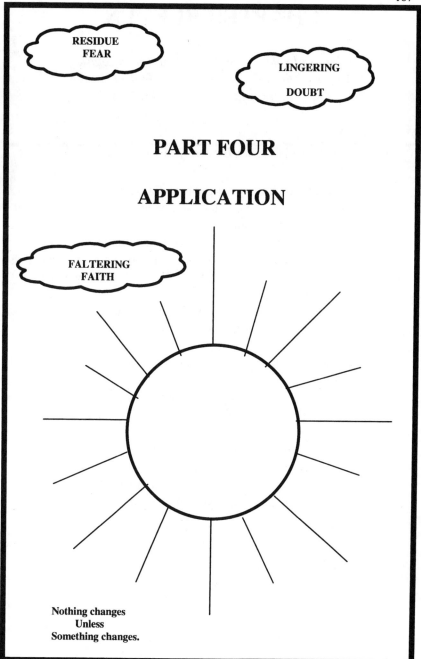

CHAPTER ELEVEN

"Why did you do that?" . . .I heard a voice ask.
"Who said that?". . . I replied, as I looked around,
saw nothing, and thought that I was crazy.

OVERVIEW

After you have read Chapter Eleven, you will be able to:

1. Identify the structure in your internal dialogue
2. Recognize what ego state you or someone else is operating from based on how they are talking
3. Understand situations that used to confuse you when someone switched their tactics or set you up (including your own reactions)
4. Work with and change the feelings of being "small" when an authority figure talks to you
5. Learn to deal more effectively with your children and parents
6. Keep on level ground with your love object
7. Deal better with social change
8. Increase your ability to be congruent with thoughts, feelings, and behavior
9. Increase your understanding of your wants, needs, and boundaries
10. Maintain a balance between work, relationships and leisure
11. Learn how:
    a.The Critical Adult's messages permeate the culture's verbiage
    b.To protect yourself from the culture's negative messages
    c.To turn the message into a positive statement about yourself
    d.To change the negativity in your messages to others

INTERNAL DIALOGUE

How many times have you heard voices, looked around, and saw nothing? Did you brush it off? Think you were crazy? Or did you listen to them? So many have learned to dissociate from themselves by not listening to their intuitive voice and they attribute it to an outside source. Many, when they first get into recovery or therapy, and begin to reconnect internally, describe listening to this source as being outside their bodies as an observer, witnessing newly realized behaviors, patterns, or changes to self-defeating strategies, and being in awe of themselves. The voices one hears is his internal dialogue. It fires off every waking moment, and adds meaning or interpretation to any situation experienced by the human being. It is the part that: ads commentary, stirs feelings, makes judgments, and attaches fear or acceptance to any event. In its commentary can be experienced internal harmony or dissention. It is what I affectionately call one's "Entertainment System."

In the past it created great difficulty for me because I didn't understand its purpose. It added confusion, doubt, and fear. On a good day, if thoughts, behavior, and feelings were congruous, I was in harmony. On a bad day, I was fragmented at best. After I learned to understand my Internal Dialogue, it was no longer a roadblock. It became a guide and a tool that would give me access to all my experiences - to create a way to assess a situation today, based on my past experiences, and formulates options that were adaptive. It also gave me entrance to my feelings and opened me up to all the colors of life. This was difficult because feelings are a two-edged sword: You feel the good with the bad, and I had baggage I wasn't willing to look at. Over time, I was able to see it as a guide, and as I went through my feelings at a greater level, was able to allow this guide to bring me deeper and deeper into my feelings.

Society, or the culture, is uneasy with the concept of one of its members hearing "voices", has a prescribed behavioral treatment for these types of deviants, and its called medication and psyche units. To one going through an acute phase of schizophrenia, this is appropriate treatment. It's not for someone confused about his internal dialogue. Some doctors will not recognize the confusion unless one can verbalize his understanding of the voices as being self-talk. When this internal dialogue is first experienced as confusion, as the mind becomes a battlefield of different opinions - some think they are becoming crazy and if they report the confusion —

will be diagnosed as insane and locked up forever. By a show of hands, how many of you have felt in the past, or feel today — that same way? How many? Not much honesty out there. This book is certainly needed. Let me ask again. How did you feel when you first noticed that a part of you observed everything you did and most times would make a comment on it? What happened if you disagreed with this part? How many times did you argue with it and say "no" to what it asked or demanded? How did you feel? Felt crazy didn't you? Bet you didn't tell too many people about what was going on inside. Did you? Now let's have a show of hands. That's better. It's easier to be honest when you're not afraid. See, this book does help.

An example and a warning through a funny story . . . When I was receiving supervision during my pre-license experience, I had the honor to be supervised by an excellent psychiatrist. He challenged me in every way, provided a wealth of information and experience, and helped me to see there were many ways of seeing things. Mine was just one of those ways. He would call it my theology. One week as I was explaining a transference problem in my therapy group, the feelings it raised in me, and what transpired internally; he went into his best clinical pose, played with his mustache, and asked in his most elegant, poised, and professional voice, "How long have you been hearing the voices, Lou?" Inside I started to laugh, thinking he's assessing me for being a schiz. Another voice went off and said, "Play with him, Lou." (My Adolescent is really bad.) And at the same time I replied, "Don't get crazy, Doc. It's only my internal dialogue and I'm not a schiz." He looked back, still in his assessment mode, and stated, "Just checking."

I had a lot of fun with this and he eventually loosened up, but it got me to thinking how easy it is for someone to be misdiagnosed if they told the attending psychiatrist that they heard voices, instead of calling it their internal dialogue. I was working at the time in a dual-diagnosis psychiatric unit with multiple relapse clients and had to be very careful because of the vast differences between the way the doctors interpreted the clients and how we worked with them. This example of psychiatrists assessing the patient as hearing voices and the therapists working on those same voices as internal dialogue instead of pathology is a good example. There is a world of difference when two view the same presentation so differently: One sees it as a tool, and the other views it as a mental aberration. It made me work very carefully in this area, and I used humor as one of my main tools for both the psychiatrists and the patients.

I did very extensive work with the patients' internal dialogue. I helped them to label the voices, understand their significance, and to utilize the information given by the voices as a self-awareness tool, a stress-reducing strategy and how to increase problem-solving skills. In staffing and supervision, I emphasized what I was working on and made several distinctions between internal dialogue and auditory hallucinations because we would occasionally have schizophrenics on the unit that would de-compensate and regress in an acute phase.

One of the interventions used to normalize the patients' (in-hospital treatment) or clients' (anyone seen out of a hospital setting) internal dialogue was to tell the story about the doctor and me. Everyone in group would laugh. Some would be strained. This would happen because the topic raised a lot of fear in a population that thought it was crazy to begin with, and in some ways could add more evidence to their case. I would tell a couple more funny stories, warn them about therapists who hear and talk to voices, and then go to work teaching about the various voices that fire off in our heads.

Like them, the reader needs a conceptual framework to jump off into the material. The preceding chapters were that framework:

1. Stating the problem and its process
2. Outlining the structure of perception and how it precipitates behavior
3. Utilizing a developmental model to enhance clarity in psychodynamic concepts
4. Demonstrating the operating system and examining its components
5. Exploring personality development, its structure, and determinants
6. Traversing the development of the three ego states
7. And now exploring the derivative of this process which is the human's internal dialogue. Are you ready to work?

STRUCTURE

There is a structure to the voices and it follows a developmental model. In its matrix are three distinct voices: the Child, Adolescent and Adult. The Adult has two personas: one critical — the other nurturing. The order is important because each stage acquires an additional voice as the human gets older. There would be one voice in childhood, two in early adolescence, three to four in late adolescence and all the way through, until death. They are chronologically ordered: the Child, Adolescent, and the Adult. The Adult has two voices depending on which mode the person is in. One is a critical voice and the other is a nurturing one. The nurturing one is also called the "observer" (Bern, 61, 64).

I've also noticed that the Nurturing Adult is usually connected to a person's spirituality. The analogy is, *if* we are a part of God, Higher Power, or energy of the universe....The Nurturing Adult is the segment of the personality and the conduit into the connection of our communion with this entity. I don't do religion very well and the preceding was not religious in nature. It was spiritual. Whatever works for you — works for me. To me, it's not how you connect, only that you do connect. We all find our own path. Mine is just one of many. This book, on the other hand, can disperse great light on your path if you are ready.

Internal Dialogue of the Child

The Child Ego State is small and soft. Sometimes it is nonexistent. It manifests from what was seen by the child *AND HOW IT WAS INTERPRETED.* It's usually attached to the individual's feelings. It fires off when one is scared, mesmerized, spontaneous, shamed, fearful, curious, playful, withdrawn, trusting, violated, needy, or insecure and any other feeling that engenders childlike behavior or *the feeling that the adult is very small.*

Some simple examples of the adult's internal dialogue originating from the Child Ego State is when you speak to the boss about a raise or have a problem, and your throat goes dry, voice lowers, fear, doubt, and insecurity goes off inside your head. You are now in your Child, its voice is what you are hearing, and you are now five years old. Know that feeling of smallness when you get stopped by a police officer and the voice in your head says, "What did I do?" over and over. That's your Child. Know the feeling you get after an argument with your lover or spouse and you hear in your head, "What if they leave? What am I going to do?" That's also your Inner Child's voice.

How do you feel after a disagreement with your parents? Are you big and empowered or small and insecure? Be honest. This is a difficult area because your Inner Child loves his parents and it doesn't make a difference what they did to you or how your Adolescent or Adult feels about it. That small part of you, that we call the Inner Child or the Child Ego State, *ALWAYS LOVES HIS PARENTS*! You don't have to trust your parents, only acknowledge this love for them.

Do you know how many people have spent years in therapy trying to rectify this conflict? Many! All you have to do is to validate the Child and the internal battle disappears. Too simple you say? Wrong! Take my framework, get a good therapist, a strong twelve-step support network and program, do some experiential work with your Inner Child, and watch the healing begin. Listen to the inner conflict quieting down. Don't believe me? Try it. Then write to me and let me know the results. (My sponsor tells me I have an ego problem. What do you think?)

Based on what you have learned in the book so far, what part of me wrote the last paragraph? Assess me! Write it out. Let's see what you have learned. I'll give you the answer. It may be in code, somewhere in the book, or at the end of this chapter. It all depends where my Little Kid wants it. He feels mischievous. This always happens when I have fun. I'm having fun now by playing with you. Are you? What did you learn from this lesson other than your Adolescent and Critical Parent saying I'm crazy? If you think this is bad — wait until we get to the chapter on relationships! I'll try not to stir you up too much.

Internal Dialogue of the Adolescent

The Adolescent views himself as being ten feet tall and bullet proof and its voice denotes the same connotation. When riled, the Adolescent is very antagonistic, aggressive, and ego centered. It will push someone out of the way or run over them. The reverse is true of disempowered Adolescents. They go inward and become self-destructive. Their dialogue is based on the above descriptions.

Let's carry the preceding examples from the Child section to this one and observe the Adolescent's response. The response can come from two sides. The first would be an aggressive voice from the side that acts out. The next will be the disempowered side turning the anger inward and possibly sabotaging itself.

Know what happens to you behaviorally when you speak to the boss about something? Your Little Kid is insecure and your Adolescent has to act on this fear. Know when you're sarcastic, arrogant, and the boss says you have a bad attitude? That's your Adolescent. Do you know when you back down, call yourself all those names, and then become passive/aggressive on the job, or self-destructive? It's the "acting in" part of your Adolescent who's in charge. Remember when the boss said to be in his office at 4:00 P.M. without an explanation? The first voice you hear is the Child. The next is the Adolescent either quitting the job or knowing he deserves to be fired. You know what fires off in your head. I'm only giving it a name and how to access the information it stores to develop adaptive coping strategies and non problematic decision-making skills instead of building up a head of steam and quitting or getting fired.

Getting stopped by a police officer can generate the same internal dialogue. Most people stay in their Child because it's the safest thing to do. Others go right to their Adolescent and that's when things get real hairy. If you have both individuals operating in their Adolescent mode — trouble begins real quick. This is probably one of the most explosive street situations. Thanks to the excellent training a police officer receives today, most of these situations are kept in check.

What about your response, after a fight with your lover or spouse, when you think they are going to leave you and you break up with them first or ask for a divorce. That's your Adolescent. You know the voice: "Forget them," it says! "You can live without them," it replies angrily! "They're like a bus," it further states; "One comes along every twenty minutes." The other side to leaving is staying in the face of evidence that the relationship is over. When you don't leave, the Adolescent turns it inward, as self-destructive behavior.

With parents, it's the same old story, over and over. One capitulates, gives himself up, and does what the parents want, or, goes opposite to their wishes. In this case, the adolescent reaction is worse than the parents' request because many times, opportunities are missed or substance abuse is used. All of these reactions occur because the adolescent is trying to jam it up their parents' rear end and all they are succeeding in doing is jamming it up their own. Remember, family systems therapy and the adolescent as the IP (identified patient)? When the adolescent reacts in the dysfunctional family, everyone looks at him, instead of the real problem that's going on. At this time they are merely a symptom of the problem. When the adolescent acts out they become a problem to themselves by diverting the necessary energy it takes to learn and grow and then invests it in the maladaptive behavior of a Problem Loop. In the process, they hinder their own growth and virtually perpetrate themselves as they stop their own growth.

Internal Dialogue of the Adult

NURTURING ADULT   When the Adult is in charge — reason will prevail. Common sense will be used, and past strategies reviewed. All the dialogue associated with mature thinking will prevail: It will be positive in nature, solution oriented, and soft not wishy- washy, firm not hard or dogmatic, open minded, adaptive, and looking for a win-win situation without giving up themselves. This is a highly mature posture and the hallmark of the Nurturing Adult. Let's bring the previous scenarios forward, from the Adolescent to the Nurturing Adult and observe how they will be facilitated.

Work - In the first situation, the boss was being approached about a raise, problem, or the employee was asked to meet with them later in the day without an explanation. During this time, the Child's insecurity came on line and became very fearful. This stirred up the Adolescent who became sarcastic and arrogant when it didn't quite go his way. *ALL OF THIS FIRES OFF IN THE HEAD FIRST — BEFORE — IT'S PUT INTO ACTION!*

It's during this time the Nurturing Adult talks to all of its parts. It looks at what the Child is afraid of, validates the feelings, and then sorts out the reaction from the facts. Based on their conclusions, the Adult will sooth the Child's feelings, give it the necessary information that's needed to quell the fear, and go on to the next step in the decision-making process. At this time, the process will go on even though the Child is still afraid. This lack at trust by the Child, toward the Adult, does not hinder the Adult. At some point the Child will have to learn to trust the Adult. This is a hard process when someone has spent his life dissociating from his feelings and it takes a great deal of time before the Child begins to trust its Adult.

The next phase of the decision-making process is listening to the Adolescent. I can tell you right now, that the more powerful the Adolescent presence is felt, can be directly correlated to the amount of times the Adult tried to ignore them. And you know how hard it is to ignore Adolescents. The solution-oriented Adult would first ask the Adolescent, "Why are you here?" The Adolescent will respond. It may be that there's exploitation going on, or the Adult is not getting an adequate enough compensation for the services demanded. It may be a pattern of unproductive vocational choices that the Adult continues to make in spite of several failures, and the Adolescent is trying to warn him. It could be disempowerment, or it could be as simple as a boundary violation. Once the Adult listens to the Adolescent with a keen ear, it is usually apparent what the Adolescent's concerns are. As the concerns are acknowledged by the Adult, the Adolescent backs off, warning he is at arms length and can come back in a moment if needed. This veiled threat should be taken seriously and it's an unwise Adult who doesn't listen. The Nurturing Adult will not ignore the

Adolescent's concern and will affirm the Adolescent's right to be part of the process. The Adults appreciation is demonstrated when he elicits the Adolescent's help by using his energy to tackle the problem instead of fighting. Decisions based on this process are usually innovative, adaptive, and highly functional.

Authority Figures — In the second example when the adult is stopped by the police officer, the Child becomes fearful and the Adolescent wants to react. Once again, the Adult takes in all data given by both the Child and Adolescent and combines it with its own observations. Based on this, the Adult will sooth the Child's fear and tell it, "We are not going to jail for life." The Adult will elicit the energy of the Adolescent to find out why they were stopped, and to respond with appropriate behavior. If you were stopped for a minor violation, it was usually a broken taillight. I've gotten stopped and because I keep a few small tools in the car and some spare bulbs, have fixed the car on the spot and never gotten an inspection ticket. Accidents do happen. Nobody goes to jail for life or has to argue with a police officer over a broken taillight. Nor does anybody have to learn to change a broken taillight. My Adolescent likes to do those things, and my Child doesn't like to go into inspection stations. Even though I drive a late model luxury sedan, and don't remember the last time I changed a taillight, I still carry the equipment in my car today.

Relationships — They are the most difficult to conquer. The thought of losing one triggers off past unresolved abandonment issues and gives rise to the most revengeful entity that man has ever seen. It's the stuff nightmares are made of. It's the catalyst for planning someone's death or thinking up a thousand ways to get back together. It's what drives people crazy. I'm only going to examine the rudiments of relationship dynamics in this section because I'll devote several chapters to it later on in this book.

When that special, wonderful, and DIFFERENT someone in your life says the relationship between you and them is all over - several dynamics come into play:

1. It's a loss and has to be treated as such
2. Getting over it (poor wording) or resolving it - is a process
3. The breakup will trigger unresolved losses that transpired over the lifespan

Loss is cumulative. When one tries to go over it (not a play on words) instead of going through it and gaining resolution — it only accumulates more. Each time someone superficially tries to get over something they are usually trying to bypass the pain. How many times have you heard someone say, "I'm over them," and then rebound into another bad relationship? *The only way out of the pain is through it and it usually takes some time spent alone with yourself to sort out what happened, clean up your end of the street, and make the necessary changes to yourself in order to have clearer choices in relationships.* This time alone could start at one year and extend to five, in order to do the work it takes to stop the downward relationship spiral. Right about now a few of you have thrown the book away, burned it, puked, and said, *"NO WAY!"* Some have said, "I'll give it a try." Others are saying, "It's a different idea." It doesn't matter what you think, only that you have choices in whom you pick to be with. Do you have choices? Read on.

When a relationship ends, it's the Child that usually gets hurt. It's their voice you hear when you're thinking, "What will I do? How will I live without them? I'll never get another person like them. I'll be alone the rest of my life." The second voice that sounds off is The Adolescent, and you hear in your mind, "Forget them! Who do they think they are! The bum! The pig! I'll show them! They didn't deserve me! They were no good anyway! I'll kill them!" Instead of hearing helpless and hopeless from the Child, it is anger and sometimes rages from the Adolescent, depending on how many times this has happened and what significance the relationship played in one's life. The more times it has happened, the greater the reaction. The Adolescent that doesn't act out usually turns it inward and becomes self-destructive with an: "I'll show you" attitude, and goes into depression, experiences substance abuse, can self-mutilate, becomes overly involved in work and "doesn't have time" for relationships, becomes promiscuous, or becomes the victim in another toxic relationship.

At this point, there is much confusion going on in the mind and heart as all these voices are shooting off the questions and angry remarks into thin air. The Nurturing Adult steps in at this time, quiets down the noise, and starts to sort things out. *By taking charge over the confusion, the novice steps into the Adult role. If one remains helpless and hopeless, they are in their Child Ego State. When they continue to be angry, revengeful, or self-destructive, they have fallen into their Adolescent mode.* This is an excellent self-assessment tool that can help anyone sort out the issues raised by its individual parts when a relationship is ended.

After the carnage is muddled through, the Child and Adolescent are separated, and each one addressed individually. During the process, the Child is affirmed, as each fear he raised became answered. In a soft voice the Child is told, "We'll go on and make a life without them. We'll find someone else, or be happy with ourselves, and never be alone. We are lovable. It wasn't our fault they changed. It's O.K. if you still love them. I won't let them hurt you again." With a respectful voice, the Adolescent's concerns are addressed with the following dialogue: "I knew they hurt you and you're angry at me for picking the same kind of emotionally unavailable person. I'll take responsibility for my behavior, but I need your help to remind me when I pick the same type of person over and over. This time I will listen to you. No, we can't kill them. Remember our allergy to electronic locks." When you use this type of dialogue on the Adolescent, they know that you are taking full responsibility for yourself, and at the same time not invalidating the Child's love for the person in the broken relationship. This is important because *all* parts have to be in harmony before the Adult can become congruous in thoughts, feeling, and behavior. From the conversation between the ego states, the following occurs:

1.   A plan to go through the pain of the relationship's dissolution
2.   Identification of the role one played in its demise
3.   A plan to get on with one's life

This process is what emotionally mature, responsible adults use to generate creative, adaptive solutions to their problems. They remain functional without regressing or using dysfunctional behavior as a stress reducer to take the focus off themselves. The focus is shifted externally, when they create another situation they can be immersed in, instead of dealing with the issues being raised by the terminated relationship.

Family — The family is another difficult area to work with one's internal dialogue because there are many facets involved. Depending on the person's age-stage, the differentiation between the voices gets increasingly more subtle as the person gets older. This occurs when boundaries between the ego stages merge, as the individual becomes congruent within them, and has, naturally, over the course of time, through experiencing similar circumstances as their parents had, become able to resolve some of the earlier issues with them without therapy or self help.

At younger stages the voices are clear. The adult feels like a Child when in the presence of his parents, and can also be reduced into feeling very small during a phone call. The Adolescent then wants to fight his way out of the mire the Adult placed him in, when he slides into being a Child around his parents. This can lead to fighting with them over this perceived disempowering, or becoming self-destructing and saying, "I'll show them."

The Adult claims the power at this time by reminding them that they're grown-up, not little kids, and give appropriate responses to anything their parents may have said or done to invoke the small person's feelings. The Adolescent at this time will be quiet, watchful, and approving because the Adult is doing their job and the Adolescent doesn't have to do it for them. Note: If the reaction at this time is large, simple facilitation can't quiet it down, shame has probably been triggered. If this is the case, some work will have to be done on the antecedents, in order to disempower its stranglehold on the individual.

For some, this family power will prevail over the individual throughout the life span. For others, there will be complete detachment, bordering on disengagement, in which the family will have no influence over them. For most, it will be somewhere in between. Some days you'll feel like a grownup. Other times you won't.

As one matures, he claims his inalienable rights of individualism over the family's tyranny, the battle subsides, and one becomes a grownup who is whole within himself. This is nothing short of progressive human development in which the human, spawned from the seed, grows to being able to reproduce, and become the soul he was designed or predestined to be. To be, or not to be — is always a choice. Do you have one? Do you know what it is? If you have a Nurturing Adult — you are certainly on your path.

During this time of convergence, the Adult usually affirms the Child and validates the Adolescent. As successful outcomes of independence are experienced and the individual remains a viable member of the family, the internal conflicts diminish until they are gone. Periodically, residue of a past issue will surface, or be seen from a different perspective, and the voices will be resurrected. At this time, the Adult will facilitate those issues with poise and equanimity and they will recede as quickly as they surfaced, without any damage to one's internal structure or family relationships.

CRITICAL ADULT — This is the voice in your head that responds with negativity, becomes critical and judgmental toward everything that goes on, and second guesses the decisions you have made. It's the voice that haunts you in the middle of the night, rehashing every single moment of the day, until you fall asleep exhausted from the belittlement.

Its roots are in the culture and emerged from an archaic time which prescribed the axioms, "Self-praise is no praise." "Pick yourself up by your own bootstraps." And the infamous, "Don't give them a compliment — it might go to their heads." The sad part about it is they were meant to help, to give someone they loved humility, and to keep them grounded. It had the reverse impact. It stifled growth, inhibited ambition, reduced self-esteem, lowered self concepts, and engendered shame. How could something that had such high intentions — create such low results.

This negative verbiage system is the hallmark of the Critical Adult. It was the culture that prescribed it. The parents assimilated it and taught it to their children, who taught it to their children, who taught it to their children, and we go round and round ad nauseum until the loop stops here. Today we can see that all parents did the best they could with what information they had. Previous generations did not have the information explosion we experience today, or the proliferation of ways of receiving help. They had the Folk Culture as reinforcement only. This only reiterated the predominate culture's view and usually only prescribed ways of complying, not explaining, and certainly not exploring the ramifications of edicts.

We challenge today. Not satisfied just to go along with the culture, when to continue only brings pain. We examine our actions and change what we must to remain internally connected and keep our integrity. To do less is spiritual suicide at best.

There are several ways the Critical Adult sabotages the individual's effort to develop and be appropriate. Its original intention was to help. It actually comes from a place of love and wants nothing but the best for its children. Its delivery comes up short and is highly critical and judgmental. When you are able to see this, and respond accordingly, the Critical Adult quiets down.

I've had many clients and even other therapists go ballistic over the above intervention. Some even called me naïve to think that the process is that simple. It is. Don't fight with the Critical Adult. Thank them for their concern, and they will be quiet. This not only applies to one's internal dialogue, it also applies to the original critical parent and that's one's mother and/or father. Try the following the next time one of them becomes critical and starts to stir up the shame from your Child and the anger from the Adolescent: Just say, "Thank you Mom or Dad. I know you love me and want the best for me. I'll certainly take in the advice or comment you made." Watch them: Like a balloon, they will deflate and become docile.

How are you doing with the concept? Have you lost your breath? Have a lump in your throat? Angry? Curious? Think it may have possibilities? Try it. I know it's successful. This is one intervention that people in program have less trouble with than those in therapy. It's probably because the issues are not as extreme or the amount of energy invested is less. To those in program, it's usually taken as shared experience that works and they have little difficulty utilizing it. When it's suggested in therapy, the client usually balks, has a hard time with the concept, reacts like it's a moral issue to even consider it, and exclaims that he would rather die before capitulating. Some just sigh and with resignation, bemoan that it will never work. It's a good assessing tool to determine what issues the client has with his primary caregivers and how deep it's entrenched, based on the depth of the reaction. It's also a good barometer of what type of Adolescent they possess because it's this part of them that reacts to the strategy.

Work — The Critical Adult operates on two levels in work. The first is internal, highly demeaning, and doesn't give credit for successful endeavors, or minimizes out the gain as luck. This voice will very rarely let you take credit for work accomplished. It taunts, "You could have done better. Look at the big mistake you made." These are usually tiny mistakes that are magnified tenfold. If you get a raise — it's never enough to this part of you. If you get a promotion, the voice exclaims, "You were lucky! It's a mistake! Anyone could have gotten it!" When, in fact, you worked very hard to get it. With new ideas the Critical Adult is usually shooting them down when they are actually very good.

The Critical Parent is also on the march against the job and fellow employees. The job is never the right one. Pay is inadequate. The hours worked are too grueling. The boss is never satisfied. Etc., etc, etc. Fellow employees get the brunt of this barrage for the entire shift. Nothing anyone else does is ever good enough. There are negative comments galore about their looks, grooming, clothing, voice, or personal habits. God forbid that they have a physical flaw or some kind of different personal characteristics. Here you also see a lot of "back-handed compliments." This is when a compliment is given in a negative way or the compliment is taken back by a negative qualification. They usually sound like this: "You did a good job, *but*, it took you a long time." "Thank you for the favor even though I had to wait for you." "Thanks for coming. Oh, by the way, John was here an hour sooner." You all know what they sound like. Remember, the intention was praise and to keep you humble at the same time. Its impact is negative. The praise is taken back and the person begins to build resentment toward the giver without even knowing why.

This critical voice becomes the catalyst for: missed opportunities, apprehension, applying for a better position, insecurity about asking for a raise, not maintaining one's personal boundaries, having unrealistic expectations about a productive work load, and failure to develop an adequate support system with other employees. Critical internal dialogue is the hallmark of the unsuccessful employee. It keeps them in menial positions, under employed, not appreciated, least considered, and under paid.

Authority Figures — According to the Critical Adult, whenever the individual is in conflict, confronts, or negotiates with an authority figure - the individual is wrong to do it and considered inferior. Usually, this is shaming and disempowering to the adult. When this dialogue sounds off, it lowers self-esteem and depreciates self concepts. Remember, this consternation is for the best interests of the host. The individual is being schooled. After all, "You can't fight city hall." The Critical Adult exclaims, "Why try?"

This is the voice that keeps the individual victimized by the system and afraid to take a stand or stick up for their rights. Many times people in city hall make a mistake. If you don't assert yourself under these circumstances, you lose. It's nothing personal when a mistake is made. It's just a mistake. To the Critical Adult, this is heresy. *City Hall or the Government "never" makes a mistake* according to this voice. To make a mistake is to die. This part of the Critical Adult is very childlike and its roots are in the cultural background of many immigrants. It was spawned in a previous time when people were killed for challenging the culture. When someone was schooled in the old days about not fighting city hall, it probably saved their life.

Today it is an archaic belief which has its roots entrenched so deeply within the individual's psyche, that it's hard to keep it out of today's situations, occurring in the twenty first century.

This ego state also creates a subterfuge to minimize the impact of being powerless over fighting city hall. Its strategy is to create a diversion to make it seem that the individual is capable of fighting city hall by taking a moot or insignificant, harmless, or non-threatening issue and going "to the wall with it." This only makes a molehill into a mountain to rescue one's integrity, but leaves the main issue alone. In the process, the turbulent event is minimized and turns the mountain into a molehill. This avoids all potentially dangerous contact with the establishment, maintains the individual's internal structure, and saves his life. If you doubt this, just ask some immigrants about some of their experiences with their former governments before coming to the United States. Remember, none of this has to be going on today. It went on in the past; it's alive in the mind, and real today subconsciously.

Relationships — This is a fertile area for the Critical Adult. There are far too many opportunities, in today's world, for this segment to dominate. Many times today people seem detached, able to shift gears very quickly, and remain superficial. This makes it very difficult to start and maintain a mature intimate relationship in either work or play.

There is the instant bonding between those who share experience in the same areas like the various self-help programs, therapy groups, sports, school, clubs, certain vocations, early life events, and going through a major catastrophe together and surviving. There is also the instant bonding in a sexual relationship, when the intensity of the relationship and the sex is so high, that no end is perceived. I'm not judging the examples. Many terrific and long-time relationships have begun in the same way. Most times, great individual effort is expended to maintain the relationship after the bonding episodes are over. This takes commitment, dedication, purpose, and substance. How many people do you know today who have those qualities? Do you? It's hard to make this kind of a commitment, and expend the effort to maintain it, in a world that drains you of your time and energy just to exist.

The faster we travel, the quicker we expect the outcomes to occur. We live in an instant gratification society which adheres to the motto, "If we don't get it now — we don't get it at all." Relationships aren't like that. They take time to develop, nurture, and sustain. No wonder there are so many relationship problems today, and with them comes the Critical Adult's berating, moving down the track like a freight train, bowling over everything and everybody with their negative dialogue.

The dialogue moves in two directions. The first is self-depreciating. The second is directed outward toward their partner and it's very critical and judgmental toward them. Many have used this state to work out their parental issues on their friend or lover. This is actually where Psychoanalysis (Freud, 52) comes in with transference and projection. Something their partner does triggers off a past event or trauma; the past feelings are then attached to the current situation; the present love object is now blamed for the current pain which has been magnified greatly. If you ever wondered about how something became blown up — there's the answer. The pain from the original hurt was transferred onto the present situation and projected onto the new love object. This is all done in conjunction with the Critical Adult, and will be explored further in the chapter on relationships.

Family — This area remains germane as each developmental stage has some kind of connection back in the family and has the Critical Adult in overdrive trying to keep up with all the opportunities to "school" the family member. This area (the family), like authority figures, has its roots in the culture, and maintains a high regard for respect.

The authority figures in the family take on the same life and death characteristics as the cultural icons engendered in times past. This is a hard relationship boundary to break. You can project the multitude of problems a developing human will acquire each time it has to push a boundary or limit with the family and is met with the resistance of a dogmatic structure.

This persistence is continued throughout the life span and is felt in every interaction with the family until this part is understood and quieted. I deliberately didn't use "confronted" because it's not appropriate terminology. It really is more of an understanding that quiets the battle that rages in the mind. Once it's reframed to my concept, accepted because it's viable, and practiced, it's more of a joining. When you think about a person coming together, accepting all its parts, isn't the Critical Adult one of its parts? To reject it — is to reject a part of self. Today, this concept is no longer conjecture; it is a fact, empiricism, and an important piece of work that has to be accomplished if one hopes to quiet his internal battles.

A mature adult who has completed the individualization and the separation process with the family of origin will only have minimum difficulty with this part. For them, when the conflict arises, they will evaluate the evidence, check out their computer banks for previous relevant experiences, dispute the negative dialogue of the Critical Adult, and complete the task or make the decision. When this adaptive, solution-oriented process is utilized: the growing person's self concepts will be validated, self-esteem will rise, self-confidence will be generated, personal integrity will be solidified, and one's internal structure will remain intact.

The maladaptive individual, using a problem—oriented coping style, will remain focused on the negativity and fight and fight and fight until all energy is spent. At this point, he will capitulate either through lack of energy, which is forfeiture, or, just give up, which is disempowerment. Either way, he has lost the battle when all he had to do to win was to understand and develop good emotional boundaries.

ANSWER FOR WHO WROTE THE CHILD SECTION

The part of me that wrote the last couple of paragraphs in the Child section of this chapter was the Adolescent, in conjunction with my Nurturing Adult, which allowed my Child to feel whole. What triggers off internally is my Child has witnessed many losses and becomes fearful when he thinks someone is going to leave. Leaving under the old belief system was usually experienced as death because even if someone didn't die, a way of life died. My Adolescent would cover up the pain by acting out, and medicate it with whatever was available, including persons, places, and things. My Critical Adult (the sum totals of all significant others) would judge him and beat him to death. My Adolescent would further react, and all hell broke loose.

Today, my Inner Child has been taught that leaving is not dying — though sometimes it feels this way. That people are like seasons — they come in your life for awhile and then leave. Some stay. Most go. They are angels, sent from my Higher Power, whom I choose to call God, to guide me through a certain part of my life. The part of me that verbalizes the above words is my Nurturing Adult. My Adolescent is quiet at this time and also in reserve and standing by if I need him.

The lesson my Adolescent learned since I came in self-help and therapy is that his acting out scared the Child. Even though he was protecting him - *the actions frightened him*! The energy from the acting out had to be re-channeled. Just as the Child had to have reframed the experience of someone leaving, so did the Adolescent on how he protected the Child.

This is how my Adolescent protected the Child in the paragraphs and gave you a lesson at the same time: I used his intensity to write instead of him acting out, gave you a powerful message, and did it in conjunction with my Nurturing Adult (Remember. My child knows how people die because of their compulsions. This book is one of the tools needed to stop mental, physical or spiritual death). I personally feel that in the process, I'm connected to my Higher Power who gave me the words, to pass on to you, because I didn't plan on writing what was on the page. My Critical

Adult's voice is silenced and my Child was able to come out in play, because all parts of me were in harmony and I was connected to God. How did you do with the assessment? Let me know.

ANOTHER LEARNING EXPERIENCE

In therapy, as in recovery, there are many things we have to learn. The lesson to be learned here is that the Child *ALWAYS* loves the parents. We as adults *have to* validate that to be in harmony with ourselves. Once done, there is no longer a battle…. just the fact that the Child continues to wish for better parents. The rest of the ego states can feel any way they want. It's O.K. and doesn't have to invalidate them. Until one can come into acceptance about one's parents "doing the best they could, with what they had, for where they were" - the above is a good strategy for letting something go that *can't be changed* - which is the past, and freeing up the energy to be applied to something that *can be changed - THAT'S YOU TODAY*!

WHEN WE LET GO OF THE PAST -
WE CAN CHANGE OURSELVES TODAY!

ASSIGNMENT 14:   What voice predominates in your internal dialogue? Is it a fearful Child who gives himself up easily? Is it the angry or provocative Adolescent who tries to coerce or seduce his adversaries? Does the Critical Adult shame your Child, taunt your Adolescent or second-guess your Nurturing Adult with every decision it makes? Is your Nurturing Adult activated yet? Does it know how to affirm the Child, validate the Adolescent, set healthy boundaries and limits on them and quiet the noise level of the Critical Adult? If yes - how and under what circumstances is the appropriate ego states activated? If no - what do you need to practice in order to "make it so"? Internal harmony simply means that: the Nurturing Adult is able to check in with the Child to see how they "feel"; determine any "boundaries" and "acquire" the energy from the Adolescent; take the input from the Critical Adult as a possibility instead of a judgment; and make the final decision based on the feedback from the entire internal structure. How do other people in your life give you messages? They would include parents, children, spouse, lover, significant other, friends, co-workers, bosses, and even institutions. Look at the beginning questions again.

Do this work with your various relationships and you will probably be surprised at what you see. The clarity will eventually be phenomenal.

SUMMARY

Internal dialogue is the self-talk that prevails in every human being's cognitive structure. Some call it thinking. Others call it confusion. It goes on every waking moment of someone's life. The only way to silence it is to sleep, or, take serious mood-altering drugs. These voices are not to be confused with a schizophrenic's auditory hallucinations.

When examined, the dialogue has a structure, which corresponds to the ego states of my developmental paradigm: The Child, Adolescent, Critical Adult, and Nurturing Adult. Each has its own distinctive voice and purpose. The Child will let you know the feelings of a situation. The Adolescent will determine the appropriate response, based on overkill, unless healthy boundaries and limits are set. The Critical Adult usually delivers a shame-based message, derived out of the values of a turn-of-the-century culture which expounded on one's ability to "pick themselves up by their own bootstraps," or, "Never give them a compliment for it might go to their head." Their mantra was, "Children should be seen and not heard." Their overall intent was to motivate, build character, and warn about the dangers of not being productive. The Nurturing Adult affirms The Child, validates The Adolescent, extracts a positive message from The Critical Adult's dialogue, makes decisions based on their holistic needs and brings internal agreement to the evolving human being's mind.

I believe that Westerners, as a culture, have learned to ignore their internal dialogue. As a result, they are alienated from their inner core, confused, and spiritually bankrupt. This disconnection is really dissociation. When it occurs, one cannot know himself, have balanced relationships with others, or complete his spiritual tasks.

In order to reconnect with this lost attribute, one has to recognize the loss, gain the necessary data to understand the nature of the voices, apply the results to life situations, and learn from whatever mistakes he made. This is a simple concept. Why do so many have difficulty with it? It's the building blocks of learning. Learning about one's internal dialogue is no different.

Once a person's internal dialogue is labeled, the effort is placed on increasing one's skill in attaching the meaning of the message to the present situation. As reconnection to oneself occurs, any decision made on a life event will be an adaptive one based on the individual's holistic needs.

CASE STUDY

The following case study will illustrate how one's internal dialogue continues to covertly operate in our culture under the most benign conditions and inappropriate places. It also uses humor to demonstrate a strategy for counter-acting its negative impact.

Brent and his wife Sandy were visiting a popular tourist attraction in Florida. One of its highlights is a variety-type show that includes some very talented performers. The show is held in an amphitheater that's set up for excellent viewing because of the steep slope. The crowd is usually boisterous and follows the high energy level of the performers.

Brent and Sandy are an attractive upper-middle-class couple in their forties who present very well. They have three very beautiful children and are admired as a family whenever they attend anything together. This particular day, Brent and Sandy were on a date and wanted to let their Inner Children play without their biological children around.

The day was perfect. The weather cooperated. Even the kids wished them a good date as they left for school in the morning. Both were looking forward to seeing the show because they enjoyed high-energy entertainment. The seats they chose were good ones. It was during the week, so the crowd was thin and there were plenty of empty spaces between the seats and the rows.

During the first part of the program, Brent noticed that Sandy had quieted down and seemed to have less enthusiasm. As he checked it out with her, she pointed to some older couples, three rows down and to the left, who seemed to be chatting among themselves and occasionally looking their way. "Sandy's voice was on the low side," reported Brent, and he described her as a little girl whom someone had hurt, as she informed him that "those" people were giving him dirty looks each time he applauded and cheered.

Numbness is the first feeling Brent reports having as Sandy is describing what the older couples were doing. Shame began to rise as Sandy finishes and Brent remembers his Nurturing Adult separating out from the feelings, and telling his Inner Child that he didn't make a mistake, he isn't a mistake, and it's their stuff that was coming up.

The shame subsided, Brent exclaimed, as he surveyed the situation. A quick look at the four couples reveals no outward sign of emotion. All appeared to be pretty stoic. No handholding or touching could be seen. Every 30 seconds one of the women turned in their direction and gave them "THE LOOK!" You know "the look" I'm talking about? The one that your parents give that reduces you to a little Child….the one that raises shame in the individual at warp speed. The one that makes you want to change your behavior instantly, no matter what you're doing or if you're right or wrong, just to make "the look" go away.

"This whole observation process took only a couple of minutes," Brent reported. He smiled back at the lady who was giving him "the look." He then laughingly turned to Sandy and explained he thought they were trying to control their enthusiasm by their actions. Brent is now laughing as he describes Sandy's response. He further states that his wife has been in a twelve-step program for several years, and has what he describes as a "black belt" in these issues, because she's really solid within herself, and still maintains good contact with her family. "It took a lot of work to get there," he states with much admiration in his voice, and further states, "I'm proud of her."

Sandy's whole demeanor change as Brent lovingly explains what he thinks is occurring. First it is shock and disbelief that registers on her face. And then a mischievous smile takes over as she whistles, applauds, and cheers the performers.

"All was back to normal," claims Brent, and they enjoyed the rest of the show with the same zest that prevailed prior to "the look." In fact, Brent reveals that they seemed to have a better time because both their Adolescents were defying the parents. Both could observe the couples' huffing and puffing with indignation when the "looks" didn't work.

Later on during the day, the same couples are observed trying to give the same looks to them with an added look of intimidation by one of the males. Brent states that he is in his Adolescent mode, is going to "kick all their a_ _ _ s" and moves in to confront them. Brent then starts to laugh as he describes them "moving fast" to get away from them. That was the last time they saw them at the attraction.

Brent also observed that this occurred several times throughout the day with other people. There seemed to be a proliferation of seniors that day and they weren't very accommodating to the jovial environment.

When Brent and Sandy were going home that evening, they discussed the events of the day, and laughingly said they wished they had those couples' children's phone numbers so they could tell them how to drive their parents crazy when they tried to control them with "the look." Try it yourself. Look around you. Tell me what you see.

The situation that occurred with Brent and Sandy should not have occurred. They were at an attraction that was designed to elicit the responses they were producing. They were appropriate to their environment and the kind of people these kinds of establishments want to attract. They went there to have fun - they did. And because some older couples were raised in a culture that *"children should be seen and not heard,"* they almost had their day ruined.

CHAPTER TWELVE

Grief is a process.
The only way out is through it.
There are no shortcuts!

OVERVIEW

When you have completed this chapter, you will be able to recognize:

1. Grief as a process, the natural unfolding of awareness and the connection spirituality plays in its matrix
2. Impact of the ego states of each stage's resolution
3. The therapeutic value of *denial* when used as a shock absorber
4. When *anger* is healthy, while being used, to vent the energy from inaccessible feelings
5. How *bargaining* allows for mediation before the full impact of the loss is experienced
6. How *depression* becomes the place feelings are accurately identified and expressed
7. When *acceptance* is not the final stage for an individual ego state

In the process of the above stages, you will gain further understanding of emotional maturity in relationship to life events or losses and be able to:

1. Visualize the Grief Process as a roadmap. *On it,* the stages of the Grief Process become its mile markers. *In them,* one can determine his current position in relationship to resolving any issue, situation, or loss
2. Recognize if you or a loved one is stuck or moving through the process
3. Determine when you enter the Emotional Twilight Zone and how to get out of its loop by using the Adult Ego State
4. Identify the factors that influence one's path through the process
5. Use the Grief Process as a therapeutic framework to help others heal

THE GRIEF PROCESS

So far in this book, you have been brought down the path to awareness and recovery. Each step was designed to help the reader *conceptualize and use a path* I see so clearly. Each facet of the process can be compared to a highway. We start off our journey of self-discovery on a road. The road can be winding, narrow; sometimes it runs out of asphalt and becomes muddy. Other times it's like a traffic jam. Everything is stopped and there's nowhere to go except to hang in there until the traffic begins to let up. Another metaphor one could use is a pie, and every piece of recovery is a segment of the pie. When the pie is filled, the person is complete and ready to face his problems in a functional and adaptive manner.

If we use the road imagery, it would start off as a single lone road with just enough room for one car. When one is in self-centered fear, the road zigzags, and one meanders over it in order to avoid the littlest bump in the road. In healing and recovery, the road is expanded to a four-lane highway, and straightened out. It's paved, and a lot of work went into engineering to avoid the pitfalls which have fallen on other roads.

PHASE ONE   of the road building process describes the components to the problem, how they impact the individual's growth, and if left unattended, would continue to impede his progress. This would be tantamount to completing the engineering survey on the road so it didn't get washed away or flooded each time it rained.

PHASE TWO   describes the developmental process and how the human grew and evolved over the life span. The equivalent of this on the road construction would be the bed they lay for the right of way. The depth of this bed on the highway is usually determined by the frost line. In healing, the predication would be the depth of the issues explored.

PHASE THREE   lists the ingredients that make up the paving surface of the road. In my paradigm, it would be identifying, accessing, and utilizing the ego states to develop innovative and adaptive strategies to life's problems instead of reacting with dysfunctional behavior in order to cover up one's inability to deal with the problem.

PHASE FOUR   would be actually paving the road. At this time each lane is laid separately until it's a four-lane highway, complete with a breakdown lane and full shoulders on each side. In this section, the Grief Process is one of those lanes. It's a part of the road one has to go through in order to traverse one's life, because with all change, good and bad, positive or negative, comes the need for a process to accept the change. The Grief Process is the instrument used to help the person complete the Journey.

WITH ANY CHANGE COMES THE NEED
OF A PROCESS TO ACCEPT THE CHANGE.
THE GRIEF PROCESS **IS THE ROAD ONE**
TRAVELS TO GAIN THAT ACCEPTANCE.

PHASE FIVE   is the problems one will encounter driving down the road. Each one will be described in the next section of this book. It will include driving tips on how to recover from an incident or how to avoid it altogether. This will be accomplished by exposing the problematic areas of your life's road, and moving into the solution by offering success-oriented, adaptive, and non-dysfunctional solutions.

NOTE: The term *loss* as a noun in the Grief Process, will be reframed to an adjective, and as a substitute, *event* will be used in its place. The connotation of loss in the Grief Process matrix is usually attached or associated with death. I wanted to separate the loss from death, from the one sustained when any change is experienced in one's life, because it limits the concept of experiencing the Grief Process in all life's changes, which is essential to my counseling paradigm. This will be explored further on in the book.

GRIEF AS A ROAD IN LIFE

Another point that's crucial to my model is that: any event which occurs in one's life creates its own path as an *exit* from the main road, that would have continued had not the event occurred, and an *entrance* back onto it after the process from the incident is over. Figure 12.1 is a depiction of the detour.

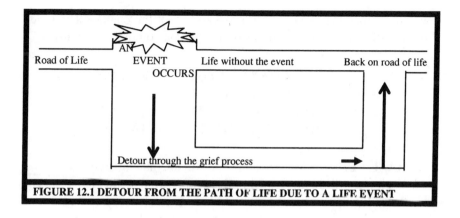

FIGURE 12.1 DETOUR FROM THE PATH OF LIFE DUE TO A LIFE EVENT

The detour can be further illustrated because it creates a road of its own. That section of the road is labeled, "the path of the Grief Process." It has its own entrance, several markers, and an exit back onto life's main road. Each stage of the process is a marker as one leaves one to enter another. Each stage also has its own parameters, and I view them more concrete as a road instead of a stage one travels back and forth between as Kubler-Ross (1969) observed.

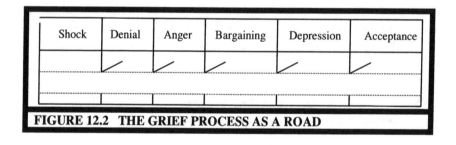

FIGURE 12.2   THE GRIEF PROCESS AS A ROAD

In Figure 12.2, the Grief Process is illustrated as a road. Each segment has its own toll booth, and once you pay the toll, by experiencing the appropriate level of awareness and feelings (determined by one's internal structure), the door or passage opens to the next section, and the person travels through.

In the next section, we will watch the road of the Grief Process expand to a four-lane highway in which each ego state has its own lane, and moves at its own pace commensurate with its capabilities and limits. The depiction of what they will encounter is integrated in Figure 12.3.

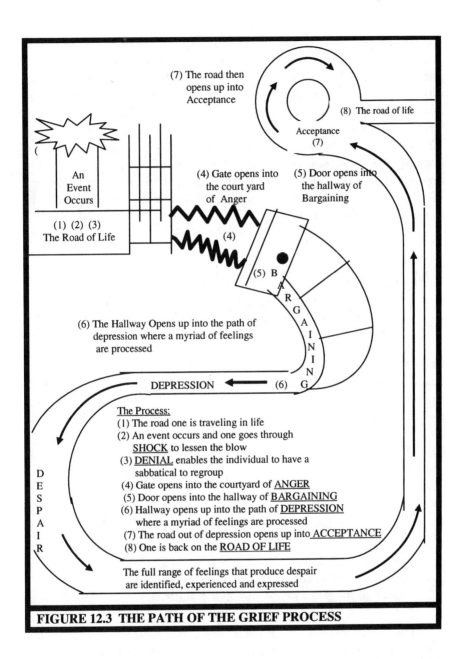

(7) The road then opens up into Acceptance

(8) The road of life

Acceptance
(7)

An Event Occurs

(4) Gate opens into the court yard of Anger

(5) Door opens into the hallway of Bargaining

(1) (2) (3)
The Road of Life

(4)

(5) B
A
R
G
A
I
N
I
N
G

(6) The Hallway Opens up into the path of depression where a myriad of feelings are processed

DEPRESSION ← (6)

D
E
S
P
A
I
R

The Process:
(1) The road one is traveling in life
(2) An event occurs and one goes through SHOCK to lessen the blow
(3) DENIAL enables the individual to have a sabbatical to regroup
(4) Gate opens into the courtyard of ANGER
(5) Door opens into the hallway of BARGAINING
(6) Hallway opens up into the path of DEPRESSION where a myriad of feelings are processed
(7) The road out of depression opens up into ACCEPTANCE
(8) One is back on the ROAD OF LIFE

The full range of feelings that produce despair are identified, experienced and expressed

FIGURE 12.3 THE PATH OF THE GRIEF PROCESS

What one experiences as he traverses the Grief Process is not arbitrary (Kubler-Ross, 1969). He will go through it. Each state will taste the wrath of the stages of the Grief Process, confront his own fear, and move or remain stuck, depending on his limits of maturity, wisdom, and experience. All of this process occurs at the individual's own level. The process can be enhanced with education and unconditional acceptance *if* the person has the ability to move at a faster pace. (Remember, this is at their pace and not the therapist or helpers.) If not, both will enhance the unconditional support being given and greatly facilitate trust if the emotional boundaries or limitations are respected. The additive factor to this construct occurs later on in the process, as increased trust will motivate the individual to move more quickly, or, break up emotional impasses sooner, because trust was established early. This kind of a strategy is not only appropriate and demonstrates unconditional regard for the person (Rogers, 1961), it connects with all three ego states and promotes harmony throughout the counseling process.

EMOTIONAL MATRIX OF THE GRIEF PROCESS

When we add the emotions of the three ego states to the matrix of the Grief Process, we now include a dynamic that changes a person's mood quickly and frequently. As the change occurs, each of the ego states will simultaneously be in different stages of the Grief Process. I believe that this quick change of the person's presentation, due to the fluctuation of his emotions, answers the question of why Kubler-Ross (1969) observed the Grief Process as fluid and without boundaries, and I see it as having distinct boundaries with a predictable process. Figure 12.4 illustrates how the emotions of the three ego states are intertwined in the configuration of the Grief Process

During the various stages of the Grief Process, each ego state can become stuck due to:

1. **Immaturity**
2. **Enormity of event**
3. **Lack of in-depth problem-solving skills**

In this inconsistency, the individual will present as being stuck in one area of the process, but doing well in others. Losing a parent is a good example of the ego states' interactions with each other in order to lessen the magnitude or ramifications of a future loss.

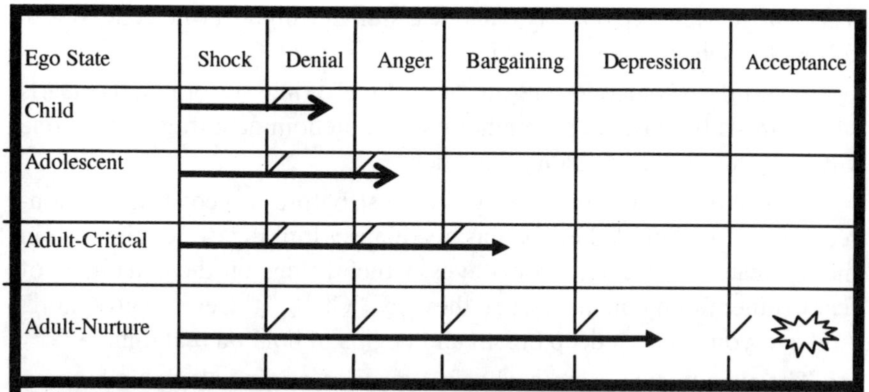

Ego State	Shock	Denial	Anger	Bargaining	Depression	Acceptance
Child	————→					
Adolescent	——————→					
Adult-Critical	——————————→					
Adult-Nurture	———————————————————→					✸

FIGURE 12.4 EMOTIONAL COMPOSITION OF THE GRIEF PROCESS

In later situations, when the Adult is trying to deal with a loss, the Child's feelings will surface quickly because he feels like an orphan. The Adolescent attempts to remain in the anger stage in order for the Child to be protected from the overwhelming feelings being dragged up by the new loss. The Nurturing Adult will accept the facts of the loss, disappear at times when the feelings are overwhelming, or, become preoccupied trying to stop or clean up the Adolescent's actions. The Critical Adult will remain negative throughout the whole episode.

The above are all mixed feelings. Any one of them can dominate. There is no real time frame — only the flux that is present in all human emotions. Stress at this time is increased as the baggage of the loss of a parent is carried forward in the "natural" process of internally resolving the grief. Most do not realize how much the unresolved grief from a significant loss impacts their daily interactions in a present-day situation until they have therapy, read a book, or become involved in self help. Once they are aware of it, the insight becomes an invaluable tool in maintaining one's integrity during emotionally overwhelming situations.

THE EMOTIONAL TWILIGHT ZONE

There is one other construct that confounds and inhibits accurate identification of which segment in the Grief Process the bereaved is currently occupying. My new construct is called, *The Emotional Twilight Zone*. It's a state that causes one to change more rapidly "than a speeding bullet."

The change occurs so quickly that one acquires whiplash when one tries to follow the shift of the mood swing.

The shift of someone entering "The Zone" brings terror into the hearts of therapists because its presentation is the predominant trait of someone with a Borderline Personality Disorder.

This shift is what the family sees just before a recovering or non-recovering alcoholic/addict begins his relapse/drinking cycle. The shift in mood creates "that look" in his eyes, which brings on those feelings of fear to other family members, and they say, "Oh S_ _t! Here we go again!" And everyone takes a deep breath and begins to hold on real tight.

The phenomenon occurs when the traveler moving along his Journey through the Grief Process, touches some of his deeper feelings in the depression stage, and regresses to an earlier and safer state. If the issue is relatively unimportant and the feelings moderate, the regression will be a minimal one back to the previous stage. If it is an important one, the backward recoil could encompass two stages. When overwhelming feelings are experienced, the subsequent reaction could bring him back three stages into denial. It is during these circumstances that the relapse cycle begins because the enormous pain he is trying to escape from comes up like a "ton of bricks" and "hits him in the face," then "knocks him off his feet."

In Figure 12.5, The Emotional Twilight Zone is depicted in the *Stages,* and its path is illustrated in the *Reaction*. Within it, the dazed person bounces back and forth between the stages like "The Rubber Band Man." Whatever helps him best to facilitate the feelings is used as the strategy of the moment. It gets real crazy in there, and I have seen people, including myself, do their best "rock and rolling" when they enter its course. Confusion reigns as they bounce from depression to denial, and then back up the process again. Some, if they don't get help, have the maturity to transcend the feelings, or find themselves unable to face their demons; will bounce back and forth several times before:

1. They can go through their feelings or
2. Act out in such a way, that the behavior of the acting out, covers up the pain from the loss, and/or lasts long enough to stuff the pain as the painful episode subsides.

Plug this process into your relapse prevention plan or group, and let me know if you get as good results from it as I do. If you do, you will identify the antecedents clearly and be able to institute quickly, more effective remedial action, based on the ego state's presentation in the developing relapse scenario's path.

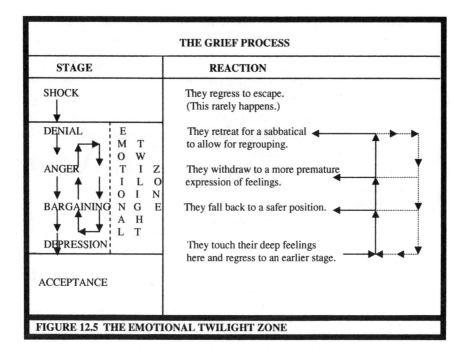

FIGURE 12.5 THE EMOTIONAL TWILIGHT ZONE

CASE STUDY: Bill, our recovering addict who relapsed after two years of good, clean time, came into therapy shortly after "Going back out there," and exclaimed, "I don't know what happened to me! One moment I'm O.K. — the next I have some blow up my nose."

In probing Bill with the usual questions, it's apparent that he's confused and clueless. Using my framework, I listen for the stage he's in the Grief Process, and what ego state he's operating from. It's obvious to me that Bill's in the Emotional Twilight Zone and that he's bouncing between ego states. While he talks, I sort out the confusion to determine what his internal needs and strengths are.

Bill has two years of program, and I know I can tap into his *Adult* with it. For a non-program person, it would be any past event they handled successfully. The Child is easiest to hear. A problem that some people encounter with the relapsed person at this time is that they judge the Child's feelings as self-pity, and react because they don't want to feel manipulated. Most times, under relapse circumstances, it's not self-pity, just raw feelings that have been exposed, and they're trying to cover them up. There is a world of difference between being stuck in one's feelings, and self-pity. If you use my concept, as a filter, when you work or explore your own self-motivations, ask: "Are they using their feelings as emotional black-mail to manipulate me, *OR*, are they stuck and don't know what to do?"

I use a pain management model for addiction or abuse. This means that a person drinks or drugs to cover up the pain of:

1. **What abuse they received from others**
2. **What was not adequately given to them in childhood and adolescent development**
3. **What they did as a reaction to what was or wasn't done for them in the form of:**
    a)What they did to others
    b)What they did to themselves

Ninety-nine point nine percent of the answers of why someone drinks, drugs, or uses any number of things obsessively and compulsively can be found in the above listed questions.

Identifying their ego strength, sorting out the pain and then validating it, begins the process of what the antecedents were to the relapse, and developing a functional strategy to facilitate it when it arises again. This is basic relapse prevention, which follows Gorski's (1982, 1984, 1986) model. My contribution is adding the ego states and the Grief Process in order to work more quickly and effectively to identify the precursors to the relapse.

Bill was able to use his Adult Ego State to label and identify his feelings, using a 'feelings' list I supply when someone is stuck. As he disclosed the events of the preceding month, it became clear that something happened to trigger off his relapse cycle. To narrow down the time frame, we went backwards to discover when and if he began to have feelings of discontent, started going to fewer meetings, or backed off from some of his involvement in the program.

The time period was quickly attained, and prior events to it were explored. The only significant event that occurred was that a friend from childhood had just overdosed, and he couldn't make the funeral because it was on the other coast. Another small item that occurred during this time period was a promotion in work that gave him more responsibility.

Upon probing the significance of the death of his childhood buddy, Bill talked about painful memories surfacing of his 'using' days, and his dismissing them as "water under the bridge," and that, "they were behind him." Using the ego strength of the *Adult*, and validating the pain of the

Child, I was able to guide Bill to slip into his feelings, avoid the resistance from the *Adolescent*, and do some work with his feelings.

This whole process took a 50-minute hour. In three more sessions, Bill had processed through the event, and developed a more adaptive strategy to use the next time something else was triggered. This is very effective relapse prevention counseling, and is consumer oriented because it is short, identifies the activating event, and provides an excellent return value for money spent on therapy. A by-product of the process is that it increases self-esteem, awareness, and self-monitoring skills.

One additional note: Bill had two years of recovery that I could build upon. With a newcomer, the process would be double because of the lack of basic skills, and it could go triple depending on the issues, motivation, and possibility of being duel diagnosed with a psychiatric diagnosis.

Another component to Bill's relapse was the feelings that arose over the promotion. The first to impact him was the rise in the level of feelings he experienced because he was happy. The increased ability to feel because of the happy circumstances also allowed more intense feelings due to the loss of his friend while his normal shields were down and he was vulnerable. The openness also allowed more of his history to be exposed. All of the issues that affected his relapse were identified, worked on, and closed off. They will be more manageable for Bill later when they surface with less intensity.

GRIEF AS A THERAPEUTIC FRAMEWORK

The Grief Process contains six stages: shock, denial, anger, bargaining, and depression, and acceptance (Kubler-Ross, 1969). It is invoked each time a change occurs in one's life. The event can be large or small, the impact positive or negative, the results good or bad. It makes no difference. The process will still happen. There are several factors which impact the process and they are the:

1. Severity of the event
2. Duration of its effect
3. Issues attached to, or triggered by, the incident
4. Maturation level of one's internal structure
5. Repertoire of Problem-Solving skills and strategies

The above factors will be explained in order for the reader to understand what mitigates how a person goes through the Grief Process, and when one can become stuck or derailed from completing it.

Factors Involved in the Process

THE SEVERITY OF THE EVENT: How severe an event is will determine the amount of time one takes to go through the Grief Process. If it is a small event like the loss of a nonessential possession, the process will be short. If it is a large event like the death of a family member, it will be long. Timing of the event is also a determinant to the degree of loss felt. If a parent dies when he is old, the loss will be less than if he died when he was young. This happens because it's the natural order of things, and expected. Loss of a career can invoke the same response when a person's job is obsolete, because of technical advantages.

Good things can also stimulate the same reactions. A job promotion is one of them because the worker is leaving the comfort of old friends and a familiar surrounding to travel into uncertainty. All that's left behind will have to be grieved. Winning the lottery is tantamount to a death, because one will leave behind a whole way of life for a new one. I bet you didn't think that highly desirable attainment could bring on such powerful feelings that would have to be processed just as negative events do.

THE DURATION OF ITS EFFECT: The length of time it takes for the event to be over is crucial to the process of grief. Any loss that occurs over a period of time slowly wears down the individual's coping strategies and creates within itself more losses. In this process, all of the human's energy is diverted to, "hanging in there" through the loss, and all other areas of life are ignored or put on hold until after the loss occurs. At the same time, one's coping strategies are continuously taxed, with the daily struggle of the event, missed opportunities, unattended to responsibilities, and projected losses. This overwhelms the average person, and in order to survive, he has to shut down, and become task oriented. The above not only transpires during death, it also occurs when one loses a job, moves to a distant place, divorces, goes to war, becomes incarcerated, or any other situation that would extend the grief of the actual loss. They are too numerous to list, and the ones I chose to illustrate the concept cover: family, relationships, vocational, and societal losses.

THE ISSUES ATTACHED TO OR TRIGGERED BY THE INCI-DENT: Any unresolved issue or "unfinished business" attached to the issue will exacerbate its impact. At this point, the loss becomes a trigger that mirrors or mimics a past event, and instead of having the feelings from the present event only — *ONE ALSO EXPERIENCES THE MEMORIES FROM THE PAST EVENT AS WELL!* The confusion that arises for the unwary individual is overwhelming and takes major work to separate and sort out the feelings. This is very difficult to accomplish without therapy or a twelve-step program.

Minimal tools are given to children as they are being socialized by their primary caregivers, because the societal messages to the grieving are, "get over it, put it behind you, and just get on with your life!" There is no judgment being made on the author's part — just a reporting of the facts. On the other hand, those who read this book and assimilate its concepts will be better equipped to reduce grief's impact because they will be forewarned. Sometimes, just the knowledge that one is not crazy or alone, is enough to stop the downward spiral into shame and depression. As in any other serious issue, it is recommended that one seek help in any situation that persists and is overwhelming.

THE MATURATION LEVEL OF ONE'S INTERNAL STRUC-TURE: In Part Three of this book, we explored the development of the ego states. This is one's internal structure. If one has not advanced beyond childhood and shuts down when grief strikes — the same pattern will be followed in adulthood. The same is true for a person who is mired in Adolescence and reacts when grief occurs, instead of experiencing the event and going through the feelings of the Grief Process. When one is in his Adult, he will have the skills to facilitate the process via previously learned strategies that enable the grieving person to mediate the rising feelings in an adaptive and non-dysfunctional way. Each of the ego states will be explored, in all stages of grief process, in order to identify their deficiencies and/or to build upon the stages' attributes.

REPERTOIRE OF PROBLEM—SOLVING SKILLS AND STRATEGIES: As in the preceding factors, successful facilitation of the increased stress or problems, which are generated from important losses, multiple events, or triggered memories from past events, is determined by the repertoire, depth of problem-solving skills, and strategies. This is a hallmark of an emotionally mature responsible Adult. Without an amalgamation of strategies, gleaned from life's experiences, only the most benign losses will be acknowledged and processed. The larger ones that invoke feelings of being overwhelmed will be avoided. The subterfuge begins when the individual enters a Problem Loop to avoid the feelings from the loss, and uses the energy from the subconscious feelings to create another problem as a diversion from the painful loss. Figure 12.6 illustrates the probable responses when responding to major losses in an adaptive or dysfunctional manner.

Diversion is also considered a viable strategy and has to be acknowledged and validated as such, because without the repertoire of more adaptive skills — dysfunctional behavior that allows the person to continue — now becomes a skill! In fact, *is one of the greatest survival skills one can acquire in his arsenal of strategies, and cannot be discarded without acquiring living skills to facilitate the feelings in an adaptive manner.* Remember, to be overwhelmed, translates into death to the Child Ego State. Without additional strategies, one has to develop an emergency contingency, in order to transcend the loss. Diversion is a great tactic. It allows one to bypass the trauma he can't handle, and in the process, "they live to fight another day." *The only problem with it is, long after the need for the survival skill is necessary, its maintenance gets in the way of the evolving human developing more adaptive skills.*

LOSS OR CHANGES OCCUR

ADAPTIVE RESPONSE	*MALADAPTIVE RESPONSE*
Admit the loss	Minimize or deny the loss
Feel the loss	Create a diversion to cover up the feelings
Go through the process	
Enter into acceptance	Use all energy and resources to facilitate the diversion
Continue to work on any residue feelings or raised issues	Another layer of impacted grief is created after the diversion is terminated

FIGURE 12.6 Probable Outcomes in Responding to Major Losses or Changes

**AVOIDANCE BY DIVERSION IS
AN EXCELLENT SURVIVAL SKILL.
IT'S ONLY PROBLEM BEING THAT IT'S CONTINUED LONG
AFTER THE NEED FOR IT ENDS. ITS PROCESS HINDERS
THE DEVELOPMENT OF MORE ADAPTIVE LIVING SKILLS.**

SHOCK

*Shock is Nature's Emotional Absorber.
It prevents becoming overwhelmed
and quickly glides into denial.*

Shock is the first stage of The Grief Process, or may be better stated as the entrance or gateway into its realm, because it quickly rolls into denial. It is important to recognize this stage because it is nature's shock absorber. It's the place where all internal systems of data intake and process are shut down in order for the living organism to survive a completely devastating blow. It is also the most primitive strategy because a person shuts down and shuts out the world in order not to hear, see, feel, touch, or process the event. It also invokes some of the scariest feelings to the Child Ego State, when, as a survival skill, uses dissociation to tune out the pain.

Becoming jammed up in shock is only problematic when the individual becomes psychotic, loses touch with reality, and needs to be hospitalized because of the duration the loss of reality is experienced. This will only happen in a few cases, and usually requires massive trauma or multiple losses in which the last event will be, "the straw that broke the camel's back," and the overwhelmed person will check out of reality in order to survive. Sometimes it will happen to a mentally ill person, because his normal stress-reducing skills are already overtaxed trying to facilitate the symptoms of their illness. It can also occur with individuals who are experiencing multiple stressors from major segments of their lives and have already maxed out their repertoire of coping skills. When the major loss transpires during this life segment, the person breaks down in a situation he would customarily be able to transcend, because his energy has been depleted by other major situations.

Impact of the Ego States

There appears to be no trace of the Adolescent or Adult ego states operating in the shock phase of the Grief Process. In fact, there doesn't appear to be any process at all in its matrix, only a reaction that shuts the person down when the impact from the event is overwhelming. This is a pure Child state. The longer it lasts and the depth of its reaction can determine the emotional maturity of the person. Depending on the presentation, the level can be anywhere from preverbal to age nine. Most child or human development text books will give you a list of the indicators for emotional growth. If you are in counseling (or lived in a dysfunctional family), use the childhood emotional benchmarks to determine what degree of emotional maturity they have and/or what year the trauma entered into their lives and they shut down to survive. This is probably one of the simplest and most succinct assessing tools you can use. Complicated or sophisticated is not always best. Usually they get in the way and take energy away from the counseling process. Almost like they are self-serving only and exist to perpetuate themselves instead of facilitating recovery or healing.

Potency of the Five Factors

The five factors that impact The Grief Process are not germane in this phase, except number one, because the severity of the event is perceived as so overwhelming, that it never went beyond this segment. It's possible for some of the other factors to be latent due to previous events that remained unresolved. In this case, they would exacerbate the reaction from the overwhelming event because the individual's full capacity to respond to the threat is not fully on line.

DENIAL

Denial is a sabbatical from intensive feelings.
It allows a process of gradual integration
to prevent an overload in human beings.

Denial is the first full stage of The Grief Process, because the initial shock that's felt when one encounters a grievous event is quickly transformed into its cocoon. This stage is a portion of nature's shock absorber in which the individual is shielded from the full impact of the event. It's a place where some people have to stay, for a period of time, to gain or build up the strength it takes to acknowledge the full loss of the situation. The culture, individuals, and yes even therapists, make the mistake and feel that it's good to take a person out of denial as soon as possible. "You're in denial!" is their war cry, and their mantra is, "Break their denial." It's almost like a chant. "Do it or die!" they say. "You can't live in denial," they further state. *WRONG — I SAY!* Denial is only toxic when problematic behavior is generated by it. In many instances it is the "*appropriate*" response to the situation when the full impact of the event will overload the sufferer.

Most times it's not the facts of the event a person will deny — it's the full personal impact they want to avoid. When the whole range of its ramifications are bared, with the unvarnished truth exposed, it now becomes too much to assimilate in the early stages of grief. Nature has provided denial as a sabbatical from a harsh reality and allows the human being to take it in as they can handle it.

To those of you with a Higher Power or God — this is when He doesn't give you any more than you can handle, and "*always*" meets you on your level of ability. Spirituality will be addressed later on in Part Four as its own chapter, but it has to be noted now.

Spirituality in the Process

The Human Being does not live or exist in a vacuum or a bubble. Humans live in a macrocosm and co-exist with others on many planes, which include mental, physical, emotional, and spiritual elements. It is this stage that invokes the most need for a spiritual connection, for it is in denial that man is at his most vulnerable state. At this point, the level of denial is commensurate with man's degree of helplessness and hopelessness, his depth of disengagement from self (feelings), friends and family, and disconnection from his spirituality, which leaves him helpless and without hope.

During this time, hope has to be reinstated to some degree, in order for the human to break the bands of hopelessness he has been shackled with via the overwhelming event. Spirituality is the tool or device one uses to break these chains. In it, one is able to, so to speak, "come out of himself" (which is the paralysis of the emotions) and connect with a power or energy that enables him to dig out of the mire of depression and thereby transcend his current impasse. Once this materializes, the debilitating depression of the loss is broken, the individual climbs out of the dark hole of despair, comes into the light of hope, and continues through the next segments of the Grief Process.

The above process happens in the shadowy world of spirituality. Unlike the concrete of the material world, spirituality requires faith alone, and a trust in the power which engenders that faith, to do its works. It doesn't make any difference what that power is, what it's called; only that it's prevailed upon for help. It's in the calling out that one receives the strength to go on. This type of spirituality lends itself to all faiths because all one has to do is plug himself into the central figure of his religion. There is also power to the nonbelievers as well because they can call on their Higher Self to prevail, tap into any energy available which will generate their internal strength, and allow them to overcome the dark feelings of defeat being experienced because of an overwhelming event.

This spiritual concept will prevail in all stages of the Grief Process and will manifest in different degrees, depending on the need or faith of the individual.

Impact of the Ego States

The ego states in this stage facilitate a transition from fantasy to reality. The range of their ability is determined by the amount of maturity each possesses.

CHILD EGO STATE When the level of maturity is restricted, its normal operating level would be limited to: the Child Ego State remaining paralyzed, ineffectual, stuck, and possessing limited ability to functionally navigate the stage. When this prevails, the individual needs an exacting amount of support, which can deplete the energy of the helpers, and warrants some kind of rudimentary stress training, even if it's just constantly stating that they're using their own power. Consistently positive dialogue during this time will plant the seeds of self-esteem and create a concrete focal point that can be used as a base for successful strategies and returned to later on, to be expanded. I know this is basic. Everything has to start somewhere. This is a starting point.

ADOLESCENT EGO STATE When the evolving Adult has transcended the emotional immaturity of childhood, new strategies, based on taking some kind of action, lifts him out of being helpless and hopeless. The nature of action will be, once more, based on the degree of maturity possessed by this ego state. Generally speaking, the intensity of the reaction to the current event, usually being manifested as dysfunctional behavior, is directly related to its corresponding immaturity.

Some of the simple manifestations of this fear (remember, it's the fear from the Child that motivates the Adolescent to cover it over with a reaction) can be anger to mask the feelings; *acting out* with addictive, obsessive, and/or compulsive behavior and *acting in* with depression or any form of self-destructive behavior.

Reasonable interventions at this time would be to validate the anger and help the person to go beyond it, and to "*STOP*" the current acting out whether it's internal or external. When the behavior manifests, it's to be interpreted as the individual being stuck in this stage. The only time it's seen any differently is when the behavior begins to subside and the acting out is *less destruction or not as intensive*. This is only considered as a behavioral indication that the internal pressure is subsiding. In no way is it to be interpreted as the end of the episode. So many times I have seen others underestimate the power of this stage and thereby lack the ability to assess where one is in its process. When it is not done with insight, relapse occurs, because the grieving person was over-estimated in his level of ego strength.

ADULT EGO STATE   The Adult Ego State is predominant when the responses to the event are proactive, adaptive, functional, and innovative. When the grieving person is operating in this role, there will be a forward momentum in his actions. At first the facts of the event will be acknowledged, then the ramifications of the event will be revealed, and the mature adult will vacate the denial phase, and move into the Anger Stage. Any hesitancy to move forward will be used for regrouping and exploring options to reduce the negative impact the event has spawned. All energies at this time will be used to gather all resources, explore new options, generate innovative strategies, and to get the person on with his life. Very little time is spent enumerating the problem, with most energy being spent by remaining in the solution.

Potency of the Five Factors

THE SEVERITY OF THE EVENT: Actual impact or perceived devastation will determine how severe the event will be. Real or imagined, the event will cause the same internal devastation, because this is where the process transpires and the ramifications felt. This is not a moral issue, where if the individual was stronger, he wouldn't be overwhelmed. It's a situation in which the individual's normal coping strategies are over-whelmed and they break down. Don't forget that this is solely an internal process of intake, process, and action, and if the situation is too great, the system breaks down.

Humans are not machines — they are fragile — under devastating situations. Man was not made to be a combat soldier 24 hours a day, being hyper-vigilant, and ready to respond to any assaults on his psyche at a moment's notice. This kind of a life would be extremely reactionary, stagnant, and self-centered. There would be no room in it for life, love, family, relationships, or personal or social growth. All energy and resources would be dedicated to protection only.

I know at this point in the chapter, that any individual, who is reading the text in his Critical Adult, must be "blown away" because my assault on his concept of "intestinal fortitude," invalidates his strengths as I point out the deficiencies in his life. To those who live with the Critical Parent and have watched it limit their lives, a piece at a time, because they had to be strong, couldn't display any vulnerability, and gradually shut out most people — this will come as relief.

The construct is also validation because a piece of you felt it was happening and didn't want to admit it (the Child); another segment of you tried to do something about it (the Adolescent); and still another part of you vacillated between wanting to continue the behavior or quit because of its lack of fruition (the Adult — Nurturing and Critical). Just remember that machines break down and also need periodic maintenance.

THE DURATION OF ITS EFFECT: The duration of the effect will have a great impact on one's process through the denial stage, because the longer one remains in the trauma of the actual event, the more taxed the stress-reducing strategies become. At this time, all of their defenses are brought on line, until its repertoire is depleted, and the human is over-whelmed and/or breaks down.

THE ISSUES ATTACHED TO, OR TRIGGERED BY, THE IN-CIDENT: Problems of other issues being attached or triggered by the current event are secondary at this stage, although, it can be used as an assessment tool to identify an over-reaction from the actual aftermath of the occur-rence. Denial of anything else attached to the event is common and healthy in many ways if additional information would overwhelm the individual. This is no time to go in and dig unless you know the person and the situation that's exacerbating his current feelings, and disclosure of the pertinent information will bring him relief.

THE MATURATION LEVEL OF THE INTERNAL STRUCTURE: The ability of the Ego States to display a high degree of maturation is the hallmark of the internal structure's full-grown development. During this stage, the indicator for ego strength is the manifestation of functional and adaptive skills being used to walk the person through denial — first through the fact stage and then identifying its ramifications. The more one sees at this stage, the higher degree of maturity he possesses. If they are stuck in the fact stage and can't readily see any of its ramifications, this is usually an indicator of an immature internal structure with a disengaged Executive System (the part of the adult that makes life decisions).

REPERTOIRE OF PROBLEM-SOLVING SKILLS AND STRATEGIES: The more experience with stress the person has — the greater the chances of successful outcomes in any situation. When one is limited in his responses to crisis, he will be overcome quickly when these sparse strategies are exhausted or are over-taxed.

ANGER

*Anger is a **gateway** into the feelings.*
its energy suppresses the deep emotions
and provides a safety valve

Anger is the second stage of the Grief Process. The feelings it engenders seem to be more reactionary in nature. If this is accurate, they would serve as a buffer to the deeper feelings of despair that are more associated with great losses. A visual depiction of this action can be seen in Figure 12.7.

ANGER
SUPRESSES

Abandonment, alienation, anguish, anxiety, apprehension, bitterness, broken, cheapened, conflicted, confused, crushed, defeated, dejected, demoralized, depreciated, depressed, desperate, despondent, discouraged, disgraced, doubtful, dreadful, exhausted, fearful, frightened, frustrated, helpless, hopeless, humiliated, impotent, inadequate, incapable, incompetent, ineffective, inept, inferior, insecure, insignificant, longing, lousy, low, miserable, negative, neglected, obsolete, oppressed, overwhelmed, panicky, powerless, pressured, rejected, ridiculed, rundown, scared, shocked, shamed, sickened, swamped, tense, terrified, tormented, uncertain, uncomfortable, uneasy, unhappy, unloved, unqualified, unsure, upset, uptight, washed up, whipped, worried, and being worthless.

FIGURE 12.7 — FEELINGS ANGER SUPRESSES

The list was deliberately made long to enable the reader to feel a full range of feelings and emotions. How did you feel when you read the list? If you are as open as I am, you experienced some of them as you read, played old tapes, possibly had old memories appear, and even rehashed an old dilemma where the outcome could have gone in different directions. This is a very powerful experience and you're only reading a book for knowledge. I wonder what would happen if all those feelings and events surfaced during a significant event which produced great loss? This now gives you an appreciation of what anger covers up.

If we remain open to the concept that anger masks deep feelings of despair — add to its matrix a process for those feelings — we can now postulate that anger is the gateway to emotion, because it's generally the first feeling one experiences when one exits the Denial Stage of The Grief Process. The illustration of this process can be seen in Figure 12.8. We will use this as a model in the other stages of The Grief Process to depict how feelings are exposed, experienced, and medicated throughout their Journey from awareness to acceptance.

EVENT OCCURS	
STAGE	**PROCESS**
SHOCK	Allows the individual to escape the full blow
DENIAL	Provides a sabbatical for regrouping
ANGER	Anger is a gateway into the feelings. Its energy suppresses the deep emotions and provides a safety fuse.
BARGAINING	The bargaining process allows for mediation before the full emotional impact is felt
DEPRESSION	Full entry into one's feelings is experienced as they are accurately identified and expressed.
ACCEPTANCE	Acceptance of the event is completed.

FIGURE 12.8   PROCESS OF EXPOSING FEELINGS

Impact of the Ego States

The ego states in this stage, mediate the amount of time the individual needs to safely transition into his deeper hidden feelings. The amount of time mandated is regulated by the degree of development his internal structure possesses.

CHILD EGO STATE The Child is hidden in this process. In fact, it's the recipient of all its benefits. Any elongation of this stage is due to the immaturity of the Adult and the inability of its Executive System to devise a functional and adaptive strategy through the event.

ADOLESCENT EGO STATE The Adolescent is the main character of this phase. It's reacting with anger safeguards the Child from overwhelming feelings, and provides an avenue in which the energy from the feelings can be expelled with a minimal amount of threat. This is *functional* because it's a survival skill when it prevents breakdown by ventilating the toxic energy. It's *dysfunctional* when the reaction takes on a life of its own and perpetuates itself for its own sake. This is when a survival skill gets in the way of developing living skills. Some examples would be when one *acts out* by drinking, drugging, crazy behavior, etc, *OR*, a*cts in* through depression or self destruction. At this time, the reacting behavior would mask the pain from the original event, and at the same time, create another layer of pain due to their obsessive and compulsive behavior.

A paradox that's created in the Adolescent's reaction occurs when the reaction to cover the pain (designed to protect the Child), now scares the Child *almost* as much as the original event. Almost is a deliberate word: Until the pain the Adolescent is masking by his acting out is greater than the pain he is hiding....he will continue in his present dysfunctional behavioral strategy.

ADULT EGO STATE The Adult's ability to facilitate the event is the main determinant in how long the individual takes to traverse through this stage. If the Adult has a considerable Executive System — the path will be short and direct. If it doesn't, the trail will meander longer, as the immature ego states try different dysfunctional and/or maladaptive strategies, to handle the feelings from the event. The hallmark of emotional maturity in this stage is the Adult's ability to transit it in a minimal amount of time. In this manner, anger is considered a feeling. When it's prolonged, it's a reaction to cover up the deeper feelings.

Potency of the Five Factors

THE SEVERITY OF THE EVENT: The severity of the event can be directly correlated to the amount of anger displayed or the subsequent reaction to cover it up. In less severe events or situations that lack a heavy investment, the impact will be minimal.

THE DURATION OF THE EVENT: The duration of the event will signify how many strategies it will take to transcend the anger and move through into the next stage. The downward spiral the individual will experience as his coping strategies run out can be observed behaviorally. After all the cognitive strategies are exhausted, the overtaxed ego structure will try to ameliorate the stress by diverting attention from the event. This will begin simply by stirring the pot and creating dissension with others. As the duration increases, the reaction turns to fighting, *acting out* with drinking, drugging, eating, etc, or *acting in* which turns the anger inward as depression. Progression of the compulsive behavior would also be witnessed as the stress from a long-term event is experienced.

THE ISSUES ATTACHED TO, OR TRIGGERED BY, THE INCIDENT: The greater the attachment — the greater the reaction. This can be indicated by the individual remaining stuck in Anger. It's also a major component of The Emotional Twilight Zone, and causes the confused person to bounce in and out of stages without receiving the benefit of any process. Usually what happens is the present situation attaches itself to a past event and the combination of events exacerbates the current feelings to a far greater degree than the situation would warrant. This is when you or someone else over-reacts to something minimal and don't understand why.

THE MATURATION LEVEL OF THE INTERNAL STRUC-TURE: The level of maturity can be determined two ways. *The first* is the depth of the reaction and the duration of the episode that follows it. *The second*, how quickly and innovatively the Adult facilitates the resulting anger or reaction. During this time, the hallmark of maturity will be the amount of time it takes to identify when one is over-reacting, stopping the reaction, identifying the antecedents to the reaction, and then devising adaptive strategies to better facilitate them in the future. The functional strategy here, of course, would be to feel the feelings, not to act out or in, and to transition the stage in an adaptive manner.

The Repertoire of Problem-Solving Skills and Strategies

Without several successful stress-reducing strategies, the organism will become overwhelmed in a serious or far-reaching event. It is impossible, without becoming dysfunctional in some way, to mediate high-impact situations without a significant amount of successful strategies. The major problem incurred here is when an individual raised in a high-stress environment, devises sophisticated survival skills, which Freud (1955) calls 'defense mechanisms.' Instead of going through the stressors, great lengths are taken to avoid them. These usually are encompassing and leave the socially oriented parts of the individual's life empty, because most energy and resources are depleted in the avoidance spiral.

BARGAINING

The bargaining process allows for mediation
before the full emotional impact is felt

In bargaining, one, more or less, gets to talk to himself. Unlike all those psychiatric diagnoses that were designed to label and treat the various ways people do talk to themselves — this one is considered normal because it's labeled internal dialogue. It's the dialogue encountered during the conversation we are concerned with. If it is positive in nature, the process will be an effective one. When it's negative, the reaction will be problematic at best. The ego states, the Five Factors, and the Emotional Twilight Zone all have great impacts on the process because it takes a fully-grown Adult to traverse this stage in an adaptive fashion.

Impact of the Ego States

The ego states in this stage can greatly curtail the process because this is where the Critical Adult does its greatest sabotage. When all ego states participate in harmony, one's feelings (the Child), behavior (the energy from the Adolescent,) and thoughts (the Adult) are congruent. There will always be an acceptable level of differences between the ego states because we are dealing with different levels of development. As in raising children, there is usually conflict when competing needs clash. The most important task at this time is that *"EVERYONE"* has input. The same transpires internally — *"ALL"* ego states need to be heard. The Adult makes the final decision based on past successful strategies, input from the Child and Adolescent — yes, even the Critical Adult — and makes a decision by determining what's best for one's *"WHOLE"* self.

The process is usually a win-win situation because it's generally a compromise to prevent age-stage needs from blocking adaptive and functional Adult decisions. The process becomes dysfunctional when the Child and Adolescent rule the Adult, and decisions made today are based on unfulfilled early developmental needs. There are ways to get those needs met. It's just not adaptive to get them met in this stage. Combat between the ego states is one of the main ingredients for entry into the Emotional Twilight Zone, because the individual exits into the next stage with a fragmented internal structure. One can skate by under these conditions with smaller issues. It spells disaster with important ones because without a harmonious internal structure, the human will become overwhelmed. The relative position of each ego state during this dissension is illustrated in Figure 12.9.

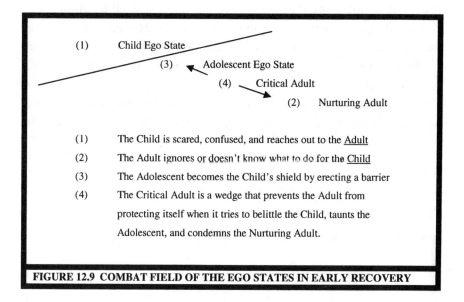

(1)   Child Ego State

(3) Adolescent Ego State

(4) Critical Adult

(2)   Nurturing Adult

(1)   The Child is scared, confused, and reaches out to the <u>Adult</u>

(2)   The Adult ignores or doesn't know what to do for the <u>Child</u>

(3)   The Adolescent becomes the Child's shield by erecting a barrier

(4)   The Critical Adult is a wedge that prevents the Adult from protecting itself when it tries to belittle the Child, taunts the Adolescent, and condemns the Nurturing Adult.

FIGURE 12.9 COMBAT FIELD OF THE EGO STATES IN EARLY RECOVERY

CHILD EGO STATE   When the issues are minimal and the Child remains out of fear, doubt, and insecurity — the process can be a smooth one. It's when the issues have deep ramifications, that the Child displays its greatest immaturity, when it becomes mired in fear. This is the part that keeps saying, "What if" or "I can't." Sometimes it begs to stop because it's projecting and fearful of an unknown outcome. The Child has to be validated. Its feelings are real. It doesn't make any difference if they are reality based or imagined via projection — *THEY ARE STILL REAL TO THE CHILD!* If left unattended, the Adolescent will begin to rise, and the Critical Adult will begin its negative barrage.

ADOLESCENT EGO STATE The Adolescent can be utilized two ways during the bargaining stage. The first is *functional* when its energy is harnessed to get through the negotiations. The second is *dysfunctional* and maladaptive when the Adolescent is allowed to be the dictator and demands like a tyrant what outcome it expects from the Adult. At this time, its own gratification is only considered. The expense to others is not even a factor as the demands inundate the Adult. The basis for this reaction is fear. During this time, the Adult has to constantly redirect the Adolescent's energy, and at the same time, sort out its needs. This is a difficult process at first and gets easier in later recovery.

The Adolescent during this discernment has two functions. The first is protecting the Child, and the second is trying to get its hedonistic needs met — *NOW*! At this point, most internal chaos can be relegated to emotional immaturity. At this time, firm boundaries, healthy limits, and non-problematic direction have to be given by the Nurturing Adult in order to generate enough energy to facilitate the loss in a functional manner.

In early recovery, the Adolescent balks at the process because the Adult hasn't enough of a track record to be trusted.

Another factor that has to be considered if the Adolescent doesn't quiet down is to look for any boundary that may have been violated. Usually the energy of the Adolescent protects the boundaries, and when they become violated without the Adult acting, the Adolescent enforces the boundaries with its familiar over-reactive style. When the Adult is able to fulfill its parental role, the Adolescent lowers the wall, and remains in place as depicted in Figure 12.10.

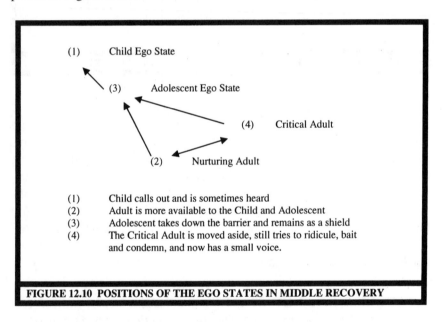

(1)	Child calls out and is sometimes heard
(2)	Adult is more available to the Child and Adolescent
(3)	Adolescent takes down the barrier and remains as a shield
(4)	The Critical Adult is moved aside, still tries to ridicule, bait and condemn, and now has a small voice.

FIGURE 12.10 POSITIONS OF THE EGO STATES IN MIDDLE RECOVERY

ADULT EGO STATE When the Adult acts emotionally mature and is responsible, it is a full grown adult. Presentation of the opposite behavior by the Adult, precipitates its splitting into two fragments, and produces a critical half. *This segment is the personification of all past authority figures who tried to direct or implant wisdom to the fledgling, although did it in a negative way. When the Adult is not doing a competent job — the*

*Critical Parent appears. As the Adult is able to fully discharge its role —
the Critical Parent disappears.*

For the Adult to portray an emotionally mature, responsible adult, he
has to listen to and affirm the Child, harness the energy of the Adolescent
by setting healthy boundaries and limits for him, while recognizing his
adult needs throughout the event. When this is consummated, the Critical
Adult dissipates by melding with the Nurturing Adult. In this way, the
Adult is whole again because he is incomplete when the ego states are
fragmented.

At this time, the Critical Adult becomes a resource instead of a hindrance, when it provides the wisdom that was imparted upon it by the past
authority figures. With the added information, the Adult can apply the past
experience to the new event, in order to enter the next stage of the process,
and successfully facilitate it in an adaptive fashion.

This reframing of the Critical Adult into a resource for the Nurturing
Adult is a key intervention to quiet one's internal dissension and promotes
healing between the generations. This is where the rubber meets the road
in recovery. Anything else indicates there is still a lot of work to do. This
isn't a judgment — just a hallmark of recovery — and can be a formidable
challenge. Figure 12.11 is a visual depiction of the outcome to this process.

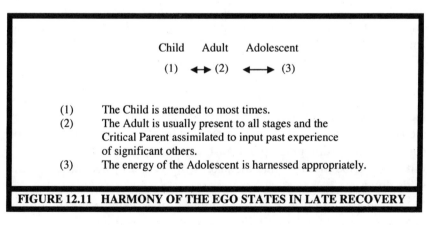

Child   Adult   Adolescent
(1) ↔ (2) ↔ (3)

(1)   The Child is attended to most times.
(2)   The Adult is usually present to all stages and the
        Critical Parent assimilated to input past experience
        of significant others.
(3)   The energy of the Adolescent is harnessed appropriately.

FIGURE 12.11   HARMONY OF THE EGO STATES IN LATE RECOVERY

Potency of the Five Factors

The plethora of facets the Five Factors engraves onto the event, changes
its magnitude, intensity, and depth. What begins as a simple issue exacerbates greatly, when the factors begin their impact. Used as a framework

for identifying underlying cause, the factors when explored, can add great clarity to the individuals understanding of their own reactions and issues.

The severity of the event taxes the individual's Executive System greatly — unlike a small event that uses minimal energy or ability to facilitate. Size, along with *the duration of the event*, forces the individual to expend more and more of its energy to ameliorate the resulting feelings which seem to grow larger with each passing time period.

Issues attached to or triggered by the event greatly exacerbate its impact, and mystify why the human has shut down or over-reacted. It's easy to see the added impact the severity and duration can have on the event. It's equally as easy to administer appropriate interventions in support, validation, new skill acquisition and enhancement of current skills. Although the added burden of an attached or triggered past event to the current situation requires some psycho dynamic intervention, it should occur "AFTER" the individual is out of the initial denial and impact from the event, and *doesn't destabilize his current Executive System's strategy for facilitating the event*!

There is no deep work involved in this process. You have to *identify* the feelings causing the impasse, *sort* them out from the work already done, and *normalize* their current process by sharing that it's common to attach loss from past events to present situations. In session, I illustrate this concept by using imagery. In it I use dropping an anchor into a lake, dragging it along the bottom, and picking up objects along its path. The anchor is the current event, and as it's being dragged, it breaks loose or picks up unresolved past issues. The client usually sees the imagery and attaches it to his current blockage.

I then use the resulting action of the anchor being dragged as part of the imagery, by describing how the silt at the bottom, being stirred up by the anchor, clouds the clear lake water, and how that can be related to the current event — dragging up old stuff, and dirtying the present episode. I further describe that life, like the lake, will eventually become clear and settle down.

At this point I normalize the awareness, give them permission to put any issues on hold unless it's *directly* related and pertinent to successful resolution of the current event, and *CLOSE THEM UP*! Usually the relief they get from knowing that they're not crazy or going there, is enough to satisfy their needs, and the impasse is broken. Very rarely does it require any deeper intervention. If they can't experience closure to this stage, I would back up to explore anything that might have been missed earlier in their process.

The time span of the above process will be determined by **the matura-tion level of the internal structure** and the PARENTING SKILLS of the therapist, because any developmental impasses met during this time can be countered with affirming the Child and validating and redirecting inap-propriate behavior by the Adolescent. This action will also neutralize the Critical Adult, because there will not be a need for it to intervene. Remem-ber, the Critical Adult's role is to impart previously learned information, and there is no need to engage when the therapist or the Nurturing Adult is demonstrating good parenting skills and "taking care of business."

The last element of the Five Factors becomes significant only when the magnitude of the current event is overwhelming or perceived as such, because the greater the consequences of the event, the larger **the reper-toire of problem-solving skills and strategies** needs to be in place.

Emotional Twilight Zone

Misdirection in the Bargaining Stage of the Grief Process sets up the individual to fail in successfully negotiating the next phase of the process. This propels him back into earlier stages, vacillating between them, until the skill to advance is acquired or the consequence of their reaction has lasted long enough for the resulting feelings of the loss to subside. Going back and forth between the stages is what constitutes The Emotional Twi-light Zone. A successful intervention, at this time, is just to ground them in the fact — *that they take care of it now — or take care of it later. Either way they will take care of it.* This is especially true with chronic relapses because most of them have never realized how they have to account for their behavior.

DEPRESSION

*Depression is the stage where feelings are
accurately experienced, identified and expressed*

In order to successfully complete this stage and enter the final step of the process, one has to become *the Nurturing Parent to himself*, and bring all ego states through the process intact. This is a big job because of the many passages that exist. One can get easily lost if they are preoccupied with other business, and fail to see the signposts. It takes good parenting skills in order to remain focused, centered, and grounded in stress.

During this time, the Adult has to remain a full-grown person, affirming his feelings, and maintaining adaptive, functional, and appropriate behavior. In the process, the Child and Adolescent will be heard, feelings will be experienced and processed, behavior will remain appropriate to the situation, and boundaries maintained. In using an effective Executive System, the Critical Adult usually remains quiet or has a small voice.

Completion of this stage is simple — going through the feelings and being O.K. with oneself on the other side. The Five Factors will continue to impact the consequences in a lesser degree, because most have been addressed in earlier stages and if some resolution has occurred, will have a cursory impact only. If the opposite is true and the factors avoided, most feelings will be raw and exacerbated.

The lack of good parenting skills and successful avoidance of the Five Factors, will jet propel the human being into the Emotional Twilight Zone "faster than a speeding bullet." These are the main causes for not attaining acceptance, in which resolution is not completed, or generating dysfunctional behavior as a shield to avoid the pain from the event.

There are no adaptive shortcuts out of depression. One has to grow and go through the pain or leave to skirt the issue or discomfort.

**A TWELVE-STEP PROGRAM ADAGE SIMPLY STATES:
ONE EITHER GROWS OR GOES IN THE PROGRAM**

Growth is a difficult undertaking during this time and its hallmark is the human being's ability to transcend the pain instead of running from it. There is nothing wrong with looking for shortcuts, cutting one's losses, or trying new strategies, as long as they're functional, adaptive and don't engender problematic behavior.

ACCEPTANCE

Acceptance is a process.
Each level of awareness has its own process.
Accepting the process is its hallmark.

Acceptance is merely the end of a long road. It's a place where you are O.K. with yourself. It's like coming home to a safe environment, in which you can take off your shoes, sit back, and be comfortable with you. It's like leaving the world behind. We can relate this to one's process: the individual has gone through all the stages, traveling through a strife-ridden world, and now it's over.

Over simplified? I don't think so. Try it. You may like it if your process can tolerate it. Remember — some humans cannot do peace. They have to have conflict in their lives or they can't function. In fact, the greater the disharmony, the more alive they feel. We all know people like this. Make a list of them and see what's revealed. Don't forget you, if your behavior mirrors my description.

• Acceptance comes in many levels:

1st Level: The facts of the event — admitting it actually happened

2nd Level: The immediate losses incurred

3rd Level: The future losses that will happen

4th Level: What will never happen again because of the loss

During these levels, one goes through the Grief Process for each item that's revealed, but in a shortened period. Some of this is so subtle that it only takes minutes from awareness to resolution.

• Losing one's parents can be an excellent example of the levels:

1st Level: That they died and will not be physically present again

2nd Level: That they are now parentless

3rd Level: What you won't be able to do together in the future

4th Level: Any omissions during childhood that will never be fulfilled

We can interweave several other issues, along with the various facets of the issue, and you can see how much a human being has to work on before he gets *complete* resolution, if, it's possible. *We are a work in progress boys and girls. Go easy on you*!

ASSIGNMENT 15: What are your reactions in the Grief Process? Does your Child become stuck in shock or denial? If yes — when? Does your Adolescent become jammed up in anger? If yes — how does it happen? If no — how does he go through the anger? Think of an actual experience that happened and write it out. When you write, the process becomes concrete, instead of a hazy response. I also want you to be not only aware of your process, but to take the credit for it as well. Is your

Nurturing Adult emotionally available for your Child? Does the Adult set healthy boundaries and limits on the Adolescent during the process? Is the Critical Adult antagonistic toward them? If yes — when does it happen? How can you change it? What item during this chapter surprised you? Did your thinking change? Are you managing better today because of the information in this chapter?

SUMMARY

The Grief Process is not only a process — it's a road as well. Along with the road comes a structure. Its matrix includes the Child, Adolescent, and the Adult. In the process, each ego state travels at it's own pace, until it reaches its destination of Acceptance. The time it takes is fluid and depends on: the severity of the event, the duration of its effect, the issues attached to or triggered by the incident, the maturation level of one's internal structure, and the repertoire of problem-solving skills and strategies that it possesses.

In the Grief Process, each developmental ego state goes through the six stages according to its ability to facilitate the feelings that surface over the loss. Each stage moves at its own pace and its movement is not judged. Without making a value judgment, one can accurately assess his forward progress in any issue, seek help or new strategies if needed, or, leave it alone as a natural process, based on his true ability to transcend the loss, and know where he is with any issue or loss. Each stage has its own issues, impediments, and resolution.

Stages one and two (Shock and Denial) have similar issues. Each stage is one of nature's shock absorbers that keep the emotionally frail human being from becoming overwhelmed and dysfunctional in a great loss. These stages are usually associated with the Child Ego State because it is predominantly feelings that encompass its process. Issues arise when the person lacks the emotional maturity, stress-reducing strategies, or ego strength to break the impasse and move forward

Stage three (Anger) is predominantly associated with the Adolescent because it is a teenage trait to express one's feelings as anger, or, to turn it inward as self-destructive behavior. Anger can also be viewed as a healthy expression when it's used to vent the energy of impacted feelings that have no other way to be diminished.

Stage four (Bargaining) is the beginning of the Adult or intellectual process of resolution. In it, one can mediate the event prior to feeling the full emotional impact of the loss or event. During this stage there is a natural unfolding of one's ability to facilitate feelings. It occurs when the Child becomes more exposed to the Adult's influence after the Adolescent releases its full protection. The release is gradual after the Adult lives up to its responsibility to provide adaptive solutions and sets healthy boundaries and limits on the Adolescent. At this point, the fully empowered Adult is able to redirect his Critical counterpart, identify his feelings, and maintain his internal integrity and external boundaries.

Stage five (Depression) is the stage in which an emotionally mature adult will facilitate the feelings and maintain appropriate behavior during the event, or, an emotionally charged Adolescent will take over once the Adult has abrogated his right of decision and propel them into The Emotional Twilight Zone. This is the pattern one travels when he can't tolerate the intensity of the feelings. In it he regresses from Depression to any of the previous stages of the Grief Process when the feelings get too overwhelming. Then, when able, travels back into Depression. If the feelings have not subsided, they repeat the process again, and go back to an earlier stage. It's a loop they travel with no ending, round and round they go until the energy from the feelings is dissipated. There is no learning in this process — only survival — and it will have to be revisited later in order to release the emotional influence it carries in the individual's life.

Stage six (Acceptance) is the final stage of the process. In it the Adult accepts the facets of the event it can handle. Usually the time varies for each ego state's attainment of the stage. It doesn't make any difference where the states end up — only that the person understands their position. With some issues, acceptance will not happen for all the ego states. This is normal. No value judgment is made when an issue is not resolved because everyone is different, and can be affected by a myriad of factors.

CASE STUDY

Polly P. came into therapy because she couldn't sleep, lost weight, was having difficulty with her current relationship in trying to remain emotionally present, frequently cries for no reason, and at times feels herself going numb to things around her. In completing a psychosocial, it's revealed that Polly lost her mother 15 months ago and her father doesn't appear to be doing well. In fact, Polly states that he has expressed several times, a desire to 'join' his wife, after each time he talks about not having a reason to live any more because his wife is dead.

Polly was placed in a grief group composed of clients who were stuck in various segments of their process. The group was a continuous, open-ended group, so there were people in each stage of the group process. The size of the group went between 12 to 15 members and had a male and female therapist co-facilitating it. The group process used was a combination of Psycho Dynamic and Transactional Analysis. The current counseling model of this book, using the ego states to identify their internal structure, and enlisting the Grief Process as their road map, was used extensively throughout the life of the group. Psychodrama was used weekly, after the resistance was identified, in order to develop a strategy to break the gauntlet that was created by the impasse. Education and insight were cornerstones of their foundations, and each group member was given significant written material about the group and the process it utilized.

In therapy, Polly talked easily about *FACTS* of her mom's death, and appeared to have rudimentary insight and process. When the initial prodding about *FEELINGS* began, Polly stated adamantly that she had put "the loss behind her," and further warned me "not to go there." When Polly was confronted about this resistance, she could offer no explanation, only the fact that she thought she did enough grieving over it.

Polly agreed to participate in group therapy, and after the usual transition time, was given an assignment to write a letter of goodbye to her mom and to read it in group. Polly took two weeks to write the letter and only completed it because she was given an ultimatum. At this time firm boundaries were imposed about being ready for group therapy. She was told, if the assignment wasn't completed by the second week, she probably wasn't ready to work in a group process, and would be terminated.

She was able to read the letter to another female peer in role play, and while reading it, broke down and sobbed for over 15 minutes while the woman substituting for her mother held her. During this time, Polly wailed about all the things her mom had done for her, and what she would miss the most. Later in the group as we were processing the loss and closing her off, Polly was not able to go beyond the immediate personal loss of her mother, in spite of the difficulties being experienced by other family members since the death, when her sister started to drink too much, her brother was having problems on his job, and her father no longer wanted to live.

Polly was given all the educational tools: was able to verbalize understanding of the stages of a group, expectations of group members, stages of the Grief Process, and the ego states. During the first four weeks, Polly completed the first stage of the group process by establishing trust, and was ready to enter the working phase. This was accomplished as she gained knowledge, decreased her pain when she identified and experienced her loss, and gained competency in working with my model.

The next four weeks were the Working Phase. In it Polly was able to complete three psychodramas in which she discovered that her:

1. *CHILD*: was in denial of the ramifications of her mom's death in the fact that the rest of her immediate family was having great difficulty in their lives since her mother's death, and the possibility of her father dying because of his age, current physical condition, and giving up hope.
2. *ADOLESCENT*: was covering up these feelings by "acting in" to protect the Child.
3. *ADULT*: had sought therapy to get some help because she didn't know what to do, even though the Adolescent was resistant.

During the next four weeks, which is the utilization of what was gleaned in therapy, Polly was able to complete two more psychodramas, and establish the following with her different parts:

1. *CHILD*: validate the Child's fear of losing her dad, although remained fairly detached from the deep feelings of possibly being parentless by stating, "I'll cross that bridge *if* I come to it!" This statement during this stage of therapy is viewed as a *boundary*, given by the Adolescent, to protect not only the Child but the Adult's internal integrity as well. The apparent resistance is reframed to a boundary because it's appropriate, due to the large amount of work she accomplished in therapy.
2. *ADOLESCENT*: The Adult had to get to know, trust, and affirm the Adolescent's power. In the process, the Adult bonded with the Adolescent in order to harness her energy to develop more adaptive coping strategies, and avoid any more "acting in." During this time, in psychodrama, the Adult had to commit to an acceptable strategy for overcoming the loss, and putting her life back together. At the same time, the Adult pledged to pay more attention to the Child, and to acknowledge when the Adolescent wanted input, instead of brushing her off as she did after her mom died.
3. *ADULT*: By entering and working in therapy, the Adult grew, self-esteem increased, and Polly's Executive System (Automatic

Decision-Making Process) was greatly enhanced because it included all three aspects of her internal structure. Its behavioral demonstrations were:

a) That she allowed the Child to feel and protected her in an adult manner, with appropriate emotional boundaries, when unnecessary work was challenged.

b) That she used the strength of the Adolescent to go through the pain, acknowledge her part in the dysfunction, and listen when boundaries needed to be placed, even on the therapist.

c) That she sought help and entered therapy, worked while she was there, decided on appropriate boundaries, and utilized the insight uncovered in group to develop appropriate, innovative, functional, and adaptive strategies to heal and go on with her life.

During closure with the group, Polly thanked everyone for the part they played in her healing, verbalized the role the counseling model played in freeing her from her depression, reconnecting her back with herself, and how she will use it in the future. Polly was also at that time symptom free, displayed a bright affect, could verbalize hope, was able to sleep without much effort, and reconnected emotionally with her significant other. At the end of the group, Polly also exclaimed that the rest of her family was going to try 'those' Hospice Grief Groups because she seemed to be doing better. Not that they really needed it, because after all, "it was behind them," and they, "didn't want to go there."

Conclusion

As you can glean from the case study, I use a simple observational technique, based on the premise that each developmental ego state is alive, well, and interacting within us — can be used to determine where a person is along the path of the Grief Process.

My observation is as follows: The predominate ego state *of* the moment, presents as being in one stage, and as feelings and emotions change internally because they are *always* in flux, presents as being in another stage to correspond with the changing feelings.

WHEN INTERNAL FEELINGS CHANGE SO WILL THEIR EXTERNAL MANIFESTATION. EACH WILL CORRESPOND TO A DIFFERENT PHASE OF GRIEF EVEN THOUGH THE PERSON HAS NOT MOVED IN THE PROCESS.

During this time, a mood swing would manifest, as an analogon to the internal change, and present as another stage; when, internally, it is a different ego state revealing its position — *NOT A CHANGE IN THE STAGE OF PROCESS THEY'RE IN*. This is extremely important to map out. If not, many issues will be missed, and opportunities to grow passed by unaided.

The above can be verified through body language, verbiage, and presenting behavior of the client, or yourself, once my concept of the ego states moving through the Grief Process at different rates is plugged into your scan. This information will, if used, increase accurate assessing skills for therapists and enhance self-monitoring skills for individuals.

CHAPTER THIRTEEN

The Spirituality of Human Beings is based upon three Factors:
1. Their relationship with self
2. Their connectedness with others
3. Their belief and use of a power greater than themselves
   because "Faith without works is dead."

OVERVIEW

After you have completed this chapter you will be able to:

1. Conceptualize spirituality with a cognitive framework
2. See it as a path in life
3. Recognize when you or someone else is off their path
4. Know when you lack spirituality and why
5. Learn how to keep it once you have it
6. Explore the roadblocks that keep you from following a spiritual path
7. Identify the impact of the ego states of your spirituality by learning what issues each brings to the tapestry, and what you can do to break any gauntlet created by one
8. Observe the many different roads one can take on his spiritual journey when fear steps in and faith leaves

SPIRITUALITY

Spirituality, in many ways, is the last piece to the puzzle of why humans are on this planet. Without it, humans merely flounder around, in search of "the Invincible Foe," and just as Don Quixote tried, ended up fighting windmills, and come away empty. Man, in his search for meaning in life, remains unable to elicit an answer without adding a spiritual component to his quest.

Spirituality in this context is just admitting that there is a power out there in the universe, and that it is greater than you. This power can start out as something simple and intangible as faith, or move to a more complex model and use energy which would be more tangible. *IT CAN BE ANYTHING YOU BELIEVE IN.* There are no limits here. The second tenet would be that you would reach out to that Higher Power for help in your time of need. These two pieces will open the door to spiritual awareness and growth.

There are many roadblocks to attaining a spiritual connection:

1. Fear of what one will find
2. Adverse modeling by primary caregivers
3. One's lack of a relationship with self
4. Isolation from others
5. Inability to use what one believes in

WHAT IS IT?

Human beings, throughout time, have asked many questions about their existence: Why am I here? Is there a plan and a purpose to my life? Is this life the best I can give myself? WHO AM I! Many have asked and sought the answers — only to end up in the ashes of frustration like Don Quixote. I too, prior to recovery, followed false gods. Sometimes they were money, property, prestige, jobs, other people, fads, or anything I could do in a socially acceptable compulsive and obsessive manner. The predominant culture actually reinforces this toxic behavior when it reveres socially acceptable values that keep a person so busy, that if God were to appear today, as he did with Moses in the form of a burning bush, the harried individual would call the fire department on his cell phone, and then wander aimlessly, wondering why God would abandon him in his hour of need.

One has to slow down, catch up with himself, in order to develop a spiritual connection.

Spirituality is nothing more than physically stopping, quieting your mind, and allowing yourself to connect with whatever positive force reveals itself to you. Most times this will be a feeling. One in which you trust, that as long as you follow a path that keeps you in this feeling, you will remain connected. The feelings are ones of peace, serenity, and security. They permeate one's life as long as the individual stays connected to this power and follows a path that maintains the feelings.

The illustration in Figure 13.1 was the easiest visualization I could conjure up. Anything else would be too esoteric. Look carefully at the depiction and begin to conceptualize your own path. At step one you were doing your life in whatever fashion suited your needs. No value judgment is made here because "one person's poison is another person's nourishment." In step two, you stopped for a moment, became aware of this book "*somehow*," (maybe by a "*coincidence*" but I don't think so), began to read it and due to the nature of its teachings, you are beginning to become impacted by it. If you're a therapist, mentor, parent, spouse, or a sponsor in a twelve-step program, you will also recognize others who can benefit from the book's wisdom. In step three, good feelings arise and you desire to maintain the connection. Hopefully, this simple descriptor can be used to reinforce or conceptualize your own Higher Power.

In step five of Figure 13.1, appears the two possible roads one can travel, when a life event occurs which has negative consequences. In Road A, one travels down a path of fear, breaks contact with his Higher Power, wanders down the road until the feelings from the event dissipate, and eventually reconnects back onto his spiritual path. In Road B, one remains in faith, goes through the feelings from the painful event, and maintains contact with his Higher Power.

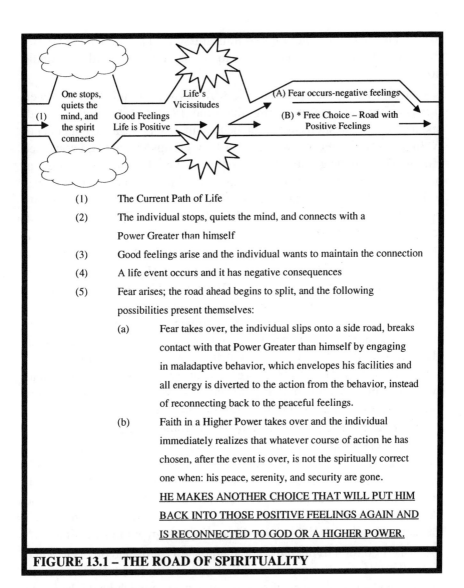

(1)	The Current Path of Life	
(2)	The individual stops, quiets the mind, and connects with a Power Greater than himself	
(3)	Good feelings arise and the individual wants to maintain the connection	
(4)	A life event occurs and it has negative consequences	
(5)	Fear arises; the road ahead begins to split, and the following possibilities present themselves:	
	(a)	Fear takes over, the individual slips onto a side road, breaks contact with that Power Greater than himself by engaging in maladaptive behavior, which envelopes his facilities and all energy is diverted to the action from the behavior, instead of reconnecting back to the peaceful feelings.
	(b)	Faith in a Higher Power takes over and the individual immediately realizes that whatever course of action he has chosen, after the event is over, is not the spiritually correct one when: his peace, serenity, and security are gone. <u>HE MAKES ANOTHER CHOICE THAT WILL PUT HIM BACK INTO THOSE POSITIVE FEELINGS AGAIN AND IS RECONNECTED TO GOD OR A HIGHER POWER.</u>

FIGURE 13.1 – THE ROAD OF SPIRITUALITY

RECOGNIZING WHEN YOU HAVE SPIRITUALITY

My own concept of God, Higher Power, or a Power Greater than myself, has changed throughout my life span. In my childhood, the God of my understanding was a Catholic one. He was judgmental, critical, and ready to doom me to hell for the slightest transgressions. I kicked Him out of my life at about age nine and He wasn't to be asked back in until my middle 40's.

At 40, I went on a "search and destroy mission" for this Higher Power. It was a three-year quest. During that time, I listened, listened, listened, and then asked questions. It was in the listening that I began to understand. At first my Higher Power was the self-help groups I attended. I could see Him working in the group. These people had what I wanted. They were at peace with themselves and describing a path that would maintain it. I was in turmoil, didn't know how to change, and couldn't see it getting any better. The group was also a place that I felt emotionally safe. This was a feeling I hadn't experienced for a long time. It was also a place I could sit still, be quiet, and connect with whatever power permeated that room.

While I listened, I remembered my first adult Higher Power. It was in the TV show "Baretta." When Robert Blake would get frustrated, he would look up and say, "Louie, ya gotta do somethin' with this." I liked that. I could identify with the role he played and began to use it myself. It was good but couldn't be sustained because it lacked substance. It was just an idea and I used it. This was different from my emergency God whom I bargained with when something went seriously wrong in my life. Whatever pact I made with Him during the crisis — was broken right after the intensity of the situation diminished or the problem was resolved.

My next adult venture into the realm of Higher Power was when O-B-ONE-KENOBE told Luke Skywalker in "Star Wars" about "The Force". I understood about "The Force". It was something I experienced in childhood. When I needed help with problems, sports, people, or situations, all I had to do was to relax, let this wonderful and safe feeling come over me like a veil, and I could do anything. It was also during this time that I foresaw a long life, and that I would accomplish great things with it.

What I do for a living, how I do therapy, this book and others to come were all predestined for me. I saw all of this as a child. I felt "The Force" in adulthood and at the same time foresaw my accomplishments. Just as in childhood the adversity entered my life; the connection broke when I had nothing to sustain my faith and triggered off my fear.

Today I'm back to being that child. The feeling of being connected has returned and I call my Higher Power, God the Father, because I feel I'm His son.

Just like a dad, He makes me feel guided, protected, special, and loved. In His presence, I'm never alone. I've chosen to share my personal experience finding my Higher Power because I didn't want to write it as an observer. I don't think my story is much different than anybody else's. We all search, have experiences, make decisions, and travel our life's path. Some do it alone. Some find comfort along the way. Today I choose never to be alone again.

In Figure 13.2 the connectedness is illustrated as an interaction between one's self, others and a Higher Power. It is a two-way exchange as each gives and takes from the other. The receiving from God, is when one becomes a channel and passes on the intuitive guidance that is given when in communion with Him, instead of giving self-seeking information to the one looking for guidance.

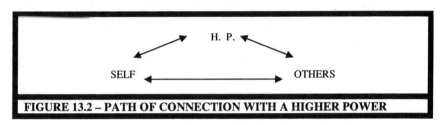

FIGURE 13.2 – PATH OF CONNECTION WITH A HIGHER POWER

Did I explain what spirtuality was in a way that can validate your current assumptions or give you something tangible enough to hold on to with such an inttangible concept? I hope so. Get a feel for the concept. Like a piece of delicious hard candy, let it roll around in your mouth to savor its fine taste before you chew it up. Who knows? Maybe you'll have a spirtual awakening before you know it.

Application of the Book

The practical application of the book's concepts will occur in steps three, four, and five of Figure 13.1 (p.323). Out of these concepts you will develop the tools to maintain your positive feelings of connectedness during step three, when a problem arises from one of life's vicissitudes (A Twelve Step Program term for this occurrence is "life on life's terms"), *without* succumbing to the fear in step four and traveling down the negative road in step five (choice A).

This book, at the junction in step five, gives you an adaptive choice in which you can stay in the positive feelings and remain on your spiritual path instead of taking a side road which will divert you from your primary spiritual intention.

The concepts in this book and its main thrust are highly spiritual in nature. Its content allows you to scrutinize the following:

1. Where are you in your life's path?

2. Where would you want to be?
3. What choices do you have in its direction?

These are profound questions, and for some, may have serious ramifications because of the adversity one's path has given him. Very few *can't* return to their primary spiritual path. *MOST CAN!*

In my practice and the twelve-step programs I've attended, I've seen death occur, and mostly due to an individual's inability to transcend his past. This book offers much hope that anything is possible. It gives one a way to look at the past and work it out instead of giving up and choosing spiritual death. This will ultimately lead to physical death because the depth of the loneliness one experiences when he is completely void of all human and spiritual contact is too much to bear, and death usually follows. Those of you who have been in the depths of depression, or, witnessed a client or loved one in it, know exactly what I'm talking about.

HOW DO YOU KEEP IT?

The path of spirituality takes faith, trust, and experience to remain on course. There are many pitfalls along the way that can sidetrack even the most devout of believers, as facets of his spirituality were ignored or were not relegated to importance when his nature would jeopardize doctrine.

Faith in itself can "move mountains." Alone, "faith without works is dead," is almost contradictory. I believe what it states is that something that can't sustain itself is doomed to extinction. This is not a conflict, but a furthering of the process which allows one to keep what he has, instead of losing it, when the overwhelming adversity comes into his life.

Trust is a component of "the works." It allows for a tangible element, almost a foundation, on which one can build, instead of its being elusive like a puff of smoke. Please remember at this point that the language is metaphorical and being used as imagery, *NOT AS A PUT-DOWN TO BLIND FAITH!*

At this point — trust is the process. It allows for a continuous assessment if faith is working, under what conditions, and how it can be repeated. This concept adds a cognitive component and in it the head and the heart become connected. Something that religion doesn't always accomplish when it asks one to go on blind faith alone.

I offer the above to you because a human is made up of both a head (cognition) and a heart (feelings) and to think that one can operate on 50 percent of his facilities, when it comes to sustained spirituality during adverse conditions, is a disservice to the human psyche. It's in the process of trust that one begins to concretize his faith. It allows a human to know when it works and what causes it not to. In this way it can be replicated. The tangible indicators during this time would include feelings of peace, serenity, protection, and an innate feeling of being on course: life would be going in a forward direction, functional strategies would come into one's consciousness, and the future would appear to be bright.

The last component to "the works" is the consistent experience one gathers while going through life's difficulties "*AND*" using his spiritual intuition and knowledge to transcend the overwhelming problems, instead of yielding to fear by entering into ineffective, dysfunctional, maladaptive, or problematic behavior.

It's at this juncture in the human life span, that self-centered fear drives or sidetracks the human being from his spiritual course and:

1. Uses all energy and resources to:
   a)Perpetuate the problematic behavior and
   b)Later, clean up the carnage left in the acting-out behavior's wake
2. Instead of following a spiritual path to:
   a)Go through the adversity
   b)Gain experience with life
   c)Use the experience to become the person one is destined to be

Roadblocks

Some of the roadblocks to maintaining a spiritual course in the face of human adversity include:

1. Not having faith
2. Not having trust
3. No concept of a Higher Power, God, or Spirituality
4. Adverse experiences with religion
5. Negative modeling by primary caregivers or cultural icons

Of all the roadblocks that are encountered on the recovering person's quest to find a spiritual path — past modeling has been found to be the biggest hindrance. Many people have been led to believe in a judgmental and critical God who was waiting to trample them for any infraction of the tenets of their faith. Others have watched hypocrisy as pious church members model a "power of example" on their Sabbath and then revert back to negative behavior the rest of the week. The leaders of the various faiths have fared no better. All one has to do is to look at the many scandals over several of the past decades to realize that they are as crazy as any other mortal. There are some notable examples, although not enough to trickle down, as evidenced by our moral decline over the past thirty years.

The modeling of the human's primary caregivers, in less than child-centered homes, is also the culprit. During these times, the parents inadvertently became the template for God as the child matured and developed his own spiritual connection to a Higher Power. The primary caregiver had this type of power over the children, by nature of the adult's size, and importance to the child's security and thereby his life — THEY ARE GODS AND RELEGATED AS SUCH BY THE CHILD!

At this point in time, it doesn't make any difference what intention the parent had — *IT'S THE INTERPRETATION, BY THE CHILD'S PERCEPTIONS, THAT COUNT!* There is no blame being given here. I'm only reporting the facts. Parents do the best they can with what they have. This is a fact. Another fact is that OJT (On the Job Training) for parents really sucks. Too many times the wisdom comes after the damage has been done. One can *stay in the problem* by denying the facts or beating themselves up for not knowing "OR" he can *come into the solution* by admitting the problem, changing the behavior, and passing on the wisdom to others — "INCLUDING" their children.

If you want a good model of being connected to a Higher Power through spirituality, sit in a twelve-step meeting and listen, or talk to, someone who projects it without saying. You will know them by their peaceful looks, verbalizing faith, living a functional and adaptive life, and fulfilling a goal which will help others. Listen for fear as they talk. There will be little. Any adversity in their lives will be met with equanimity. Their lives will not be perfect. They will have difficulty as all humans do. What they will do differently is to correct bad decisions quickly to avoid going down those negative roads. In order to maintain their direction, you will hear them connected to their feelings, feeling deep levels of emotions that some may judge as unnecessary. This is one of the hallmarks of spirituality. The others are: faith, trust, and experience. Without them, they would find it almost impossible to sustain a path on spiritual terms when deep adversity strikes in their lives.

Adverse experiences with religion can be overcome with my framework. This reframing can add to, be in place of, or smooth out the road, in any human's belief or faith by giving it a cognitive foundation. On this base, one can add the components to his house and build his structure called spirituality. The pieces to this building would be the individual's feelings. Each one serves a purpose: some are small like nails; others are large like beams and planking. Others are the finished material, shingles, and paint. *In order to build this house, one has to "want" to come out of the problem and go into the solution.* Too many times those who have had negative religious experiences want to tell their story over and over, re-traumatizing themselves in the process, instead of trying new roads that will bring a different experience. Negativity keeps one stuck in the problem because as he enumerates it over and over, he remains in his head to avoid his feelings. Religious misinformation stirs up a plethora of issues because once again, the "parents," in the guise of the church, have let them down.

The other roadblocks can be overcome through an experiential intervention in which one believes, trusts, and experiences spirituality vicariously in a twelve-step program when one: believes because someone else believes, "talks the talk" by talking about a Higher Power, and "acts as if" when he says he has one when he doesn't. *This is a cognitive-behavioral experiential intervention in which one quiets down the negativity and opens himself up to spiritual possibilities. It's "cognitive" because it alters the thinking process, and its "behavioral" because of the change in the person's actions which were dependent on the old thoughts.*

THE IMPACT OF THE EGO STATES

The impact of the ego states on one's spirituality when a problem is present in his spiritual concepts is usually synergistic because of the deep issues the confusion raises across the developmental life span. Nowhere else do these issues surface as quickly and bring up all the "big guns" of someone's issues. The reaction's roots are so deep and basic, that it triggers off massive shame immediately once the loop has begun.

When this shameful downward spiral has begun, it takes a concentrated effort, with a highly cognitive system, to put on the brakes and stop the episode from further deterioration. This is possible "AFTER" the shame's origins have been exposed in psychotherapy or a twelve-step program, and the individual has gained a working knowledge in psychodrama of the ego states in their internal structure.

Working the steps in a twelve-step program can give someone a rudimentary understanding of his feelings, triggers, and give many cognitive and behavioral skills to stop the downward spiral into shame. The individual needs therapy or new information to bring the process to the next level of growth. This book is written with the hope that it will give the new information to the struggling members who need it to break the gauntlet that shame has placed in the path of developing positive spirituality or spiritual concepts.

The Child Ego State

The Child is the heart of the issue in one's confusion over spirituality. It's the segment of the adult's makeup that was vulnerable and wounded. The Child was the part that believed in the church, God, dogma and rituals. It was the segment which held the hope that all would be right in his world if he believed hard enough. It was the side that was disappointed so greatly, that shame was the resulting feeling, and in shame, the Child internalized: *"there was something wrong with me that couldn't be fixed."*

The inadequacy of organized religion that doesn't provide a foundation on which to build faith is just as inept as the dysfunctional family which expects blind allegiance from its children. A child internalizes the external deficiencies of his primary caregiver and institutions as internal inadequacies, and shuts down. What emerge later on developmentally are an angry adolescent and a dysfunctional adult.

In order to provide a healing environment, the issues have to be uncovered, the Child's feelings validated, and the inadequacy placed where it belongs, "WITHOUT" shattering the Child's love. In this way, the Child can heal without re-traumatizing it inadvertently, if, in one's haste to help, the Child's love object is put down. Further along in his process, you will observe the Adult, truly recognizing that *everyone did the best they could with what they got*, and that it was O.K. to forgive and still love his parents. This will happen after much healing has occurred. In fact, it's one of the best indicators for healing, because *if they haven't forgiven them, they haven't forgiven themselves*, and are probably stuck somewhere in their process or have an additional agenda they're holding onto. Sometimes this is some form of abuse. Either what was done to them or what they did to themselves or others. This secret will be locked away in the Child.

FORGIVENESS IS THE HALLMARK OF HEALING.
WITHOUT IT — ONE IS STUCK!

The Adolescent Ego State

The Adolescent is the one that gets belligerent toward the church and puts up a fight or stops going. This action is a direct result of the wounds that were inflicted upon the Child when he was shamed because of the institution's inadequacy. The reaction can be acting out (refusing to go), or acting in (shutting down). Either way, it's effective because he no longer takes in the influence of the church.

This is sad because spirituality can be a great force in a teen's life, helping him to bypass misguided assumptions (fear-based information designed to control rather than to guide) and remain on his spiritual path, and finding out what his talents are and using them for the betterment of other human beings. Too many times the Adolescent is angry, doesn't know why or at whom to direct it, and lashes out at the easiest possible target — which is usually the family. This anger, channeled through his spirituality, now becomes the energy to explore his potential, identify his talents and open up possibilities. Freud called this sublimation. In spirituality it's substituting the unacceptable call of instinctual drives into the energy to produce socially acceptable behavior. An example: an angry teen, instead of fighting, works the anger out in sports and becomes good at it.

Spirituality opens up many possibilities that blind faith does not allow for. Look at its potential. Instead of the teen striking out in fear, he redirects that energy, through faith, to complete his developmental tasks, to become the person he thinks he is. It's not over simplistic. It actually works. I've taught it to many teens, that years later, are still doing well. Their lives are not perfect, they are *not* going down the old paths, and they *are* trying new ways. That's success!

**SPIRITUALITY IS A TOOL TO HELP THE ADOLESCENT
TO COMPLETE HIS DEVELOPMENTAL TASKS
AND BECOME THE PERSON HE THINKS HE IS**

The Adult Ego State

The Adult is the portion of the internal structure that has to successfully facilitate a barrage of feelings and reactions into an effective, creative, and functional decision-making process that will provide adaptive choices in the best interests of the whole person and allow him to maintain his direction along a spiritual path. This is a big job. It takes practice, experience, and faith. It is also a collaborative process in which the Adult gives and takes with the two other ego states. Figure 13.3 is a visual look at that process.

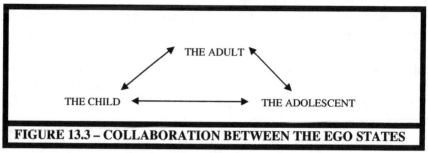

FIGURE 13.3 – COLLABORATION BETWEEN THE EGO STATES

THE ADULT IN RELATION TO THE CHILD   Along the path of spirituality there are many side roads the human being can take. *It's up to the Adult to determine what path he encounters based on faith and maturity instead of the Child's fear or the Adolescent's reaction.*

So many times the road to faith is based on the "fear" of the Child. This confuses the Adult by clouding his decision-making process, and he follows false gods because they are familiar to his Child part. This process is purely an emotional one: one in which all logic and reason are suspended as the Child plays out his parental issues with the church. At this point the church becomes the parents to the Child. In this projection the church will heal his wounds and fill up the empty hole in his heart because the Child thinks the church will never let him down as his parents did.

This childlike thinking is a subconscious process; one's hidden agenda, which gets triggered over the course of his involvement with the church. At this point it's up to the Adult to validate the feelings of the Child in wanting to get involved, but, make a decision slowly, based on experience instead of the enthusiasm of just wanting to join. The Child at this point has to be cautioned about going too fast. This is hard because the Child can't think abstractly. At this time the intellect (Adult/cognitive) has to rule over the emotions (Child/heart) in order to prevent another repeat of childhood when the caregivers and institutions fell short of their mark in providing adequate care and guidance.

One breaks the chains from his past by having choices. When one is little they lack choices and to follow because the adults are the gods. *One is victimized by this process.* Later, when one is older, bigger, and has more resources — he has choices. No longer is he held hostage to an arbitrary or capricious caregiver who seeks to control rather than guide. As an adult, if one follows that same path he was forced to follow as a child, he is no longer a victim, *he is participating on a voluntary basis* and HAS TO

TAKE RESPONSIBILITY FOR IT. In this way the Child is no longer making decisions for the adult. The Child has input. It's a full-grown adult that makes the final decision with the Child's best interests in mind.

THE ADULT IN RELATION TO THE ADOLESCENT The Adolescent is the final segment of the triad. In its matrix is the system that brings energy into the human tapestry called life. The energy can be used to generate dysfunctional behavior in the form of a fear reaction in which one is taken off his spiritual path "OR" expended in an adaptive style in which the energy is used to produce creative strategies that maintain the individual's spiritual course.

The adult has to use all the communication skills he can muster when the Adolescent blows up, because the event is a highly charged emotional issue for the Child. Adolescents traditionally overreact, and the wise adult listens carefully to the message being given throughout the emotional episode. Generally they are setting boundaries, overreacting in order to compensate for what they perceive as a putdown, and wanting to be taken into consideration when a decision is made.

The Adult at this point "has" to listen to the Adolescent's concern. The Child was hurt by "God" and the Adolescent doesn't want it to happen again. The Child wants to trust — the Adolescent doesn't, and rightfully so. *The evidence is already conclusive — If it happened once — it can happen again*! It's the Adult's job at this time to convince the Adolescent to relinquish control so a new strategy can be explored. Usually, just talking to the Adolescent will allow him to let go with a cautionary note, that, "I'll be back if you don't fulfill your adult responsibilities."

During this truce, the adult will move carefully, building evidence to sustain his faith, and remaining on his spiritual path. This can be an overwhelming amount of internal strife to contend with. If it is facilitated in an emotionally mature adult style, the Adolescent will continually lend himself to giving over the energy to remain on his spiritual journey, with the exception of burring up when he thinks the adult is being used or his boundaries are being violated. It's best at this time to do a reality check, to see why they surfaced, and ask: "Why are you here?" or "What did I miss?" The Adolescent will tell you. Assure him that you will take care of the problem he sees even if you don't believe it.

At this time, check in with the Child, because you may have slipped into this ego state and want to do nice-nice or go on blind faith when the evidence won't support it. Also, do a 360 degree visual scan. You might find that someone in authority may be violating your values, ethics, morals, or boundaries. It may be as simple as an inappropriate request for money, time, or space. It may be a flagrant abuse of power, "in the name of God," which will send up all the cautionary flags, bells, and whistles. *Heed them! If you don't — THE ADOLESCENT WILL!*

THE ADULT MAINTAINING A SPIRITUAL PATH In order for the Adult to remain on a path of light in his spiritual journey, he has to remain *AN EMOTIONALLY MATURE RESPONSIBLE ADULT.* In the process of being one, he will listen to his feelings (the Child) and maintain his energy (the Adolescent) in creating effective solutions to life's problems which can divert him from his spiritual path.

Easy said — hard done, when emotionally charged issues cloud his objectivity, and one's internal structure is at odds with each other. The Adult, during this strife, has to sort out the past from the present with both the Child and Adolescent in order to ground them, set appropriate limits to focus them, and have them remain centered on the Adult instead of being off in "the Twilight Zone" of the past trauma. Now, one's internal structure is in harmony, and will be spiritually connected with the resulting peace and quiet.

The Adult can now follow his spiritual path. When he deviates from it, his negative feelings will rise, and he will make a course correction immediately to put himself back on track. It's like getting off on a highway, instinctually knowing you made the wrong turn, and taking the entrance ramp back onto the highway. If, at this time, one begins to doubt, he will travel further along the wrong road looking for sign posts that will assure him he took the right road. The signs never come, and one eventually turns back or asks for directions.

This book will become a blinking yellow cautionary light, erected "*before*" each exit that takes you off your spiritual path, to warn you about the deviation you are about to make. Some will heed the warning well in advance. Some will swerve just in time. Some will take the exit, feel the digression, and return on the entrance ramp. Some will feel the departure, remain on their errant course looking for validation, and will eventually seek directions back. Others will shut down, stuff, or deny their feelings "*AFTER*" ignoring the warning sign, and remain on their aberrant, fearful course until the energy of the distraction diminishes and they return back to their spiritual path — *IF POSSIBLE!*

When you check out Figure 13.4 "PLEASE" make note of several juncture points that have far-reaching consequences along someone's deviation from his spiritual path. The first point occurs in number six when suicide becomes an option. At this time they usually can't see any hope, even addiction offers no relief, and suicide is contemplated. *AT THIS POINT ONE SHOULD SEEK HELP! This is the biggest red flag one can send out as a call for help! Heed it!*

The second pivotal point is at number eight, which identifies the usual outcomes of the diversion from one's spiritual path. This does not vary too much because one "grows or goes" in recovery. Either he finds a way to take care of the pain in an adaptive manner, or he finds a way to take himself out of the equation. Death, of course, is the final answer. It doesn't make any difference if he commits suicide, overdoses, gets killed in an accident (yes — you read that right!), contracts a serious illness (AIDS is an example), gets murdered mysteriously, gets killed being a hero (firemen, policemen, military people), or any of the other thousand ways to die in a socially-prescribed way. Death is death. Reasons for it are immaterial. They're still dead.

The relapse cycle is the third divide. It also has three splits off its path which confuses the recovery process because the newcomer presumes he won't slip. The person in the middle stages has a rudimentary sense about recovery and feels it's enough not to slip. And the old-timer gets complacent. All three reasons are enough to send anyone down the tubes of relapse.

NOTE: Take a moment at this time and follow the path you, friends, co-workers, family members, lovers, or spouses take when adversity enters into your or lives. Did they or you take the *high road* or the *low road*? If one took the low road (deviating from their spiritual path): how long did it last and how far down the road did you all travel? The length one travels in their fear determines the depth of their issues. This is an accurate assessment tool. It can work for you to determine how much work one has to do to return to a spiritual path. *Without help....one maintains only....until the next crises!* When the crisis occurs, one will return to the *low road*, increase the stakes and regress even more. It's the nature of the beast. Check Figure 13.4 to see what's "yet" to come for you.

ASSIGNMENT 16: What does spirituality mean to you? Define its concept and break down its structure. This will give you a cognitive framework to work from. How do you connect with your Higher Power or God? If it's through feelings, what do you do when something traumatic happens and you shut down? If you connect through an institution, what happens to your connection when you have an issue with them? What was the last one you had and how did you resolve it? If you didn't, how did it affect your relationship with God? Can you recognize the various ego states in your connection with a Higher Power? If yes, how do they impact it?

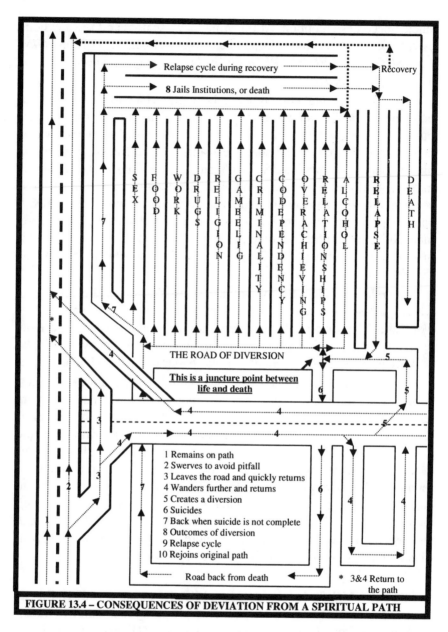

Relapse cycle during recovery .... Recovery

8 Jails Institutions, or death

THE ROAD OF DIVERSION

This is a juncture point between
life and death

1 Remains on path
2 Swerves to avoid pitfall
3 Leaves the road and quickly returns
4 Wanders further and returns
5 Creates a diversion
6 Suicides
7 Back when suicide is not complete
8 Outcomes of diversion
9 Relapse cycle
10 Rejoins original path

Road back from death   * 3&4 Return to
                                the path

FIGURE 13.4 – CONSEQUENCES OF DEVIATION FROM A SPIRITUAL PATH

Were there any roadblocks to your attaining spirituality? If yes, how did you overcome them? If they are still there, do you have a plan? Has this book or chapter helped you overcome any of your spiritual resistance?

SUMMARY

The concept of spirituality can be a highly complex esoteric one in which one can become confused with dogma and rituals, or, it can be as simple as clearing the brain of all distractions and reconnecting with our innate ability to commune with God.

The process is simple if one is living a clean life, has resolved to a reasonable degree any previous confusion in his life, and knows himself somewhat. The process becomes complicated when one is disconnected from his feelings, has major unresolved issues, is practicing obsessive-compulsive behavior in any form including substance abuse, and has a psychiatric impairment that's ignored or not being treated effectively. All of these conditions are being reported — they are not a judgment. One does not connect with God when he has a high noise level in his head. It's just impossible to hear His guidance above the roar of the confusion.

In the peace and serenity of spirituality, one connects with his Higher Power or God through his feelings. Once felt, these feelings become the barometer, and determine the traveler's path in life. When the feelings are negative, he has strayed from his path. When they are positive, the reverse is true.

In order to maintain the connection, one has to be in harmony within his internal structure. If he has a fearful Child, a vengeful Adolescent, or an ineffective Adult who cannot maintain inner harmony, the connection is not made or is broken off easily. This book will help you to become congruent within yourself. It is the book's primary spiritual purpose.

Keeping peace and serenity in today's fast-paced world is difficult at best. One has to reassess his values in order to keep down the noise level in his head. Some reassess their priorities. Some make small changes to alter the focus of their energy. Some have to make massive changes in all areas of their lives. A warning to them - Do it one item at a time. Too much change, all at once, has the same impact as a busy life — there is too much going on to remain spiritually connected to God.

There are also roadblocks that one has to break and they include: lack of faith and trust, negative modeling, adverse experiences with religion, or no concept of a Higher Power or spirituality.

Spirituality is the connective tissue between humans' spiritual intentions and remaining on the road they choose to take in order to complete themselves. There are many diversions on this road and the majority usually manifest out of fear. In the deviation, one can momentarily lose his way, take a small side trip and wander back on course (experiment with other behavior), create a diversion and go through an addictive cycle that can include relapse, jail, institutions, or choose death itself by suicide or setting themselves up to die mentally, emotionally, or spiritually.

CASE STUDIES

The easiest way to demonstrate spirituality with a case study was to write about how each of our representative samples disconnected in adversity and reconnected later on in their lives through faith, hope and trust. It has a process to it, which I can briefly touch for illustrative purposes only.

The overall process for each case study was to reconnect with his Child (feelings), set healthy limits and boundaries on his Adolescent (stop reactive behavior) and at the same time, redirect its energy. Success occurs when the Adult changes *from* entering into problem loops, *to* harnessing the energy for the power to create adaptive solutions to life's uncertainties. This success empowers the Adult to maintain authority over its internal structure. The process allows the Adult to create internal harmony and thereby reduce the noise level to maintain God's guidance and direction in his life.

DARLENE — Disconnected twice from her Higher Power. First, when she was sexually abused as a child. Second, when she went into fear as her daughter approached the age Darlene was, when she was sexually abused. Each time, her dissociation from her feelings (The Child), was the cause of her break with God, when she couldn't transcend the pain from the memories of the abuse. In childhood, the dissociation was appropriate because she did not have safe enough parents to talk to, nor would they believe her story. Rather than chance the pain increasing from the potential invalidation — it was easier to "forget about it." The parents' unavailability doesn't have to be accurate, only that her child perceived it that way, and that's what Darlene did. The second hindrance came from the Adolescent as she became crazier and more obsessed over the baby's safety — in order to take the focus off her internal pain from the ascending memories of the abuse. The first intervention was to break the control of the Adolescent by having her agree that her mom was a safe person, and she could baby-sit while Darlene came into group. This was the beginning of setting adaptive boundaries and limits on her Adolescent without encountering resistance. The second intervention was to redirect her back into her feelings in order to sort out the present confusion. This was accomplished through several experiential interventions, which allowed her to expose the abuse, and process its carnage. After Darlene was finished, she was able to reconnect with her Higher Power because The Adolescent was no longer in charge and the noise level in her head was gone now that the abuse was no longer a secret.

JOAN — Disconnected three times from God. First, as she was shamed when her parents were too busy for her and she internalized it as her fault. The second, when she became over-involved in school activities and work, thereby ignoring the balance in her life. And the third, each time she entered a "Problem Loop" with a relationship drama. In group, Joan had to be reconnected with the Child and have her belief system changed. When she worked on her Adolescent, she had to reassess her value system. Both ego states had misconceptions. The Child thought she was a mistake and worthless. The Adolescent was under the assumption that the only worth Joan had was her ability to be successful at work. Joan completed several experiential interventions during which she: changed the belief system of the Child to one in which she was no longer a mistake and had a right to be here, and altered the value system of the Adolescent to include other areas of her life. As Joan completed her work in group, the effort she expended outside her work life, opened up her connection with her Higher Power.

BILL — Abandoned God: because of the trauma he continuously witnessed as a child when Dad was drunk and abused Mom; the sexual abuse he experienced at a young age, and questioning his sexuality when he experienced pleasure with his male perpetrator; on-going substance abuse from age 12; and the fear his wife's pregnancy raised because he didn't want his baby to experience the same kind of life he had. Bill's process of recovery followed the same course the introduction outlined: connection to his Child (feelings), boundaries to his Adolescent, and the exposure of the Problem Loops Bill manufactured to create an external diversion in order to avoid the feelings of his painful past. Bill also had three areas he had to work on: 1) what was done to him (abuse) and not done for him (no affirmations or validations), 2) what he did as a reaction to what had happened to him (substance abuse) and, 3) how he hurt others. Bill was able to incrementally re-engage with his Higher Power after The Problem Loops were ended; his reactions to what had happened to him were explored and resolved; and his relapse pattern was charted out. Bill had a large investment in his relapse cycle. In it, it made no difference if he was obsessing about using, not using, his last drug, his next drug, where he could procure it, where he couldn't get it; the operant word here is obsess — and obsess he did. Each time he began to obsess, he broke his connection to his Higher Power. It took a concentrated effort to disengage him from its paralysis, and the process was a backwards unfolding. Once the matrix was uncovered, Bill had a choice at the beginning of the loop whether to disconnect in fear, or maintain his communion with faith. Generally he chose faith.

JOHN — Disconnected various times with God, similar to Bill, only it usually happened on holidays and is where John had his greatest difficulties with his emotionally disengaged and critical parents. It occurred as the cultural message John was given about families being together and loving over the holidays did not come to fruition in his home. This perception of John's Child caused him to overeat, rebel to his parents' vocational plans for him, and become underemployed. As each of the above items occurred, he became preoccupied, reacted, and then broke his spiritual connection with God. John's inability to emotionally disengage from his family of origin became a trigger to his shame and his failure to act on his own behalf became his GATEWAY DRUG into depression and then food. Like Bill, John's Problem Loops and Gateway Drugs were identified, and new behavioral strategies were put in place in order to keep the internalized response from occurring. As he stopped his parents' encroachment, he became more solid within himself, began to explore further vocational possibilities, and changed his concept of how to have a good holiday. As the noise level in his head diminished, John was able to reconnect with God, each time he made a good decision for himself.

DENNIS — Continuously disconnected from God each time he experienced his parents' unavailability. During childhood he internalized their abandonment as shame. In adolescence he medicated it with substance abuse until he became sober in middle adulthood. Dennis reconnected to his Higher Power: First, through Alcoholics Anonymous when he became sober; and Second, in therapy after his relapse. In the AA program, he attended meetings, obtained a sponsor, studied the Steps, helped newcomers, and through the process gained back his spirituality. His first taste of it came when he walked into his first meeting, saw the peace and security the other members had, and wanted it. The second was the connectedness to others he felt when he went to meetings. The subsequent connections came each time he worked a Step into his life, helped a newcomer, volunteered for service work, and chose not to drink or use a mood-altering substance when his craving returned. In therapy, Dennis completed the previously described work in this section's introduction and personified his cravings, or, as self-help labels it, his disease. In the reframing we could concretely identify his initial cravings and relapse cycle, and then determine the triggers or the antecedents to the cravings. Once freed from the tyranny of not knowing his relapse cycle, we could devise interventions to: prevent the relapse by catching its process in its initial stages, and have alternative strategies to replace the toxic nature of the cycle. In this process, Dennis was able to reconnect or remain connected to God as soon as the negativity or fear was identified and he had a choice to continue or stop the behavior.

VALERIE — Disconnected from God when she first experienced the confusion, had a fear-based reaction (the Child), and then went into depression (the Adolescent). In group, she was able to connect with her Child and Adolescent and immediately went to work with them. In the process, she was able to soothe the Child's fear and redirect the Adolescent. Valerie had good ego strength and it was based on the pleasure and fulfillment she experienced being a wife and mom. She didn't know how to go forward in her life, without, what she thought, would be a loss, when she was no longer a full-time wife and mother — even though most of her children were launched and she was back into her career goals for the past five years. With therapy, Valerie was able to reconnect back to God quickly. It started when she mediated between her Child and Adolescent, made a decision to go through the fear and use her energy to launch her last child, renegotiate her relationship with her husband and to pursue her career goals. It increased when she reframed her marriage to a first career, that the experience of being a wife and mom was a wonderful reward for her dedication to her family, and that it was permanently hers. The total connection back to God came each time she completed her developmental tasks and moved on to her next role of being a successful business woman.

JOE — Like the others in the previous case studies, Joe disconnected from God when he entered his own self-centered fear of not being good enough. The fear manifested when he married an emotionally distant woman and had to suffer through the daily agony of not getting his needs met by her. The Problem Loop stopped when he recognized his reaction and began to work on the underlying issues. This was also his first spiritual awakening. Joe's spiritual connection to God was increased each time he took affirmative action on his part to get out of the Problem Loop and to stay in the Solution (God's plan for him). Review the case studies that included Joe to identify each segment of his process that allowed his communion with God to increase.

POLLY — Became jammed up internally and disconnected from God when her Child entered denial and she refused to acknowledge the present and future ramifications of her mom's death. These were occurring right in front of her eyes and she refused to believe that: her father had lost the desire to live, her sister had started to drink excessively, and her brother began having problems on his job. In group, Polly worked on her Child and Adolescent as she remained emotionally accessible to her feelings (the Child) and stopped the Adolescent from acting-in (being depressed) when she worked on the issues that maintained her depression. As she went through the Grief Process and resolved her mom's death - she had a spiritual awakening. In this spiritual awakening, Polly reconnected back to God and strengthened the attachment with each new awareness she experienced and change of behavior she accomplished.

BRENT AND SANDY — Had minimal disconnection because of the amount of time they had invested in self-help and therapy. All they needed was the developmental framework of my paradigm, attached to their self-help foundation, and practice. This they did eagerly because it was fun to them and filled in the blanks they had in their recovery. As the syntheses of both strategies (self help and therapy) were applied to their lives, they experienced an unbroken connection to their Higher Power, whom they chose to call God.

TANYA — Disconnected from God the moment she was gang-raped and no one was able to recognize it. She maintained the break by joining her abusers. At the time of the separation, her abusers represented God for they virtually had the power of life and death over her when her primary God (her mom) did nothing about the rape and subsequent coercion. The loss of her mom's power occurred even though she didn't have any awareness of the rape because the Child "perceived" the danger of disclosing and chose to keep it a secret in order to cut her losses. The Child's reality of her environment was an accurate one: once her mom had to work a different schedule and couldn't be around to protect her, she became a target for the gangs, and if she didn't capitulate to their demands, could have gotten both herself and her mom killed. Tanya was like other adolescents who came through treatment and had their first spiritual awakening when they disclosed the abuse. Their reconnection to God came as they pressed through the ramifications their lives had experienced due to the abuse; learned new self-awareness tools, stress-reducing skills, and developmental tasks; and were able to apply the new knowledge to keep them on track developmentally. The process allowed them to heal from their past wounds and to lay the foundation for an adaptive lifestyle, in order to discover and fulfill their spiritual plan.

MARY, CONSTANCE, AND STAN — All have the same story and very different endings. All of them spiritually disconnected from God due to the increasing noise level in their heads which had been generated by the critical nature of messages the culture gave them. The process created a "hole in their hearts" which characterized a flaw they experienced in themselves. The resulting internalization of the feeling, generated by the process, created a shame-based belief system that told them every time they made a mistake — THEY WERE THAT MISTAKE! It didn't make any difference if the messages they received were overt or covert, as the process was generally covert, for it was against the "highest law in the land" to think of your primary caregivers in anything but a positive light, to talk well of them, and to show the proper respect. THE PROCESS FOR ALL THREE WAS THE SAME: Learn and apply my model to their current depression; acknowledge the deficiencies of the culture they were raised in; take in the new Twenty First Century information based on The Human Potential Movement; identify the emotional losses they incurred in their childhood; and explore how their past impacted the way they raised their children. This was not an easy task for the seniors. Most did well. Some didn't. With most, the depression lifted, and *they were grateful to have new understanding about their prior life experiences which "didn't" invalidate their accomplishments.*

MARY — Was able to complete the work in order to connect with her Child and Adolescent, and through the process, to God. When she did the work, she was relieved, for she now had someone to blame for the feelings she experienced and didn't feel crazy anymore. Mary was given The Rules covertly in her upbringing: Don't Talk, Don't Trust, and Don't Feel! The *"Don't"* rules were instilled in her as her parents continuously repeated the following phrases: "You're not supposed to be scared! Only sissies are afraid!" and "Good girls don't get angry." As she listened to her parents' messages disallow the feelings she was experiencing — Mary's integrity was shattered, and she became confused. In therapy, she could now "blame" her Child for being scared and her Adolescent for being angry without losing the integrity of the Adult. This cognitive reframing by Mary was her first spiritual awakening. The next awareness's connected her head and her heart back to God completely when she identified: the problems she experienced due to her parents' imperfections, forgave them for their humanness, and simultaneously was able to receive the love intention of their messages; and the problems Mary's children experienced due to her imperfections, made her amends, and changed how she viewed and treated her grown children.

CONSTANCE — was not open-minded. She wouldn't explore her feelings (the Child), experienced increased symptoms (acting in), and had to be given additional medication (the Adolescent). She resisted every attempt to connect her back to her feelings, stating, "I already dealt with that and it's behind me!"

STAN — was the same way except he did his male thing, became aggressive and shut down. **BOTH** refused to do any family work, take in the new data, or follow their treatment plan. Both were discharged from the program. Both are dead today: One from an avoidable accident, the other in an operation that had no mortality rate to it. I don't judge their demise — I only report it. The medical or psychiatric conditions I target in this book – do kill. It's not always someone just learning how to stuff more unresolved grief inside them: when they are filled – something has to happen. Death is one of those happenings.

ACTION

HIDDEN FEARS
OVERCOME

One comes out
the other side of adversity-
into the light of God . . .
Freed from the bondage
of their past pain.

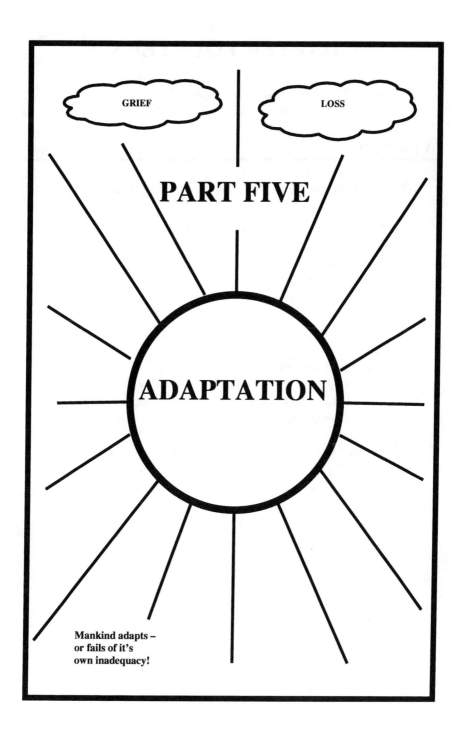

GRIEF

LOSS

PART FIVE

ADAPTATION

Mankind adapts –
or fails of it's
own inadequacy!

CHAPTER FOURTEEN

One is too many.
One thousand is not enough!

OVERVIEW

When you have completed this chapter, you will be able to:

1. Define addiction using three different criteria
    a)DSM-IV
    b)Twelve-step definition
    c)The author's model
2. Understand the author's Pain Management Model of addiction
    a)Recognize its structure
    b)Impact of the culture on the alcoholic/addict's Stress Management Style
    c)How shame underlies the alcoholic/addict's addiction cycle
    d)Visualize the cycle of addiction and identify its roots
3. Learn how to re-parent yourself and guide others by avoiding problem-oriented thinking and develop solution-oriented strategies
4. Learn how to effectively assess the addiction spiral
5. Develop effective strategies to combat addiction
6. Identify gateway drugs in self and others

ADDICTION

*The Cycle of addiction is the finest tool
to keep one separate from himself.*

This chapter will use a wide framework for the definition of addiction and will encompass *ANY PERSON, PLACE, or THING* that can be used in an *OBSESSIVE AND COMPULSIVE MANNER, IN WHICH THE RESULT-ING ACTION ALLOWS THE INDIVIDUAL TO FOCUS EXTERNALLY "INSTEAD" OF LOOKING AT HIMSELF!*

DEFINITION

DSM-IV

The DSM-IV changed its terminology in this edition and devised a more clinical definition of addiction. It now uses substance dependence and abuse. The substance abuse criteria are very liberal. If one attended Alcoholic's Anonymous (AA) meetings, was honest enough to share personal stories that identified him as a substance abuser, he would call himself an *alcoholic* and take a *white chip*! He would meet the current criteria of the DSM-IV for substance abuse.

The criteria for substance dependence states that one has to manifest three or more of the following symptoms during the past 12 months: tolerance, withdrawal, increased use, inability to decease use, preoccupation, and continued use when it exacerbates other conditions.

According to the author's model, either criterion would indicate addiction in the human being that was exhibiting behavior in the listed categories.

Twelve-Step Definition

It can be hard to come up with a simple definition because of the suspicion between the addicts (NA) and the alcoholics (AA). It's funny, because I see NA as the children, fighting the parent AA, when both of them are the same. In case anyone hasn't realized it, *ALCOHOL IS A DRUG*! It's a central nervous system (CNS) depressant. So, who were really the first addicts? You got it — THE ALCOHOLICS!

Oh sh—! There they go, up in arms, ready to lynch the author because he committed heresy. "Did anybody read that!" they yell. "He called us drunks — drug addicts! He doesn't know sh—." *Relax.* I know a lot. I just see it differently. If it wasn't for Bill Wilson, I would be dead today. He started something in 1935 that many of us have added onto today. I'm one of those people.

The student usually comes back and teaches the professor. If the instructor is wise, he will assimilate the new information and continue to become wiser. The trouble with some teachers is that they become stagnant and won't take in the new knowledge out of fear. Hopefully, the twelve-step programs will overcome that fear, too.

Using the above analogy, Bill Wilson saved my life because I was able to use the Program. Today, almost 20 years later, I could counsel Bill Wilson and make possible a quieting of his internal strife, which his writing and tapes indicate he carried until his death. Arrogance on my part? I think not. I've learned, grown, and like Bill, am giving it back through writing this book!

AA and NA are in the same boat: AA the teacher, NA the student. The student has to learn to bring back the knowledge. NA was sidetracked because AA became *"THEM,"* the people they hated the most. The ones they said they would never be like. *THEIR PARENTS*! The only thing that changed was their drug of choice. Instead of taking alcohol in liquid form — they take it in pill form.

AA is also out of the loop in this matter and became fragmented when they couldn't assimilate, through identification, the drug addict into AA. I really believe they couldn't hear the stories from their Children, because, most of the addicts were raised by alcoholics, gamblers, or Adult Children from Alcoholic Homes (ACOAs).

The void in the information proliferation that AA began in 1935 was later picked up in the '80's by the Adult Children and Co-Dependency movement. Out of it came the National Association of Adult Children of Alcoholics, the ACA and Co-Dependents Anonymous (CoDa) twelve-step programs and ACOA-focused Al-Anon meetings.

I had the privilege of being involved with the Program as the first ACA and Al-Anon ACOA meetings began in Massachusetts and started the first Al-Anon Adult Children Step meeting. It was the first time that "Adult Children" could talk in safety about what went on and how they were affected by their alcoholic home. Meeting after meeting, the "secrets" came out, those who attended regularly no longer felt alone or crazy. They began to understand their present unwanted behavior and started to acquire choices. An additional phenomenon began to occur. People who attended our meetings by "accident" or were "referred" by friends, could identify with us, even though they were not raised in an alcoholic home. They recognized being raised in drug addiction, overeating, gambling, mental illness, adoption, some kind of parental fear, or a strict religious background, created the same syndrome as being raised in alcoholism.

It was there I saw the common bond between people who were raised in a non-child-centered home. The solution is what this book is all about — to help those to heal — who were wounded, inadvertently, by less than adequate caregivers, or, a culture that didn't realize the importance of a home being child-centered. Either voluntarily or by lack of design, the damage is inflicted. *No blame — just the facts.* This book is a derivative of The Adult Children Movement. The systems in the book are mine. The concepts my systems were generated by are from: the greatest thinkers over time, the fathers of the premises we use in psychology today, and all those who added to their original works. *MY CONTRIBUTION IS A FOURTH-LEVEL ADDITION.* Those who build on my work will be a fifth level. If I pay attention — they (the students) — will come back and teach me through their works.

Why the entire hullabaloo over what seems to be a philosophical difference of, "you say tomato and I say tomotto"? It's important! The third millennium is here. Many systems are becoming synthesized for the sake of clarity. We have much distillation occurring and out of it will arrive more effective strategies to help dysfunctional people. Nobody has to disband any twelve-step program. All, plus more, are needed! I just want fellow travelers to recognize the common similarities, in order to enhance assimilation of excellent help being given in a twelve-step meeting.

Program definition is simple and encompassing. It states: it's a disease; affects one mentally, physically and spiritually; is chronic, progressive, and can only be arrested "a day at a time" through the support of the program and the study and application of the twelve steps to one's life. The only difference which occurs is the focus of the disease (alcohol, drugs, gambling, food, sex, work, etc) in the various twelve-step programs. The addiction is the same. The process is the same. Take only one of your drugs of choice, the addiction cycle is put in motion, and doesn't stop until one abstains, or becomes incarcerated, institutionalized, or dead. *ONE CANNOT DO HIS DRUG OF CHOICE IN SAFETY.* This means he can't guarantee the outcome of his behavior when he starts to use any person, place, or thing (alcohol, drugs, sex, food, gambling, etc) in an obsessive or compulsive manner.

Author's Definition

This book uses a Pain Management Model to define addiction. In its process, one creates a diversion to mask or block rising emotional pain from surfacing. This pain originates from a past-traumatic memory buried deep in the human being's subconscious, and is resurrected when something, similar to the original event, occurs today. We call the present event a trigger because it sets the past pain in motion just like the trigger on a gun fires a bullet. The behavioral set that goes into motion — to dissipate the energy raised by the emerging pain — is the catalyst for addiction. In it, patterns of obsessive and compulsive behaviors are repeated, until the psychic energy of the triggered pain has run its course and no longer are a threat to the individual's current integrity.

The "action" generated by the behavior (drinking, drugging, overeating, overachieving, compulsive gambling, smoking, promiscuity, criminality, overworking, some mental illness) is a subterfuge to keep the individual focused *externally* on his behavior instead of "keeping the focus on himself" and looking *internally* to discover what the released pain is attached to. *The cycle created to dance around the problem and repeated each time it tries to surface — IS CALLED ADDICTION!* The length of the cycle created includes all the rituals to bring on the behavior, maintain it, and then clean up the carnage left in its wake.

THE CYCLE OF ADDICTION

Addiction has a complete cycle. In its spiral, an event occurs in the addict/alcoholic's life, his thinking becomes distorted when a past traumatic memory is triggered by the current event and the cycle begins. As his negative thinking increases, he begins to BUD (Build Up to a Drink). AA calls this "stinkin' thinkin'." The family knows "the look" all too well and can tell you almost to the day when he is going to drink. No matter how the drinking, drugging, bingeing, running, or relationship began, it usually ends up in a downward spiral.

Life becomes unmanageable during the time one becomes active in his disease because work, family, self, friends, God, and community take a back seat or are ignored entirely. This chapter will study the cycle, define its origins, assess its impact, and look at two effective strategies to combat it.

What Does It Look Like

The process of addiction is a simple one. A trigger in the environment (sight, sound, taste, smell, touch), mimics a past occurrence and releases its stored memory from the subconscious. The memory is usually a past traumatic event that's been suppressed by the psyche because it was too overwhelming at the time. These memories fall into three categories:

1. **What was done to them (mental, physical and/or sexual abuse).**
2. **What was not done for them (being affirmed or validated in a child-centered home).**
3. **What they did as a reaction to one and two (hurt themselves and others).**

As the trigger releases the impacted grief from the subconscious, the pain rises to the preconscious and begins a process that transforms the emotional pain into a behavioral response. This covert system was specifically developed as a subterfuge to mask the pain in order to prevent an immature human being from becoming overwhelmed. This method, at the point of conception, was not developed to cover an innate maturation problem. The strategy was spawned to enable the emotionally inexperienced child to shut down, stuff, and deny his feelings, as they were being heightened in the warlike environment of a dysfunctional home or by a traumatic event. *Remember, children are not combat soldiers, and were not designed physically, emotionally, spiritually, or cognitively to facilitate the stress that is generated in a toxic home*!

During the pain's climb through the Preconscious, the intense feelings are transformed into a behavioral response which occurs just prior to their entrance into the conscious and manifests in the *external* world as active addiction or *internal* as self-destructive behavior with depression, a suicide attempt, or self-mutilation.

There is a whole process that can be observed and worked with. During this time, if there is no insight or knowledge gained about his motives to mask his pain, the addictive behavior begins to manifest as the abuser starts to use his reactionary behavior to take the focus off his pain. Some of these devices are alcohol, drugs, food, gambling, sex, work, nicotine, relationships, or any behavior or thing that can be sustained in an obsessive and compulsive way.

Once the addict uses, the downward cycle begins, until he hits bottom. During the roller-coaster ride down, self, family, work, God, and community all take a second seat to his addiction. This is the first half of the cycle

— it takes him to the termination point of active using. The second half of the circle takes him back to the point of origin "before" he began active use. Pay strict attention to this segment of the cycle. It's no different from the first because the addict is still crazy. The only element that's been changed is his cleaning up instead of tearing down. "This is positive" you ask, "and seem to be because it's a forward momentum? Is it? The answer is yes *IF* one learns from the circumstances of his dysfunctional using. If he continues to relapse, the answer is no and the cleaning up is just as important to look at as the actual using was.

The cycle is complete when the carnage from the relapse has been cleaned up. The addict is now exactly where he was before he began to relapse. This is a complete circle, and all he has done is to catch up with himself just prior to his relapse. What a scary thought. Does this mean he will relapse again? *"YES,"* if he doesn't have a program to arrest his addiction "one day at a time" or insight into the antecedents to his relapse. In fact, if the same set of circumstances which were occurring before the relapse occurred again, he would relapse again! *THERE IS NO CHOICE! IF A NEW STRATEGY IS NOT DEVISED, THE OLD BEHAVIOR WILL PREVAIL — "BECAUSE IT WORKS!"* This is basic relapse prevention. Terri Gorski has a library on it. Do some additional reading. Figure 14.1 is a graphic representation of the cycle.

This cycle will continue to go round and round, through relapse to clean time, and back to relapse. Over and over, ad nauseam, until the compulsion is arrested "one day at a time" in a twelve-step program, he gets therapy, or becomes institutionalized, incarcerated, or dead. *THERE ARE ONLY TWO CHOICES — LIVE OR DIE!* People do die. Some can't make it. It's a fact. It sucks — but true! Relapse will be addressed later on in this chapter.

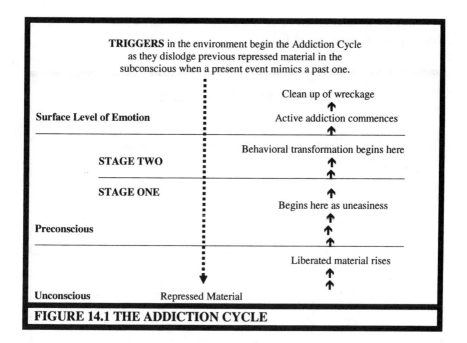

FIGURE 14.1 THE ADDICTION CYCLE

Where Does It Come From

The addiction cycle begins in childhood via experiencing a war zone when raised in a toxic family. This environment produces low self-esteem, a poor self-image, and emotional immaturity. The process occurs because the child had to shut down, stuff, deny, or dissociate from his pain while he was being mentally, emotionally, physically, or sexually abused. Its payoff to the Child is life, for to feel the pain of the abuse to an emotionally inexperienced youngster, is tantamount to a death sentence.

The second half of the cycle is derived from experimental behavior, which through trial and error during adolescence, the apprentice at life, tries various strategies in order to mask his past pain. This is where the victim becomes the perpetrator as he continues in toxic behavior in spite of the negative consequences to himself.

This concept is difficult to admit, for the adult has spent so much time trying not to be like them, he didn't realize that the opposite to sick is still sick, and it's in the middle that healthy balance prevails. What we observe in acting-out behavior is usually extreme — too far left or right. Any reaction to the offending behavior is extreme as well. A definitive example occurs as a person raised by an alcoholic, says I don't want to be one and becomes a drug addict (because it's not alcohol), instead of not using any mood-altering substances or only using in moderation. Figure 14.2 is an illustration of being out of balance.

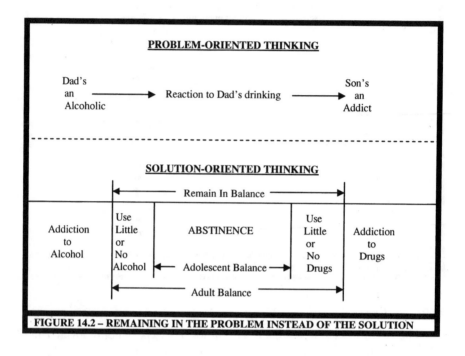

FIGURE 14.2 – REMAINING IN THE PROBLEM INSTEAD OF THE SOLUTION

This behavior is fine-tuned throughout adolescence and early adulthood. During these periods, the developing addict learns and reinforces the best ways to mask his pain. It is during this period the user crosses over some unknown bridge and loses the ability to predict the outcome of any using episode. At this point, he becomes an addict and rarely can he use again in safety. All of you, who think you can use recreational drugs or alcohol without consequences, need to attend AA or NA to hear what has happened to others who tried to control the mood-altering substances they placed in their bodies.

Those who are "normal" drinkers can drink or not, not think about the next time they will drink, or care if they do. Nor will they let alcohol change their lives, cause them physical problems, have personality changes, lose jobs, or allow it to interfere with any part of their lives with family, friends, self, God, or society. Can any of you "controlled drinkers" out there make the same statement, continuously, throughout your life span?

PAIN MANAGEMENT MODEL

The previous described addiction etiology spawns a model to examine, study, and treat addiction to anything! It's called a Pain Management Model, and except for the five percent of addicts/alcoholics that seem to indicate a genetic predisposition to addiction, the balance fit into my paradigm significantly.

It doesn't make any difference if we follow a socioeconomic, family, or psycho-dynamic model. All have one thing in common — THEY ARE INSUFFICIENT TO THE EVOLVING HUMAN'S NEEDS AND THEIR INADEQUACY DEPOSITS PAIN IN THE GROWING ORGANISMS' PSYCHE BECAUSE OF IT! This pain has to be ameliorated somehow. When it's too great for the developing person's stress management system — addiction becomes the strategy of the hour. In it, a person can survive until he develops the skills needed to facilitate the stress in an adaptive manner. Pain management, through addictions, assures the continuation of the person's life. Without it, he feels death is imminent.

Structure

The structure of the Pain Management Model is graphically described in Figure 14.1 — the Addiction Cycle. In it, a past painful trauma is triggered by a present event. While this overwhelming memory rises through the three-stage process of the psyche, it is transformed from emotions into a behavioral set. This allows the energy raised from the repressed event to vent externally without addressing the episode itself.

SHAME Shame is the energy that drives the system. It is shame's attachment to an event that makes the event so profound. When this reaction occurs, it's usually provoked by the feelings of not being protected or cared for as a child by his primary caregivers and what he had to do as an adolescent or a young adult to facilitate his misunderstood childhood feelings.

Childhood shame is too overwhelming and when it's triggered, is tantamount to being attacked and overrun by enemy forces. This particular adversary is called emotional immaturity. In it, one lacks the skills to successfully negotiate the episode which unleashed the feelings, or, the suppressed material attached to it. The trauma can be overcome in therapy and based on its severity, in a twelve-step program by identifying the antecedents, separating the past event from the present situation, and teaching new adaptive strategies. The process is learned and reinforced when self-help members study and apply the principles of The Twelve Steps to their daily living.

Culture

The culture plays a major role in the addiction cycle because of the shameful ways it portrays how feelings and painful events are supposed to be "taken care" of. "Put it behind you," it says. "Just get over it!" it exclaims. "Is that still bothering you?" it asks, several days after a significant death occurs. The message given to the grieving human being is: *there is something wrong with your feelings because they don't agree with the predominant culture! This is further compounded when the individual tries to change the feelings in order to be harmonious with the culture, can't, and then thinks there is something wrong with him that can't be fixed.* This invalidation of the "*HUMAN FEELINGS*" the bereaved feels after a significant death begins the roller-coaster ride down into the depths of shame, causing major depression or massive anxiety.

This highly toxic strategy evolved out of a culture that was clueless when it came to personal feelings. And, until the later half of The Twentieth Century, notably "The Sixties" with the advent of the encounter groups, feelings and emotions were mostly minimized, stuffed, denied, repressed or suppressed. This is a successful strategy for a survival skill. I personally feel, if you don't know what to do with feelings, then, leave them alone. That's what the culture did and I applaud them for it. It would have been dangerous, inappropriate, and cruel, to open up something that couldn't be closed.

PROBLEM-ORIENTED THINKING   In order to perpetuate the culture's inability to handle feelings, citizens of the planet Earth devised an amazing strategy. They put their focus on external persons, places, and things and stopped looking at themselves (if they ever had the ability). They then developed problem-oriented thinking, in which they enumerated the problem over and over in their heads, in order to remain out of their feelings.

There is a slight sarcasm in my description because I've seen the devastation this system has heaped upon my and other generations. At the same time, I am in awe of how a collective unconscious could have generated such an effective strategy on an evolutionary scale. My hat is off to them!

SOLUTION-ORIENTED THINKING   Today, thanks to therapy and recovery, people are changing. No longer are they hooked onto the old belief systems of staying in the problem and being "other directed." Instead, they are coming into solution-oriented thinking — a place where the problem no longer dominates the human cognitive process — with an internally-motivated, adaptive, creative, effective, and functional decision-making process to guide them. This is the goal of today's focus.

RE-PARENTING   Reframing the human cognitive system to solution-oriented thinking is accomplished by the individual reparenting himself. In the process, he gains skills and tools his parents were not capable of giving because they were too busy surviving, were never given the skills by their parents, and the culture did not reinforce these parenting values. This book, other readings, education, twelve-step programs, rising spirituality, and therapy are some of the ways one learns to re-parent himself.

The framework of this book teaches you how to get in touch with your inner self. Through the internal dialogue that prevails within the human's cognitive structure, he is able to identify his Inner Child (feelings), Adolescent (energy), and Adult (intellect or executive system). Once this is accomplished, the human being can better identify his wants, needs, and desires, and fulfill them himself. This was seldom taught in a home that wasn't child centered. Remember, everyone did the best they could with what they had. It doesn't mean one has to remain victim to deficient parenting skills. It means to acknowledge it and move on by taking care of your own needs instead of waiting for someone to fill them who are emotionally unavailable or ill equipped. Transcending the losses is good parenting skills. You wouldn't let a little child remain in a painful place. You would try to talk to him and help him out of it. Do this for yourself.

PHILOSOPHY   Study this book. It's not all psychology and science. It has a psychological base which includes philosophy and spirituality. It's philosophical in nature because we have to see where we have been to know where we are. Read the eleven volume set of "The Story of Civilization," by Will and Ariel Durant (1935/1963), to get a feel of where we come from. Many years ago, the supermarket had a "History of Western Civilization" set that I purchased for my children. This was an excellent beginning. Anything that helps to give you a feel for your cultural heritage will help.

SPIRITUALITY Connecting to a Higher Power or God is the final element that completes my system. Without it, people are seldom connected internally because of all the outside distractions that break their focus. Spirituality is really a *"sustained connection"* to the outside source of energy one plugs into to keep himself on his life path. This tenet is a major premise of my book, and without it, one cannot maintain the effort it takes to remain internally focused. Figure 14.3 is a graphic depiction of the connection.

In Figure 14.3, spirituality is the connective tissue between the head and the heart. Behavioral choices come out of this process when both are connected because thoughts and feelings, *AND THE BEHAVIOR WHICH IS DEPENDENT ON THEM — ARE CONGRUENT!* James Redfield's, "The Tenth Insight, Holding the Vision" (1996), gives you a good framework of how a spiritual culture functions, what religion tried to do with it, how the culture feared it, and the internal strife that occurs within the human being because of a lack of understanding it. A deeper understanding of oneself lowers the fear level in any new concept. When one is solid within himself, he usually has a good spiritual connection to his Higher Power and is less fearful of change.

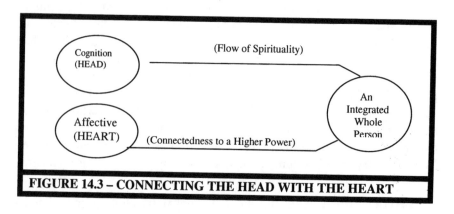

FIGURE 14.3 – CONNECTING THE HEAD WITH THE HEART

ASSESSMENT OF
THE ADDICTION'S SPIRAL

This segment is not meant to be a definitive assessment instrument. Its only intention is to give you some overall indicators as to the degree of use and the depth of the damage it has done to the addict and his family.

Degree of Use

The amount of mood-altering substances and the degree of addiction a user has can be directly correlated to the amount of help needed to maintain abstinence. The following five strategies are ranked in degree of difficulty, and their corresponding substance use is listed beside them in Figure 14.4.

ABSTINENT STRATEGY	DEGREE OF USE & POSSIBLE ISSUE		
(1) Give it up alone	Probable Misuse	–	Used for stress reduction
(2) Stop with some help	Substance abuse	–	Stress-clouded judgment
(3) Abstain through AA	Substance dependence	–	Can't use in safety
(4) First time in treatment	Chronic abuse cycle	–	Has lost any control
(5) Multiple treatments	Maintenance user	–	Heavy duty issues
	Chronic relapse cycle	–	Possible severe abuse:
			Mental, physical, or sexual

FIGURE 14.4 – SUBSTANCE ABUSE INDICATORS

Depth of Damage Done

The depth of the damage done to the substance abuser can be determined using several indicators:

1. **AA Twenty Questions**
2. **DSM-IV** list of symptoms for substance abuse and dependence
   a) The more questions answered yes to and the greater amount of the symptoms displayed, indicates a higher degree of damage
3. **Family**
   a) The greater the distancing by the family, would indicate the larger amount of damage done to it by the addict's using
   b) The DSM-IV lists family and social disengagement by the user. You can extrapolate the amount of carnage by looking at the family losses in the list of symptoms for substance abuse and dependence, and conclude that all disengagement by the user (social, vocational, interpersonal, and intra-personal) directly impacts the family, and causes greater losses and indicates deeper issues.

EFFECTIVE STRATEGIES
TO COMBAT ADDICTION

There are three effective strategies designed to bring addiction into remission. They are:

1. **Therapy**
2. **Twelve-Step Programs**
3. **Relapse Prevention Training**

The first two are designed to help the abuser who no longer wants to be dominated by a mood-altering substance and is unable to practice abstinence. They also help the abuser to identify the antecedents to his dependence and develop more adaptive strategies for stress reduction. Therapy employs clinical interventions from trained professionals, designed to elicit specific responses. A twelve-step program utilizes study of the twelve steps and shared experience of other program members to accomplish the same goal. A word of caution: with deep issues such as sexual abuse, incest, ritual abuse, extreme deprivation, suicide attempts, co-morbidity of mental illness, and continued substance abuse even in the face of physical ramifications, social isolation, and vocational losses, therapy would be the treatment of choice because a twelve-step program is not designed to handle these issues. In fact, under some conditions, invalidation may exacerbate the symptoms unless one is given training on how to deal with others and depersonalize any issues that surface while at a meeting because of it.

Relapse prevention training starts the first day of abstinence. It begins when the abuser first enters treatment for help and can be applied continuously throughout his recovery. It's also employed after a relapse, to identify the antecedents and prepare the addict/alcoholic not to repeat the same mistakes over and over, when he thinks things will be different, if he just gets it right this time.

GATEWAY DRUGS

Gateway drugs can be "*ANYTHING*" that begins the addiction cycle. The obvious ones are when the drug addict drinks, the alcoholic uses drugs, or the gambler uses a mood-altering substance and then places the first bet. All three items begin the abuser's downward spiral into the next episode. The more subtle ones are hard to identify. They are the ones that proceed the:

- Overeater's binge
- Relationship junkie's next encounter
- Sex addicts next affair
- Career criminal's next crime
- Overachiever's next goal
- Underachiever's next cycle of deprivation
- Chronic depressive's next tailspin
- Next panic attack
- Rage addicts next episode

And, so it goes, on and on, ad nauseam — until any person, place, or thing, used in an obsessive/compulsive behavioral sequence, can be listed as a drug-of-choice. If we explore the above categories, we will observe an immature adult, attempting to facilitate uncomfortable feelings, using problematic and maladaptive strategies in a dysfunctional way. Instead of going through the feelings, he is attempting to divert them through another person, place, or thing. These are powerful strategies that accomplish their primary goal, which takes the focus off him to avoid his internal discomfort and places it external when they become fixated on something outside him. This strategy is directed by the Adolescent Ego State.

Shame as a Gateway Drug

Shame is the primary mechanism that begins an addiction episode. It's not the feeling itself that starts the use — it's the process that occurs and leads up to the feeling — that causes the cycle.

The drug addict drinking, and then "picking up," is understandable, with alcohol lowering inhibitions and impeding judgment. The alcoholic falls into the same trap when using drugs by ingesting ETOH in a solid form. Alcohol is a drug. It's a Central Nervous System (CNS) depressant. It doesn't matter if used in liquid or pills — the impact is the same, and so are its consequences.

With "*other*" addictions, the behavior preceding the feelings of shame becomes the gateway drug. Some may want to call it the gateway or activating event. It's not the event that causes the shame: it's the repetitive nature of the cycle, which encompasses an event that precipitates and actuates the shame. The following case studies will illustrate its pathways.

CASE STUDY: John's (our computer programmer) episodes with his overeating are good examples of how the repetitive pattern of his self-defeating behavior invokes the feelings of shame. At this juncture, the shame arises from his inability to emotionally take care of himself. The process occurs when stress increases on the job, his parents visit, or during the holidays.

The immaturity manifests when his parents visit and he doesn't set limits on their stay, or boundaries on their attitude toward him. John's dad is usually "disappointed" in his son because he didn't follow in his foot-steps and become a lawyer. John's mom is no different when it comes to his friends and associates. They are usually "judged" as "not being our type of people." No matter what type of friends he had over the years, John reported, "My mother was never happy with my choices." John has been living on his own for several years and wonders when he will "cut the apron strings."

John's Gateway Drug.   Emotionally, John is still tied to his family of origin. Even though he was physically launched several years ago, his emotions are enmeshed with his parents' feelings. During his parents' vis-its, John continues to subjugate his feelings to their whims, his shame is activated, and he overeats. It's the repetitiveness of the episode that galva-nizes the shame, when John doesn't intervene on his own behalf by either; mediating it *internally* and not "buying into the lie" as when his parents disapprove of his vocational and interpersonal choices, or, *externally* when he doesn't set boundaries and limits on them. *JOHN'S FAILURE TO ACT ON HIS OWN BEHALF IS HIS GATEWAY DRUG!* To begin the change, John had to:

First —   Own the enmeshment and commit to working on changing

Second —   Follow through with the results of his work

Third —   Explore less problematic strategies when he was over-whelmed by his parents

We also took the results of his work and applied it to the conflict he had with authority figures and the mixed feelings he had over the holiday season at Christmas.

In the first stage of therapy John cried profusely over the losses in his childhood, discovered how his reaction (eating) caused its own set of losses, and for the things that may never materialize in his relationship with his parents. During this time, John had to maintain good boundaries with his parents or his work would have been sabotaged.

During the second stage, John's deficits were re-framed into assets and used for a foundation in the esteem-building process. John was amazed during this period because he always considered himself a coward for not taking any action. He never knew that inaction was the appropriate response in situations when one is powerless. Some actions can be dangerous to the psyche if they are not equal to ones level of maturity.

At the third stage, John worked long and hard. There were several impasses that he had to work through to keep his forward momentum going. It seemed each time he made progress in developing new skills; he would begin to sabotage it, and had to work diligently in order to stop the self-defeating behavior. During this final stage of the process, John could clearly see how his inaction became his gateway drug, and took the final steps to changing it.

ASSIGNMENT 17: What does addiction mean to you? If someone you know has a mood change when he uses alcohol or drugs, and continues to use in spite of this adverse condition — do you consider this abuse or dependence? How about you — if you do the same? How do you handle emotional pain? How do your spouse, significant other, and children handle it? How did your parents handle it? These are some sensitive areas — "*PLEASE*" be gentle with yourself and your family. Do you recognize the cycle of addiction in anyone? Yourself? Did you recognize your parents' problem-oriented thinking process? Your own? What do you do when you have mixed feelings over an issue: As described in the chapter as a spiritual battle when your head (thoughts) tells you to do one thing and your heart (feelings) tells you another? Does the conflict raise the noise level in your head and keep you ill at ease with yourself, others, and God? What can you do in each case, with 1) yourself, 2) others, and 3) God, to quiet the internal noise and reconnect with each? Tough questions! You may not have the answers. That's alright. At this point you have the question, an understanding of the process, and hope. The answers will mostly reveal themselves throughout the rest of the book if you are ready and want them. Whatever the outcome, the seeds have been planted.

SUMMARY

There are numerous definitions of addiction. Included in them is the DSM-IV interpretation where addiction is categorized into two headings — abuse and dependence. Both categories have their own criteria and the results of the assessment are clinical in nature.

Another explanation for addiction comes from the Twelve-Step Program of Alcoholics' Anonymous which states that alcoholism is a disease, is chronic and progressive, never abates, and an alcoholic only gets a daily reprieve if he goes to meetings, studies the steps, and helps newcomers. The program contends that one cannot drink in safety because he can't predict what will happen after he takes his first drink. A program adage is: "the man takes a drink — the drink takes the man!"

The author uses a Pain Management Model to define addiction. In its matrix is a definitive process that allowed the psyche to avoid feeling great emotional pain by transforming the pain's energy into a behavioral response. Addiction began when the behavioral response became the internalized reaction to the stress and no other choices were considered possible by the overwhelmed individual.

Shame is usually the activating feeling of the addiction cycle. In it, a trigger in the environment releases the memories from the subconscious of a past event that was unresolved and suppressed. As the feelings from the buried trauma begin to surface, they become inundated by additional feelings of shame that were attached to the event when the victim's primary caregivers did not protect him.

The basis for the feelings of shame was spawned in childhood as the child internalized his lack of protection as "something wrong with him or it wouldn't be happening." The behavioral response was generated in adolescence when the developing Child was no longer able to handle the feelings internally and had to use an external process to dissipate the energy generated by the rising feelings.

The culture played a dominant role in the development of a Pain Management Strategy because it lacked the expertise to effectively deal with feelings until the Human Potential Movement of "The Sixties" opened feelings and emotions up to scrutiny and process. One of the culture's greatest strategies was to blow up insignificant events into major issues, by utilizing their energy to enumerate a small problem over and over in order to avoid the painful feelings of traumatic events. The process allowed them to stay in their head and avoid their feelings.

Alternatives to the maladaptive coping strategies can be found in the re-parenting process as the individual begins to restructure his cognitive process and uses solution-oriented thinking. In this process, he develops living skills designed to create adaptive solutions to life's problems instead of continuing the old survival skills that were designed to avoid feeling the impact of the problems. A by-product of the process is that the evolving human no longer remains developmentally stuck and self-actualizes.

Addiction also cuts the person's connection with himself, others, and God. When he is in his addictive cycle, the noise level is so high in his head that any communion with God or a Higher Power is impossible. Within this mental gymnastics lies a spiritual battle: *Good* (maintaining his spiritual path) against *evil* (succumbing to self-centered fear.) In the process, the head disconnects from the heart, enters a problem loop that generates the addiction cycle, instead of remaining connected to the heart that wants to find an adaptive solution to the current crisis in order to remain connected to himself, others, and God.

Accessing the addiction's spiral will allow one to determine to what degree of using mood-altering substances the dependent person regressed to by identifying the effort it takes to stop using and the damage done to family relationships while the substance abuse was occurring.

There are three effective strategies designed to bring addiction into remission, work on the underlying issues, and prevent them from returning: with therapy, twelve-step program participation, and relapse prevention training. During these three modalities, one will learn: what his triggers are, how his using cycle operates, when to intervene in the process, new stress-reducing skills, gain a new perspective on life through the twelve-step process, increase his self awareness, enhance his relationships with self, others and God, and identify his relapse process.

In the relapse process, one can identify his "Gateway Drugs." This is the drug, action, or circumstance that will begin his relapse cycle. The underlying feeling when a person experiences his "Gateway Drug" is shame. It is usually raised by the Child when the Adult fails to protect him and goes off on another obsessive and compulsive binge because this is not the action of a responsible adult. In the process the Child gets abused by the Adult's behavior when he internalizes the Adult's behavior as "something being wrong with him that can't be fixed" because he didn't receive adequate protection from the Adult.

CASE STUDY

Dennis is a 45-year-old married alcoholic with three children who re-lapsed after five years of sobriety. Prior to the relapse, Dennis thought he had enough time in the program and had his "drinking problem" under control. When questioned about why he drank, Dennis exclaims that he doesn't know why and reports that nothing major was going on in his life at the time that would "make him drink." He just remembers thinking that "maybe" he could do some controlled drinking, even though a "little voice" kept warning him against it. His next memory is waking up in detox and being told that he was brought there by someone from AA because he was coming off a bender and they were afraid he would go into the DT's.

Dennis was in detox for three days before he came to group. When questioned about the antecedents to the relapse, it was clear that Dennis only possessed marginal self awareness, had minimal stress management skills other than the basic tools of the program, had not identified his core issues, and did not recognize his cycle of addiction. It was also clear that Dennis had his reservations about alcoholism being a disease, which left a lurking reservation that "maybe," somewhere down the road, he would be able to drink responsibly again.

The first treatment goal for Dennis was to identify his cycle of using. This was done in two stages: the first through traditional group therapy in probing the timeframe prior to the relapse to gain a degree of personal insight and possible environmental triggers into the relapse's antecedents; and second, to take the results of the probing and use the information to personify Dennis' cycle of addiction in psychodrama.

It was in psychodrama that Dennis was introduced to his Adolescent when he materialized out of the work we were doing with his addiction cycle. Dennis was startled, called it his "Dark Side," an evil twin, and wanted it to go away. The Adolescent held his ground and declared that he would destroy Dennis if he didn't listen to him. This confrontation by the Adolescent to Dennis' Adult had a profound impact on him and opened up a whole new level of awareness.

This unfolding was the real goal that was intended for Dennis. If I had tried to impart the awareness directly, he would have shut down (Child), or become "resistant" (Adolescent). These actions would have been his boundaries, protecting his internal integrity from new information that would overwhelm his present emotional coping strategies. When it un-folds naturally — it just happens. This is the main reason I don't try to break through a person's denial. The goal is to teach the skills they need to facilitate the potential emotional pain from the suppressed trauma. Teaching precedes the emerging awareness, before they are cognizant of it, in order to prevent resistance in treatment.

At this point in therapy, Denis had five years of AA that I could build upon. I also knew he had an angry Adolescent inside that was tired of carrying the Adult Dennis because the Adult lacked self awareness of his disease of alcoholism and the personal etiology of his addiction. All of this would be realized latter. Right now he was clueless.

My therapeutic strategy was not to go against the Adolescent prematurely, bond with him through validation (stating the disease is a survival skill), and maintain appropriate boundaries. I even openly talk to that part as Neurolinguistic Programming (NLP), (Bandler & Grinder, 1979) suggests doing.

In the first phase of therapy, I address it through: talking about respecting boundaries, informed consent about my counseling style, and validating behavior as a survival skill. This acknowledgement also reduces resistance because of the stigma attached to addictive behavior. The reframing transforms addiction into a choice, and they now can take responsibility for the behavior because it can be changed. When addiction is looked at as a moral issue (you should know better), great shame is attached to it, it's difficult to own the behavior, and a natural resistance occurs.

In the second phase of therapy, I directly address the Adolescent in any issue. I never go through the Adult unless I am attempting skill-building parental tasks by instructing him on how to set some boundaries and limits on the Adolescent. It's the maturity level of the Adult that has to perform the task — not the therapist, sponsor, spouse, or friend. There are limits to applying even the most profound knowledge. This book has those same limits.

Dennis was now open to his cycle of addiction, the Problem Loop it created, and was ready to look at why he was addicted to alcohol.

During the first phase of therapy, Dennis was given significant information about the Pain Management Model of addiction. It was taught through lectures and enhanced experientially through psychodrama as he watched other group members work in group. When he was working on his cycle and the problem loops created, he was introduced to the other parts of his internal structure: the first was the Critical Adult who had a negative comment about everything he said or did; the second was the

Child who bruised easily, experienced shame in the bruising, and then shut down. At this point the Nurturing Adult was barely noticeable.

When Dennis was able to feel the pain of his Child, identify the shame that followed the pain when it was unattended to by his Adult, he could then tie The Pain Management principles into his observation, and became aware how he drank to hide from the emotional pain that overwhelmed him. As we explored Dennis' present situation for triggers to past unresolved trauma, he discovered that his oldest son was the same age as he was, when he started drinking and having the most problems with his father's alcoholic behavior. This was a painful period of Dennis' life and took a lot of work in therapy to clean it up.

As Dennis completed the work of identifying his core issues, going through his past unresolved pain in group, and gathering new intra-personal skills — the Nurturing Adult began to materialize. It was at this point that Dennis recognized how he relapsed and was able to develop a strategy to avoid another relapse "A day at a time." *At this point he no longer had a need to mask his unresolved past pain with mood-altering substances; was on his way to becoming an emotionally-mature responsible adult who could experience the daily problems of living without using a mood-altering substance to deflect the emotions of the situation; and could develop creative solutions to transcend an encounter with a painful situation or memory.*

Dennis was fun to work with. He had a good foundation from Alcoholics' Anonymous that could be used as a new design for living — living free from the bondage of substance abuse and dependence. What he lacked was the ability to transcend his internal pain from a dysfunctional childhood when he couldn't identify his core issues using just the program. In therapy, Dennis was able to gain the intra-personal skills it took to open up and resolve the issues; the program of Alcoholics Anonymous was not designed to do. Today, free from the tyranny of the past pain, Dennis is able "a day at a time" to apply all the tools of the program to remain clean and sober.

CHAPTER FIFTEEN

Psychotherapy is the key to
Unlocking the secrets
That maintain a human being's
Bondage to his past trauma!

OVERVIEW

At the end of Chapter Fifteen, you will have a psycho-dynamic/developmental counseling paradigm. In it you will:

1. Understand the process of therapy and understand how it impacts each developmental ego state in all three phases of healing
2. Know how to use verbal cues to help yourself and others
3. Know what areas are generally explored in therapy
4. Have insight into borderline personalities
5. Know what the counseling process is in the new paradigm
6. Visualize the Grief Process as the road one uses to resolve anything that happens to him over the life span.
   a) Assess when a person is stuck, using the stages of the Grief Process as signposts or mile markers, along a road that will identify where he is or where he should be
   b) Identify an impasse in resolution through the process the ego states take in the Grief Process
7. Recognize the ways the paradigm increases the therapist's effectiveness
8. Understand Relapse Prevention using the Pain Management cycle, structure, and process

THERAPY

Therapy is an effective modality to help the user who is addicted to a mood-altering substance (alcohol, drugs, food) or persons, places, and things (gambling, sex, relationships, action, criminality, work, over-achieving, or prestige) to begin to:

1. Explore alternative strategies to his current dysfunctional stress-reduction strategies
2. Identify, work on, and resolve the antecedents to using mood-altering substances
3. Identify current environmental problems, which exacerbate his stress
4. Develop adaptive strategies for life's difficulties without using problem loops
5. Determine how the effective delivery of the above, in conjunction with a twelve-step program, will engender abstinence

There are also two levels of therapy that seem to prevail. The first is almost a life skill theme in which the user needs to acquire new strategies for living without problem loops, requires validation and affirmation as a human being, and to explore and develop a new purpose in life, or at least, to meander down another path other than his addictive one.

The second level of therapy appears to be centered on those who have experienced severe deprivation or emotional, physical, or sexual abuse. These types of antecedents usually require extensive therapy in a treatment setting. This is where 28-day treatment centers are effective. Ninety-day and one to three year programs are fruitful for the hard line addicts, who developed a lifestyle out of using, didn't have the repertoire of skills needed to change it, and for whom less restrictive environments produced no results.

A partial hospitalization program (PHP), is taking the type of patients today that used to be serviced by in-hospital stays, due to government funding cutbacks and managed care. The main problem with this change is there is a greater chance of relapsing, as deep issues are uncovered when the client does not have a positive support system at home, to keep him shored up until the next group. In residential treatment, there is a 24-hour, seven days a week, professional support system to help the raw client through his adversity.

The other main problem with a PHP is that a client has to be incrementally opened and closed on a daily basis in order to avoid de-compensation and deliver effective therapy. It usually takes ninety days of a PHP to effect second-order changes. Anything less than this, with chronic addiction, is ineffective treatment and usually results in compliance only (first-order change) and breeds relapse. The baseline for treatment needs can be summed up quickly. *The more that was done to them — the less they received — the more they did to themselves and others as a reaction to the former — the higher the treatment level they require*! **It's that simple!** Anything less is "ineffective" treatment, borders on being criminal, (based on today's studies), and enables at best.

The path of recovery, therapy opens, is very spiritual in nature. I know some therapists don't want to hear the spirituality "stuff." It's okay to be uncomfortable. To me, it's just another opportunity to grow. Look at how you do therapy? What drives you? What makes you good? To you natural therapists: How do you think or feel you got your talent? These are simple questions that have profound impact. Do you think you are alone? Do you feel there is a greater good operating? Look at the nature of your field — *to help others to make profound changes in their lives and become productive human beings*. If that isn't spirituality — I don't know what it is. To those of you, like me, who also believe in spirituality — this becomes our ministry. We just won't tell the others, who don't believe, that it's theirs, too.

PSYCHO-DYNAMIC/DEVELOPMENTAL PARADIGM

The counseling paradigm that I've developed is a comprehensive one that can be used as a total treatment modality with addiction education, a twelve-step program, and some form of experiential therapy (preferably psychodrama).

Psychodrama can personify the conflicts between the ego states and the drama they provoke. The paradigm can be utilized as an adjunct to any other counseling strategy by modifying your own model with mine to enhance effective communication between therapist and client, thereby increasing its efficacy. This is accomplished when both have a common language. Psycho-jargon and nomenclature has its place between professionals in clinical settings, but adds to the confusion when used in therapy sessions.

Utilizing my model will enhance the client's awareness of his internal structure (what drives his thoughts, feelings, and behaviors) and issues. It will give you more reliable information when the reporting agency (the client) is not confused. The following is an example of how the client can report more accurately what is going on internally, during any event, **after** he has been taught the model.

CASE STUDY: Remember John, our computer programmer with weight problems after interacting with his parents? The following session took place the day after he made a stressful phone call to his parents.

THERAPIST:"How are you doing today, John?"

JOHN:"I don't know." His face appears sad and one foot is moving rapidly.

THERAPIST:"Your face and body language indicate there is something disturbing you."

JOHN:"I don't feel anything. What do you see?"

THERAPIST:"You have to tell me, John."

JOHN:He starts to grip the arm of the chair, shrugs his shoulders, and his body animation continues.

Now the direct contact with the ego states begins.

THERAPIST:"How is your Child?" (Inner Child is shortened during training)

JOHN:"He's sad today because I tried to talk to my parents on the phone last night. They just minimized my feelings. I don't know why they do that!" He shrinks down into his chair and his voice becomes hesitant like a little boy.

THERAPIST:"How's your Adolescent doing with this?"

JOHN:Sitting up in his chair and suddenly angry: "He's pissed off! Don't they ever listen? You think I would learn my lesson after the one hundredth time of trying! I must be stupid!"

John is speaking very critically with a stern look on his face.

THERAPIST:"Who just spoke, John? Who made that last statement?"

JOHN:"Oh, my God. It's him! It's my dad! I've become him again?"

The sadness on his face deepens and his eyes well up with tears.

THERAPIST:"What are you feeling now, John?"

JOHN:"My Child is devastated." He begins to cry, but tearfully continues. "I'm just like him. Each time I make a mistake, I beat myself up, just like my dad does. My Critical Adult really comes up when this happens."

THERAPIST:"What happened to your Nurturing Adult? Can you see him when this happens?"

JOHN:"I can't access him when this happens. He seems to disappear. I can see what's happening inside of me when the battle begins. My Critical Adult beats up the Child when I make a mistake. He (the Child) then hides and is followed by an angry Adolescent. My Critical Parent attacks them both: he tells my Child that it didn't hurt that bad and scorns my Adolescent for trying to stick up for himself. This is when I usually start to eat."

THERAPIST:"Would you like to do some work with this in group to see if we could engage the Nurturing Adult during this time and change the usual outcome?

JOHN:"I'd like to!!" Immediately his face changes to a stern look, "But I'd probably mess it up — I can't seem to do . . ." John stops in mid-sentence as the therapist holds his hand up in a "stop" gesture.

THERAPIST:"John, tell your dad to hold on for a moment while you decide if you want to work this out in group."

JOHN:Very simply, "Yes."

THERAPIST:"Good — be here next Wednesday at seven in the evening and we'll get you started."

Look at what happened! Isn't it exciting! John went *from* not being able to identify his feelings, *to* labeling them, processing, and gaining insight. It's a short process that gives many rewards to the therapeutic relationship. Most systems used today take a longer time to achieve the same level of insight, as my paradigm does.

This dialog is also a process. As one uses the paradigm for a filter, the client can be observed along a continuum. In the next section, the client's verbal statements are used as an indicator to assess how far along the recovery continuum he has traveled.

PROCESS OF THERAPY

The process of therapy has three distinct phases. During these phases, one learns how to deal with situations using different strategies by: creating adaptive solutions and acquiring choices instead of using dysfunctional or problematic behavior. During the process, the client will learn about himself and others, identify any self-defeating behavior, and explore road-blocks to recovery. These three phases are:

Phase One: Establishing trust and learning about the therapeutic process.

Phase Two: Working phase: discovering oneself, working through the blocks to recovery, and acquiring new skills and strategies.

Phase Three: Implementation of new learning to existing problems and closure.

In the following breakdown of the phases, we will explore the confusion created by the various ego states, when they color the issues that arise throughout therapy. There are many books written about the phases clients will transition during individual and group therapy. There is no reason to re-hash their content. The professional reading this book will know them. The novice or self-help person will glean more than enough information. In fact, this book covers the entire process of recovery. All one has to do is to draw a continuum to assess his progress, by using the various scales and imagery described in this book.

Phase One

THE CHILD   It's the Child in Phase One that the therapist establishes trust with. Without this process, there would be no therapeutic alliance between the client and his helper. This is a sensitive period in which the therapist has to be hyper-vigilant so as not to be judgmental or critical. In this process he becomes the Nurturing Adult to the client's Child Ego State. The client feels emotionally secure when a safe environment is developed, trust is accomplished, and an effective relationship has been established.

THE ADOLESCENT   In Phase One, the Adolescent is the ego state that displays the resistance by reacting to a perception or interprets insensitivity to the Child. The Adolescent reacts aggressively when his boundaries are violated. This is difficult to observe without the filters of this paradigm because traditional therapy views the boundary violation as resistance. Once the altercation is explored with the Adolescent, without criticizing, judging, or **shaming**, the boundary can then be verbalized and validated. At this point, it **doesn't matter whether the therapist agrees with the boundary or not. It is still a boundary!** Sometimes tight boundaries are difficult to understand until you are aware of the context in which they were developed.

When the boundaries are skewed, as they usually are in early therapy, client teaching of appropriate boundaries will avoid a head-on collision and keep resistance lowered. I usually find a way to work on another client with the same issues in order to a effectively teach without resistance, and in processing; the group can confront the boundary. This is a back-door approach that allows the client to examine his own values internally without having to fend off what he perceives as an intrusive therapist.

The process creates trust with the Adolescent because you didn't "bang heads" with him while the therapist is in the power position. He respected the client and displayed it by not using the power against him or his peers.

THE ADULT The Adult in Phase One needs education and modeling of effective parenting. At the onset, both are accomplished by the therapist. Further into therapy, as other group members enhance their own parenting skills, they become available to each other as role models.

Phase Two

THE CHILD During this segment of therapy, the Child accomplishes his greatest work by labeling his feelings and identifying any abuse or unmet needs experienced during childhood. This is the period when most of the issues surface and the client is most vulnerable. At this time, psychotherapy is used to dig out the pain and expose it to the light, to enable the festering sores to heal. Roll play can be used to explore the peripheral areas and psychodrama utilized to reveal the structure of the process and break its impasses. This element of therapy involves awareness, insight, and tons of feelings work.

THE ADOLESCENT During Phase Two, the Adolescent becomes aware of how his reactions maintained dysfunctional behavior long after it was needed, learns appropriate boundaries and limits, and relinquishes control to the Nurturing Adult. This is difficult to accomplish in traditional psychotherapy because the Adolescent can't visualize the concept through verbal interventions. He has to see the concept in action, and psychodrama is the perfect medium for it. It is extremely profound to watch someone become aware of his or her behavior and then **immediately** correct it. Now he is cognizant!

During the last several years, I've used psychodrama to personify the structure of the ego states, identify power and control issues between them, and expose the antecedents to the individual's dysfunctional behavior and the motivation behind it. The Adolescent was usually the key to breaking any impasse.

THE ADULT   The Adult grows exponentially during this phase because all ego states are entering into harmony. In this period, the Adult learns about his feelings and experiences them (the Child), explores his problematic behavior and develops alternative strategies (the Adolescent), and generates new parenting skills which spawn an effective Executive System that can explore and create adaptive strategies to current and past difficulties (the Adult).

Phase Three
AN INTEGRATED WHOLE   During this last phase, the client becomes an integrated human being. No longer is he fragmented: his thoughts, feelings and behavior are now congruent, and what used to be an internal war-zone is now quiet. In its process, the Adult works in harmony with the other ego states and makes the best possible decisions based on his holistic needs instead of the fear of one ego state. In order to accomplish this feat, the Adult has to be in touch with his feelings (the Child), and aware of his boundaries (the Adolescent). The subsequent behavior of the Adult, which is exhibited in the process, is usually appropriate, adaptive, and functional.

BORDERLINE PERSONALITIES

Borderline personalities are the most feared clients a therapist treats. They have tight boundaries and blow up at, seemingly, nothing. They shift gears at the drop of a hat. You are their greatest gift one moment, having all the answers. They shift, and the next moment you are the scum of the world. This means they are volatile, exhibit mood swings, *and are considered dangerous because of this instability*. Right? Wrong! They are adults who have an overly developed Adolescent Ego State.

Once the borderline manifestations have been reframed to Adolescent acting out behavior, effective interventions can be applied, and the therapeutic relationship can begin. There is no greater satisfaction than an eager-to-learn client, when effective therapy is delivered to this population.

Effective therapy includes validation of their boundaries, bonding and gaining trust through verbalizing their implicit boundaries, setting appropriate boundaries and limits on their behavior, and teaching them the skills they lack through modeling and education instead of confrontation. Most of them were raised in a toxic environment, guessed at what normal was, and developed their boundaries out of the ashes of the various defeats they endured, instead of an adaptive system based on internal needs.

One of the most effective interventions that I found was to show them the DSM-IV criteria for Borderlines and watch them shake their heads in agreement. When my clinical supervisor suggested this, I thought he was crazy. The intervention was so successful that I posted the page on the clients' bulletin board. Substance abuse therapy with Borderlines can be taxing at best. When I posted the criteria, we could then have fun with being Borderline. We had so many clients identify with the criteria that we were going to have tee-shirts made exclaiming, "So, I'm Borderline — you got a problem with that!"

The other main factor that helped reduce the impact of the diagnosis: we were a twelve-step philosophy-based, partial-hospitalization program (PHP) that utilized twelve-step principles during psycho dynamic interventions. This eases the burden of having to take a rigorous stance because the program wasn't in a psyche hospital and the DSM-IV diagnosis was regarded as a cluster of symptoms only, and not treated as a disease.

During client education, the stigma of having a psychiatric diagnosis was reduced when it was explained that the DSM-IV classifications were nothing more than a cluster of symptoms designed to enable the professional helpers to talk a common language, and to design clinical interventions to reduce its impact on the functioning of the client.

**THE DSM-IV CLASSIFICATIONS
ARE A CLUSTER OF SYMPTOMS
WHICH ENABLE PROFESSIONAL HELPERS
TO DESIGN CLINICAL INTERVENTIONS**

VERBAL CUES

The following statements will give you a sense of where the client is in his process. Some of the inflections can change because the ego states are fluid most of the time, except in extreme situations where one predominates. In later recovery, all of the states will be closer to the surface so you will observe them more easily. This occurs because humans do have mixed emotions. What has changed from the past reactions is: a full-grown adult moderates the current feelings as an emotionally-mature, responsible adult and the emotions remain in a manageable range. The following are indicators:

- **Entering Therapy:**
"I don't know why I behave that way."
"I don't know what I'm supposed to feel."
"I don't even know what to think anymore."
- **Basic Awareness:**
"I have mixed feelings."
"I become sad and it changes to anger."
"I end up confused."
- **Teach the Paradigm:**
"My Child is sad."
"My Adolescent is angry."
"My Adult is lost. It's like they're not there."
- **Effective Use of the Paradigm:** (Midway Point)
"My Child was hurt by their action."
"My Adolescent wanted to retaliate."
"My Adult is trying to figure out what to do."
- **Increased Adaptation:**
"My Adult is negotiating."(Is evidenced as they do it.)
"My Adult is taking action." (They begin to take action.)
- **Internalized Response:**
"My Adult is in charge."(They make adaptive decisions.)

This process's speed will be determined by the complexity of the present situation. With issues that are encountered on a frequent basis, a new strategy will be developed quickly, and none of the internal structure will require intense facilitation. When the issues engender "core issues," mediation among the ego states will be required and all of their voices will be interspersed throughout the process. Sometimes, when an issue appears to materialize out of nowhere, one of the ego states has:

- Lacked insight into the process
- Became confused
- Voiced its opposition to the current intervention

AREAS TO BE EXPLORED IN THERAPY

There are three areas to be explored with a client. Without completing it succinctly, a thorough picture cannot be completed. They are:

Psycho-dynamic   What goes on in a human being's head? What trauma has not been addressed? What is the nature of the impacted pain? What is missing in his developmental process?

Physiological   Is there a physical cause of the impairment? Physical exam, blood work, aging, current medication, all need to be scrutinized.

Environmental   Is there anything occurring at home, on the job, in relationships, or within any significant organization or institution that impacts the person, that could be generating or exacerbating the current psychological manifestations?

Some of these areas meet resistance because the culture generalizes: the human being should be able to rise above his environment, or, there is not a physiological reason for a psychological manifestation. Some even feel that depression, anxiety and hallucinations — only emerge from a physical imbalance. This part is the medical model, which follows their major tenet of "better living through chemistry," even though people tried that in "The Sixties" and it didn't work! They prescribe pills to cure the symptoms. Some of these professional helpers feel that a minimum of psychotherapy is needed for recovery.

Anyone trying to help the client to facilitate change in his life, break the impasses in his forward momentum, and maintain a path to self-actualization, misses a great deal of opportunity to help when they omit any of the three areas. I'm not saying anyone is wrong. I was taught that my counseling paradigm is my belief system and as Corsini (1986) states, ". . . there are many forms of therapies as individuals . . ." What I am saying is to provide effective therapy, in a consumer-driven system that "all" three areas have to be explored.

THE COUNSELING PARADIGM

> "Psychotherapy works best when one
> tries to match the developmental level of a client
> with his or her own level of understanding."
> –Grace J. Craig

The Model

The model suggests there are three segments to the human being personality: The Child, Adolescent, and Adult, Ego States. These states are driven by an unconscious process that contains three levels of awareness and orders our reality by organizing external stimuli into understandable data. The first level is what we actually see in our present reality. The second level is the preconscious where our thoughts are formulated "prior" to our awareness. The last level is the subconscious where all past memories, events, or traumas are stored.

It is the mandate of the therapist to promote positive, functional, and adaptive changes in the client by using efficient techniques during the therapeutic relationship. Quality therapy teaches the client to develop effective strategies to counteract problematic situations that have overwhelmed his usual coping systems.

Effective therapy is accomplished when the therapist helps the client to solidify his internal structure, develop more creative and resilient coping strategies, and identify past traumatic blocks that stymie his growth. A major impediment to this growth process is the perceptual system, which has internal safeguards that allow it to safely deny and repress any information that will overwhelm the organism. This defense mechanism operates on the same principle as an electrical circuit breaker: when the load is too heavy, the breaker pops, and the electricity is shut off. The human perceptual system accomplishes the same purpose when it sidetracks the toxic data into the subconscious.

To effectively facilitate the changes needed to dissolve the obstruction, the therapist works on energizing the client's internal structure in order to use his own internal strength to facilitate change. In the process, the Nurturing Adult is mandated to become an Executive System for the psyche, in order to moderate internal strife, and make adaptive decisions for its holistic needs. During the process, thoughts, feelings, and behavior are usually congruent as previous unresolved germane issues (residing in the subconscious, structure of an ego state, or residue from impacted grief or trauma), are identified, processed, and released from the depths of the subconscious to begin the healing process.

THE COUNSELING PROCESS

The counseling paradigm utilizes a developmental framework in which the human being will follow a predictable pattern of growth over several periods of time. Throughout these time periods, each stage of growth is dependent on completion of tasks from the previous period because development is cumulative over the life span.

During the human's physical growth, psychological changes occur as his internal structure is developed and molded by experiences in his environment or how the situations are perceived. As the human being's internal structure is forming, it generates three age-stage ego states: the Child, Adolescent, and Adult. Each ego state has various tasks to perform in order to complete its job and deliver a competent individual into the next stage. It is when these stages are not complete that development becomes blocked or skewed and problematic behavior begins. Freeing up these impasses is the main thrust of the new counseling paradigm.

The Ego States

During the counseling process, the ego states are each targeted for specific work. Like the overall developmental process, therapy is also cumulative, in which new information is added onto previous or existing knowledge. The work completed on the Child is used as a base for the Adolescent's behavioral response that, in turn, is used by the Adult as the emotional, cognitive, and behavioral foundation on which mature decisions are made in everyday situations of life. If any previous segment is incomplete or skewed, so will be the subsequent decisions made by the next ego state. Decisions are only as effective as existing strategies allow them to be.

THE CHILD. The Child works primarily with feelings and is impacted by any subsequent abuse that may have occurred. The feelings of the human conscious are developed out of this process. Without feelings, the Adolescent will be able to behave in any way fashionable because he doesn't feel, and the Adult will remain numb or be confused about his emotions.

THE ADOLESCENT. The Adolescent carries out the Child's reaction of what was done to him or not done for him, in order to survive the trauma of being raised in a non-child-centered environment. This occurs because it wasn't safe for the child to feel. The inability results in the Child shutting down and the Adolescent subsequently lacking an emotional foundation upon which to work. The developing human also continues his reactions into adulthood, as he lacks the sublimation (deferment of pleasure skills) that is the hallmark of mature behavior. The two major goals for the Adolescent Ego State are to develop appropriate boundaries and limits, and to relinquish control of his dysfunctional behavioral responses to the Nurturing Adult.

THE ADULT. The evolving Adult is expected to make mature decisions on the problems of life and lacks the essential tools to do so. The two deficiencies carried forward through the preceding two ego states has left him in internal dissention, when, he cannot work with his feelings and lacks an adaptive behavioral repertoire. The Adult has to acquire these insights and skills to develop new strategies in order to re-parent himself. In the process, he will learn to moderate his internal strife by:

- **Working with his feelings**
- **Moderating his behavior**
- **Developing adaptive strategies to life's vicissitudes**

The Consciousness

Overseeing and impacting the internal process of the ego states is the consciousness. It is the segment of the human being's internal structure that directs external stimuli to its designated compartment and is made up of three stages: the conscious, preconscious, and subconscious. During these stages, all that is perceived by the consciousness is identified, sorted out and classified according to emotional and physical content. During this dissemination, the following occurs in each state.

THE CONSCIOUS In the conscious of the internal structure, the human being is able to be mindfully aware of what he sees, hears, tastes, smells and touches. Hidden from this segment are the pieces that have been censored out, through the filters of the perceptual system that were deemed overwhelming or too stressful for the organism's survival. This category of toxic data is sent directly to the subconscious.

THE SUBCONSCIOUS   All data that is too overwhelming for the person to handle is suppressed in the subconscious. All painful or overpowering feelings, events, or traumas are stored in this corner of the mind. These memories are not a problem until one is filled up with the baggage of impacted pain and there is no room for any more, then, a present situation triggers off a past hurt because it resembles the past event, or the past pain attaches to the current loss and exacerbates its impact.

THE PRECONSCIOUS   This is the place that hosts the transformation of a repressed memory into a behavior set. The process occurs as the fragmented memory breaks off from the subconscious and rises through the preconscious. It then transforms the rising overwhelming emotions into a behavioral response. This segment is targeted by the paradigm because it's the main area where dysfunctional behavior begins.

Counseling Goals and Tasks

A therapist following my counseling paradigm has specific tasks that have to be accomplished in order to promote the client achieving an adaptive lifestyle that generates effective stress-reduction strategies. The therapist will:

1. Help the client to become familiar and work with his internal structure
   - Identify the three ego states within himself
   - Teach the structure and process of the consciousness
   - Identify the client's problem loop
   - Expose the client's shame
   - Explore the impact shame has on the human perceptual system and how the meaning of a present situation is altered by it
2. Educate on the Grief Process
3. Demonstrate how the Grief Process turns into the road to healing by using techniques on how to visualize its path as a tunnel, bridge, or road
4. Explore the client's belief system and how old skewed beliefs impact his current behavioral responses or perceptions in current situations
5. Identify the current power struggles between the ego states and develop interventions to disperse the power fairly
6. Increase the presence and availability of the Adult Ego State
7. Identify and release frozen feelings from impacted grief in the Child

8. Model effective parenting and communication skills for the client to emulate
9. Teach stress-reduction skills to replace the current problematic strategies
10. Work to help the Adult set appropriate boundaries and limits on his Adolescent and Child ego states.
11. Encourage the Adolescent to relinquish some of his control and to defer to the Adult when final decisions are made
12. Identify, release, and begin the healing process on any past abuse or trauma, which currently impedes the forward momentum in the client's life

During this time in therapy, the practitioner acts like a detective in a good mystery story and discovers each clue, which will unravel the truth as the story progresses. The similarities between the two can give you a framework to help the client identify and work with his internal structure.

WHO — The Adult Ego State makes up the human's internal structure

WHAT — The consciousness or Perceptual System drives the internal process

WHEN — Anything that overwhelms the individual's present coping skills

WHERE — Manifests externally on the road of life

WHY — The whole process is set in motion to avoid crippling pain

When all of the above questions are answered, the following will occur:

1. The client will acquire a conscious access to his internal structure and begin to utilize its process to learn and grow
2. The therapist will be able to access the client's internal structure and will use it to promote positive mental health and
3. Identify any emotional blocks to his forward progression in life.

The above process can work for both the therapist and the client if both have deficiencies in their internal structure. The only stipulation with utilizing the concept is the therapist has to internalize it before he can teach it to the client. Figure 15.1 is a visual illustration of the human being's internal structure.

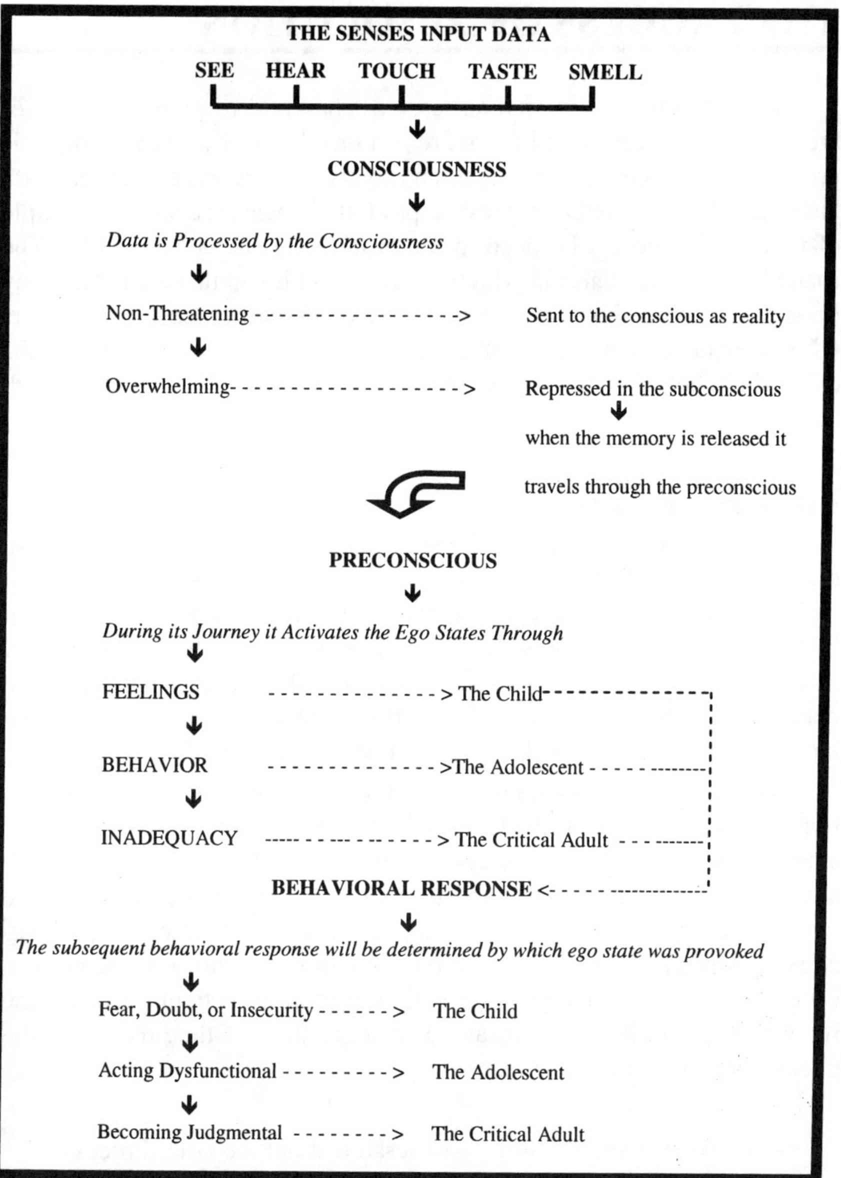

THE SENSES INPUT DATA

SEE   HEAR   TOUCH   TASTE   SMELL

⬇

CONSCIOUSNESS

⬇

Data is Processed by the Consciousness

⬇

Non-Threatening - - - - - - - - - - - - - - - ->   Sent to the conscious as reality

⬇

Overwhelming- - - - - - - - - - - - - - - - - >   Repressed in the subconscious

⬇

when the memory is released it

travels through the preconscious

PRECONSCIOUS

⬇

During its Journey it Activates the Ego States Through

⬇

FEELINGS   - - - - - - - - - - - - - > The Child- - - - - - - - - - - -

⬇

BEHAVIOR   - - - - - - - - - - - - >The Adolescent - - - - - ---------

⬇

INADEQUACY   ----- - - --- -- - - - - > The Critical Adult - - - --------

BEHAVIORAL RESPONSE <- - - - - ------------

⬇

The subsequent behavioral response will be determined by which ego state was provoked

⬇

Fear, Doubt, or Insecurity - - - - - - >   The Child

⬇

Acting Dysfunctional - - - - - - - - - >   The Adolescent

⬇

Becoming Judgmental - - - - - - - >   The Critical Adult

FIGURE 15.1 – MAP OF THE HUMAN BEING'S INTERNAL STRUCTURE

THE PROCESS OF RESOLUTION

Once the client's internal structure, behavioral response, and issues are identified and explored . . . there is a process to resolving them. This process is equivalent to a road which travels along a predetermined path, has defined points, and many rest stops along its way. It even has a couple of rotaries for those who need to travel in circles for a little while. The road also has three lanes in which to drive, and it's in this area that many become confused about the stage they are in, in their process. This occurs when they change lanes, because each lane is an ego state, and when the client shifts between them — his presenting behavior will correspond with the shift.

The Grief Process

Each issue that rises out of the subconscious, is triggered by a present event, and follows a path to become resolved. Resolution does not magically appear. It is hard work, a process, and everything doesn't get resolved in the first round. Learning the process is like trying to find your way around in a new city. First, you need a map or ask directions, and after you make several different trips, the directions become internalized and you know your way around without any aids or assistance.

The Grief Process is the road the human travels down to gain resolution with his issues. Just like learning a new geographical area, one needs a map to learn the route. The six stages of the Grief Process (shock, denial, anger, bargaining, depression, and acceptance) are the road. After this road is traveled with several issues and later processed in therapy, its path becomes internalized to a point where the client can identify where he is in each issue, and the therapist can help him more effectively because the reporting system is now accurate. The acquisition of the process by the client is an analogue to the recovery process:

- Obsession over the drug — obsession about the Grief Process
- Obsession about meetings — obsession about using the Grief Process
- Learn what's under the compulsion — learn what triggered the issue
- Gain new stress-reducing strategies — learn to use the process with all issues

It's also the task of the Executive System to mediate this system. If the Child or Adolescent is in charge because the Adult is not a viable presence, the subsequent process will serve one state only, and an immature system will result. It's tantamount to letting a little child or an immature adolescent drive a bus with a load of people, in a major city, during rush hour. Nothing but carnage can occur. The resulting immaturity is why the Adult becomes stuck. It occurs when he lacks sufficient development and hasn't the skills or strategies to negotiate life's problems.

The inability to follow mature strategies did not happen in a vacuum. It's one of the main deficiencies of his family of origin when they didn't provide the information because they lacked it themselves. Even if the individual came by some of the knowledge, it wasn't usable because he was too busy surviving and lacked living skills to apply it. This process is overwhelming at first because:

- It's a new concept and learning something new is difficult
- It's concrete and won't allow you to stray without pain
- It increases your awareness exponentially each time its used
- When used — past issues surface as your skill level increases
- It's hard to regress once you start down its path

Figure 15.2 is a visual representation of the path.

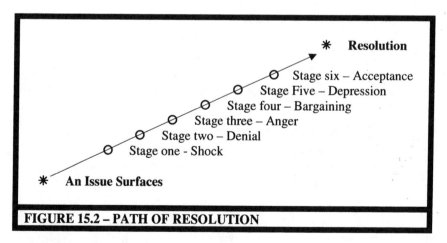

FIGURE 15.2 – PATH OF RESOLUTION

The Ego States
The lanes in the road of the Grief Process are engineered by the ego states. They determine if its path will be a straight one; how many lanes it will need; where the rest areas will be built; if and when a side road, rota-

ries, and exists are needed. Exact knowledge of the destination is not necessary. Self-actualization is life's goal. What that means is different to each human being and will be in accordance with his life plan. Attaining one's life goals will eventually answer the question asked by fellow travelers: "Why am I here?" Its answer is illusive to most, because the noise levels of the world's ways in the human being's mind blocks the spiritual connection that guides one to its answer. One does not have to isolate in a cave to achieve the communion. All he has to do is to clarify self-actualization as a value, and maintain a forward course to attain it by eliminating anything that diverts him from this primary spiritual path when it causes the noise level to increase in his head. Problems, people, places, things, situations, past traumas, are all dealt with one at a time, and processed, resolved, or eliminated. In this manner, all that is impedance to spiritual growth is eliminated or modified over a period of time. In the final stage of this process, very little will knock you off of your spiritual path, and you will maintain the connection that guides you along your road in life.

The fear, doubt, and insecurity generated by the struggle are what activates the ego state's fear. In the process, any deficiencies of the ego states will increase the odds of a problematic response instead of an adaptive solution. It is the clatter between the ego states, generating the confusion, which blocks connection to a spiritual source of guidance. The dissonance is identified through the following construct:

- The Child, when feelings can't be mediated
- The Adolescent, when behavior can't be modified
- The Adult, when adaptive strategies can't be created

The impasse is explored through probing and working with the presenting ego state and usually results in the following:

- The block is broken and forward momentum reestablished
- The issue is identified and the client can now complete the remedial work needed to break the impasse in future situations or recurrences of the fear returning

Figure 15.3 is a further illustration of the path leading to resolution and includes the ego states. Each one of the entities makes a significant contribution to the process and changes its presentation during each stage, which matures with progress, or remains stuck or regresses when obstructed

---

*   *Resolution*

        O   **STAGE SIX – ACCEPTANCE**
      O   The Adult
      O   The Adolescent
     O   The Child

     O   **STAGE FIVE – DEPRESSION**
    O   The Adult
    O   The Adolescent
   O   The Child

    O   **STAGE FOUR – BARGAINING**

  O   The Adult
  O   Thc Adolescent
  O   The Child

   O   **STAGE THREE – ANGER**
  O   The Adult
 O   The Adolescent
O   The Child

 O   **STAGE TWO – DENIAL**
O   The Adult
O   The Adolescent
O   The Child

O   **STAGE ONE – SHOCK**
*   *An Issue Surfaces*

FIGURE 15.3 – PATH OF RESOLUTION INCLUDING THE EGO STATES

CASE STUDY: The case study in the beginning of this chapter is a good example of the expected outcome when clients learn about their inner workings. It helps them to explore their feelings and identify the problem loop that precipitated dysfunctional behavior. This is the foundation on which the client will resolve current impasses, develop adaptive solutions, and restore forward movement in their lives.

The next stage of the process is to identify where the raised issues are in the client's recovery process and expose any dissention between the ego states. When this stage is finalized, the client will have a working knowledge of his internal structure and will be able to utilize its attributes to create effective, adaptive, and functional stress-reducing strategies to life's difficulties. After John completed the first stage, he was able to:

- Identify the elements to his internal structure and how they impact his current interactions

- Identify and label his feelings
- Identify his problem loop and the antecedents to its activation

John finished the first phase of awareness in individual counseling and completed the rest in group counseling. He experienced the usual transition problems and overcame them easily because he understood what ego state was reacting and could accurately report the internal strife. John remained grounded during the initial group interventions and built up trust with the group members at a high rate, because his fear didn't overcome him.

In the second phase of therapy, John was able to identify the underlying issues of abandonment, verbal abuse, and emotional deprivation that he experienced in his family of origin. He also worked on the damage he self-created by reacting to the deficiencies in his childhood when he created a dysfunctional lifestyle that blocked attainment of a peaceful and creative life. John was able to map where each issue resided on his path toward resolution by accurately reporting their position in the Grief Process.

John was next able to explore the various issues in order to identify where each ego stage was and what confusion, dissention, or harmony they brought to the issue. In a few of the simple issues, the ego states were congruent. With the more important ones, the schism was greatest when the fear was the highest. John completed several psycho-dramas in which he completed the re-parenting process when he:

- Worked on effective communication between the ego states
- Re-balanced the power structure between the Adult and the Adolescent
- Became more available to the Child and set appropriate boundaries and limits on the Adolescent
- Established trust with the Adolescent
- Quieted the Critical Adult without destroying it

During the final stage of therapy, John was able to apply the new knowledge he gained in self-awareness to develop adaptive strategies, in order to combat self-defeating behavior. The behavior generally manifested when either his primary caregivers or significant authority figures would try to control him. If the control was not addressed at the time, it would trigger the shame that propelled him into his problem loop of depression, overeating, and sabotage.

Cognitive and Affective Components

The process of resolution has two distinct components that need to be completed before resolution is experienced by the integrated whole personality. They are the cognitive (thoughts) and affective (feeling) components to the human being's psychological structure. It really doesn't make any difference where the therapist starts because the final outcome will always be the same: thoughts, feelings, and the subsequent behavioral response predicated by them will be congruent. Traditionally in therapy, men gravitate toward left brain activity and usually begin with their thoughts or logic. Women, on the other hand, are right brain oriented and start with their feelings. Each will have to learn to use both sides. With men, logic can impede the feelings process, and with women, I over E (intellect over emotion) can diminish the impact of a traumatic situation through understanding it better. I'm not making a value judgment. I'm just reporting what I usually observe in therapy. Figure 15.4 depicts the path an issue follows in order to complete the cognitive and affective components of its resolution for the integrated whole.

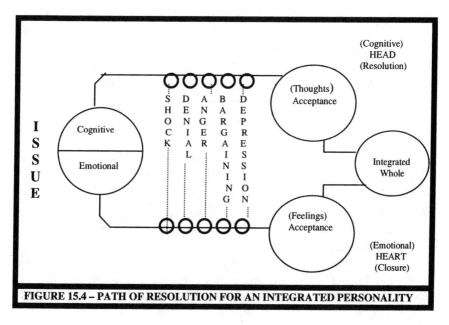

FIGURE 15.4 – PATH OF RESOLUTION FOR AN INTEGRATED PERSONALITY

COGNITIVE SUBSTRUCTURE   This is the thinking element of the individual's personality. It's the part that orders, sorts out, and makes sense out of any event that occurs in the human being's life. The process includes greater understanding of the event, responses, and consequences. In the process, three levels of awareness will be traveled through:

Level One — The event itself
Level Two— Losses from the event
Level Three— Far-reaching consequences from the event

In each of these levels, the individual will reach conclusions that will help him go to his next level of understanding. It's the same as completing a complicated task three times. Each time you finished, you would have a greater understanding of the project. In the cognitive process toward resolution, the first level leads to the second until the whole picture is viewed through the awareness of the third level.

AFFECTIVE SUBSTRUCTURE   The human being feels the aftermath of the event in this mode. This is the division of the personality structure that brings color to the tapestry we call life. It enhances living, adds a deeper meaning, and brings contour to a flat surface. Emotions make our dearest memories come true. They also personify our biggest fears. It creates dreams and nightmares alike. Traveling through its process, one advances through the same levels as cognition. Each level reaching a deeper level of expression until most of the feelings have been felt and processed to a degree that they no longer overwhelm or impede the forward progress of the bereaved individual. They are:

Level One — The impact from the event is experienced
Level Two— Losses from the event are felt
Level Three— Further consequences of the event are gone through

At this time, review the illustrations in Figures 15.1, 15.2, 15.3 and 15.4. They describe:

- The human's psychological internal structure (p.317)
- The cognitive process of perception and how it can change reality, lend new meanings to situations, and impact or modify thoughts, feelings and behavior
- The path of resolution (p.319)
- The impact of the ego states on acceptance and resolution (p.321)
- The cognitive and affective components of the human personality (p.323)
- The three levels of understanding to cognitively resolve an issue
- The depths of feeling, occurring in three levels, needed to reduce an issue's impact and stop exerting its influence on the human being's forward progress in life.

- The three levels experienced in the cognitive and affective mode
  is tantamount to going down a highway three different times and
  each trip brings new knowledge of the route

We will now add one more layer to the construct. It will enlighten you
as to "why" the process has been so confusing and add to the therapist's
repertoire of facilitative skills by accomplishing the following:

- Increase the ability to accurately assess the impact of an issue
- Determine where the client is in his process
- Identify impasses in the individual's internal organization
- Enhance his ability to create effective interventions to promote
  healthy change.

Diversity of the Ego States

The ego states are the steering committee of the human's internal organization. It's the division that acts upon the entered data from the
consciousness, and the segment of the personality that mystifies, confuses,
and angers all that try to understand it. While the ego states are interpreting the new data, each segment (Child, Adolescent, and Adult) has its own
influence, and like three cars on the same highway, each will determine its
own course. *The most important element of the construct is the specialized
agenda each ego state follows*:

- *The Child* — **anything to do with pain or impacted grief**
- *The Adolescent* — **ties in with all maladaptive behaviors**
- *The Adult* — **when there is little or no effective leadership**

When the format of the ego state's agenda is tied into the process of
resolving an issue, it becomes an accurate assessing system in which to
pinpoint blocks and possible elementary work the client has to complete
in order to move on in his process. If you wonder why they regress, it's in
the failure to complete the elementary work they need to maintain internal
integrity. If they lack the basics they can't go forward in their process.

CASE STUDY: The work our computer programmer accomplished in
group is a good example of how the various ego states can impact or impede the client's progress in therapy and also indicate the type of
intervention needed to facilitate any impasse.

The Child ego state will be the target of the intervention when the client appears stuck at a certain point in his feelings. At this time, attention will have to be given the Adolescent and the Adult as well. Their behavior (the Adolescent) or lack of availability (the Adult) to the Child can create the roadblock. During these times it is unsafe for the Child to continue and he usually shuts down or remains guarded. This is what happened to John when he was shifted from individual to group therapy. He acquired a basic understanding of the mechanics of the ego states, although lacked the ability to utilize them in his attempts to break his current gauntlet. In psychodrama, the personification of the Child Ego State disclosed that he feared the eating binges of the Adolescent were going to kill him, and wanted them stopped. He also described the abandonment he experienced when the Nurturing Adult was not available to him and he felt all alone. He further reported the shame he had to endure each time the Critical Adult berated him. John's Child expressed a desire to have all three change their current practices, although was doubtful that it would happen. The following goals were generated out of the intervention:

- To stop the Adolescent's eating behavior
- To help the Nurturing Adult become more available
- To quiet the Critical Adult's verbal barrages

The Adolescent responded quickly to the Child and refused to change his behavior until the Nurturing Adult decided to take more responsibility. Before the Nurturing Adult could respond, an argument quickly ensued between the Adolescent and the Critical Adult, after the Critical Adult started to antagonize them all. The Nurturing Adult at this point was taken out of the drama and placed in the observer's role after another peer was chosen to play its role, in order for him to see his internal dissention. The following goals were formulated during this segment of the drama:

- To establish a degree of trust with the Nurturing Adult
- To relinquish some power to the Adult
- Set appropriate boundaries and limits on current behavior.

The Adult — John's Adult Ego State was forced to take a good look at the personification of his internal chaos while he remained in the observer role. In the role, John admitted that he didn't know what to do. With additional work, over several weeks, John was able to accomplish the following goals with his ego states, and brought harmony to his internal structure:

1. Became more available to his Child Ego State, by:
   - Not suppressing his feelings through eating

- Allowing the Child to be present during decision making
- Quieting the Critical Adult
2. Established trust with the Child by:
   - Remaining consistent in the new behavior
   - Setting limits on the Adolescent's behavior
3. Re-parented the Child by:
   - Acknowledging the Child had pain and giving him permission to talk about it
   - Affirming his right to be alive
4. Earned back power from the Adolescent by:
   - Learning new strategies and applying them to problems
   - Establishing the need for appropriate boundaries and limits
   - Acknowledging the leadership the Adolescent provided after the Nurturing Adult abrogated his responsibility
   - Quieting the Critical Adult
5. Established trust with the Adolescent when:
   - The Adult's new behavior was consistent over time. (It was important at this time that the Adult had minimal regression back into old behavior, for the Adolescent would start to emerge each time the threat was present, and the Adult had to be reminded about using his new behavior.)
6. Re-parented the Adolescent through demonstrating a new way of life by:
   - Adopting a food plan
   - Attending OA meetings
   - Attaining a sponsor
   - Agreeing to make phone calls before overeating
   - Validating his right to make a contribution to the whole

This case study gives you an idea of the work that has to be accomplished in order to understand the structure of the human personality and design effective interventions in order to overcome the ego states' chaotic influences at times when fear and confusion paralyze their ability to make adaptive decisions.

Journey of the Ego States

During John's process in therapy, he had to first acquire all the essential information, before he could progress beyond his original plateau. John had to learn how to use his new insight in his daily facilitation of life's vicissitudes, and to identify the roadblocks when he couldn't. This was accomplished in therapy when he unstuck his frozen feelings, decreased his problematic behavior, and began to make decisions based on holistic needs. During his journey in therapy, John followed a path called the Grief Process, and like a major highway, had a separate lane for each of the ego states that allowed them to travel at their own pace.

There are other roads the ego states can choose to travel along as a diversion in order to escape the reality of their existence. Each path has its own agenda, reasoning, and consequences, and it is not our place to judge it, only to use it as an assessing tool. **REMEMBER — all behavior is useful. If it weren't working, the behavior would change!** Below is a list of possible avenues the human can explore along his path in life as he attempts to make effective decisions and resolve his issues.

MAIN ROAD   This road is the straightest path taken. On it, one goes through each state until the process is complete and the issue or situation is resolved. During the journey, the ego states will find various stages to "park" until they are ready to journey forward. I use the work "park" instead of "stuck" because the layover is merely a sabbatical until the human being has mustered enough strength to continue along in his process. This is the place where all humans are different and we have to respect the individual's process, lest we push him along too quickly and become part of the problem instead remaining solution oriented in our therapeutic work.

There are also three levels to this process, three ego states influencing the path, and up to nine possible positions the individual can occupy simultaneously as he travels toward resolution.

Level One — The facts of the loss or change
Level Two— The feelings from the situation
Level Three— The far-reaching impact of the event

Figure 15.5 is an illustration of how the road is structured and the various side trips the ego states can encounter along their paths.

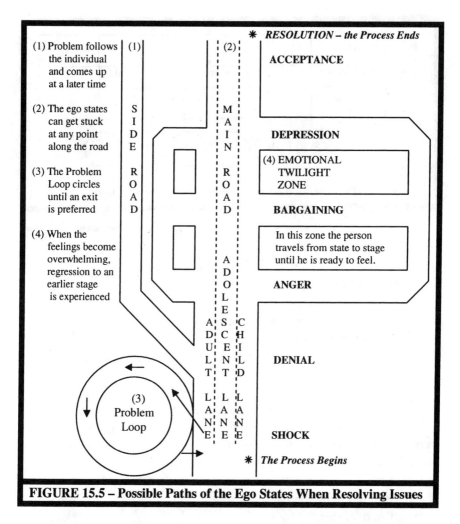

FIGURE 15.5 – Possible Paths of the Ego States When Resolving Issues

Each person will move through these stages and levels at a different pace. As the therapist learns to integrate these constructs into their assessing filters, the therapist can: determine more accurately and quickly where a person is in his process, know how to develop more effective interventions, and know when the client no longer needs the therapist's services because some grief issues can be a life-long process. The prime determinant for terminating therapy is the absence of problematic symptoms. It's ok to still have residue feelings over a loss. It's not OK to continue in dysfunctional behavior, because this is a problem loop and not what resolution looks like. Figure 15.6 is an example of how the ego states can rest in the three levels of the six stages along the road we call the Grief Process.

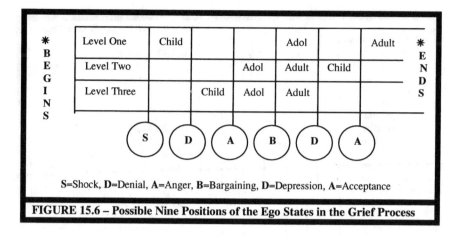

* B E G I N S	Level One	Child			Adol		Adult	* E N D S
	Level Two			Adol	Adult	Child		
	Level Three		Child	Adol	Adult			

S＝Shock, D＝Denial, A＝Anger, B＝Bargaining, D＝Depression, A＝Acceptance

FIGURE 15.6 – Possible Nine Positions of the Ego States in the Grief Process

SIDE ROAD This path manifests in several ways:
- Geographical cures
- Vocational changes
- Divorce, new relationships, or family changes
- Following a different spiritual path
- Changing one's thinking or behavior as a reaction and not a process

No matter what device is used to bring the fearful individual into a Side Road….its goal has one function….to avoid or minimize the pain from the loss or the change. Some of the client's statements heard by the therapist just before the client enters a Side Road are:
- "It's not important."
- "It didn't really bother me."
- "I'm over that."
- "I put it behind me."
- "Is that supposed to bother me?"

The statements are endless. Rendered, they sound like minimizing or rationalization, which is the Bargaining Stage of the Grief Process. The Side Road is an internal choice. In it, the client remains internally intact by allowing himself more time to "*absorb*" the impact from the painful event without becoming dysfunctional and creating a Problem Loop. The strategy allows the client to resume his life by avoiding the overwhelming pain. What will precipitate his return to the chaos created by the Twilight Zone's protective process, occurs if he becomes dysfunctional and starts to employ a Problem Loop, when his avoidance is no longer, 1) working as a facilitator of his painful feelings or, 2) diverting the impact of a stressful event.

THE EMOTIONAL TWILIGHT ZONE The Emotional Twilight Zone materializes when any state enters its depression phase becomes overwhelmed and regresses to an earlier stage. The distance traveled back in the process is usually one or two stages. Rarely does anyone go back into denial. If he does, it's only momentarily, until he has had a reality check. He can circle between anger, bargaining, and depression until he is able to tolerate his own feelings: by going through them instead of running away. In figure 15.5 the process is depicted as a double loop. In the illustration, the jump back can be one or two stages. It's not important how many stages they retreat . . . the regression is designed to keep the individual out of his feelings. This is also when the client verbalizes his craziness as sad one moment, angry the next and then wishing it were different. Around and around he twirls — like a merry-go-round, until he feels, creates a Problem Loop, or breaks down (requires hospitalization).

THE PROBLEM LOOP This is the dysfunctional strategy one chooses after all the mileage of The Emotional Twilight Zone has been expended and is the last desperate attempt to divert the pain from the loss or the event. This is also when psychic pain is transformed into a behavioral response. Internally, the transformation process is generated in the preconscious, and manifested in the now. The loop is *"anything"* that can be ritualized in an obsessive and compulsive way in which the possessed individual can continuously focus on: completing, avoiding, and agonizing over the undesired behavior. In this manner, the tormented human being masks his inner pain with an external response. As the obsession becomes more ritualized, the individual's focus is externally directed on his medication of choice, and he is no longer in touch with himself internally. This dance in the problem loop will continue until it is no longer useful to him as a medicator. The only problem is that it takes therapy and/or a twelve-step program to break the obsession and if they are not sought, one usually ends up in prison, the hospital, or dead. Program Adage: Jails, Institutions, or Death can be the results of ones addiction.

The Completed Process

Resolution, the completed process of integrated (cognitive and affective) acceptance, is the final goal of the journey. This occurs when the ego states have worked through The Grief Process in the three levels of awareness. There is no correct method of achieving this goal, except to work them through. Also, acceptance is not a destination, it's a journey and it doesn't matter how fast the ego states progress through the tiers of its matrix. The only matter of importance is that the person learns about himself in the process, he grows, and in the final analysis, can facilitate the stress from a painful event easier, each time it's encountered. The process is also called, *"emotional maturity."*

To all you task-oriented individuals: the final goal is not to end up with all the ego states completing the journey of the Grief Process, through three levels of awareness, sitting on the home-plate of acceptance, in an integrated whole personality. This is a case where the process is more important than the destination, for it is in learning its matrix that the human being will benefit. It's of no consequence what ego state rests in what stage or level of the process, for it's only a place, *not damnation*! When the ego state has the maturity to move on — *it will*! Figure 15.7 illustrates the completed process of resolution.

The two constructs used to illustrate the process in Figure 15.7 were designed to give you a feel for the material. They are:

- Loss from a death (Cognitive: 1, 3, 5. Affective: 7, 9, 11)
- Recovering from abuse (Cognitive: 2, 4, 6. Affective: 8, 10, 12)

The statements usually heard in the client's reporting during the stages of recovery were meant to be indicators only. There are no absolutes. Once the constructs are included in your therapeutic filters, they will greatly enhance your insight, assessing skills, and interventions.

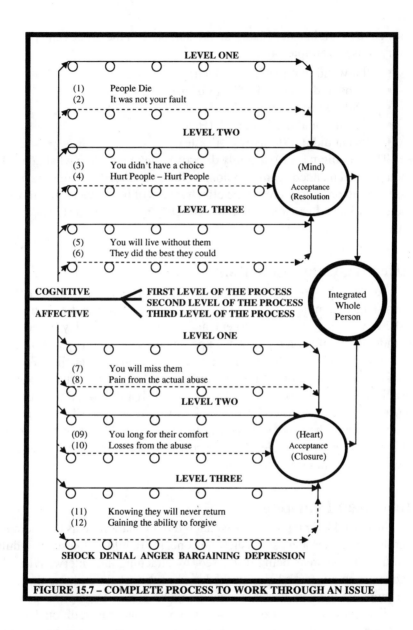

FIGURE 15.7 – COMPLETE PROCESS TO WORK THROUGH AN ISSUE

THE PARADIGM'S EFFECTIVENESS

The paradigm works effectively in both areas of the brain. It employs logic and consistence to utilize the left side and imagination and creativity to engage the right side. Changing the language in the probes can provoke every sense. Examples are:

- "How did that feel?"   (Touch)
- "What did it look like?"   (Vision)
- "Did it have an aroma?"   (Smell)
- "What sound did it make?" (Hearing)
- "What did it taste like?"   (Taste)

The paradigm is also a highly directive one in regard to what goals the therapist had planned for the session. At first, structured sessions are highly essential, in order to increase the effectiveness of the services given, when the client lacks the same frame of reference as the therapist. The model will bridge this gap efficiently.

Effective Communication

To start the process of therapy, trust has to be established through consistent communication. The model allows the therapist to use established concepts (Child, Adolescent, and Adult) in an everyday framework, without the confusion the novice experiences, as he learns psychological terms (psycho babble) in other counseling strategies. This allows for effective communication in a timely manner and engenders trust sooner, as less inadequacy is experienced by the client. If I described the last sentence with the terms used in this book, it would be: The Child feels trust sooner because he is not shamed due to a lack of understanding the terminology; thereby the Adolescent doesn't have to become defensive to the therapist by exhibiting "resistance."

Increased Learning

Increased learning is also engendered in the paradigm as the therapist verbally activates and establishes the concepts (Child, Adolescent, Adult) throughout the areas being discussed, by attaching and interweaving the ego states to all issues being probed, and continuously utilizing these descriptors in their summaries. Piaget would be proud! During this process, the client's knowledge base increases at a greater rate than traditional psycho babble because of the continuous attachment to pre-existing knowledge. This process greatly expands their existing concepts, instead of having to develop new ones.

Greater Productivity

Sessions produce greater results in less time, as the paradigm gives the clinician greater flexibility, easier access to the clients' internal processes, and less resistance if used appropriately. If one learns the model effectively, the following benefits will materialize:

- Less resistance will be evoked
- The paradigm can be used as an assessing tool because only the deeper issues will trigger resistance
- To help identify the clients' implicit boundaries
- Increasing trust by verbalizing and respecting the implicit boundaries
- Augment the ability to probe the implicit boundary, to identify and gain greater insight into the clients' hidden agenda or issues

Expanded Flexibility

Individual or group sessions provide diversity. A choice in treatment modalities allows for greater flexibility . . . when the therapist or group facilitator can "fine tune" his own professional assessment of what the client needs to heal, process, or explore . . . against what he can effectively tolerate. How many times have you (the therapist) tried an intervention and found it ineffective because the client needed additional basics before he could go any deeper. An example is when the beginner has completed some rudimentary feelings work; process and/or solutions are attempted and the client becomes resistant. All that has happened is: you didn't complete the feelings work; the issue has attached onto another, or the individual's internal structure hasn't matured enough to handle the process. At this juncture, the therapist can lead the client in any direction he chooses in order to break the impasse, as long as he possesses the skill it takes to get the client through the resistance.

Enhance the Developmental Process

When a client becomes stuck in his process, it's usually the Executive System (decision-making system) of his internal structure (Child, Adolescent, and Adult) that is stuck. The following presentations usually manifest during the therapeutic process:

The Child	Gets stuck in his feelings
The Adolescent	Becomes mired in overreacting
The Adult	Disappears or can't make an adaptive decision

CLINICAL NEEDS — When the client growth becomes impeded by his internal confusion: the therapist can accomplish his greatest strides, as he enables the client to continue his forward momentum, "*if*" the therapist knows what to look for. During this crisis in therapy, each ego state has to be treated differently, depending on what state is present and what its **current needs** are:

The Child during this confusion has several needs to fill:

- More work needs to be accomplished on his feelings
- Exposure of the Adolescent's behavior that frightens him
- Help the Nurturing Adult to be more present to him
- Quiet the Critical Adult's assault on his tenderness

The Adolescent has several needs to acquire during this episode:

- Validation of the difficult job he has done
- Awareness of how his "protective devices," designed to shield the Child from pain, actually hurt him once the trauma was over and recovery became blocked
- Learn age-appropriate responses
- Develop alternative strategies to current self-defeating behavior
- Define healthy boundaries and limits
- Disengage from the battle with the Critical Adult
- Re-engage with the Nurturing Adult to facilitate an orderly transition of returning power back to him **after** trust is re-established

The Adult during this period, is either nonexistent, dominated by the Critical Adult, or has a small role. His needs at this time are to re-engage with the other ego states of his internal structure. This is accomplished when he:

- Allows the Child a voice in all matters
- Earns back power from the Adolescent by demonstrating consistent behavior
- Establishes appropriate boundaries and limits for the Child and Adolescent
- Protects the Child from outside abuse, self-defeating behavior of the Adolescent, and emotional battering from the Critical Adult
- Protects the Adolescent from his own reactionary behavior and the verbal onslaught from the Critical Adult
- Becomes the Executive System and makes all decisions based on internal harmony
- Learns good parenting skills

Concise Probes

Very few counseling paradigms allow as much flexibility as a developmental one seems to provide. It is based on the clear goals of a developmental process, which allows the human being to grow and adapt through all situations, and seems to provoke the least resistance. The concept that humans grow and develop over a measurable time span appears to be comfortable to clients and usually eliminates or cuts down self-depreciation. Using this concept in therapy, we can assess the needs of the client today, which grew out of the deficiencies of the past, implement appropriate interventions to counteract the damage and start the healing process. We can use descriptive language, targeting specific ego states, assessing along a recovery continuum, thereby engaging in precise therapy in order to accomplish therapeutic gains along a clinical path.

The Child needs the language of feelings and affirmations. Without them, there is very limited communication. In fact, if they are not used, resistance is immediately raised.

The Adolescent understands validation. It needs to be given credit for the job it has already done protecting the Child, when the Adult abrogated his responsibility by not taking charge. The Adolescent also requires a reality check. In it, the following will have to be addressed:
- How his reactions have added to the Child's fear
- The need for functional boundaries and limits
- Education about adaptive behavior
- Information on how to transfer power to the Adult

The Adult understands logic. Prior to therapy it is disengaged from its feelings (the Child) and doesn't understand its behavior (the Adolescent). As the Adult is reunited with its feelings, internal trust begins, when it allows the Child to voice his emotions. Integrity is built up as the Adult remains connected to the Child (his feelings). At this juncture, the Adolescent begins to relinquish control and self-defeating behavior starts to diminish. The understanding of this process and its implementation, allows the Adult to take charge of his internal structure, and to develop a highly effective Executive System.

RELAPSE PREVENTION

Relapse prevention training occurs when the addict/alcoholic enters treatment or a twelve-step program. Both help to identify the triggers that lead up to using, and offer alternative behavior instead of continuing down the same path, which will eventually lead to relapse. The primary goal of the training is to prevent the actual relapse. It doesn't make any difference how many times the relapse has occurred — the training is the same. Once the substance abuser recognizes his relapse cycle, he can avoid it by maintaining a "constant vigilance" and a "one day at a time" lifestyle that is clean of all distractions which can bring him down the relapse path.

Terry Gorski's model is highly definitive for those of you new to the field or recovery and I would strongly recommend becoming familiar with his work. The material in this section will utilize my model to identify the antecedents that jeopardize continuous sobriety and further precipitate a relapse. To the author, relapse is just another form of pain management and it can occur in the structure or the process. If it's the structure, new strategies to old behaviors need to be instilled. If it's in the process, impacted pain or a dreaded secret is usually the culprit and needs to be exorcised. There is also an overall structure and intent for the relapse, which follows along the construct of my Pain Management Model.

Pain Management Construct

The relapse cycle begins within the addicted person each time life gets better and he begins to clean up "the wreckage of his past." The cycle is simple: as things improve in his life following sobriety, the rising positive feelings also "drag up" the negative ones, and the negative feelings overwhelm the individual because recovery made him vulnerable. What has actually occurred is that his feelings level has increased and previous material that was suppressed through his substance abuse is now free to rise into the conscious. This is the main reason people in early recovery have so many mixed feelings, become confused, and wonder if recovery is really worth it. It's during this time a problem loop manifests as the relapse cycle begins. Figure 15.8 is an illustration of its process.

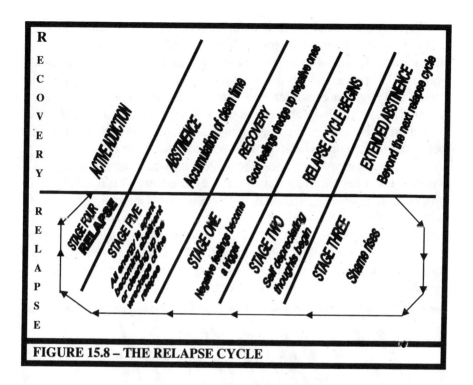

FIGURE 15.8 – THE RELAPSE CYCLE

The relapse cycle at this juncture of the recovery process, is reframed to a medicator in which the addict will hide from his lack of effective stress-reducing strategies or hidden pain. In order to go beyond the continuous loop of multiple relapses and move into extended abstinence, we will examine the structure and process of the addict. In this way, we can determine what appropriate interventions are needed to break the cycle.

STRUCTURE When we examine the internal structure of the substance abuser, codependent, food addict, etc., we look for the ego state(s) that are "*not*" working as a unified whole. If the problem is in the structure, we usually find a diminished, disempowered, or ineffective Adult. When this prevails, the Adult has abrogated his responsibility as the Executive System, and the Adolescent has moved in to fill the vacuum. When the abandonment is exposed, the Adult has to be encouraged to take back his power with new problem-solving skills and stress-reducing strategies. These life skills have to be acquired in order for the Adult to gain the tools to facilitate his ascension back into an authority posture. The Adolescent also has to be convinced to share his power with the Adult and to refrain from reacting while the Adult becomes competent with his new skills. This should eliminate another relapse if the problem is in the structure.

PROCESS   When work is completed on the structure and relapses continue as the addict verbalizes his desire for abstinence; it's time to look at his internal process to identify where the block(s) are to maintaining sobriety. The process at this point is usually elusive. Identifying what it is hiding and beginning an intervention toward diminishing its power over the addict is difficult — at best. We have to take another approach. The new strategy is exacting because the impasse we are trying to identify has been transformed into a behavioral response (relapse). In order to identify its components, the therapist needs to explore its behavioral response backwards in order to gain an awareness of its antecedents. *This is a backward process into awareness*! The main problem with this intervention strategy is that it's always after the fact, and we are forced to examine what precipitated its momentum toward relapse instead of witnessing the actual circumstance. The insight will come later if the relapses continue. The initial goal of this type of strategy is to shorten the time spent in relapse. Figure 15.9 is a depiction of the process.

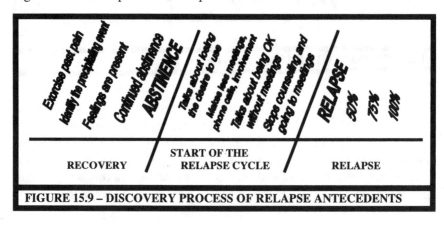

FIGURE 15.9 – DISCOVERY PROCESS OF RELAPSE ANTECEDENTS

Relapse Prevention Training

RELAPSE — Relapse training begins in the final stage of the process. In it, the helper (therapist or sponsor) tries to instill enough information into the addict to enable him to catch his relapse sooner and prevent further erosion of previous gains. They say that a twelve-step program ruins one's disease — so does therapy. Both decrease the addict's ignorance and raise his bottom in the recovery process. Each time the addict experiences a relapse cycle with **increased awareness**....his emotional bottom increases. This is why there are percent figures in the right hand side of the illustration. Each percent will be the amount of time the relapse lasts. The subsequent relapses are shorter because more work has been done in between and the addict is more knowledgeable. Don't forget that we are working on the structure at the same time. No one relapses in a vacuum. We are attempting to explore all components to the problem (structure and process). When we accomplish our goal, we will unbalance the addict's present unknown structure and process, and internally something will begin to change. The amount of relapses usually determines the depth of the pain. The range I generally observe is Stage One through Four (Figure 15.8) with each relapse becoming shorter. Sometimes, the last one is only one drink, pill, or joint. The average amount of relapses I see is two. Generally with the work we do in therapy, the addict cannot use without intense pain. A popular adage used in the program states: "when the pain of what you're going through becomes worse than the pain of what you are hiding — you will look at *anything!*" This is what we try to accomplish with relapse prevention when the pain of relapse is more intense than what is inside. At this time the relapse stops and we clean up the residue pain.

Prevention Goal - This is the primary clinical goal to shorten the abuser's relapse cycle in raising his bottom through education, awareness, and confrontation.

BEGINNING OF THE RELAPSE CYCLE — This segment describes what occurs just prior to the actual physical relapse. Most of the statements made by the potential relapser will minimize the helpful components of recovery. Many addicts relapse emotionally long before they use . . . you can hear this process in their verbal statements. **First they talk** about their distorted thinking with **the behavior close behind.** This can be a long or short process. During this time you will need a lot of assistance keeping the abuser on track. If they are in a twelve-step program, they will be constantly confronted by others who have **been there, done that, and received a T-shirt.** The challenge continues overtly with direct confrontations, and covertly when other substance abusers disclose their previous thinking, attitudes, and where their subsequent behavior took them.

This is the stage in which "dry drunks" remain. It's where the thinking is distorted, skewed, egocentric (self-centered) and the abusers do everything but physically abuse a substance. During this phase they are in a holding pattern of continuous confusion, paralyzed to go forward in recovery, yet fearful to retreat/relapse. Stay with it and miracles can happen.

During this phase, the Critical Adult is usually active. The main thrust of therapy is usually cognitive. RET (Rational-Emotive Therapy) spreadsheets (Ellis, 1962) are concrete enough to challenge even the most stubborn. Tangential thinking can be tracked with written logs of when the particular pattern began. Group members in therapy and a twelve-step program, will become the greatest change agents for these cognitive distortions. This is also the place the abuser will "*Grow*" by admitting his cognitive distortions or "G*o*" by leaving to eventually use, hence the phrase **"grow or go."**

The exploration attempted during this stage is a backward process and designed to identify when the cognitive distortions, (what AA calls **"stinkin thinkin"**) actually begin. The reverse process of discovery usually occurs in four phases:

1. Almost total withdrawal from the program and counseling
2. Talks about not going to meetings and counseling
3. Attends meetings infrequently — misses counseling appointments
4. States that he lost the desire to use

At each juncture in the process, the helper tries to ascertain what was occurring just prior to the thinking or action. The main probe the therapist uses is to ask, "What was going on prior to those thoughts coming into your mind?" The answer will help the clinician determine what the precipitating factors were to cause the addict's current slip.

Prevention Goal — The primary clinical thrust of this stage is to work backward in order to ascertain when the cognitive distortions began in each of its four phases. The goal of each section is described below, starting with phase four, it being a reverse process.

Phase four:	Attend more meetings and therapy sessions
Phase three:	Challenge the lack of importance for program and group
Phase two:	Maintain involvement in self-help and in therapy
Phase one:	Confront the denial of their thinking.

ABSTINENCE — Is the stage of recovery in which relapse prevention work begins. During this time the abuser tries to discover his using cycle and hopefully what precipitates it. Some do — some don't — it's only important that one tries. Another time prevention is explored, occurs when the addict attempts to complete his fourth and fifth step in a twelve-step program. During therapy and Step Five....whatever initiated his cravings was explored. If what precipitated the desire to use was uncovered, it was explored at the same time.

The main thrust of therapy after the abuser is detoxed or "cleaned up," educated on the model, substance abuse, nutrition, spirituality, codependency, the disease concept, and assimilates the twelve-step process of a recovery program, is to:

1. Develop alternative strategies to self-defeating behavior by teaching or enhancing any deficient life skill in his present stress-reduction system
2. Identify the using cycle
3. Probe for the antecedents to the cravings
4. Identify the impacted grief
5. Exorcise the overwhelming pain

Prevention Goal — The primary goals are to educate, teach, and discover the using cycle, its antecedents, and clean up unresolved issues or impacted pain from the past.

ASSIGNMENT 18:   This assignment targets the three major groups of people I feel will be "drawn" to this book. Anyone else reading this book, maybe . . . just maybe . . . it's not a coincidence you were drawn to this book. Everyone needs some handrails in life — something to help you through a difficult time. Maybe the concepts in this book are those handrails? Not to slight you, I can give you some questions to peruse: Were you "drawn" to this book? If not — how did you find it? Have you learned anything new from it? Has it reinforced your present concepts or helped you clarify concepts you were struggling with? Was the book worth reading? Write to me how it helped you.

1. *THERAPISTS* — Do you follow a model when you are doing therapy? Do you know where your client is along a continuum between pathology and good mental health? Do you have specific interventions designed to alleviate the stress that binds the client's progress along his life's path?
2. *COUNSELEES* — Does your therapist follow a counseling model you can understand and follow? Does he help you to understand your thinking process; identify, label and bring you through your feelings? Does he help you to align thoughts, feelings and behavior? If you can't attain internal harmony, does your therapist have the expertise to help you accomplish it?
3. *SELF-HELP MEMBERS* — Did this chapter help you to help yourself better? Did it help you to help others the way your Higher Power wanted you to do? Did it help you to identify or relinquish self-seeking behavior?

SUMMARY

Therapy is a healing modality. In its process, the developing Human Being can break free from the pain of his past traumas and self-actualize into the person he was destined to be. The paradigm explored in this book has a Psychodynamic/Developmental base which states: one grows over his life span, completes the tasks of eight different stages and self-actualizes to accomplish his spiritual task that The Celestine Prophecy (Redfield, 1993) calls the birth vision. The psychodynamic contribution is how the human's internal structure . . . his psychological makeup and personality traits . . . impact the developmental process.

In unimpeded development, the evolving Human Being completes his tasks and stages, and no therapy is needed. When the process is stuck or sidetracked in obsessive/compulsive behavior — help is needed. If the delay is short and the process is able to continue — some additional support is probably needed. When the delay is indefinite and growth is halted — therapy is usually needed. The longer it takes to get unstuck in therapy — the deeper the issues — the more intense and longer-lasting the therapy has to be.

There are three stages of therapy: establishing trust, working phase, and the implementation of the new knowledge. During these three stages, one learns about his internal structure; gains the ability to dialogue with the different ego states; enhances his relationship with self, others and God; is able to recognize his path in life and determine where he is along this road, with any issues, using the stages of the Grief Process as mile markers. In the Grief Process, one travels through its six stages, from shock through acceptance, to gain resolution with any life issue.

The key to breaking the impasse which renders one developmentally stuck is to identify the issue, ego state, and stage of the Grief Process he is stuck in. There are also three areas impacted by the impasse: thoughts, feelings, and the subsequent behavioral response initiated because of how the original situation was interpreted. The goal of therapy at this time is to generate an internally congruent behavioral response that will break the current impasse instead of miring in its own internal confusion.

Two areas of the impasse that usually require therapy are: first, *as he remains stuck in the Emotional Twilight Zone* . . . usually circling between anger and depression when he is unable to tolerate his feelings; and second, *when an ego state gets stuck in one stage and impedes the progress of the other two* . . . further creating a "Problem Loop" (behavior) which is designed to release the energy of the impacted feelings without addressing them. The smoke screen they create enables the human to divert the pain's rising energy without uprooting the original impasse. In the process, one can pretend to be competent because an action was taken.

Some of the new paradigm's contributions to therapy are: effective communication between therapist and client, increased learning, greater productivity, expanded flexibility, enhancement of the developmental process, and more concise probes.

Relapse prevention is part of the matrix of therapy. The increased self-awareness gives the addicted person a series of cues that allow him to assess himself when he begins to travel down the road to relapse. Along with the insight comes education and training. Both are designed to stop or help the addict go through the increased craving by not using mood-altering substances, instead, to use a variety of: cognitive exercises designed to nurture, validate and stop the negative thinking of the potential relapser; and behavioral tasks which will substitute for the usual behavior sequence the addict demonstrates as he travels down his relapse cycle.

During this time, a Pain Management Model is emphasized because of the painful nature of recovery when the addict has hurt himself and others; others have hurt him, and naturally occur as he tries to clean up this wreckage of his past. Rising positive feelings are another factor to this process. When they rise, they can't increase in a vacuum. All feelings rise at the same level — both good and bad. It's when the negative feelings rise along with the positive ones that the addict remembers his painful past in memories that include: what was done to him, what he did to others, and what could have been had he not reacted to the pain with an addiction.

CASE STUDY

Darlene, our 32-year-old married mom, came into her first therapy session stating she felt crazy. She was able to acknowledge her current over-protectiveness of her seven-year-old daughter was neurotic, confessed she was powerless over her own behavior, wanted to modify it, and couldn't. She also pleaded for some help to stop the disintegration that was going on inside of her and with male relationships including her husband and brother. In their deterioration, she found herself pushing them away from her and her daughter. She knew there was no logical explanation for her reactions. As she verbalized the facts, she also reported that her feelings tell a different story. They say there is something wrong.

As Darlene is focused by the therapist, she reports the underlying feelings are: someone is going to hurt her child, it's a male, and she has to protect her child from the harm he is going to do to her. As Darlene talks, she presents as a lost little girl, who is confused, and doesn't trust anyone. Upon further probing, she can't identify who it is or what they are going to do to her. She only knows there is danger for her little seven-year-old and has to act on it or "she will die."

Probing for significant environmental events proves unproductive: no major event has occurred, no deaths, anniversaries, moves, job changes, promotions, marriages, developmental milestones, or financial changes. Probing her about her childhood produced nothing suspicious, except that it seemed too much like "the Walton's." She was confronted about her uneventful childhood and sarcastically apologized for it not being traumatic. She was then confronted about her defensiveness, retorted with, "Do all therapists have to go on archeological digs in order to find a solution to a present-day situation," and then became quiet. At this time the therapist explained the questions as appropriate for his therapeutic style and asked her if she wanted to continue and go on with the assessment. She answered yes. The therapist at this time noted the resistance in his head, gave informed consent and set a boundary when he talked about his therapy style, and respected her boundaries when he asked her if she wanted to continue.

Darlene stayed in individual therapy for two sessions before she was placed in group therapy. During these sessions, the therapist was able to assess the problem and develop a treatment plan for her.

The first stage of group therapy progressed uneventfully for Darlene. She was able to establish trust with the group easily, remarked about how the group seemed to be connected in a way that felt good to her, could verbalize understanding of the developmental paradigm we use in group, and received valuable education on obsessive and compulsive behavior in a vicarious manner due to the composition of the group, including twelve-step members. It was also during this stage that Darlene started to help other group members by taking roles in their psychodramas, and she inadvertently opened up her own issues.

The first time this occurred was when we were working on another female in group, and Darlene was playing the other woman's Child Ego State. As we processed the group at the end of the drama, she started to talk about the strange feelings she experienced while in the role. At this time she was given an assignment to write a letter to her Child Ego State with her dominant writing hand, asking her about the feelings. After this letter was finished, she was asked to allow her Child to reply by writing another letter with her non-dominant hand, and bring both letters back to group the next session. At this point Darlene has entered into the second phase of group work.

During phase two of group work, Darlene was put in touch with many of her lost feelings. She cried throughout the groups. When process was attempted, all that she could report was that the feelings were dark, she felt closed in, and was afraid. Any further attempt at more awareness was met with resistance. She was given another written assignment to address the resistance. She also resisted the intervention by taking three weeks to complete it, after she was threatened to be discharged from group for non-compliance. While in limbo, waiting for the assignment to be completed, she was given: additional reading assignments in order to build up her intra-personal skills, some remedial group work with the developmental model, and plenty of validation from the group.

It was while we were working with the results of her writing to her resistance, she met her Adolescent, who informed her Adult that nobody was going to hurt Angela (the seven-year-old daughter), and then shut down by refusing to expound on the warning.

At this point in therapy, Darlene could verbalize understanding of her ego states, apply them to situations when she took roles for others, and was not able to personalize them for herself in current or past situations. This is a natural occurrence in therapy when one is bright, presents well, and appears to be further along in her process than she actually is. It did signal that Darlene needed additional information or process in order to eliminate her blocks to assimilating and using the new data.

The team reviewed Darlene's treatment plan, current progress made in therapy, what areas the resistance seems to rise in, and determined that although she made excellent strides in her feelings and learning the model: she was blocking her process of uncovering what was under her current reactive behavior toward her daughter. A backdoor approach was decided upon by the team because they knew if Darlene was confronted directly, her Adolescent would intervene and continue to block the awareness process.

The intervention decided upon by the team was to lure her into a psychodrama by intriguing her Adolescent with the possibility that her current behavior was a "Problem Loop," beneficial to her "somehow," and to explore if she was willing . . . "the Loop's" benefits to her. The team felt this was an innocuous way of addressing it and could appear to be fun, instead of pain, because Darlene was fascinated with how the group members who were in self-help used the Problem Loop in their lives.

The Problem Loop was personified with each stage having a voice. Half way through the drama it was clear that each voice of the Loop was also the voice of one of the ego states. The director made the shift of the voices by re-labeling each stage of the Problem Loop to an ego state (Child, Adolescent, Adult) . . . replaced the Adult Darlene with another group member she chose . . . placed the original Adult of Darlene into the observer position . . . and replayed the dialogue from the problem loop as their newly associated ego states while Darlene looked on from her new role.

Darlene looked upon the drama in amazement as it unfolded. It was as if . . . she was seeing it for the first time. During her observation, her face went from surprise, shock, anger, fear and then she began to cry. She was immediately switched with the Child alter, continued to cry, and became angry when any attempt was made to process the feelings. She maintained the anger when she was switched to the Adolescent. During the switch in roles: the Adolescent was validated for protecting the Child; the resistance was reframed to a boundary that the Adolescent did not need to maintain, as the Adult had sought help for the hidden pain by coming into therapy; and the Adolescent would still not relinquish control by reducing the anger.

The Adolescent was switched to the Adult, given all the pertinent facts of the current impasse, and urged to take some action with the situation. The Adult capitulated to the strength of the Adolescent and fear of the Child, and shut down. It was at this point that the therapist gave her a choice to end the drama or to go on to explore some possibilities. Darlene chose to continue. (This demonstrated ego strength and probable success of the intervention.)

Not altering the drama's structure — the therapist directed the Adult to converse with the Child and try to get her to talk about the pain. The Child was given a secret message from the therapist to either not talk, or, to say that she didn't trust the Adult (this was the Child's real message to the Adult when she wouldn't process her feelings and the Adolescent had to save her.) Upon the therapist's direction to the Adolescent, she was to come and take the Child away from the Adult and tell her that the Adult wasn't capable of protecting her and stated a few problem loops she was going to participate in to accomplish it.

As the Adolescent drew the Child away from the Adult and walked to the other side of the room — the Adult went into action. She walked right up to the Adolescent, talked to her gently but firmly, stated her limits and boundaries when it came to her feelings, and took the Child gently by the hand. The Child was reluctant at first. The Adult remained gentle but insistent, brought the Child back beside her into the center of the room, where the original drama took place, and asked the Adolescent to join her and be by her side. The Adolescent complied without any direction.

At this point, the Adult took over the drama, sat head to head with the Child, and gently encouraged her to talk. As the Adult started to cry, the therapist switched her into the Child's role, and had the Adult Alter repeat the words the Adult Darlene said to the Child. Darlene, in her Child Ego State role, started to talk and by the time she finished: had disclosed being sexually abused by an uncle for five years; how she was afraid to report it because the rest of her life was so perfect; thought somehow it was her fault she was abused; would be blamed for it going on for so long . . . she would then lose her perfect life . . . AND DIE!

Her little girl (Child Ego State) during this time had learned how to dissociate from her feelings when she was being abused, by going to a secret place in her mind where she was safe. Her Adolescent was the one who stopped the abuse by telling the uncle she was going to the police if he ever did it again. He hurriedly moved away to another part of the country and was killed in an automobile accident.

The combination of the dissociation and the uncle's death allowed the developing Darlene to "forget about it" because the abuse was "water under the bridge" and she could "put it behind her." This cognitive process became an overt decision made by an abused child, and transformed by an internal covert process composed of two ego states in order to keep the knowledge of the abuse buried and out of reach from the awareness of the future adult. It was an excellent survival skill and needs to be validated. Until Darlene had the ability to handle the feelings and ramifications from the abuse — it was dangerous to see them.

In the last phase of therapy, Darlene was able to process the losses from the abuse and begin to heal. As she continued in therapy, she was able to allow her daughter more space, stop enforcing limited contact with males, and could verbalize and believe that her brother would not abuse her daughter.

All of Darlene's expectations of therapy were met: her thoughts, feelings and behaviors were congruent, the disintegration of her self concepts and male relationships were stopped, and her life was on a forward course again.

CHAPTER SIXTEEN

A twelve-step program
Is a new design for living.
Within this spiritual approach,
The steps become its
System of recovery.

OVERVIEW

The overview of the twelve steps in Figure 16.1 can help to conceptualize their intention to help the development of spiritual growth within the recovering individual. In the growth process one will: develop trust in a power greater than himself, clean up his side of the street, and move *from* being a user of others out of a self centered fear — *to* helping others overcome the same problems they were besieged with.

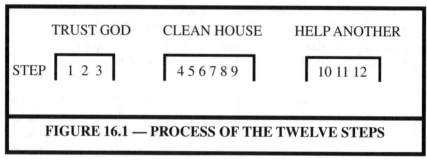

TRUST GOD	CLEAN HOUSE	HELP ANOTHER
STEP 1 2 3	4 5 6 7 8 9	10 11 12

FIGURE 16.1 — PROCESS OF THE TWELVE STEPS

When you complete this chapter, you will have an understanding of how a twelve-step program works, helps, and be able to identify various problems you can encounter:

1. The twelve steps help the recovering person to grow individually
2. The twelve traditions help him to grow with the group and family
3. The twelve concepts help him to conduct business in the fellowship and grow within the non-program predominant culture
4. Helps him to establish mental, physical, and spiritual boundaries
5. Helps him to view trust as a process and determine whose trustworthy (including himself)
6. Helps him to overcome problems of choosing and keeping a sponsor
7. Helps him to develop a support system of twelve-step program members
8. Identifies what happens when you outgrow people in the program
9. Identifies how you never outgrow the program

TWELVE STEP PROGRAM

A loose definition of a twelve-step program would be:
a group of people, joined by a common problem,
who meet weekly to share their strength, hope, and experience
on how to overcome their common problem.

TWELVE STEP DOCTRINE

The four components of the twelve-step program are a set of spiritual, moral, and ethical principles that embody the wisdom of the ages. They are a philosophy that, if adhered to, will bring a more positive and rewarding life to the human being who is following them. The first fellowship to start was Alcoholics Anonymous in 1935, when a recently sober alcoholic named Bill Wilson came to the conclusion that the only way he was going to maintain sobriety was to help another drunk. During this time, he was in Akron, Ohio and was referred to another chronic alcoholic. This turned out to be Dr. Bob, the co-founder of Alcoholics Anonymous, and the first meeting was held. In 1987, there were 76,000 groups, three million members in 139 countries following the principle embodied within the Alcoholics Anonymous program and finding a sober, more peaceful, and rewarding life.

The twelve-step philosophy is broken into four components. The first portion of the doctrine states that anyone following its tenets will maintain a daily reprieve from the disease's oppression. The second part of this belief system is in the principles taught through the twelve steps. Their dogma ensures a person's recovery from the damage already inflicted upon him by his disease (The Promises of AA, pp.83-84, The Big Book, 1976) if he follows the system of recovery embodied within him. The third tenet is the Twelve Traditions which guide the individual's relationship with the group and can also be a conductor to healing within the family (Narcotics Anonymous, It Works, How and Why, 1993). The fourth section of this philosophical system is the Twelve Concepts — and in them is described a set of principles of how the groups can apply the spirituality of the program in business matters among themselves or the fellowship as an organization. This trust can also be used in the home or on the job. (Paths to Recovery, Al-Anons Steps, Traditions, and Concepts, 1997).

A New Design For Living

The prime tenet for using the program as a new design for living is: through shared experience, members can abstain "a day at a time," from the person, place, or thing they are addicted to or obsessive over. Another major tenet is that the compulsion is a disease — chronic (never goes away), progressive (gets worse), and it can only be arrested a day at a time. They also believe that this daily reprieve can be accomplished if one makes a commitment to the program by going to several meetings a week, joining a home group, becoming active in service for that group, obtaining a sponsor, helping newcomers and others still suffering from the addiction (twelve-step work). Their teachings also include, without a twelve-step program, the addicted individual will end up in "institutions, incarcerated or dead" (Alcoholics Anonymous, 1976). These tenets embody the first of four components that encompasses the doctrine of the twelve-step philosophy.

CASE STUDY: Bill, a 27-year-old addict, is a classic example of what happens when someone doesn't follow the program. In early recovery, Bill was glued to the program. He attended 90 meetings in 90 days, acquired a sponsor, adopted a home group, was able to be of service to the group by doing various jobs, tagged along on commitments, and participated in twelve-step work by talking to newcomers and going to institution meetings and telling his story. Bill was able to maintain a high level of commitment for 18 months. As a reward, Bill enjoyed good clean time: his relationship with his wife had improved, he had received a promotion on his job, other family members and friends were recognizing his changes and were beginning to trust him again.

Just about the time Bill was experiencing his greatest achievements, his attitude began to get negative as he started to talk about recovery getting old. The first to pick up on his mood swing were his wife and sponsor. His wife cautioned him about "going down old roads," and Bill assured her that he was just tired. His sponsor confronted him on the change, warned him about the pitfalls of early recovery, encouraged him to maintain his meeting level, and suggested completing a comprehensive Fourth Step. Bill verbally agreed with all his sponsor's suggestions, and over the next six months did just the opposite . . . progressively backed out of the program until he was attending one meeting every other week, stopped participating in service work, and relapsed three days before his second anniversary.

When Bill came into therapy, he was three weeks clean from his last relapse, after having two years of abstinence prior to using again. Bill stated that he was enjoying his life before he relapsed and even though it only lasted a month, he felt like he gave up his life again. With initial probing Bill couldn't identify the antecedents to the relapse, only that his attitude became negative, and he woke up one morning in a crack house with a spike in his arm. Bill's wife and sponsor were both highly supportive of him and stated that they felt he could do it again with the experience of having two years clean. Bill made the commitment to re-engage in the program at his previous level, work the steps with a greater enthusiasm, and attend therapy. Had Bill followed the new design for living as it is outlined in the primary text of NA and the Big Book of AA, chances are, "a day at a time," *he would not have relapsed.*

A System of Recovery

The next three segments of the philosophy open up a spiritual path for the individual to attain peace and a working relationship with God and self (steps), family and friends (traditions) and society (concepts). Embodied in these principles lies the healing Journey in which one can return from whatever Hell he puts himself into. These are also called The Three Legacies:

ONE = RECOVERY ... *Steps* were designed for individual recovery

TWO = UNITY .... *Traditions* help the recovering person with relationships

THREE = SERVICE ..... *Concepts* are a guideline to interact with society

THE TWELVE STEPS The twelve steps are the primary system of recovery in a self-help program. Their principles are the personification of acceptance, hope, faith, honesty, integrity, willingness, humility, courage, charity, vigilance, serenity and service. They manifest as a deepening spirituality within the Human Being studying and applying them to his life. Broken down, the twelve steps help with the following:

STEP ONE: Helps one to see the problem he is struggling with and how much it has cost him in trying to control it alone.

STEP TWO: Helped him to understand, in a gentle unfolding, how insane his control was when he did the same thing over and over and expected something to change.

STEP THREE: Helped him to understand what spirituality could be when it defined one's *will* as his thoughts and feelings, one's *life* as the behavior that was generated out of those thoughts and feelings; and identifies issues that kept one separate from God when he couldn't go to him for relief of the obsessive/compulsive thoughts, feelings and subsequent behavior.

STEP FOUR: Helped one to look at himself in a way that was never before possible.

STEP FIVE: Helped one to develop trust in the program, himself and God.

STEP SIX: Demonstrated: that everyone does the best he can with the tools he has been given; all behavior was and is useful; that change is a process and usually doesn't occur until another behavior replaces it.

STEP SEVEN: Teaches that true humility is being teachable.

STEP EIGHT: Shows that awareness only comes when one is ready for it, he won't be given anything he is not equipped to handle, and suggests that he has to put his name on the list of people he has to make amends to.

STEP NINE: States that you can't get better at another's expense. No amend can be made if it hurts the other person to reopen the wound. That one can make an indirect amend by changing the offensive behavior. That life will change for the positive when the first nine steps are completed.

STEP TEN: Demonstrates the importance of keeping one's side of the street clean in his daily interactions with others. A by-product of keeping the moment clean is that the lack of negative consequences keeps the noise level in one's head at a low volume and allows him to do the work on the antecedents of his self-defeating behavior. The process helps him to clean up the past and prevent it from influencing today's agenda.

STEP ELEVEN: Allows the recovering person to remain in communion with a Higher Power. It also identifies ways to discover what that Higher Power wants him to do to help himself and his fellow travelers. This also hinders self-seeking.

STEP TWELVE: Helps one to stay out of self-centered fear and self-seeking when he helps others go through the same problems he is conquering by sharing how the principles he has learned in the program helps him to have a better life.

THE TWELVE TRADITIONS The traditions are the second point on the healing triangle of the three legacies. Just as the twelve steps help the individual in his personal recovery, the traditions help facilitate change within the family and outside relationships. If their principles are adhered to, various changes will appear over time, until a complete transformation can be observed in the individual. This is actually a secondary gain of the program . . . when relationships heal . . . after the abuser sought help to become abstinent.

THE TWELVE CONCEPTS The twelve concepts are the third segment of the recovery triad. In their principles, they provide a system to maintain personal harmony, while conducting business with other groups and can the predominant culture.

CLARITY FOR NEWCOMERS (and also long-timers)

Like every other institution on this Starship Earth, a twelve-step program can be a microcosm of the predominant culture, if one is not careful. I believe, in our Journey, that those we meet can provide to us a negative or positive experience, depending on which side of them we tap into. Program people are no different. They are human and subject to all human frailties. The major advantage they have over non-program people is that they have at their disposal, a system of being aware of and changing the undesired behavior.

Boundaries

One acquires or clarifies his boundaries through the shared experience of other program members. In the sharing, they learn how boundary violations contributed to their disease, and later, what violates them mentally, physically or spiritually.

MENTALLY No one has a right to beat you up mentally. This occurs when someone you respect because they appear to have a good program, berates you for a difference of opinion or because you made a mistake. Most will not. Most will share their personal experience about how they overcame the same problem, in an effort to help you find another way to attain less problematic outcomes.

If you find yourself attracting negative people, look at what you do to draw them in. What generally occurs in this scenario is that your biological Critical Parent was usually the primary caregiver. Your Child, who is the one interacting with these adults, is needy. In order to get his needs met, he moves toward something he knows....**someone that is familiar**....and the person they generally seek validation from is usually **the Critical Parent.** If you wonder why dysfunctional people find someone else to complement their codependency — the above is the reason. I'll address this in depth in the chapter on relationships. Once you know the problem, look for other solutions by:

- Not letting critical people into your life (have tight boundaries)
- Talking about the problem at meeting level
- Running it by your sponsor, therapist, and support system
- Listening to how others stopped going to critical people
- Watching how others interact and gravitate toward the ones who are remaining positive with themselves and others
- Risking to connect with more positive people

The only thing that will happen when you successfully complete the transition is that you will experience some anxiety.

The thoughts that prevail during the anxiety are, "it's a dream — not real — you are not worthy of positive friendships — or something will happen to end it." Hold on! This is only the leading edge of feelings that manifest as irrational fear, fueled by prior experience, are made real in the process and try to sabotage you. This evidence (feeling its real because it happened before), is false. These feelings are only the memories of past events, visitors from your history, *AND FALSE IN THE MOMENT*! As you hold on tight, dispute the irrational fears, your true feelings will surface. They will be the sadness of what you experienced throughout your life span *AND THE NEEDLESS MISTAKES YOU MADE WHEN YOU REMAINED IN NEGATIVITY BY DRAWING IN CRITICAL PEOPLE AND REPELLING POSITIVE ONES*!

This is a big issue. Hold on tight and go through it. The rewards are greater than the pain — for once you go through the pain, a world of positive experiences is waiting for you. To avoid the discomfort — the opposite is true. One can continue to allow the negativity into his life and wonder why his life doesn't get any better.

PHYSICALLY Physical boundaries are the same as mental ones. One has to know them in order to enforce them. Some people come into program without any boundaries. Some were never taught because their primary caregivers didn't have any. Some were abused and their boundaries were constantly violated.

Some will violate your boundaries. Most will not. If you feel "funny" or "uncomfortable" about what someone is physically doing to you — *STOP IT! YOU HAVE A RIGHT TO DO IT!* They are probably violating your boundaries and you don't know it because you are just beginning to identify them. The easiest way to stop them is an outstretched hand in the form of a handshake. If someone tries to go past that, turn it up into a stopping motion and order them to stop. It works. The program does force one to do his inventory…. even the boundary violators.

If you find yourself continuing to draw this kind of people, it's generally the Child who is needy, attracting what's familiar, or the Adolescent wanting to get his sexual needs met. The main problem with both is that the violation, if left unattended, can lead to shame and relapse. The sexual acting out will cause the same results. Both are gateway drugs and need to be identified as such. Neither can be played with, denied, or minimized because of their potential devastating consequences. Both ego states can be handled in the same way the emotional boundaries were transformed. It takes a strong Nurturing Adult to handle this area. Any less, the Child will remain needy and the Adolescent will act out. Both will rule the Internal Structure, dictating the needs of the 7 and 13-year-old to the Adult who will not intervene, and all three ego states will wonder why things are not different in their lives.

SPIRITUALLY Spiritual boundaries become violated when well-meaning members try to recruit for a religious organization or philosophy that works for them. There is nothing wrong in what they follow — it only becomes a detriment when they try to preach it in the program. Most newcomers are confused about God. Some hate Him. Others no longer follow the God of their childhood. Many don't trust Him. It doesn't matter where someone's beliefs are when he comes into program. It's only important that he learns and applies the program to his life.

Spirituality is developed as one "gets" the program. He learns about a Higher Power through someone who is willing to guide and love, instead of judging, criticizing, and condemning him. Most times the group is what the newcomer feels is his Higher Power….with its members, everything is possible….new answers and solutions, acceptance, love, and purpose. After the newcomer's initial reluctance, most will have a personal relationship with God after they ask Him back into their lives.

Through the spirituality of the program, some will return to the God of their childhood. Others will seek a new faith. Some, for the first time, will have a faith. It makes no difference which choice they make for the results are usually the same: a spiritual relationship with a Higher Power who loves, comforts, and guides them throughout their lives. And through this relationship, peace and harmony are attained in their daily living. This allows them to grow and actualize into the people they were destined to be, as they complete the job they envisioned prior to their birth (Birthvision).

There is another way one can be spiritually violated and that is through diversion. This deviation occurs when one's attention is taken away from the study and application of the program to his life. It occurs when someone:

- Becomes preoccupied with another
- Is used by someone self-seeking (prestige, power, sex, ect.)
- Takes up their time needlessly
- Goes off on a tangent and proclaim its merits
- Has a personality clash. (Program states: principles above personalities)
- Is dominated by the group or an individual
- Uses one's status or power to sway someone
- Uses any means that diverts another from attending, studying, or applying the program to his daily life.

Diversion usually occurs subtly....sometimes it's blatant....most times it's not. The devices used are as "cunning and baffling" as the disease is. I can't emphasize enough its insidious nature. The simplest rules to follow are: when one is a "vexation to your spirit," or "things" seem to usually come up which constantly drain your energy; when there is not enough energy to take care of yourself; this is generally a spiritual diversion.

SUMMARY All boundaries, mental, physical, or spiritual, are nothing more than one learning about himself in relationship to self, others, and God. In boundaries, one creates a space between himself and the outside world, which protects his internal integrity. In the space created — one takes in his spirituality. Without this space one is engulfed by another - their ideas and actions - and nothing can penetrate it. It's like being covered by an impenetrable force field. Nothing can breech its density. This can also be a defensive cloak, when new ideas are not able to enter, and the old Problem Loops remain inside.

The program is a place one can learn these boundaries through other members' shared experiences. The safety generated at various meetings allows the new boundaries to be tested without the fear of ridicule. Watch as others in the program drop their veils of codependency. This starts as they recognize and set boundaries and continues when they keep themselves separate by "knowing where they begin and the other ends."

Overall, boundaries can be imagined on a physical plane. It's easy. All one has to do is to extend your right arm out fully, place your hand in a stopping motion, and draw a circle around yourself at the distance of the outstretched hand. That is your boundary space. It will include mental, physical and spiritual boundaries. In any situation, all one has to do is to visualize this space to see if it looks, feels, or sounds like anyone is violating it. Figure 16.2 is a graphic representation of them.

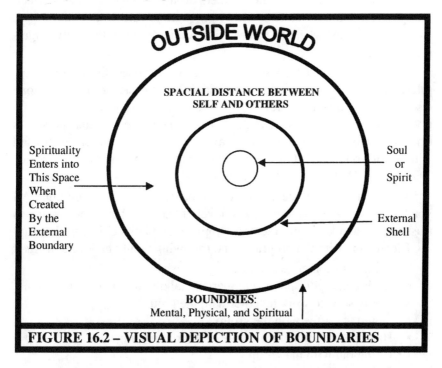

FIGURE 16.2 – VISUAL DEPICTION OF BOUNDARIES

ASSIGNMENT 19: What are your boundaries? Try to personalize some of the information of this chapter to ascertain yours. Some will be easy; others will be elusive until you know more about yourself. Physical boundaries are easy to test. Allow someone you trust to help you with determining yours. Have them walk toward you from three different directions: front, back, and side. As they walk toward you, the place you begin to feel uncomfortable is your boundary. Mark it on the floor. Don't be surprised by what you see.

Mental boundaries are more difficult. An easy way to determine the violation is to make note when someone's action toward, or, around you, diverts your mind from the positive thinking you were trying to maintain. Spiritual boundaries are similar except they involve feelings instead of thinking. Take heed when the positive feelings you experience from the program are suddenly ended because of someone else's behavior and you return to self-centered fear. The action of that person has just caused you to disconnect from your Higher Power. Their behavior violates your spiritual boundaries.

Trust

Trust is a process. Most newcomers do not know how to trust when they first enter program. They either gravitate toward what's familiar or automatically trust when the information sounds good, without investigating it further.

The process of trust is a simple one: give someone a little about yourself and if it's not used against you and doesn't come back through someone else — the person can be trusted at that level. Each time you do this, you give more of what you are. If the trust is maintained — that person is trustworthy to the level of trust you have tried. Not everyone can be trusted with all of you. That's OK! If you only have a few trustworthy friends YOU ARE LUCKY OR A GOOD JUDGE OF CHARACTER.

If your trust is violated, you don't have to "throw the bum out." All you have to do is go back to the last level of trust at which the person was trustworthy, and keep him there. A simple example would be in developing friendships with the program. The following would be levels of trust:

- Talking to someone at a meeting
- Giving him your phone number and talking to him over the phone
- Doing service work together with the group
- Going to coffee with the group
- Having coffee together before or after a meeting
- Going out with the group
- Doing something together

The above is not meant for a guideline on how to start a sexual relationship. It is a way to develop an intimate friendship with another program member AND ENJOY ALL THE OTHER LEVELS OF FRIENDSHIP

AND FELLOWSHIP THE PROGRAM HAS TO OFFER. Once the process is learned in program, it can be used in all parts of your life.

Most people will fall into the first category. You enjoy them at meetings, look forward to hearing them speak, talk to them at meetings, and that's all. Some will do service and provide you a chance to observe their character in action. You will also have a safe place to try out the process if your group goes out for coffee after the meeting. Here is another place one can observe if someone is just "talking the talk" or they can be trusted.

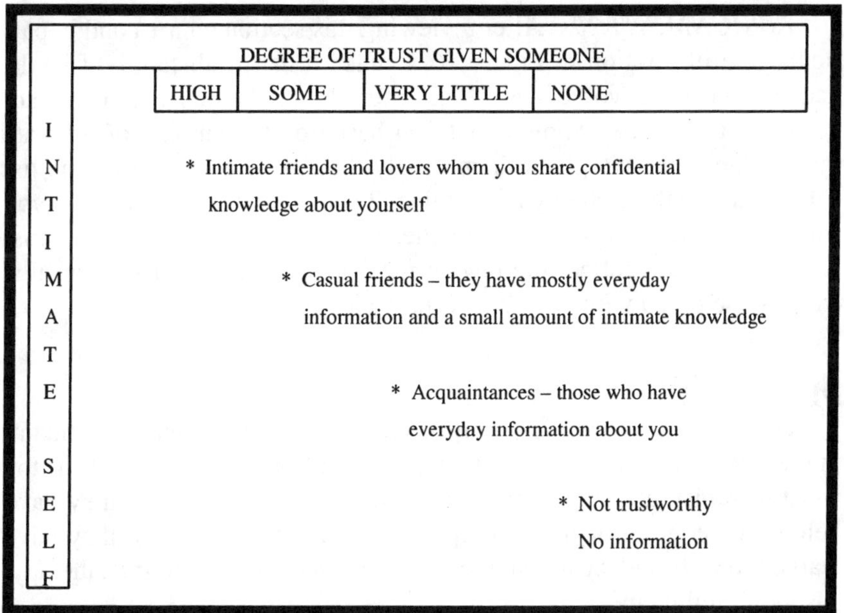

	DEGREE OF TRUST GIVEN SOMEONE			
	HIGH	SOME	VERY LITTLE	NONE
I N T I M A T E S E L F	* Intimate friends and lovers whom you share confidential knowledge about yourself	* Casual friends – they have mostly everyday information and a small amount of intimate knowledge	* Acquaintances – those who have everyday information about you	* Not trustworthy No information

FIGURE 16.3 – TRUST SCALE

When you meet a friend before the meeting, it usually signifies the beginning of a deeper level of trust. More intimate things are discussed and one becomes more vulnerable. The last two levels concern social events. Groups do get together and attend social events together: picnics, covered dishes, sports events, dances, etc. These are usually safe because there is safety in numbers. When members start socially interacting together, there is usually a high degree of trust, friendship, and intimacy. If married or divorced, sometimes they can do things with their families. When trust is broken at this level, it is usually devastating when old tapes play and shame rises. If it does, all it means is someone trusted too fast, and needed more time to observe the true character of the other person. Figure 16.3 is an outline of letting someone in.

The process of trust is easy to conceptualize. In order to visualize it, just envision the same illustration we used to describe physical boundaries: an outstretched arm and the hand in a stopping motion. Where the hand stops is usually two feet. It's at this point you allow casual friends. Intimate friends, lovers, and trusted family members are the only ones allowed past the barrier. Acquaintances are placed between two and four feet away. Untrustworthy people are kept in the next room or an additional barrier is placed between you and them.

ASSIGNMENT 20:   After reviewing this section on trust and in particular the illustration in Figure 16.3, make a list of all family, friends, acquaintances, co-workers, etc. Place each one on the trust continuum according to what they know about you based on the amount of intimate knowledge you have given them. Study the list. Is everyone on the list trustworthy to the degree you trust them? If the answer is no, why do you trust them? How can you move anyone, according to the scale and the trust criteria, to better reflect the degree they are trustworthy. How can this exercise help you with new friends now and later in the future?

Sponsorship

Having a sponsor in program is like getting a new friend, confidant, guide, mentor, and sometimes therapist. Sponsors don't like to hear the word therapist, although what else would you call them after they have helped someone through a bad episode, using the knowledge they have learned so well, and the individual didn't go out there. It's program therapy. Just don't tell them.

Like all relationships, one with a sponsor is built over time, using the same guidelines outlined in the previous two sections. Trust is established slowly, giving only appropriate information at each stage, to ascertain if the sponsor deserves your trust. If you want to keep your sponsor at program level and use a therapist for more intimate problems — IT'S OK. THIS IS GOOD BOUNDARIES. Many are good with the program and fall short with effective strategies for non-program situations.

A sponsor's true role in the program is that of a guide, one who's been through the forest of the disease before you, found the path that leads out of the darkness of despair and into the light of recovery . . . and is willing to take your hand and lead you out. Al-Anon and Alcoholics Anonymous have excellent pamphlets on sponsorship. Pick them up for further reading.

Not having a sponsor has been likened to playing Monopoly, passing "Go," and not collecting the $200. Another analogy would be only taking half a pie when you were offered the whole thing. There are two problems that consistently come up for the newcomer and long-timer alike, when a sponsor is not attained:

1. Lack of trust
2. Fear of success

It's also suggested in the program that one picks a "*SAME SEX*" sponsor because of the intimacy that transpires between them. I feel it's imperative to adhere to the suggestion. Opposite sex sponsors add a dimension to the relationship that is not spiritual in nature, when it diverts with the action of sexual intimacy, instead of helping with shared experiences and guidance.

LACK OF TRUST   The Child Ego State is the reluctant part of the internal structure that doesn't want to trust. His evidence is the betrayal exhibited by those he trusted in the past. This is where the Adult has to try new ground, not head toward what's familiar: "to do what you did — to get what you got," and generate more positive outcomes. In this case, trust will be a process. The Child will have to be supported through this phase, as his fear increases, while the Adult learns to trust.

In this process, the harmony of the internal structure will become greater as the Adult continues to make mature decisions based on holistic needs, instead of the self-centered, fear-induced needs of one ego state. In this way he can provide adaptive outcomes and throughout the experience remain available to the Child.

Sometimes, the Child will have unreasonable expectations of the sponsor. He will see him as a god (the parent), able to do some exciting things with the program and seem to have all the answers. He puts him on a pedestal. What the Child has done is to set him up to fall. The sponsor is human. He will fail in some areas. No one has all the answers, except God, and sometimes I think He makes up the answers as He goes along (humor). The Child, at this point, needs limits placed on him. He needs to be told "the facts of life" and assured it's OK for someone he trusts to be human. THE CHILD WON'T DIE IF THOSE IN HIS LIFE ARE NOT PERFECT. The Adult understands this — the Child doesn't.

The other problem experienced while trying to establish trust with a sponsor is the transference that occurs when a sponsor, or one who has the potential to be one, has the attributes of one of the person's primary caregivers. The sponsor does things that are similar to the parents: same talk, gestures, looks or features, attitudes, accent, cultural likeness, ethnic similarities, walk, etc., and to the Child — THEY ARE THE PARENTS *"BECAUSE"* IT FEELS LIKE THEY ARE! This is real to the Child and has to be validated. It doesn't mean the Adult is going to act upon the feelings, just because the Child feels them. It's just a validation to a part of him that has different perception. This is when feelings are not facts and the Child has to be gently told this. To act upon these feelings without a reality check by the Adult, is to place the Child back into "driving the bus." If it happens, the Child is in charge of the Adult's life; all decisions are made based on the fear from the Child instead of the balanced holistic needs of the Adult.

When the transference occurs (the Child is now in charge), the negative attributes of his primary caregiver are projected onto the sponsor or a potential one, and he is verbally attacked or avoided. In either case, the loss is to all when we enter a spiritual component to the equation. Usually, spiritual forces are at work in the program, putting people together, in order to facilitate change and promote healing. This spiritual agenda is ignored totally when the Child is in charge, running out of self-centered fear, when no Adult is in operation to steer him back into fulfilling his spiritual goals.

The loss is immediate to both, when distrust based on fear, happens between them. The newcomer loses a lot of potential growth in the program. The sponsor doesn't get the opportunity to reinforce his program beliefs. Both lose the potential healing that transpires when two people injured in the past, one through omission — one through commission, has a chance to be part of a healing exchange, when his sponsor is able to be more supportive than his primary caregivers were. BIG LOSS!

ASSIGNMENT 21:   Has the above ever happened to you? If yes — when? How could you have changed it? What did you lose? What was the transference (what reminded you of them)? What did you project onto them (blame them for what they didn't do)? How can the experience help you to pick a sponsor now?

FEAR OF SUCCESS   The fear of success encompasses three layers which include the Child, Adolescent, and an uninvolved or distant Adult.

• **First Layer — The Child**   The first layer immerses the Child in fear as he perceives recovery as moving too fast. At this point, the Child's fear is of "fear itself;" doesn't understand what's going on — just knows that it's too fast and if it keeps moving at this speed — the anxiety he's feeling will kill him. The feeling under the anxiety is one of being out of control — and he is. If recovery keeps moving, he will not be in charge — the Adult will. The subconscious memories that drive this fear are the evidence to back up the feelings. Didn't the same thing happen when he was small — every time things moved too fast he was hurt. The Adult has to go through these feelings and maintain his pace in recovery before he can develop the emotional maturity needed to quiet the Child's fear. Sounds familiar doesn't it. *It can happen in any phase of living and you won't know the outcome until the situation you chose to go through is over.* This process is the hallmark of emotional maturity. Fear is not overcome until courage, faith, and hope are applied to a difficult life event and one goes through it.

• **Second Layer — The Adolescent**   The Adolescent balks in this layer because he doesn't want to give up his toys. Usually, he is not using a mood-altering substance. He has switched to this secondary drug of choice, which is generally persons, places, or things. Some of the toys can be sex, relationships, money, prestige, work, accomplishment, or any pleasurable or fulfilling activity, event, or circumstance that if brought to an excess (can be used obsessively and compulsively to keep the focus external) diverts him from his healing path.

The spiritual malady created with this behavior occurs when the individual deviates from his spiritual tasks (healing and helping others) through the activity created by the errant behavior. Some examples would be: someone having an affair with a married person — coming to an understanding through the program that it has to be terminated — and not wanting to end it. Another would be when work becomes encompassing and all other facets of the person's life are ignored. The program stresses balance — holds one accountable for omissions as others share their losses at meetings — and makes it very uncomfortable to perpetuate problematic behavior (even if it's a good one like work).

During this time of excess, the Adult has to place limits on the Adolescent by bringing the behavior back to balance or stopping it in the case of self-defeating habits, in order to return back toward his spiritual path. This won't be easy. The Adolescent's purpose is to protect the Child. He accomplishes it when the Child's feelings are anesthetized through the action of the excess behavior. Don't be surprised at what surfaces for you after the behavior is stopped or balanced.

• **Third Layer — The Adult** Fears are generated in the Adult when he begins to recognize the abuse he suffered in relationships with addicted, distant or disengaged: spouses or partners. The pain engendered by these relationships is profound and commensurate with the longevity of the relationships. Some are married for 50 years before they are aware there is something wrong with how they are feeling and seek help to find release from their pain.

At this point, recovery stops in order to remain in the toxic relationship or marriage. They proclaim they don't want to leave because "they still love them" or are in fear when "they don't want to be alone." In both cases, the program would exacerbate the confusion when unacceptable behavior, trust, boundaries, entitlement, safety, rights, and appropriate relationships are discussed and modeled. The fear can be overcome. The rewards are great. You don't have to leave just because you have new information. Sometimes, it can be used as a foundation for healing the past and establishing a new and better relationship today. When a couple has been together for a long time, it's worth the effort. It will take two. When there is only one participating, the breakup becomes more imminent as they grow apart in the program. It's a hard fact to overcome and as a twelve-step person, I leave it alone when I recognize it in others. As a therapist, I confront it and help them to discover what's behind the fear. This gives them a choice and I believe all human beings deserve choices in any decision they have to make in life.

Support System

Developing a support system is a similar process as creating one with a sponsor: trust is a process and boundaries are maintained. Instead of it being one person — it is many. A sponsor is part of a support system. Other members that could be included in a support system are more seasoned members who engender nurturing and seem to take on a parenting role. These people usually seem wise, knowing, and have good shared experience that seems to help you with a presenting problem. These are the ones most members in the program are comfortable with. Some take on the form of being a lost or nonexistent brother or sister — one you can identify with, talk to, and who usually understands what you are going through. Others are spiritual guides — seem to have a conscious contact with God, and demonstrate it by how they behave and treat people. Others are "power of examples" of how the program works, and are willing to share it with others. Some you just talk to at meetings. Still others will be available to take phone calls and just "listen" when you need it. Put them all together and they equal a support system.

In developing a support system, the same pitfalls with the ego states in getting a sponsor, can prevail. The same issues and interventions can be applied. Each new person entering the support system can trigger off the same fear and abandonment issues until they are resolved to a satisfactory degree. *This desensitization will occur as one uses his issues as an opportunity to grow instead of a reason to run.*

The same issues that trigger you off can set off the person you are reacting to. At this time, you will have to separate yourself from them in order to sort out the information and identify whose issues belong to whom. This is hard at the beginning and gets easier as you go along. *A rule of thumb in handling these issues would be: if someone comes at you with something out of nowhere — it's their issue: if you have a large emotional reaction to something they say or do — it's your issue.*

This separating out of another's issues from their own is problematic at best for newcomers. Enough energy is spent just trying to stay clean and to put the focus on them: that another's reactions to them, or their own personality clashes with another, are just too draining. It is nothing but a diversion to take the focus off themselves, and diverts them from their primary spiritual purpose: to remain clean and sober and use the results of the experience to help others remain abstinent.

Later on in the program, after sobriety is a daily fact, one will be able to easily field these difficulties with poise and dignity.

Outgrowing People — Not the Program

One word of caution: If you stay in the program long enough and apply it to your life, you will at various times outgrow most of your support system and even your sponsor. This does not mean that some are better than others — it means that people grow at different rates. Some grow faster than others. Some have fewer issues and less history to deal with. Others have more.

It's also not abandonment for you or the other person if you outgrow them. It's normal. Someone in the program was talking about the people that went through her life since she was in program and related them to angels that God sent to her: some were meant to stay a season, others a year, still others much longer. This was a healthier way of looking at people who left the program or people you outgrow and leave behind.

It's also not uncommon for one to have had three sponsors: the first as a newcomer, the second when he became more serious, and the third seems to be a permanent sponsor until he retires and moves away or dies.

No matter how many people you grow beyond, you will never outgrow the program. It continues to produce — the more you cultivate. Each time your awareness rises, you will find another way to use the program. It never stops. Each time you think you know it all — another opportunity to use the program will present itself. It will amaze you how you didn't see it before. The more teachable one is - the greater the possibilities.

SUMMARY

A Twelve-Step Program's matrix is the template for a new design for living to those who have been hurt or confused by past events and reacted with self-defeating behavior. They want to change today, but can't. Their old ways of dealing with problems just maintained their previous maladaptive behavior instead of providing effective strategies to overcome the problem.

The Twelve Steps, Traditions and Concepts generate a system of recovery as the dysfunctional individual applies their principles to his life and achieves more desirable results when encountering life's problems. The Steps provide the framework for individual recovery. The Traditions provide help to the group and subsequently the family. The Concepts help with the program's business matters and apply to the culture as well. Together, they form The Three Legacies.

Boundaries to the individual can be mental, physical and spiritual. Most people who grew up in less than child-centered homes very rarely learned boundaries because their parents had none, and the children's were consistently violated, or never existed. One determines his boundaries by how he feels and also how he reacts to someone else's behavior.

Trust is a process. Those who did not witness the process in their childhood usually end up trusting untrustworthy people because they are familiar. When someone is familiar to them, it is usually a protection of their primary caregivers on to an acquaintance and they trust them without knowing why. The process of trust occurs as you give some information about yourself to someone and they don't try to hurt you with it, nor does it come back to you from anyone else. The more you are able to give another about yourself without being violated or betrayed by them — the more trustworthy they are. One learns how to trust himself in how he is able to trust others without getting himself hurt.

There are several issues that surround the individual's inability to obtain a sponsor. Most of them revolve around trust and the fear of success.

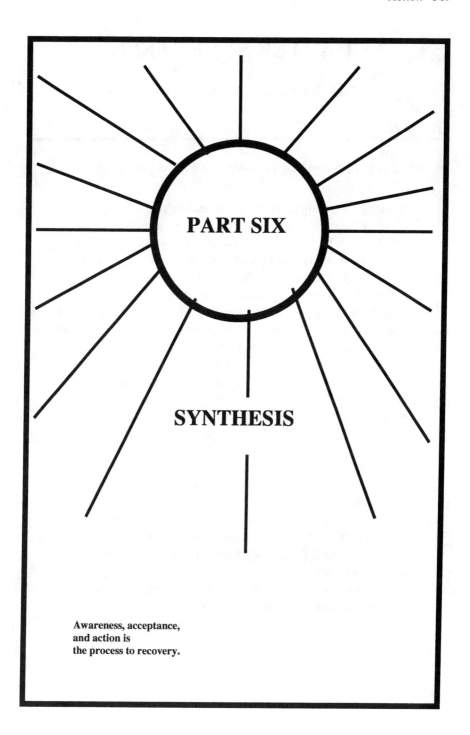

PART SIX

SYNTHESIS

**Awareness, acceptance,
and action is
the process to recovery.**

CHAPTER SEVENTEEN

Relationships are both heaven and hell

OVERVIEW

When you have completed Chapter Seventeen, you will be able to:

1. Acquire a working definition of a healthy relationship
2. Identify the various needs one tries to fill in relationships
3. Recognize when someone is trying to manipulate or attempting emotional blackmail in order to get his needs met instead of:
   a)Asking for them to be fulfilled
   b)The reasons for their inability to be direct
4. Understand why the "Me Generation" is so insistent on getting its needs met in an instantaneous way and doesn't display maturity by deferring some of its gratification
5. Learn how to mature in relationships with self and others
6. Learn how you remain stuck in codependent relationships
7. How the Controller becomes controlled by their control, or, attempt to control another human being
8. Understand the spiritual foundation of relationships:
   a)How they develop, maintain, and breakup
   b)How not to violate your partner spirituality
   c)What spiritual symbiosis, appears as, in the matrix of the relationship
9. What confusion the ego states bring to relationships
10. What are the toxic outcomes for each ego state if left unattended
11. How the Central Personality works in the construct of one's internal structure
12. How one's capacity to make decisions is developed over his life span and influenced by the three ego states
    a)What happens when one ego state dominates the process

RELATIONSHIPS
PART I : THE STRUCTURE

Relationships "ARE" both Heaven and Hell. Nowhere else can some-one acquire as much pleasure and pain at the same time. How many times have you heard: "I was doing so well by myself and thought it was time to start a new relationship. How wrong I was!" I disagree. It wasn't a wrong choice to begin a new one. The problem usually lies in several areas:

- Taking in emotionally unavailable partners
- Gravitating toward what is familiar (picking the same type of person)
- Not knowing what a healthy relationship looks like
- Lacking personal insight in being unaware of your wants, needs, and desires
- Letting the Child or Adolescent pick your partners
- Feeling you don't deserve any better
- Subconsciously sabotaging any healthy relationship

All of these areas will be explored in regard to the following:

- Determining who you are first
- What a healthy relationship looks like
- How codependency impacts the relationship
- What your needs are and how skewed development sabotages their healthy fulfillment
- How to separate your issues from your mate's (friend, family, co-worker) agenda
- Identify if you are out of your day and playing old tapes (good tools)
- Know when you are reacting to an old memory instead of the current event
- Recognize how the ego states impact the process in a relation-ship
- What spirituality is between couples
- How spirituality is maintained between partners
- What ruins relationship spirituality
- How lack of spirituality eventually breaks up the relationship
- Some examples
- What happens in the workplace

SELF DISCOVERY

Definition

We can define a relationship as: An intimate friendship between two individuals that can be sexual or not, in which two people love, respect, admire each other and want to spend time together. In it, both parties will have their realistic needs attained without giving themselves up, or, at the expense of the other. In the process, both will be able to maintain their person-hood in the form of dignity, integrity, sexuality, identity, spirituality, and direction in life. During the relationship, both will be affirmed, validated, encouraged, and assisted when necessary, to accomplish their personal, vocational, and spiritual goals. Each time a transaction occurs between the two — no energy will be drained by the other. In the relationship, both will bring a complete human being . . . whole within themselves . . . although the sum of the two as a couple will be greater than individuals . . . as their individual potential increases in their couple-ship.

Too much, you say? No way, I state! Without these ingredients . . . "*TWO*" people participating . . . there is no relationship. How many times have you settled for less? If you are normal — the answer is — many! We "don't know something until we find out." Relationships are no different. We can't change unless we know what to change. The following is the process of change:

- **Awareness.** Out of denial that something is wrong or not fulfilling
- **Information**. What a healthy relationship looks like
- **Insight**. What's inside of someone that prevents its attainment or causes sabotage
- **Application**. Practice the new strategies in your current relationship

The first two segments of the process have already been completed as you read and assimilated the above definition and at the same time identified the shortcomings in your present relationships. The following assignment will help you solidify the gains already made in identifying the problem and help you focus on the solution during the next section of this chapter.

ASSIGNMENT 22: Make a list of your previous relationships. According to the definition, write what needs were met, not met, and why it ended. A pattern will develop as you complete the assignment. Bring the inventory to the next section to identify what you need to work on to break the self-defeating patterns.

Problem and Solution

The two main ingredients that prevail in unfulfilling or toxic relationships are:

1. **The individual doesn't know what his adult needs are**
2. **He gravitates toward the same type of emotionally unavailable person**

In these toxic or problematic relationships, the individual attempts to have juvenile needs met from emotionally unavailable people. It's like going to a store, not knowing what you need, buying the items that look good, and wondering why you didn't get what you needed. Another way to visualize the deficiencies is to use the analogy of going to an empty well for water, over and over, and wondering why you're still thirsty. This chapter will help you identify the antecedents to repeatedly entering into problematic relationships with emotionally unavailable partners; in order to get immature needs met. Both the inability to identify needs and repeating self-defeating behavior are defined as the basis of most relationship problems and we will explore their solution next.

Needs

Every Human Being on this Starship Earth has needs, whether they acknowledge them or not. On the basis of their birth alone . . . they are *"ENTITLED TO HAVE THESE NEEDS FULFILLED"*! No one has a right to impede this process in another Human Being. The only prerequisite to their attainment is that the person knows what they are. These needs encompass mental, physical, and spiritual realms.

Mental — Mental needs include all areas of one's internal structure, and it incorporates being emotionally safe. In these needs, one requires the freedom to: think his own thoughts and not to be swayed or confused by another's aggressiveness; to clarify his own self concepts and not be dictated to by another, who insists he be something else.

Physical — To be physically safe is a person's birthright. Without safety first . . . other needs cannot be met. It is the lowest, in the order of

Maslow's (1959) Hierarchy of Needs. If one is enduring physical punishment . . . all energy is expended on survival. If a person lives in an unsafe environment . . . most of the focus is maintained externally . . . to protect, instead of looking inside to discover one's self. If the right nourishment is not secured . . . the physical body can deteriorate.

Spiritual — Self-actualization, the highest need of Maslow's Hierarchy, is extremely spiritual. What higher communion with God can the Human attain than to nourish and maximize his individual talents and be a service to his fellow man? The spiritual needs include being loved, cared for, appreciated, along with being useful and making a contribution toward mankind. A spiritual malady begins when someone or something blocks these needs from being met. Relationships are fertile ground for needs being blocked, as the individual's energy is diverted to the action or toxic nature of the relationship, instead of remaining in a safer environment to identify and fulfill their needs. It requires a quiet cognitive system to maintain a spiritual connection with God. Any less, the inspiration ends, and one is left alone in self-centered fear.

MANIPULATION   When needs are not met on a consistent basis (usually when one is raised in a dysfunctional family or remains in problematic relationships) . . . another channel has to be opened to acquire them. This additional strategy is manipulation. In it, one learns to manipulate another to get his needs met . . . INSTEAD OF ASKING! This was a good strategy when raised in an ineffective family because it was the only way one could procure them. Manipulation now became a survival skill. The only problem was that manipulation doesn't teach the healthy way to acquire one's needs, and necessitated its perpetuation long after it's needed. If you are involved with someone who manipulates when it's not necessary . . . he was probably raised that way. Manipulation is also the byproduct of an immature executive system, in which the juvenile strategies of the Child and Adolescent prevail; instead of being facilitated, through adult negotiation.

EMOTIONAL BLACKMAIL   Children are the most honest examples of emotional blackmail. It occurs when your four-year-old boldly exclaims: "I hate you unless I can have the candy!" Adolescents are equally emotional as they yell: "I hate you because you won't let me stay out all night!" Both are understandable, even age appropriate, for growing and developing children trying to define and get their needs met. Coming from a 25-year-old who has just received his second DUI and still wants to drink, is different. The excuses you hear from your spouse, after losing a second job in six months, and the bills are piling up, is also not age appropriate.

Emotional blackmail is usually overtly stated with: "If you don't do that . . ." or, "I won't love you if . . ." is their opening statement. It happens covertly as one withdraws emotionally, physically or sexually when he doesn't approve of his partner's actions.

The process is nothing more than a "mind game" and subtlety is the most devastating type of abuse. Much damage is left in its wake through confusion: when the problem remains unsaid . . . the partner is forced to guess . . . and the mindset of the player can be changed at will. This is a major setup and only generates perverse satisfaction for the perpetrator. Emotional blackmail is tantamount to silent rage and emotionally, through confusion, creates the same kind of damage. The reason it's so damaging lies in the process of the mind. It's here that the confusion becomes "larger than life" and overwhelming. Instead of being brought to "right size" and becoming manageable.

INSTANT GRATIFICATION   The "me" generation has its roots in the dysfunctional family. The phenomenon occurred over the child's life span as the primary caregivers made promises they didn't fulfill. The child learned that if his request wasn't given at the point of asking — *IT WOULDN'T BE RECEIVED*! In his despair, he learned not to trust a promise. In reaction to the anticipated loss — high levels of anxiety were usually experienced. The child then whines until his needs are met or he is forced to stop.

During this deprivation, if his needs are met at the whim of a caregiver, the infrequent fulfillment becomes a setup for later on in life as he tries to get adult needs fulfilled, and thinks he has power to change the other person's actions. Variable interval reinforcement is the most successful schedule used in behavioral psychology when continuation of the targeted behavior is desired. This is what happens to the child as he actually begs for what he wants and receives it. He interprets it as having power over others, when in reality it was only a whimsical decision made by a preoccupied caregiver.

When his initial badgering is unsuccessful . . . he will attempt manipulation and emotional blackmail. The overall strategy is refined in adolescence and internalized in adulthood. This dysfunctional strategy to get needs met is outlined in Figure 17.1.

CHILD REQUESTS A NEED FROM CAREGIVERS

REQUEST DENIED – PROMISE MADE

CHILD EXPERIENCES HIGH ANXIETY
KNOWING IT WON'T BE FULFILLED

CHILD ATTEMPTS THE FOLLOWING STRATEGIES

1) Whines to receive it NOW!

2) Tries to manipulate.

3) Attempts emotional blackmail.

THE VARIOUS TRICKS ARE ADVANCED FURTHER

ADOLESCENT REFINES THE DECEPTION AND
ESCALATES HIS ASSOCIATED BEHAVIORS

ADULT USES THE DESIGN AS HIS
INTERNALIZED RESPONSE

FIGURE 17.1 – DYSFUNCTIONAL PROCESS OF FULFILLING NEEDS

DELAYED GRATIFICATION   The hallmark of maturity in relationships; is delayed gratification when fulfillment is at the expense of another; is a necessity for a healthy and fulfilling relationship with self and others. One cannot use another to advance himself unless the process benefits both. This is a spiritual concept and prevails in all healthy relationships. To attempt otherwise, places the Child in shame and creates a disharmony between the participants, when the dissonance is felt subconsciously. Remember how something is perceived: what the filters of the conscious are, how the data is ordered, and how the resulting feelings from the process are transformed into a behavior. This is what occurs internally for the exploited partner. Later, the disharmony will be displaced, by reacting to something trivial and greatly removed from the event.

During the time, gratification is placed on hold for the "common good" of the relationship, one question seems to prevail: "When is it my turn," they ask? It's a good question and can only be answered by the individuals themselves — WHEN THEY KNOW WHAT THOSE NEEDS ARE! Without their needs becoming concretized, they are "between a rock and a hard place" and become "damned if they do and damned if they don't," as each situation becomes more confusing. The state of flux prevails when one doesn't know himself and needs another person to complete him. If he feels empty when left alone, he will do anything not to break up the relationship. This includes giving himself up by subjugating his needs to another's whims. This enslavement eventually kills any substance in the relationship, and what remains is bondage only.

In order to overcome this self-defeating behavior, one needs to place the focus on them and discover what their own wants, needs, and desires are. This will be a large endeavor for those raised in a dysfunctional home, for their entire focus has been just the opposite . . . to avoid the despair of not getting them met over their life span. For others not in as deep, who have a rudimentary understanding of their needs: they have just been sidetracked by a pretty face or a handsome smile. To get back on a spiritual track . . . admit the diversion . . . regroup . . . and continue their journey. If you are stuck, you may need more help than you realize. A twelve-step program and/or therapy will usually break the impasse.

ASSIGNMENT 23: Check out how your needs are met. Are your strategies healthy or dysfunctional? Do you coerce, manipulate, or emotionally blackmail to have them fulfilled, instead of asking? Do you know what they are? Are they met in your current relationships? Are your partners available to you mentally, physically and spiritually? Do they get their needs met at your expense? Do you give up your needs to help them get theirs? The answers to these questions will continue to help keep you focused, when used in conjunction with the previous assignments.

Maturation

Awareness and emotional maturity are a process. If they are not spawned developmentally . . . during their age-appropriate stage . . . accomplishing the recognized tasks . . . THEY WILL HAVE TO BE DEVELOPED NOW! The process will have to encompass:

- Relationships with self and others
- Identify and avoid codependent entanglements
- And remain on his spiritual path while attempting relationships

"That's too big to handle," you cry. I didn't say you had to do it all at once . . . ONLY THAT YOU SEE IT (be out of denial) . . . AND . . . IF

YOU WANT TO . . . CHANGE! It's your decision, not mine. Only you can make it. My job is over once the information is presented to you in a succinct manner. Unless, of course, I'm your therapist, and I use on you all those probing questions this book presents. God — that's hell! For some it's been a "fate worse than death" when their disease was ruined after successful therapy, and they couldn't practice their old behavior without knowing why they were doing it.

RELATIONSHIP WITH SELF (Intra-personal)   The intimate relationship one has with himself begins in the following self awareness:

- Knowing one's feelings, needs, and internal structure
- Honoring those feelings by using them in one's everyday life
- Identifying one's needs and acquiring their attainment with moderation, honesty, poise, dignity, and integrity
- Acquiring balance by becoming familiar with and using one's internal structure

One is spiritually fit when he has this intimate knowledge about himself. The accompanying peace that follows, allows him to keep the noise level in his head and the action in his daily interactions, at a low intensity. In this manner, a spiritual connection is maintained throughout most transactions with self and others.

RELATIONSHIPS WITH OTHERS (Interpersonal)   Relationships with others become problematic when something happens to cause one to question his own behavior, thoughts, or feelings. He reaches out to an outside source for clarification and the source has a vested interest in extending tainted information for self-seeking purposes.

The problem is he doesn't know himself well enough to depend on his own intuitions and is forced to rely on or give credibility to:

1. An external interpretation of the situation
2. Second-guess on what the appropriate response might have been

It's during this confusion, most relationship problems occur, when the solicited information is tainted or a guess was incorrect. If this happens, his issues surface in the translation or advice, and he falls short of being an objective participant. This is difficult for both people to understand because they become trapped when trying to interpret a situation or give advice. All one can do is to share his experience, strength, and hope and allow his partner the dignity of his own choices.

In relationships, when questioning one's own behavior, thoughts, and feelings toward another, all you can do with your partner is to ask how the suspected behavior affected him, and based on his answer, to let it go or make an amend. The rest is an inside job. The "rule of thumb" to follow to remedy the situation would be to:

- Keep the focus on yourself
- Stay in your day (If old thoughts come up — QUIET THEM)
- Check out how you feel about the situation
- Check if your needs are being met
- See if your boundaries (mental, physical, or spiritual) are being trampled
- Check if you are being used, exploited, or abused
- Change your behavior in any situation to direct you away from pain and move you toward the pleasure that peace and security brings.

If your present relationship is painful and you remain in it — you probably don't know:

- What a healthy relationship looks like
- That you are operating from a false childhood belief system
- You may be punishing yourself for something that happened to you in your past

Relationships are supposed to be pleasurable; needs are supposed to be fulfilled with dignity; and the common good of the couple-ship should prevail for both.

EQUITABLE RELATIONSHIPS ARE: PLEASURABLE, ENHANCE NEED ATTAINMENT FOR BOTH PARTIES, AND THE COMMON GOOD OF THE RELATIONSHIP PREVAILS IN ALL INTERACTIONS!

CODEPENDENT RELATIONSHIPS   Codependent relationships are not effective, functional, or adaptive. They are defense mechanisms only. Survival tools at best. They trap and destroy "*BOTH*" parties who attempt to maintain one. They are equivalent to a hostage situation only . . . in which spiritual growth is hindered . . . as all available energy is diverted into controlling, or trying to break the control. During this time, very little energy is left to maintain a forward direction in life.

The reality is: while the controlling loop is maintained, nothing else is strong enough to penetrate its barrier of action. In the enveloping nature of the interactions:

- Both participants are held hostage to the situation
- Both partners are being controlled by the process
- Neither one wants to admit his role in the dysfunctional scenario

The Controller — The aggressor becomes controlled by the passive nature of his partner's behavior. All effort has been utilized to keep his partner under control and THE REST OF THE CONTROLLER'S LIFE IS IGNORED! His total focus is on the controlling.

Isn't this enslavement, when an entire life is subjugated to one behavioral set? I wonder — who's the controller and who's being controlled?

The Controlled — The victim passively dominates the interaction by ALLOWING the controller to dominate his life. (It doesn't make any difference if it's *overt* and he knows it — or *covert* as a defense mechanism that has been orchestrated by the internal structure — there is culpability.) In order to perpetuate the farce, the victim has to:

- Avoid acknowledging his power
- Remain the victim
- Not take responsibility for himself

In this process, the victim, passively, becomes the aggressor and the controller becomes victimized by his own shortcomings of needing to control other people, to quiet his personal internal fears. The loop this creates is incredibly entwined and unless one has the filters my theory offers, they remain clueless to the awareness of how and why the dynamics work, and thereby lack the tools to break their enslavement. The need to enter into or maintain a dysfunctional relationship can originate from:

- Lack of knowledge about a healthy relationship
- Poor personal intra-relationship
- Low self-esteem
- Skewed self concepts
- Being abused (any type) during childhood
- Sabotage through personal retribution for past wrongdoings
- As a device to: MASK THE MEMORIES OF A TOXIC PAST,

WHEN THE DRAMA FROM THE *PRESENT* RELATIONSHIP
OVER-SHADOWS THE MOUNTING PAIN OF THE *PAST*
TRAUMA AND DIVERTS IT BEFORE IT SURFACES.

**CODEPENDENT RELATIONSHIPS ARE COVERTLY
DESIGNED (Subconsciously) AS A MASK, TO
COVER UP PAST PAIN FROM SURFACING
TODAY, BY USING THE TOXIC INTERACTIONS
OF THE CURRENT RELATIONSHIP DRAMA
AS A SMOKESCREEN FROM THE RISING PAIN!**

Spirituality In Relationships

Spirituality between couples occurs as a result of the harmony they attain in their couple-ship. In this peace, both are allowed to grow at their individual pace, and are not diverted from their spiritual path by their partner's behavior.

Many couples manage to maintain a spiritual course. It doesn't have to be perfect! In fact, life is never perfect and always perfect at the same time: It's never perfect to our expectations; always perfect in its natural unfolding.

When one of the couple is separated from his spiritual path through the negative behavior of his partner — ALL SPIRITUALITY BETWEEN THE TWO AND ITS CONNECTIVENESS TO A HIGHER POWER — CEASES TO EXIST! There is evidence to believe in a natural spiritual symbiosis as the heart of all relationships, when toxic relationships eventually dissolve, and healthy ones remain viable. Without spirituality, a healthy relationship seems to rarely develop.

**SPIRITUAL SYMBIOSIS OCCURS IN A COUPLE
WHEN "*BOTH*" WORK IN HARMONY TO HELP, OR
NOT DIVERT, THEMSELVES OR THEIR PARTNER
FROM THEIR SPIRITUAL PATHS**

Slavery usually occurs in relationships that are spiritually dead. It doesn't matter if the bondage is to self in the form of self-centered fear, or, the enslavement is to others as they are trapped into being controlled. Both are self-destructive. The relationships they spawn only engender hostage taking. Becoming a prisoner is not pleasant. *IT IS AN EFFECTIVE SUR-*

VIVAL SKILL WHEN THE ACTION OF THE COUPLE-SHIP IS USED TO KEEP YOUR FOCUS EXTERNAL — IT'S A POOR LIVING SKILL!

In this process of entrapment, the controller has the opportunity to displace on you his anger toward the primary caregiver, whom he has issues with. By the way, who you resemble or symbolize (the hated caregiver) is projected onto the hostage....which is *"YOU"*....if presently involved in one of these relationships. That sucks, doesn't it?

It's during this time, the victim completes his victimization of himself and the controller through projective identification, when he:

1. Gives up his power by allowing himself to be captured
2. Projects the responsibility onto the controller by stating: "They are all alike." The victim can now legitimatize his childhood belief system through the evidence of the current behavioral outcome.
3. It is here he can minimize the pain of not getting his childhood needs met, through the rationalization that everyone is out to hurt him.
4. By setting himself up to encounter the same situations over and over, he will not feel the full impact of his past losses. This pain will eventually surface if success is felt in a healthy, mutually fulfilling relationship.

SPIRITUAL DISHARMONY — Only a small amount of the enmeshment is overt. Most happens covertly (subconsciously), impedes the natural order of events, and becomes a spiritual sickness. This same subconscious process, internally, harbors much resentment toward each partner . . . one for being the victim and the other for becoming the perpetrator. It doesn't matter if both are set up. It only matters that they played the game. It's in playing the game....in awareness or denial....that the resentments are built up into walls. This internal scoreboard is the reason most dysfunctional relationships end. It happens when the animosity built up during the destructive nature of its path, *is later drawn upon to terminate it.*

WHY YOU CAN'T ESCAPE — When we use a human's internal structure to illustrate the process, we can identify how avoiding the pain of unresolved issues or trauma becomes its goal. In the internal structures process, the subconscious hides the pain. The problems that manifest are:

•   The environment will not allow the suppressed memories to remain at rest

- There is constant bombardment of stimuli to the psyche that resembles the repressed materials
- Old feelings and memories are triggered off by the new data

As the overwhelming feelings of the suppressed memories begin to rise through the preconscious, its energy is transformed into a behavior set, which utilizes the emotional energy as fuel, to complete the behavior. This behavior set, utilizing the customary human relationship dynamics as a setting, will encompass the following areas:

- Beginning a new relationship
- Stirring the pot in a present one
- Ending an old involvement

Each time the relationship rituals are activated, its resulting action will absorb the energy of the ascending pain. This diversion will allow the human to facilitate the overwhelming feelings of the past trauma and not break down. The impact felt by the strategy is:

- It knocks him off his spiritual path
- It's an excellent defense mechanism to avoid pain
- It's a negative living skill when the behavior it promotes is self-defeating
- Problems become more acute each time a dysfunctional strategy is generated
- Another layer of history is added....that will later have to be resolved

To sum it up: A toxic relationship is one of the actions a person uses to survive when he wishes to avoid the pain of emerging feelings. The cost of the behavior is his person-hood, identity, values, morals, dignity, freedom, self-respect, self-esteem, self concepts and diversion off his spiritual path. **To engage in its process is a trap**. *The only way out is not to divert one's present pain, eventually clean up the past, and live in the day no matter what it brings to your table.*

CONTRIBUTIONS OF THE EGO STATES — All three ego states contribute to the spiritual disharmony which occurs when a relationship is out of balance or not equitable to *"ALL"* participants. Each ego state's fear, immaturity, and responses or lack of it, adds to the confusion and blocks attainment of more positive outcomes. This trap of diversion is orchestrated by the ego states in the following four-act play:

ACT ONE: The Child — The Child begins the play in "Act One" as his dread from a present situation or past trauma is manifested as self-centered fear, lack of faith, or immaturity. In this reaction, the Child hides by shutting down, rationalizing (the basis for shame when he feels it's his fault), discounting, or dissociation.

ACT TWO: The Adolescent — "Act Two" begins as the Child's alarm is being facilitated internally, when the Adolescent becomes dominant, because the Adult has abrogated his authority or is too small to be effective. At this time, the Adolescent becomes the Executive System in order to decide what course of action to take to relieve the stress. At this point, the Adolescent has two choices of how to address the fear:

> *ACT INWARD* — When feelings are depressed, he becomes the victim, and allows himself to be controlled in a relationship by a dominating partner who will take charge of whatever responsibility his hostage will allow.

> *ACT OUTWARD* — Become the perpetrator and dominate the relationship as much as possible.

These actions are no longer gender specific. Welcome to the Twenty First Century where either sex can be an "equal opportunity victimizer! If we add the power of passive/aggressive behavior to this arsenal, we begin to develop more respect toward non-forceful strategies. The sex that envisions himself as strongest (traditionally it was men) should look again because control, at best, IS ONLY AN ILLUSION!

ACT THREE: The Critical Adult — "Act Three" begins with the Nurturing Adult's failure to take action, by not facilitating his internal strife as a mature Executive System. Instead, he abrogates his power through inaction. At this point, the Critical Adult rises to shame the Child and antagonize the Adolescent through verbal abuse. It's in this act that the spiritual battle begins, remains as a "problem loop," and won't be terminated as a stress-reducing strategy until Act Four when the relationship junkie starts therapy and/or enters a twelve-step program and *STOPS* the behavioral defense mechanism.

ACT FOUR: The Nurturing Adult — In "Act Four," the Nurturing Adult will take charge to help the Child to feel; the Adolescent to stop his behavior; and quiet the Critical Adult. *It's in this healthy parental role that the need to perpetuate dysfunctional behavior is finally ended.*

TOXIC OUTCOMES — Don't delude yourself about the damage done by this process — EVERYONE GETS BATTERED! This includes all three segments of a human being's internal composition, when, INATELY, all elements know the game. Externally, anyone can be in denial. Internally, it's different — *EVERYONE, EVENTUALLY, BECOMES ACCOUNTABLE FOR HIS BEHAVIOR!* It happens in the following ways:

The Child — Is looking for love and gets abused or re-traumatized when he chooses what's familiar, fails to listen to reason, and trusts untrustworthy people.

The Adolescent — Wants to stop the behavior, have the Adult take over, and is becoming scared at the level of intensity needed to maintain the game each subsequent time it's played.

The Critical Adult — Wants to help, even though the message is negative, and tries to put everyone on the right road. In their dialogue, all of the ego states become emotionally battered.

The Nurturing Adult — Wants to clear up the internal confusion, stop the dysfunctional behavior and lacks the tools or is not developed enough to change things. It will ultimately take charge, responsibility, and facilitate the changes necessary to emotionally grow up and make adult decisions.

The Adult will also pay a large price for his inactivity when the cost of his inattention is revealed to him as:
1. He develops greater skills in facilitating his internal confusion
2. He attains mature outcomes as he ceases his dysfunctional behavior

This awareness will only unfold as he succeeds. For in his success he will allow himself to see the lost possibilities, or, become aware of the havoc that was caused by his lack of insight and knowledge.

All new awareness's are difficult, because as the denial is dropped, more is usually revealed. It's a natural unfolding that must continue if the Adult is to mature. Any hesitation with the Adult will stop the process. Any more damage done because of inaction will add another layer onto an already overwhelming emotional pile. If this occurs, the Adult will experience "fear of fear itself" and may become paralyzed, unable to take a proactive course for himself. If he can't, he will avoid making a correct, intuitive, adaptive decision and opt to make a problematic one. This course of action will perpetuate the consequences of his ineffective behavior and continue in the development of a dysfunctional lifestyle instead of freeing him to pursue a healthier way of living. *I HAVE SEEN OTHERS IN PRO-GRAM, THERAPY, AND TREATMENT — COME TO THIS APEX — AND QUIT!*

For some unknown reason (to me), they became overwhelmed, stopped their forward progress, and dropped out of recovery. I can try to hypothesize why, but don't know for sure. Maybe, some crossed a designated boundary and didn't feel they had the right to advance in life, be happy, and self-actualize.

Relationships can't grow in a victim/perpetrator environment when both are using all energy in a survival mode and none is left over to connect to a higher power. This subterfuge will remain viable as long as both parties are willing to "play the game" and avoid their feelings. When the action from maintaining a toxic relationship is no longer used as a survival tool — *IT WILL DIMINISH, BE REPLACED WITH LIVING SKILLS, AND HEALTHY RELATIONSHIPS WILL DEVELOP.*

To those of you who don't believe in this undertow; become the observer, study the makeup, continuation, and breakup of relationships around you, then use the spiritual concepts of this section to evaluate what you see, and you may become enlightened!

ASSIGNMENT 24:   From your earlier list of relationships, ask the following questions and rate your overall answer along a scale of one to ten: one meaning very little and ten being perfection. Repeat the exercise for each relationship you have been in. There are no perfect scores — only awareness! Answer truthfully — on the basis of the given information — NOT YOUR RATIONALIZATION! In the process, you will get an idea of your spiritual maturation level. The questions are:

- How was your self-relationship during your connection to this person?
- Were you treated with dignity and allowed to be you without condemnation?
- Did you have to give up anything to maintain this relationship?
- Was your relationship codependent? If yes, how?
- Was there spirituality (based on my definition)? If yes, describe it. If no, what was missing?

THE INTERNAL STRUCTURE

During relationships, one's internal structure holds the key to beginning, maintaining, and ending, "ALL" involvements, whether functional or not. The control, power, and direction they possess are spawned from the skewed developmental baggage they carry when each stage incurred losses or trauma that were never addressed.

Each circumstance lies unresolved in the psyche and brings its own "contribution" to relationships, as the Adult tries to negotiate and rectify these issues in his present relationships with self and others. When you finish Chapter Seventeen, you will also be able to identify why past relationships broke up. In this section, you will be able to understand the following:

- Which ego state chooses your current partner
- Why you keep becoming involved with emotionally unavailable partners
- When you gravitate toward what's familiar instead of changing
- Why you lack insight into yourself
- How you give yourself up in a relationship
- How the relationship spiral becomes a "Problem Loop"
- How to choose more supportive partners and maintain healthy relationships . . . BASED ON SELF KNOWLEDGE ALONE! (Trust me on this one! No one gets in without your approval. We seek out and select all partners that we acquire!)

Central Personality

Within human development, a central personality grows over the life span: It is spawned in childhood, tested in adolescence, and honed in adulthood as the growing person matures over his lifetime.

During each life stage, the central personality is dominated by one of the ego states. When development occurs along the appropriate course — the central personality is commanded by the ego state fitting to his chronological age. When growth is skewed, an immature ego state will dictate and rule. This becomes problematic in relationships when one tries to participate in one as an adult, and the Child or the Adolescent is dominant.

Ultimately, The Nurturing Adult needs to be the governing force of the central personality, in order to consider his holistic needs "BEFORE" entering into a committed relationship.

Executive System

The central personality, the core of a Human Being, becomes the Executive System of the Internal Structure (Child-Adolescent-Adult), as he completes his developmental tasks and stages. At maturity, the system will be able to:

- Mediate his feelings (the Child), behavior (the Adolescent), and thoughts (the Adult)
- Make decisions based upon his holistic needs
- Attain effective, functional, and adaptive outcomes, culled from creative and non-problematic choices

Decisions made in this manner will not engender internal strife as they are congruent with all three ego states and maintain their integrity.

When development is skewed or incomplete, an immature central personality becomes dominated by the arrested stage and the following occurs:

- Feelings, thoughts, and behaviors are incongruent. They feel one way, think another, and act still another
- Decisions are based on the changing reign of the ego states which can fluctuate minute to minute
- Usually ineffective, dysfunctional, and maladaptive outcomes are achieved in order to "stir the pot" and keep the focus off himself

This is a defensive strategy to keep ones past pain from surfacing. They are good survival skills for the individual, but hell on relationships when living skills are needed.

**FAILURE TO DEVELOP A MATURE CENTRAL
PERSONALITY, AS THE EXECUTIVE SYSTEM
OF THE INTERNAL STRUCTURE, IS THE ROOT
CAUSE OF DYSFUNCTIONAL BEHAVIOR.**

STRUCTURE The composition of the Executive System is the Internal Structure (Child — Adolescent — Adult) of the Human Being. Within it, a decision-making process is developed, to mediate internal consistency between the various needs of the three ego states. During the process, each stage contributes its share of input. Decisions made by a mature system will be democratic. In Figure 17.2, the overall structure of the Executive System is depicted.

The Executive System's main thrust is guided by the fear or the maturity level of its ego states. In them, the organism remains balanced in attaining their needs and self actualizes along spiritual lines or becomes dysfunctional and falls off its higher path.

Notice that the construct incorporates the three developmental stages around a core which contains the center of a Human Being's essence. This core is the main conduit for a spiritual connection to a Higher Power. This central point is also the conduit for spirituality transpiring in relationships.

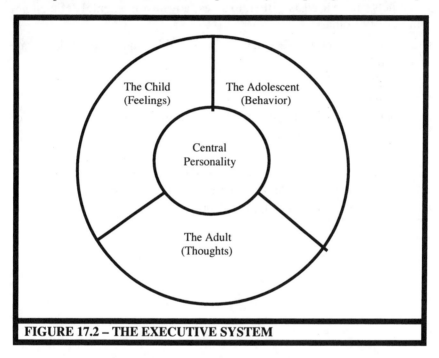

FIGURE 17.2 – THE EXECUTIVE SYSTEM

DEVELOPMENT   The Executive System's growth proceeds in the same way as the person's physical growth does . . . starts as a seed and grows outward over the three major developmental stages. In each period, the following necessary information is gathered and assimilated by its ego state:

- **The Child gathers basic information, feelings, and has concrete thinking**
- **The Adolescent acts upon the information, feelings, and has abstract thinking**
- **The Adult refines the behavior based upon his balanced needs, which change throughout the stages of the adult life span**

In this process, the Executive System grows as each stage contributes to its data entry and processing system. Without all stages entering the required data, its decisions or life strategy, will be faulty at best. It's in this deficiency that dysfunctional relationships are begun and maintained as the Adult tries to operate in various relationships without the appropriate data from self, others, or his environment. Figure 17.3 demonstrates the process of functional development and Figure 17.4 outlines the way its process becomes skewed. When you are familiar with the paradigm, both constructs can be used as a filter, to assess any developmental deficiencies within self or others.

Returning to personality development at this time has been deliberate and twofold:

FIRST   — To give you an idea of the baggage that comes in any relationship

SECOND — To help you take the credit for the roads not traveled, or responsibility for the ones that were

Relationships are usually not what they seem on the surface unless one has had: extensive therapy, or been in a Twelve-Step Program and made an effort to study and apply the principles of the twelve steps to his life.

THE CHILD

The Child experiences his feelings, and with the help of his primary caregivers, sorts, labels, and gives meaning to them. Over the length of childhood, the youngster will learn how to facilitate feelings within the limits of his thinking. At this point, the child is able to contribute his learning experiences and feelings to the Executive System.

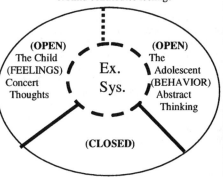

1. Child contributes feelings

THE ADOLESCENT

The Adolescent takes the learning experiences and feelings from childhood, practices ways of being, utilizes his abstract thought processes, and contributes the results to the Executive System. These behavioral sets will be the foundation of most adult behavior. They will guide the interactions used in later relationships with self, others, and his environment.

2. Adolescent tries out behavior.

THE ADULT

The central personality at this stage will have a free flow of thoughts, feelings, and behavioral strategies. As each ego state contributes to the Executive System, most, if not all decisions, will reflect the balanced needs of the individual and include mental, physical, and spiritual considerations.

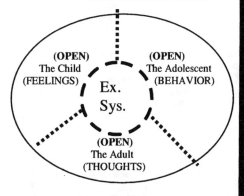

3. Adult accesses all information

FIGURE 17.3 FUNCTIONAL DEVELOPMENT

THE CHILD

The Child's main contribution to
the Executive System is fear, through
trauma or deprivation, he learns to
limit his experiences and suppress
his feelings. In the dissociation,
an estrangement from self is created,
and this emptiness (self-abandonment),
is propelled forward and magnified in
all later stages of development.

(OPEN) THE CHILD (FEAR)   (CLOSED)

Ex. Sys.

(CLOSED)

1. Fear Centered Development

THE ADOLESCENT

The Child DUMPS his fear onto the Adolescent to facilitate.The immature Adolescent has limited experience to draw upon
and utilizes ANYTHING to dissipate the
overwhelming pain EXCEPT THE ONE
THING THAT WILL HELP – TO FEEL IT!
His main contribution made to the
Executive System during this stage will be
in the ability to facilitate psychic pain through
dysfunctional behavioral strategies that are
designed to cover it up.

The Child
open to the
Adolescent only
(FEAR)

(OPEN)
ADOLESCENT
(Act out
or in)

Ex. Sys.

(CLOSED)

(CLOSED)

2. Dysfunctional Acting Out

THE ADULT

During Adulthood, the Executive System
is dominated by the Adolescent and/or
the Child. The Adult at this point is
very small or nonexistent. The decisions
made by the Executive System are fear-
based (from the Child), and reactionary
(from the Adolescent). Most are problematic at best, designed as survival skills,
and lack the ability to create adaptive
solutions.

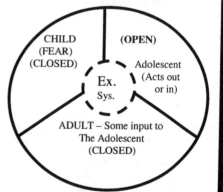

CHILD
(FEAR)
(CLOSED)

(OPEN)
Adolescent
(Acts out
or in)

Ex. Sys.

ADULT – Some input to
The Adolescent
(CLOSED)

3. Executive System Dominated by the Adolescent

FIGURE 17.4 DYSFUNCTIONAL DEVELOPMENT

DOMINATION BY AN EGO STATE   Domination by an ego state is best identified by one's internal dialogue and his subsequent behavior. The clinical term is how the client presents. Once trained, therapists have very little difficulty recognizing him. Friends and family see him in the compulsive person and don't know how to label him. They use descriptive phrases like:

- "You look hurt or insecure." (The Child)
- "You look angry," or say, "You look like you're going to drink." (The Adolescent)
- "Why are you always so critical?" (Critical Adult)
- "You treat me so well when you're this mellow." (Nurturing Adult) and then they add, "Why can't you treat me this way all the time?"

The answer to these questions is elusive and remained unanswerable until one can identify his internal structure and gain insight into what's going on inside that "made" or directs one to act that way. The last one to recognize which state is dominating the Executive System, is the struggling person. Up until this book, recovery, or therapy…. people do what they know and NO OTHER RESPONSE IS POSSIBLE. Awareness changes after recovery and the following indicators will help identify which state the individual occupies.

The Child — *Internally* he will be frightened, have very little hope or none at all, and very helpless and needy. *Externally* he will appear to be smaller than usual, use childlike thinking, won't make eye contact, and will act as the victim and present as being unable to help himself.

The Adolescent — *Internally* is usually violent or angry, thinks of himself as being ten feet tall and bulletproof, and can get away with anything he thinks about. *Externally* he acts outward against others or inward toward himself (depression, self-mutilation, etc). Negative behavior is usually the Adolescent acting out. This would include: arguing, fighting, substance abuse, gambling, promiscuity, criminality, overachieving, becoming the parent to his parents, quitting school to work, workaholism, or any behavior that can be continued in an obsessive/compulsive manner.

The Critical Adult — *Internally* is self-critical and judgmental, condemning all action taken or feelings experienced by the three ego states.

Externally acts the same toward others. Nothing anyone does is sufficient or good enough for him. In fact, when compared to him, all others are inadequate.

The Nurturing Adult — *Internally* is practically nonexistent. Tries to be nurturing of self and becomes overpowered by the dialogue of the Critical Adult. *Externally* he is able to nurture others. Mostly it is self-seeking — to make himself feel good — not to make the other person feel good. If you want to test this statement, just look at the last time you assisted someone in your life. Was the help what they wanted or needed, or was it what you thought was best for them? Therapists will have very little difficulty observing the outward manifestation of the adult's three ego states. They are trained and have a vested interest in getting the client healthy. What I am presenting is just another way to use what they already see and to put a deeper meaning to it.

For a non-clinician to become aware of these mannerisms, observe them in others, and recognize them in self, will trigger a multitude of issues. Some of these issues can be as simple as recognizing when someone is insecure, or go as far as feeling betrayed when recognizing being controlled by his partner's fear. This is especially painful for the one being controlled, when he has altered his life to accommodate his mate's, sibling's, parent's, employer's, co-worker's, or friend's request and the deference has occurred over an extended time. This victimization will stop once someone is aware of it. Even if it's not stopped completely . . . the person is out of denial. This is the beginning of self-responsibility, and with it changes will eventually come.

ONE IS A VICTIM UNTIL HE KNOWS — AFTER THAT, HE IS A PARTICIPANT

SECRET ISSUES The last facet of the personality's contribution to the relationship mystique is the "HIDDEN AGENDA." It is a process buried deeply within the psyche . . .its motives so disguised . . .that the host is not even aware of the contents. In fact, are so well concealed, when the individual is confronted with their presence . . .will vehemently deny their existence.

The next chapter will break down the agenda according to:
*   The ego state they manifested in

- The issue they engender
- Their antecedents
- How they manifest within the individual
- What problems they bring to the relationship
- How to come out of the problem and go into the solution

ASSIGNMENT 25: Who is in charge of your Executive System during various situations involving stress with work, friends, siblings, parents, spouse or significant other, authority figures (church, courts, police, school, etc.), and the culture? Write about specific events with each, what your reaction or inaction was, feelings were, outcome expected, outcome realized, and based on what you know now . . . identify which ego state was in charge. This is awareness only. Don't condemn yourself for past behavior. Learn from it. When you remain in the problem by rehashing the events of the mistaken behavior....the Critical Adult is in motion and will only trigger off the Adolescent's survival skills to medicate the pain of the mistake....and no learning will be attained. This defensive posture only engenders shame when on a subconscious level....the strategy is known....and corrective action is not taken. This assignment can help overcome the propensity of your Critical Adult to judge and condemn you for not having all the information necessary to mediate your stress in an adaptive fashion.

SUMMARY

A brief definition for a healthy relationship is: An intimate friendship, in which two individuals will get their realistic needs met, without distracting one another from his spiritual path or depreciating their self concepts, and in the process, will make the alliance greater than the sum of its parts.

These realistic needs the Human Being desires to fulfill are mental, physical, and spiritual in nature. They can be fulfilled by emotionally available partners who have the capacity to be there for them in their time of need. Never will they attempt to attain them through manipulation and emotional blackmail when their partner lacks the capacity to be available to them because it would be spiritually dysfunctional. During a maladaptive process, instant gratification of perceived needs is demanded by a fearful Child or an angry Adolescent, for unless the need is met now . . . it will never be met at all. At this time, no emotional maturity is displayed, by deferring gratification, unless the individual is shamed, threatened, or coerced.

Maturity in relationships is developed over the life span. As one physically grows, his needs change, and new experience direct him down other paths in life. During this adventure, one will grow in various areas:

1. **RELATIONSHIPS WITH SELF** *(Intra-personal):* In it, one learns about his internal structure, identifies his wants, needs, and desires, and fulfills them in a socially prescribed way. In the process he doesn't violate his own boundaries, go against his values, morals, or ethics, and doesn't break his spiritual connection between self, others, and God.

2. **RELATIONSHIP WITH OTHERS** *(Interpersonal):* To accomplish all of the above, while having an intimate friendship with another, and not to become distracted from his spiritual purpose.

When the relationship with another becomes a distraction and doesn't allow either to remain focused on himself or his spiritual path; *a codependent relationship is formed as one becomes the controller, tries to control the other, and becomes controlled in the process when all his energy is spent controlling others instead of self-actualizing.*

In the controlling, one also breaks the spiritual connection with his mate because his controlling is self-seeking in nature and not in his mate's best interests (according to God's will for them). Controlling can always be rationalized any way one chooses to see it. This spiritual disharmony is usually the course for breakup in most relationships for neither partner can grow while control is occurring. The main reason the motives for this dysfunctional behavior is hidden from the individual lies in the large investment one makes in his lifestyle to perpetuate the distraction. Once his "hidden agenda" is revealed to him....*he has a choice whether to continue the old behavior or learn new ones.*

Each of the ego states makes a contribution to the confusion. It's like watching a four-act play: **Act One**....The Child gets traumatized; **Act Two**....The Adolescent reacts to The Child's pain; **Act Three**....The Critical Adult emotionally beats both up; and **Act Four**....The Nurturing Adult takes charge by settling the discontented ego states into a unanimous whole as the individual's needs are met holistically instead of fragmented by a troubled ego state.

The Central Personality is a part of one's internal structure and is generated from a composite of all the personality traits the three ego states

(Child, Adolescent, Adult) have exhibited over the life span. Development of the Central Personality occurs as each age-stage grows and contributes their experience to it. If the information is skewed and the experiences are toxic….The Personality will be dysfunctional at best. When the information is honest and the experiences positive….an open personality will develop. In its matrix a healthy Executive System will reign, be capable of making adaptive decisions to life's problems, and self-actualize in the process. When one ego state dominates the process, it's usually fear based and includes a hidden agenda.

CASE STUDY

When Joan came into therapy, she made a commitment not to get into another relationship until she uncovered why they start on a positive note and end up disastrous. Joan's feelings of confusion were exacerbated by the fact that she was so successful in the business world and admired by many. Something happened to this capable business executive once she entered into a love relationship with a man. Joan also verbalized at this time that there must be "something inside of her" that was causing her to pick the same kind of man over and over. Some of her words were: "I must have a sign on my face — come get me!" and, "I seem to have learned how to pick men who are not emotionally available to me." This honesty, in early recovery, is rare. Generally, they come in wondering what happened and need help to sort it out.

As Joan progressed through therapy, she also avoided the temptations of other relationships forming before she was ready. While she was doing her Inner Child work, she became attracted to two different men. She was warned about being needy; allowing her Child to pick out what was "familiar" to her, and to avoid another disaster. When she saw it was her Child that needed love and that sex wasn't the need, she didn't continue in the relationship, she was able to allow the group to love her, and had her love needs met appropriately. Had she followed her libido, she would have relapsed into an old "Problem Loop"….had to let it run its course….and then start all over again — *again*! All that she would have accomplished was to remain in the victim role.

While she was doing her Adolescent work, she became seductive. She was once again warned about the consequences of her behavior, and reapplied the energy to her work in group. Joan was able to see her motives for wanting a relationship, and if she began one at this time, it wasn't because she was in love. Instead....it was for vengeance. The whole group validated the finding, with all members stating that they were relieved their partners were not like her at this time because she was so angry and would only destroy them.

As Joan completed her unfinished developmental tasks of childhood and adolescence, she became more responsible to herself and began to look for another type of man. The ones she had previously picked were men who were usually aloof and distant, or easily manipulated. It was at this point in therapy that she began to look at: what she needed in a partner; what price she was willing to pay, if any, in order to fulfill her needs. For the first time, she was looking beyond her immediate needs and trying to find out what her spiritual needs were. It wasn't an easy task because she needed a new framework to look at relationships and didn't have it.

The first objective was to show Joan what she did in her present relationships to perpetuate the old results as we began to map out her behavioral patterns. After Joan's behavior in relationships was explored, her various needs (emotional, mental, physical, spiritual) were identified, and she started to recognize her motives for the dysfunctional codependent behavior. In the process, Joan recognized how she tried to get her needs met by manipulation, emotional blackmail, and instant gratification. These were the strategies modeled by her primary caregivers and she was a good student. Once her patterns, needs, and motives were identified....the real work could begin. The work included: to acquire new skills; break up any impasses to her forward progress in therapy using experiential interventions based on my developmental models ego states; practice the new behavior in group and then use it outside in her relationships with work, family, and friends.

Joan's preliminary work was completed previously in group when she: reconnected to her feelings through the Child, regained control of her Executive System by setting healthy boundaries and limits on her Adolescent, and redirected its energy to complete her developmental tasks instead of trying to gain power and control in situations when she experienced fear.

The first impediment to her progress was in trying to assimilate the concept of spirituality in her relationships. She could see it working in the group, but couldn't determine its need in an intimate relationship with a man. It was at this point that we had to revisit the Adolescent.

In the work that followed, she became aware of her "Hidden Agenda" with men. In it, she identified the unresolved anger she had with her dad for not being emotionally available to her and the Adolescent's message that she was going to make every man pay for her father's crimes. Her hidden belief was: ALL MEN WERE THE SAME — THEY LOVED YOU AND THEN LEFT! The issue was revealed in psychodrama as Joan came into a major awareness when the Adolescent gave her the message, and the Adult Joan immediately started talking to her Adolescent ego alter. In the dialogue, Joan's Adult apologized for the misconception and the abandonment of her adult leadership role in relationships, expressed the gratitude she had toward the Adolescent for taking responsibility in the absence of adult guidance, and made a vow never to do it again.

The Adolescent was reluctant at first to give up control because she didn't believe the Adult, felt her primary purpose was to protect the Child, and she didn't feel that Joan's Adult was capable of taking responsibility for her current behavior. This was a difficult test for the Adult and needed to go beyond words. At this point, we enrolled another group member to play Joan's Child Alter Ego State and had the Adolescent explain to the Child why she felt the Adult wasn't capable of taking care of her. The Adolescent experienced a profound wake-up call as she listened to the Child telling her about how she felt when she was forced to sleep with all of those men because the Adolescent confused love with sex. It was love the Child was looking for and the Adolescent inadvertently directed her toward sex because she misunderstood the need. Another shocking revelation for the Adolescent was the fact that the Child loved "Daddy" very much and was deeply hurt each time the Adolescent berated the male substitute for him, when she became involved with different men.

Neither of these revelations would have occurred if the Adult Joan had not been reconnected back to her Child. Remember, the Child is a synonym for feelings. This is why the Adult was able to express how the Child felt.

As the Child dialogued with the Adolescent, all resistance to the Adult's takeover was dissipated. It was at this point that the Adolescent apologized to the Child for her inappropriate decisions and capitulated to the Adult with a warning that, *"I'll be back, if you abrogate your responsibility again."*

The process was a profound transformation and shifted the locus of control *from* external demands *to* internal harmony. In the process, Joan was able to identify the antecedents to her codependency and break the hold the unresolved issues had on her. Instead of being a helpless and hopeless child or an angry adolescent, she was now a full-grown adult woman who could mediate internally whatever feelings rose in a situation, and then make an adaptive decision based on her holistic needs. In relationships, the Adult Joan was able to choose a different type of male, treat him with dignity, love, and respect, and work on problems that arose in the relationship instead of acting like a fearful child or an angry adolescent. Joan was now able to connect spiritually with her love object.

Once Joan's pathology was identified and corrected, she made excellent gains in recovery because her basic skills in communication, negotiation, problem solving, decision making and interpersonal relationships did not have to be re-mediated. It saved a lot of work. Stress reduction was her only real problem. Once she reduced her psychological stress by remaining internally congruent, a few physical stress-reducing exercises, along with her budding relationship with a Higher Power, were sufficient to reduce her stress to an acceptable level for a business person in a high stress job.

CHAPTER EIGHTEEN

*One cannot experience personal
Growth at the expense of another*

OVERVIEW

When you have completed Chapter Eighteen you will be able to:

1. Recognize the Hidden Agenda in relationships
   a)State the overt intentions of the couple
   b)Identify the covert intentions of the Ego States
   c)Learn how to break up the patterns of the "Agendas" dysfunctional reactions
2. Know how the Structure of the Ego States affects the Agenda
   a)Identify which verbal configuration the couple is using to
   communicate
   b)Know what problems are inherent in the faulty communication
   between them
   c)Know how it affects the spirituality of the couple-ship
3. See the difference between functional and dysfunctional relationships when there is an imbalance of power between the Ego
   States
4. Know the difference between love and sex in a relationship
   a)Know how an abuse of power can change sex into abuse
   b)Know what to do when the need is for love and sex is offered
   c)Know how to internally facilitate the shameful feelings that
   surface when one recognizes how he set himself up to be
   sexually abused as an adult after he promised himself nobody
   would do that to him again
   d)Know how one re-traumatizes himself when he gives sexual
   favors for love or to have other needs met, that wouldn't have
   been fulfilled had they not given the sexual payment
   e)Know how The Child heals from abuse by not engaging in
   sexual acts unless it's in a loving, committed, monogamous
   relationship
5. Know how to stop the continuation of toxic relationships
6. Know how to develop new models for healthy relationships and
   acquire the skill to enter into one and maintain the
   wholesomeness

RELATIONSHIPS — PART II
THE PROBLEM: HIDDEN AGENDA

THE HIDDEN AGENDA IN RELATIONSHIPS

The "Hidden Agenda" concealed within most Human Beings — is the main reason a good relationship turns toxic or codependent — when they begin on a positive note and end up in tragedy with many dire consequences. What starts out as one's dreams coming true — usually ends up as his worst nightmare. The antecedents, issues, and process of this system is buried deeply within the subconscious and takes extensive work to uncover its workings.

Within the pages of this chapter, the keys to unlock these chains from the past are revealed. The decision to pick up the keys and unlock the shackles will depend on you — if you've had enough pain! If you haven't — they will be discarded — in order to perpetuate your current lifestyle or a similar one that has been cleaned up a little.

A Human Being's hidden agenda is contained within all previously unresolved events that occurred in his life. Its matrix is composed of the issues that were generated as a result of the following circumstances:

- Any childhood abuse (mental, physical, sexual, emotional, spiritual)
- Feelings that were frozen or unresolved
- Primary caregivers that were not there for them on a consistent basis — or when they were needed
- Despair of a missed childhood
- Uncertainty of a misdirected adolescence
- Shame of not getting one's needs met
- Behavior that was used to survive overwhelming situations
- Being raised in a dysfunctional home
- Adult behavior that violated their morals, values, standards, integrity
- Any issue that originates from the above situations. The possibilities are endless.

This agenda is driven by the unfulfilled needs of all three Ego States. Each one brings its own flavor to the stew. The agenda is not always self-defeating, even though its roots are buried in the negative mire of life. Out of the ashes of childhood defeat, grows the stamina and drive to rise above its self-fulfilling prophecies of defeat. History is replete with such instances. The plethora of self-help books written today by individuals, who overcome insurmountable odds, is current testimony to adversities' positive motivation when someone rises above his history.

Usually, the template one designs as a guide to living....that originates out of an adversarial life....is a good one! It becomes problematic, when his goals become his life, and all living is placed on hold until they are attained. This becomes an unbalanced life style and only the other side of the too much or too little coin. Some examples would include:

The Problem: A person from a poverty-stricken background becomes a financial success, driven by the past memories of being poor, and personal relationships are second to making money

The Solution: Achieving balance in his life would be to spend the money in order to enhance relationships with self and others

The Problem: When one chooses (overtly or covertly) the model of a spouse from one of his parents through the romantic eyes of a child.

The Solution: Balance would prevail as the adult looked at his parents in a realistic way.

There is nothing wrong with choosing a mate based upon good parenting practices given to him by his primary caregivers. We do have *social learning*, and how nice if one's parents were that "power of example."

The same is true for opposite situations, when one experiences negative parenting and chooses a mate which is the opposite extreme from his parents' behavior. Both conditions are problematic at best because they are a reaction instead of a choice. A choice would encompass all of the person's needs and maintain balance mentally, physically, emotionally, and spiritually.

Vocations are chosen in much the same way: do what your parents do or go the opposite extreme. Neither way is satisfying, because the decision to take either path was a reaction and not a choice.

Relationships = Confusion Multiplied by Two

During current relationships, both individuals bring their "Hidden Agenda" to the dance of love, as they attempt to get their past unrealized needs met. This is problematic at best, when neither person knows what is covertly transpiring between them, as old needs get fulfilled at the expense of the current relationship.

OVERTLY - The current events are simple:

All Ego States - The ego states of both partners want to be happy, are excited at the new beginning, and are willing to try to make the relationship work.

COVERTLY - The fear is highly complex for each partner's ego states:

The Child - Waits for signs of abandonment from his partner

The Adolescent - Waits to strike back if his partner makes the wrong move

The Critical Adult - Waits to point the finger when the relationship begins to deteriorate "or" is already "gathering" the evidence by picking at each little human character flaw that's exhibited by his mate

The Nurturing Adult - Holding his breath and waiting for the other shoe to drop. All is well in the relationship until a normal life event leaves either partner less available to the other *or* a difference of opinion occurs. At this time, the Nurturing Adult disappears. Along with him, logic or reason (the left side of the brain) disappears, emotion takes over (the right side of the brain) and fear, doubt, insecurity, anger, and negativity of the other ego states reigns supreme

As each partner in the relationship interacts and negotiates for his needs to be met, the individual ego states from both are interacting as well. This translates to six different agendas, influencing the outcome, of any interaction between the couple. Sounds complicated — doesn't it? It is! That's why one has to "keep the focus on themselves" in any relationship to determine "what's going on with them." You ask, "What about my partner"? It's not important at this time because if you don't know what's going on with you first, all you will do is to:

- React to something you don't understand
- Remain confused

- Internalize the problem as your own
- Apologize for whatever you don't understand
- Try to change whatever you "thought" caused it
- Go onto a "pink cloud" when the "problem" quiets down
- Hold your breath waiting for the other "shoe to drop"
- REACT AGAIN AND TRAVEL THE ABOVE "LOOP" — *ONE MORE TIME*!

When you have worked on your self-awareness long enough to become familiar with your internal structure, you will instinctively know:

- What ego state has just kicked in
- What your feelings are
- Why you want to act the way you are thinking about
- What the trigger was
- What your issue is
- What appropriate action to take: become reflective, set boundaries, ask for clarification, call your sponsor, go to a meeting, RUN, apologize, clarify what you said, express your feelings, see your therapist, or pray.

WITHOUT SELF KNOWLEDGE IN RELATIONSHIPS, ONE ONLY REACTS TO CONFUSING DATA AND IS HELD HOSTAGE TO ITS CONVOLUTED OUTCOME

After one has kept the focus on himself and understands his present thoughts, feelings, actions, needs, wants, desires, and motives; he is now capable of looking at himself, in relation, to another person, place, or thing. In order to be effective with this process, one has to know himself very well. THEN — AND ONLY THEN — CAN HE LOOK AT THE OTHER PERSON!

"STOP! STOP! STOP!" you yell — "How can I know the other person unless I look at them?" You can't. Until you know yourself, all you do is to look at them with a distorted vision of what you think they are or through the "rose-colored glasses" of love. One of my clinical supervisors called love a psychosis — *A BREAK FROM REALITY*! Isn't that what love is when we are attracted to the same kind of self-destructive relationships when we don't know ourselves thoroughly? Where's the reality in that process?

Which part of you dates in your relationship: Is it the needy Child who can't live alone? The Adolescent who's sexually attracted? Or the Adult who has taken the time to find out:

- Who this person he's attracted to is
- Why he is attracted to them

You have to acquire these answers if you expect things to work differently for you in new relationships.

When you understand the basic process of getting to know someone "AFTER" you know yourself....*You are ready to look at them in relationship to what you are....a Human Being....and determine "IF" they are someone you want to bring into your life on an intimate basis.*

Relationships now enter another level in life. They open up to many new possibilities instead of the same old self-defeating outcomes one becomes accustomed to receiving. In a healthy adult couple-ship, one will be able to keep himself emotionally separate from his mate's without enmeshing or disengaging, and:

- Know when he is reacting or responding
- Separate his partner's agenda from his own
- Keep past events out of present situations
- Respond appropriately within the situation
- Remain out of the problem
- Offer or look for the solution
- Gain deeper intimacy out of the interaction
- Increase trust within the couple-ship
- Experience a more committed relationship
- Bond through the process instead of separating through the dissention

Relationships don't just happen! They are hard work! The attraction is only the beginning....not the ending. What you are attracted to and why can only be answered "AFTER" you have worked on yourself. When you can say you understand yourself....you are ready to work on one. The excitement of this journey is exhilarating. Not the same as the physical or sexual attraction of her body or his looks. *IT'S FAR GREATER BECAUSE IT ENCOMPASSES MENTAL, PHYSICAL AND SPIRITUAL NEEDS AND ONE IS TOTALLY CONNECTED TO HIMSELF, OTHERS, AND THE UNIVERSE (GOD or HIGHER POWER).* It's a quiet kind of elation that allows one to totally let go control of the outcome and participate in the moment. The richness of life, in experiencing it in the now, far surpasses the action of any high, drunk, or problem loop one can devise. You be the judge. Do the work and let me know.

The interaction between the ego states of the couple will be explored in the next section. In the ego states you will gain a concrete understanding of one's internal structure during relationships.

ASSIGNMENT 26:   This is a pre-test before you read the next section. It's designed to give you an appreciation for what you already know and to help you to be aware of what is operating inside of you without your knowledge: As you re-experience the material of this section, ask yourself the following questions:

- What unresolved events in my life can cause a Hidden Agenda?
- What issues do I carry from these past events?
- How do I try to get them met today?
- What is my presenting behavior in a new relationship?
- What do I cover up in a new or ongoing relationship?
- Do I understand my ego state's reaction in a relationship when it begins, remains consistent, or something goes wrong?
- Do I know what I want in a relationship?
- Do I have a process of getting to know the other person "BE-FORE" making an emotional commitment to him?
- Do I know how to resolve a problem in the relationship without ending it?
- Can I be emotionally separate from my love object without enmeshment or disengagement, and still develop a consistent, deep, committed intimate relationship with them?
- What possible outcome can I realize if I decide to do the necessary work to begin and maintain a spiritual relationship with another Human Being?

INTERACTIONS BETWEEN EGO STATES

The interactions between the ego states are fascinating for the student, insightful for the therapists, and both heaven and hell for the unwary participants. What more, pure of motive, can it be, when: the Child in one partner — unconditionally trusts the other; the Adolescent makes a complete physical or sexual connection; or the Adult thinks he has met his soul mate? *Nothing* — if one knows himself intimately. *Everything* — if he doesn't! The following will explain why.

Structure of the Ego States

The structure of the Ego States in relationships is the manner in which both unwittingly communicate and interact. It is comprised of each individual's three ego states; creating six variations between them in any transaction, and dependent on which ego state of each is dominating at the time of the interaction. Experience a shift in mood during the interaction and the dominate ego state changes. The variations of possible responses increase to 9 or 12 if the recipient shifted as well. Have someone who is really confused, vacillating between ego states, constantly throwing you off balance with his abrupt changes, and the possibilities rise to 15 to 18, depending on how much stability you manage to maintain.

Within the relationship's matrix, one usually operates from a specific ego state, under certain circumstances, depending on the conditioned response to the situation. Examples would be: when one partner is in fear they can operate out of their Child, perceive themselves as helpless, and seek protection; if the other partner is in fear they can create an offense, and work out of their Adolescent. Very rarely would they operate in their Nurturing Adult, protecting for the sake of protection only, without a self-seeking motive, which will be extracted for a price at a later time. The price can be sex, loyalty, money, position, or giving oneself up in another situation.

In the breakdown of the interactions between the ego states, the example used, will be the generalized one that usually transpires. They will be followed up by case studies to further help you assimilate the information at a quicker pace. Figure 18.1 is the overview of the process.

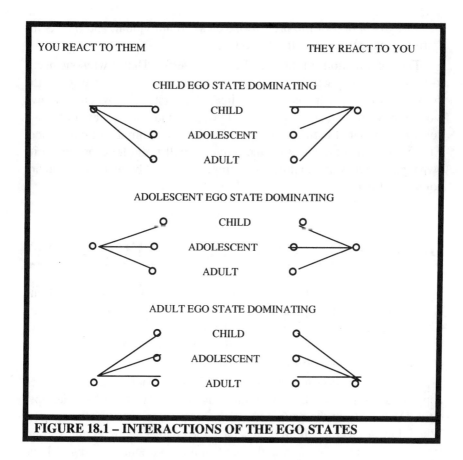

FIGURE 18.1 – INTERACTIONS OF THE EGO STATES

SPIRITUALITY BETWEEN EGO STATES It doesn't matter which ego state, either individual operates from, as long as the interaction between them is equitable and non-exploitative. When it's not, both become victimized by the process and the spirituality between them begins to dissipate. It doesn't make any difference if one is used, abused, manipulated, or enabled — the outcome is the same — *SPIRITUALITY IS DESTROYED!*

Spirituality is the second hidden agenda within couple-ships. In it, they either make the relationship work by creating an environment that "BOTH" parties accomplish their goals, or, break it by being a user, or in one-ups-man-ship, in which one is sacrificed for the needs of the other.

This spirituality in relationships fulfills two needs:

- Man gets his social needs met in relationships
- Man's connection to God is complete because He connects through people.

Any disruption of the process isolates the individual, and breaks his spiritual connection to a Higher Power.

The combinations of the agendas are powerful. That is why one needs to know his own agenda — so inadvertently — it doesn't impede the progress of another. It sounds complicated at first. It is! When you have worked at your own stuff — you will not get in anyone's way. In fact — you will step out of their way in order for them to attain their higher good. All control will be gone. And the universe will unfold, according to its own agenda, without you doing anything else except being (at rest and not doing anything).

DOMINATION BY THE CHILD EGO STATE

Operating from The Child Ego State is not always problematic if one is in a committed relationship that includes empathy. One slips into his Child when he is vulnerable, hurting, frightened, or playful. An insightful response by one's partner is what allows trust to be built, intimacy increased, and the relationship intensified.

In such a relationship, when one's "Child" is out — there are three appropriate responses that build relationships. They are not gender specific. Each party in the couple-ship can swap roles as the need requires. When they are whole within themselves, the change becomes an "accommodation" to their partner, and each remains on equal footing. I have witnessed many times, strong men becoming vulnerable — slipping into their Child, and the wife becoming a "Mama Bear" (Adolescent) and stepping in to fend off whatever hurt him. This is what truly great relationships are composed of. The accommodations would be:

Child to Child   The need that generates this combination is when one or both want to play and IT'S SAFE TO DO SO! This occurs when trust has been established within the couple-ship and either party can initiate the request.

Child to Adolescent   This configuration is engaged when the Child is scared and feels the need for protection. It happens under ordinarily stressful situations when the individual begins to feel overwhelmed and seeks the comfort of a safe haven. These life events can include: moving one's domicile, difficulty on the job, a medical or dental problem, death of a close

friend or a family member, transportation problems, a natural disaster, social unrest, launching children, aging, etc. During this time, the Adolescent
protects the Child in whatever way is necessary. Usually it is contributing
their energy, via support, to enable their partner to go through their fear.
The Adolescent creates a buffer between the Child and the overwhelming
event just long enough for their partner to muster the strength to go through
it. Sometimes it's physical, like the above example of a "Mama Bear". The
Child during these situations remains safe and the relationship is enhanced
through the interaction.

Child to Adult This presentation is spawned under two circumstances
when they: need affection by being physically close and/or emotionally
attached with their love object; seek the valued input of their mate in various situations including some that can impact both. Both of these situations
require a mature, almost parental response, in which, what is given to the
Child at that time is for their highest good and *"NEVER EXPLOITED!"*

Dysfunctional Reactions to the Domination

In therapy, we seek to unravel the hidden agenda and help to stop the
emotional damage experienced by both partners when the ego states' interactions are not appropriate, equitable, or conducive to building healthy
relationships. The changes do not begin until one is able to recognize the
problem (out of denial), takes responsibility for himself (acceptance), and
is willing to make the changes necessary to have healthy relationships.
Leaving denial and entering acceptance is a process and takes time. This
chapter is part of the process. Within it:

- The components to a healthy relationship are defined
- The ingredients to an unhealthy one are examined
- How current needs are dysfunctionally attained is explored
- How maturity impacts the relationship
- What spirituality looks like in relationships
- What occurs in a spiritually deficient relationship
- How the Executive System oversees the decision-making process
  in relationships
- What makes up the Hidden Agenda in most relationships
- How and why one of the ego states can dominate the interactions
  in any relationship
- The appropriate response when it occurs

The information presented will give you a solid foundation to admit the problem (come out of denial), go into the solution, and change the current maladaptive behavior (acceptance). Remember, the road to acceptance is the Grief Process, and each ego state moves at their own pace according to the severity of issues. You will have mixed feelings during the process. It's normal and you are where you are supposed to be.

CHILD TO CHILD   This state engenders abandonment, codependency, and victimization anytime two needy, helpless, hopeless, and emotionally void individuals try to begin a relationship while they operate out of their Child Ego State. The following occurs after the glow from the relationship's initial security begins to dim. The safety quickly ends as the partner who is less needy of the two runs out of energy and backs off to preserve his remaining reserves as love turns to disgust; *when* the Child becomes needier in the face of the coming abandonment *while* emotional boundaries are placed on their attempted enmeshment.

The issue that's prominent during this state is abandonment. Its roots are in the unfilled needs of being raised in a dysfunctional family and having emotionally unavailable, or inconsistent parents. The "Hidden Agenda" (expectation), is that the unfilled needs will be fulfilled by a mate who will: personify the attributes of a perfect parent (envisioned by the Child); will instinctively know how to fulfill their every need without asking anything for themselves; loving them just as they are, and appreciating everything they do. This romanticized projection is at best a setup, even though the ideals are worthy.

There is also an ego state change when the one who drops out of the Child State begins to set boundaries and backs off. The Adolescent is usually in charge of the process as soon as the shift is needed and goes to work immediately to set the boundary or dissolve the relationship.

It is next to impossible to maintain a relationship with both members of the couple operating out of their Child Ego State. Life is too dynamic....needs change....situations escalate....life demands you pay attention in order to survive. To withdraw....believe that life is stagnant....means death....mentally, physically, or spiritually. Children want to stop time because it gets too overwhelming. Adults face reality....accept life's challenge....move on....and remain on a spiritual path.

CHILD TO ADOLESCENT   This state generates victimization as the Child offers itself to the Adolescent for protection and then has to pay the price with its soul. During this time, the Child reaches out to what's "familiar" to him and chooses the Adolescent. The reason for the choice is spawned in the dysfunctional home when the "Child calling to Adolescent" was modeled in their primary caregivers' relationship. Usually in these couple-ships, one partner is submissive (Child) and one more dominant (Adolescent).

It's in their parents' interactions the child's blueprint for a future relationship was generated. When this happens, the forming adult has few choices and usually picks the type of mates who personify the Child's perception of what was modeled. Sometimes it's the opposite extreme of the most loathed parent (the Adolescent makes the choice here) or exactly as the most dominated and sets them up to be a victim (the Child with no power makes this decision).

This configuration is the most toxic. In it, both are victimized, able to perpetuate their sick thinking and help them to remain out of healthy relationships. With this strategy, they will never know the pain awareness will generate, when they participate with emotionally available partners. That old saying, "You never miss what you don't have" certainly applies here. The following three examples are a sample of the many problems that originate out of this process.

Spirituality Spiritually, neither partner can progress along their higher path, as they play out their childhood scripts of what a partner is supposed to be. Both innately know their agenda, and will subconsciously build up resentment toward the other as they remain stuck in old behavior; unable to break the pattern, as they are conscripted to remain playing out their old perceptions. Sometimes the resentment builds up so high that it has to be relieved. Usually it's vented through displacement when it comes out "sideways" at the person in a totally unrelated event. This is a safe way not to address the real issue.

Subconsciously, both want to be happy. When fear rises, the need is placed on hold, and one's internalized response to pain is accessed. *During this time each partner enables the other to remain in self-defeating behavior . . . instead of confronting it....growing from the process.... and moving on.* Figure 18.2 is a representation of the path one can take in a relationship when a difficult problem arises in life.

414 *More Than Words*

```
┌─────────────────────────────────────────────────────────────┐
│                    A DIFFICULT EVENT OCCURS                    │
│                              ↓                                 │
│                        ACTION TAKEN                            │
│                                                                │
│        FUNCTIONAL                      DYSFUNCTIONAL           │
│            ↓                                ↓                  │
│   FIRST – Each person takes care    FIRST – Child gives up and builds
│   of himself                        resentment as he is forced to
│                                     remain the victim.         │
│            ↓                                ↓                  │
│   SECOND – Energy is then diverted  SECOND – Adolescent takes over
│   to helping one's partner for their and also builds resentment as he
│   higher good                       assumes most responsibility
│            ↓                                ↓                  │
│   RESULTS – Relationship is deepened, RESULTS – The relationship falters
│   trust further established, and it becomes and dies as trust is violated when
│   more intimate                     each is abandoned by the other as
│                                     the relationship ends      │
│            ↓                                ↓                  │
│   BOTH PARTNERS GROW FROM           BOTH REMAIN STAGNANT FROM  │
│   THE PROCESS OF TAKING CARE        THE EVENT AS THE OUTCOME   │
│   OF THEMSELVES AND HELPING         REINFORCES THEIR CHILDHOOD │
│   THE OTHER                         BELIEFS ABOUT THEMSELVES   │
│                                     AND OTHERS                 │
├─────────────────────────────────────────────────────────────┤
│   FIGURE 18.2 – SPIRITUALITY IN RELATIONSHIPS                  │
└─────────────────────────────────────────────────────────────┘
```

Love vs. Sex Many of the problems people have in their relationships is when they confuse love with sex or can't differentiate between the two. The roots of this confusion usually originate when:

- **One was sexually abused and told it was love**
- **Sex was the only way love was given**
- **They needed to rationalize having to give sex to have their non-sexual needs met**

At this point the Child is definitely in charge of relationships, must be taught the difference between love and sex, and the new definitions applied to the dynamics of current relationships. When the new learning occurs, they will be able to love someone "WITHOUT" having sex with them, and recognize that they are using or being used for sexual relief instead of love.

When someone is used for sexual gratification only — AND THE NEED IS LOVE — THE CHILD GETS BRUTALIZED IN THE PROCESS! It's hard to imagine how this happens: the concept is a painful one for most to grasp, as they have been doing it for so long and they would never hurt themselves this deliberately. The concept is this:

- The Child has the need for love
- Love and sex are confused by the Adult
- Instead of the Adult reaching out to be loved appropriately — HE SENDS HIS LITTLE BOY OR LITTLE GIRL (Inner Child) TO BE SEXED — *WHEN IT'S THE LOVE NEEDS OF THE CHILD THAT NEED TO BE FULFILLED — NOT THE SEXUAL NEEDS OF THE ADULT!*

ONE SENDS HIS LITTLE BOY OR LITTLE GIRL (Inner Child) INTO THE BEDROOM FOR SEX WHEN THE NEED IS FOR LOVE

The imagery I receive with this concept is scary. Its ramifications shake the very foundation of someone's person-hood when he begins to apply it to his past or current behavior. It's a difficult area to break through because nobody ever thought of it "that way" before. If it's true — how can he look himself in the mirror? Isn't he the same perpetrator to himself as others were to him? Didn't he promise himself it would be different? Isn't it being a child abuser when it happens? Lots of questions and accusations surface as the concept begins to be assimilated. There is also a hint of understanding, why the Child doesn't trust the Adult, while the misdirected search for love is occurring.

THE CHILD DOES NOT TRUST THE ADULT WHEN THE ADULT USES SEX FOR LOVE

In therapy as one becomes honest about: their present behavior, how the behavior was used in the past, and what effect the misguided search for affection had on them . . . major internal conflict between the ego states will occur if the issue is not addressed. Many times the Child (feelings) are not available to the Adult because their self-defeating behavior is still being maintained. If the misdirected strategy is currently occurring, the

Adult becomes the perpetrator to the Child, when the Adult refuses to address or change the behavior. This conflict is real! In psychodrama, the parts split, and are able to confront one another. Within the confrontation....the Child is able to verbalize his invalidation because he had to give sex....in order for his love needs to be met. If the current self-defeating behavior is not addressed....great shame will be generated as the individual's internalized response to shame becomes stirred up. The resulting invalidation is also a relapse issue in substance abuse, when a failed relationship becomes a trigger, as one prematurely became sexually involved while trying to get love needs met.

Sexual Abuse   If sexual abuse has occurred — *SEX BECOMES A TRIGGER FOR SHAME*! It happens when the Adult sends his little kid (Child) for sex and the need is love. At this time, the Adult will become the perpetrator....for in his misguided efforts....his little kid (the Child) becomes abused as the unnecessary sexual act re-traumatizes him. Under these conditions . . . sex becomes a "Gateway Drug" and has to be labeled as such.

Sex now becomes a relapse issue....when the abusive nature of the act raises great shame in the subconscious....and creates a "Problem Loop" as it breaks free in the conscious. The dire consequences of the sex act....force him to re-label the use of sex to an obsessive/compulsive act....when used to get his love needs met. The same process that occurred between the Child and the Adult in the "Love vs. Sex" section applies here. The difference is when you add sexual abuse to an issue, it makes them deeper than abandonment, and usually has substance abuse tied onto them.

CHILD TO ADULT   This form usually creates an environment in which the Child, looking for an affirmation or validation from the Adult, comes up empty as he tries to get his needs met. The issue underneath the choice is: The Child is trying to get its unfilled childhood needs met through his current relationship, when, he gravitates toward what's "familiar" to him and picks emotionally unavailable partners. The resulting loss, felt, as the other partner begins to back off or set boundaries, starts the following reactions in motion:

- The current event *triggers* off his past abandonment issues
- The past emotional pain is *attached* to the present situation
- Large amounts of shame rise out of the process
- He shut down to protect himself from the coming abandonment

The real culprit in the broken relationship is the neediness of the Child. When this occurs *"nothing outside himself can permanently fill the hole he experiences inside. It's an inside job and it can only be accomplished through healing.*

THE NEEDINESS OF THE CHILD
CAN ONLY BE SATISFIED
AS HEALING OCCURS IN THE ADULT

Sometimes it's just a healthy boundary that begins the downward spiral for the Child. Other times, if the situation has been allowed to go on for a longer period of time: the partner will begin to withdraw as he feels smothered when his anxiety increases due to the enmeshment. These are difficult feelings and hard to facilitate. The process that occurs when the partner that feels overwhelmed is as follows:

- **The Adult** feels smothered and his anxiety rises
- **Their Child** thinks it's going to die and begins to panic
- **Their Adolescent** takes over and "gets rid of" the offending person when their Adult doesn't set appropriate boundaries.

Does this make sense to you? I hope it does? Relationships are a two-way street — BOTH PARTNERS HAVE TO BE CONSIDERED IN EACH INTERACTION OR IT'S ONLY SELF-SEEKING, AT BEST, AND DOOMED TO FAIL! One-way relationships do not build committed couple-ships.

When the Child has attracted what's "familiar" — he usually finds emotionally unavailable partners — ones that look good at first — and *run* when they have to be available, *or*, create a *diversion* so their behavior is not addressed. You know what kind of people these are! The ones that create a crisis, set you up, or run when you need them. Their issues are always more important than yours. They are usually the Critical Adult, and you customarily find yourself:

- Wrong in their eyes
- Always making mistakes
- Never quite good enough for them
- Mostly playing catch up
- Consistently being alone
- Frequently trying to sort out what just happened

- Thinking it will be better the next time (rationalizing)
- Secretly thinking there's something wrong and feeling it's you (shame)
- Wondering when it's going to change

Well girls and boys — it's an inside job! Picture the neediness of the Child as a great big hole inside of you. One you tried to fill with persons, places, or things, and were unsuccessful in trying to appease them. Now imagine that hole as a wound: one that was received in childhood and grew larger each time your needs were not met by:

- Your primary caregivers (usually parents)
- Those you chose to be in relationships with
- YOURSELF because you were never taught self-caring

Over time, this becomes a large gaping hole which *MUST BE HEALED — NOT FIXED*! There is nothing broken here. This is an important concept: I believe we are whole within ourselves and the only items separating us from our higher purpose, self actualization, growing up, and etc. are:

- Acquiring missing information (this book will give it to you)
- And healing from one's past hurts

As you read this book and assimilate its concepts, you will acquired much of the missing information you need in order to know yourself and others, and have choices during most situations that occur in life. The healing from past events will now transpire as one:

- Acknowledges the event
- Feels the pain instead of medicating it with obsessive or compulsive behavior (Problem Loops)
- Goes through the pain by processing it and identifying what strategies were used *not* to experience it
- CHANGE THEIR CURRENT SELF-DEFEATING BEHAVIOR THERE BY — BECOMING MORE AVAILABLE TO THEMSELVES
- Re-experiencing the pain as it opens up from greater feelings, understanding, awareness, and process

With each event and greater level of process, comes more healing until the hole is finally healed shut. In this circumstance, as in others in this book: "The only way out of something — is through it!" This is no exception.

ASSIGNMENT 27: Does The Child dominate your Internal Structure when you have a conflict with your love object? If yes....why? If no....who does? (Give examples). Does spirituality exist in your relationships? If no....why? If you didn't know before this book....how can you change to allow it in? What needs does the Child try to fulfill in a relationship? Are they past ones? If yes....how does it affect your *present* relationship? You have to be honest here (out of denial) if the assignment is to work for you. When in your Child, what are your mental, physical, spiritual, and sexual boundaries with your mate? Do you have to give sexual favors in order to have your needs met? What do you have to do to remain physically safe with your mate? If the answer is not positive....what do you have to do to change it? Does your partner enable you to stay in self-defeating behavior by stirring the pot to keep negative reactions going? How does your relationship rate spiritually according to Figure 18.2....functional....or dysfunctional? If you were sexually abused....does your partner's sexual needs trigger off your old tapes (remind you) when you were abused? Does your partner treat you like an equal? If not....what are you treated like....what are your needs....how can you make changes to be treated more in line with your self concepts and needs? Is your spouse the Critical Adult to your Child? Are you attracted to what's familiar to you....those who mirror or are the opposite extreme from one or both of your parents?

CASE STUDY: Constance, our 67-year-old housewife, is a classic example of someone having an Executive System dominated by the Child Ego State. When she came into group on the first day — it was clear that she suffered from major depression. She stayed to herself for the first week, shut down by sleeping (her medication had been stabilized prior to admission to our program), and refused to respond in depth to any probes and remained superficial with facts and highly guarded with her feelings.

During the next two weeks, she was given written assignments; opportunities in group to explore her life's current circumstances; asked to participate in other's experiential group work by taking a role in their psychodrama; family therapy in which her spouse refused to change his current relationship with her because this "depression" was her problem — not his! Nothing worked. Constance refused to engage in the therapeutic process of treatment.

Constance was informed that she would be staffed, a family meeting held following the staffing, and if she wasn't able to engage in the program's therapeutic process — that she would be discharged because she had gained the maximum benefit possible. The benefit was on a case manager basis only: all the program was able to do for her was to coordinate some services instead of helping her to look at her present circumstances, past blocks, and to do the work necessary to get out of her depression.

The staff agreed to discharge. In the discussion, the attending physician stated that she had extensive blood work to rule out a physiological cause for the depression. The program psychiatrist reported how she was balanced on her current anti-depressant medications and to change the frequency or dose would put her out of balance and sedate her only. The therapists reviewed the treatment plans, discussed the failed attempts to engage her in therapy, and reported they were out of strategies.

In the following family meeting, the family reported the results of previous attempts to get Constance some help; how it would help for a period of time and she would return into depression. They were also very frustrated because it had been going on for 20 years, tired of blaming themselves for causing it, and were giving up trying because our program had a reputation of creating miracles by helping people to get better when others had given up on them. The program was their last hope and we failed.

What happened to Constance was simple: Her Child Ego State dominated her Executive System and when the Adult abrogated her authority to facilitate the depression in an adaptive fashion, the Adolescent took charge and "Acted Internally" via depression. In this process she shut down more and more, until she was so low she couldn't make the trip back to balanced feelings: where she could interact in life as a self-empowered adult. The trip took 20 years. Once she was there, lacked the ability to make the return trip back to balance.

DOMINATION BY THE ADOLESCENT EGO STATE

The Adolescent Ego State in a relationship doesn't have to be dysfunctional. This is the mode that brings life, commitment, passion, challenge, and boundaries into an adult relationship. It's the segment of ones personality that brings to their partner:

- Protection to the Child
- Passion and intensity for the Adolescent

- Energy and perseverance to attain life's goals for the Adult

These are very positive attributes and only manifest in the mature relationship of two full-grown adults, who are completely empowered to act on behalf of all their ego states.

Dysfunctional Reactions to the Domination

ADOLESCENT TO CHILD   This condition usually spawns enabling and resentment:

Enabling as the Adolescent over-protects the Child, subverts the natural process of accountability by "fixing" any problem that arises, and forestalls the natural consequences of their behavior: *resentment* as the "fixing" diverts most of their energy or when, whatever they try to do is never enough to change their mate's current condition (the Adolescent feels they should be grateful for their effort).

The resentment originates from the ego states of each member in the couple-ship: from the Adolescent as described above and subconsciously from the Child, because spiritually they know what's occurring….although cognitively….they don't.

The issues normally attached to the Adolescent's behaviors are power, self-esteem, and abandonment. They originate out of the Adolescent's unfilled needs from their family of origin and occur as the Adolescent "fixes" the Child and acquires great power over him. If the Child capitulates, the Adolescent's power grows stronger, self-esteem rises, and the partner stays. What's really transpiring between them is the Adolescent is protecting their Child by taking a hostage in the current relationship which guarantees they won't be abandoned. (It's a power trip OK: A self-defeating one.) It's another instance where the children fix the parents and delude themselves into believing that if the parents are OK — they will be, too.

At this point, the Adolescent still believes (egocentric) they can change things externally and soothe their internal strife. They can't. It's an inside job and the effort has to be placed on them. In the past this behavior was called selfish. Today it's changed to self-caring.

ADOLESCENT TO ADOLESCENT - is the most volatile and problematic. It adds the energy, intensity, and excitement to a sexual relationship. Remember adolescence? Hormones kicking — body on fire. This is resurrected today in adulthood when two individuals try to have a relationship based on sex, intensity, excitement, or games. It doesn't make any difference if they're gay or straight, male or female, one or both is actively participating in the behavior or one is a passive recipient of the results of one — ALL ARE PARTICIPATING — ALL ARE GAINING A BENEFIT FROM THE PROCESS! Try to have an intimate relationship in that type of action when no one slows down long enough to carry one on. Good luck if you think you can.

No one is saying that sex can't be good, or a relationship intense or exciting, to be mature. This happens in many good relationships. In fact, without it, there is no relationship. The excitement of high energy relationships becomes problematic, maladaptive, or dysfunctional when the sex is the only reason for the relationship and after sexual energy dies or diminishes....the relationship or marriage is over.

An intimate relationship between teenagers or one teenager and an adult very rarely works because the evolving person has not: solidified his self concepts; had enough experience to know what his wants, needs, and desires are; nor has a level of personal understanding to separate his wants from his needs. EXAMPLE: Describe the type of person you wanted to be with at age 13, 19, 24, 29, 35, 40 or 50. Be honest. It changes. This is normal until we really get to know ourselves. When we do, the person we pick will be our soul mate. Until then, relationships will usually be in a state of flux because we are learning about our person-hood and evolving into our higher selves.

I know this is bad news to those of you who are still entranced with her beautiful curves or his deep piercing eyes and wonder why it never works out. You still get the same ending to a relationship although it seemed so different at first. How sad that we all have to grow up some time.

This combination can also be highly toxic to each other and extremely cruel. It occurs as the two adolescents clash and work out on each other, the issues they have with their parents. Anyone who remembers being an adolescent or has worked with them understands how volatile they are: one moment a cuddly child and the next, "Jack the Ripper" who wants to take off your head or at least make you bleed.

The mood swing is generated from quick changes of the ego state: in one moment its a Child....the next an Adolescent. The problem is, in knowing who's there, at what time, and what do you do with it. The shifting of ego states is enough to make anyone crazy. It sets one up to "drop their guard" and the Adolescent comes in for the kill. Nothing works in this configuration but insanity. As long as you want to remain crazy...stay in one! If you want relief...leave!

The entire dance of the Adolescents has one goal to accomplish....to keep the pot stirred up so they don't have to look at themselves. This is what usually happens in chemical dependency between couples. When both are using, it's a relationship made in heaven, as both do the dance with their individual addictions. If only one is using....the other is controlling....both are in paradise as they are spiraling around each other and neither has to look at himself. Sound familiar? It should. How many of you have participated in this type of relationship and wondered why things would not get consistently better? They weren't supposed to. This configuration is designed to sabotage the process and keep them in a problem loop so they don't have to look at whatever is going on in their past or present lives.

The mood swings generally observed in this environment usually occurs in the following process:

- Both Adolescents go head to head against each other
- One becomes fearful and drops into his Child state
- In their Child they lower their defenses
- The Adolescent can interpret this capitulation as weakness and strike
- The Child at this point shuts down. Out of the process rises the Adolescent who is determined to destroy their foe, and re-engages with their partner's Adolescent again.
- Their partner's Adolescent regroups and goes back into combat

The only variation would be when the partner's Adolescent slides into their Child and the original Adolescent mirrors their partner's cruel behavior and attacks the Child. This can be repeated ad nauseam throughout the entire relationship.

The solution is easy. When one Adolescent goes into their Child, the partner's Adolescent rises into their Adult, doesn't attack the Child, and tries to settle their differences. For the relationship to grow, the Child would have to express their feelings and allow their Adult to handle the interaction. In this way, the solution would be amicable. Figure 18.3 is a depiction of the process.

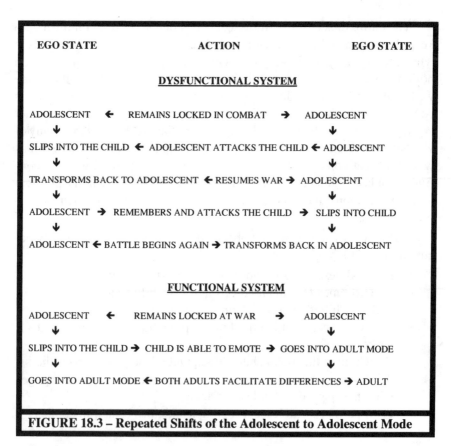

EGO STATE	ACTION	EGO STATE

DYSFUNCTIONAL SYSTEM

ADOLESCENT ← REMAINS LOCKED IN COMBAT → ADOLESCENT
↓   ↓
SLIPS INTO THE CHILD ← ADOLESCENT ATTACKS THE CHILD ← ADOLESCENT
↓   ↓
TRANSFORMS BACK TO ADOLESCENT ← RESUMES WAR → ADOLESCENT
↓   ↓
ADOLESCENT → REMEMBERS AND ATTACKS THE CHILD → SLIPS INTO CHILD
↓   ↓
ADOLESCENT ← BATTLE BEGINS AGAIN → TRANSFORMS BACK IN ADOLESCENT

FUNCTIONAL SYSTEM

ADOLESCENT ← REMAINS LOCKED AT WAR → ADOLESCENT
↓   ↓
SLIPS INTO THE CHILD → CHILD IS ABLE TO EMOTE → GOES INTO ADULT MODE
↓   ↓
GOES INTO ADULT MODE ← BOTH ADULTS FACILITATE DIFFERENCES → ADULT

FIGURE 18.3 – Repeated Shifts of the Adolescent to Adolescent Mode

\ADOLESCENT TO ADULT   This pattern is usually the most antagonistic relationship that can develop out of the various configurations the ego states operate from. It usually emerges from several factors:

1. The Adolescent gravitates toward what's "familiar" to them, and it's usually a partner that operates out of their Critical Adult
2. The Critical Adult is generally opposed to the Adolescent unless they are "perfect"
3. When the adversity between them begins, the Adolescent becomes oppositional defiant, and both meet head on in a problem loop
4. In the Problem Loop, their behavior continuously escalates; the Adolescent continues to oppose "most things" said by their partner, who in turn becomes more judgmental and critical with each new interaction between them
5. They work out their unresolved issues on each other:

The Critical Adult— When they too, do what's familiar, or are too insecure to attract and maintain an adult relationship.

The Adolescent — Continues to work out their anger issues with their parents through their current relationship, which usually recreates the same experiences, they had in their family of origin. Most are attracted to people who are carbon copies of their primary caregivers, or their opposite extremes.

Pay Off - This mode usually creates the most confusion and shame. It occurs as negative messages are given to the Adolescent as "constructive feedback," under the guise of being positive and helpful, when covertly, it is used as a means to control and suppress a youthful spirit.

The shame is generated by the constant barrage of invalidation received by the Adolescent. In the critical dialogue, a double bind is produced as they become: "damned if they do" (stick up for themselves — they lose their love object); or "damned if they don't" (do what's suggested — they lose themselves). The process replicates the helplessness and hopelessness felt as a Child and shame emerges as they feel "something is wrong with them that can't be fixed."

The payoff for the Adolescent in this toxic couple-ship includes the following:
- A self-fulfilling prophecy that relationships won't work
- Evidence that there is no one for them
- Validation that "all opposite sex partners (male or female) are no good
- Reinforcement that all men or women are the same and will eventually abandon them
- A "Gateway drug" into their substance of choice if they have a substance abuse problem
- A filter to evaluate other life events
- A WAY TO TAKE THE FOCUS OFF THEMSELVES! When they use it in this manner: the action of the "problem loop" it creates....diverts their emerging feelings as they become "other directed" and consumed by their partners actions....instead of looking at themselves.

This whole process is a smoke screen which enables the Adolescent not to feel: If they keep the focus external on another person or relationship....they don't have the time to look at themselves and see what's going on internally. *The major payoff is — if they don't know what they didn't get — they would never have to deal with the loss.*

AVOIDING PLEASURE OR THE GOOD THINGS IN LIFE — HELPS TO IGNORE THE PERSONAL NEEDS THAT WERE NOT FULFILLED EARLIER IN LIFE

Avoidance of "what wasn't" is the major goal of the defense mechanism. It's the prime ingredient of relationship sabotage. How many times have things gone well for you in a relationship and the following occur:

- Anxiety begins to rise
- Fear sets in
- You doubt it's going to last
- Wonder what's wrong
- Start to become suspicious, defensive, or paranoid
- Become certain something is going to happen and wait for "the other shoe to drop"
- Do something stupid (you really knew better) and sabotage the relationship

This is the Adolescent in charge of the relationship, and doing its job by covering up the Child's fear of being abandoned. To them it's better to cause the problem....do it to them before they do it to you. This whole problem loop becomes nothing more than a medicator or a smoke screen that enables the Adolescent to avoid anything that will cause them emotional pain.

In substance abuse, this type of relationship usually is a "trigger" or "gateway drug" into relapse. If the relationships don't mature, they usually break up. It can be any member of the couple-ship that initiates the action. Whichever partner enters recovery and starts to grow....is usually the instigator of the change in the relationship dynamics.

Therapy can also help realign the ego states, although, *IT TAKES TWO — ONE CANNOT DO IT ALONE!* There is a lot of work involved to overcome all the antagonism and invalidation that has occurred between the two. Most do not have enough positive bonding to build upon — and they usually end. It's always worth a try to rebuild. If anything, you will come out the other side knowing more about you and what you want or don't want in your life. Even though an old relationship is ending with your partner — a new one is forming with yourself.

ASSIGNMENT 28: Does your Adolescent dominate your Executive System when you have a problem in a relationship? If yes....why? Are there any other choices? If yes.... what are they? How do you implement them? If your Adolescent doesn't dominate....who establishes the boundaries? Who is in charge sexually? Do you get your sexual needs met in an appropriate way? Do you pay to have your needs met with sex? Do you make someone else pay to have their needs met with sex? Do you think your current relationship is over when the initial sexual energy diminishes from its original intensity? How do you treat your partner when he or she is in their Child? If positive....give examples. If negative....why and what can you do to change it? Does your Adolescent recognize spiritual principles between partners in a relationship? If no....why? Is fighting with your mate foreplay? Does it get you "ready" for sex? If yes....when did you learn this? Is it healthy? Does it interrupt the couple's spiritual symbiosis? Do you recognize a pattern in your life that's depicted in Figure 18.3? Is yours dysfunctional? What is the purpose (or payoff) of maintaining it? How can you change it?

CASE STUDY: Stan, a 71-year-old retired blue collar worker, came into therapy after his family threatened to put him in a nursing home if he didn't get help with his present behavior.

Upon admission, a family history was completed and indicated that Stan's current behavior was present for most of his life, although the presentation was not as severe because he worked, was active with his friends, and did not isolate. They did report periods of time that he seemed glued to the TV and drank extra beers when he did. When asked what "extra" meant, he answered, "You know — a few." When pressed for further clarification — couldn't answer.

Stan came into group and was antagonistic at best. When asked to work — refused. When pushed — wanted to fight. Every intervention possible was tried, to bond with him and establish trust. Nothing worked as he alternated between being passive in group by not engaging, to being aggressive in becoming combative. The verbal aggression was viewed as boundaries — the threat of physical violence was interpreted as fear.

Stan was given the first week of group to lower some of his defense mechanisms, and given a directive to stop the combativeness in group or be discharged. Stan replied he didn't care. Wanted to go home, have his nightly drink, and watch TV. His exact words were, "Who the hell do you think you are — trying to tell me how to live my life! I've earned the right to do nothing."

The family was called in on the second week to see what we could use for leverage to get him to engage in the therapeutic process of group. They seemed compassionate, but confessed were powerless over his behavior because he would get so mean that they would just leave him along. When his wife was asked in private about their sex life — she replied that it was nonexistent, had been for several years, and she wanted it left that way because both of their desire to have sex was gone. The statement was contrary to her physical presentation: she was in her mid 60's, looked younger, and was vivacious. The team agreed that the family had some sort of "Hidden Agenda" and wasn't willing to risk opening it up to outsiders for scrutiny. Without their cooperation, whatever the issue was, could not be used for therapeutic ammunition, and agreed not to press it.

Stan maintained his resistance throughout week two and half way through the third week, became sexually inappropriate with a 37-year-old female patient, and was discharged for the behavior.

The female was counseled as to her rights because she was considered as being sexually assaulted when he groped the sexual parts of her anatomy and requested she perform oral sex on him. She refused our offer to call the police.

Had a staff member witnessed the act, the police would have been called and the incident reported. The clients are given Informed Consent to this fact when they enter the program and know the consequences to their behavior prior to their action.

When Stan's family was notified of the event, the subsequent discharge from the program, and the action that would have been taken had a staff witnessed the sexual assault....they did not seem surprised. When questioned about the lack of surprise, the daughter disclosed her dad's behavior with other women who have been in house alone with him, and was hoping that it was just a phase he was going through. The wife just looked away as her daughter spoke, and then ordered her to stop by saying sharply, "That's enough!" Stan was unmoved by the session and was the first to leave the room when it was over. He looked angry as he walked through the unit to leave, and neither acknowledged nor said goodbye to any staff or peer.

It's easy to see that Stan was locked in his Adolescent. All behavior pointed toward it. What we don't know is why he maintained the obvious loss of energy with dysfunctional behavior; when he could have used the same energy for a positive lifestyle and been happy in the process, instead of angry, isolated, and a mean old man.

DOMINATION BY THE ADULT EGO STATE

This is the ego state we would like to see all relationships operate from. It is the one that will insure the couple-ship lasts by the following actions:

- It will mediate the stress in an adaptive fashion
- Use creative solutions to life's problems
- Remain out of the problem and into the solution
- Guarantee fairness, equality, respect, integrity, kindness and understanding
- Not unduly influence or use their partner to have personal needs met at their mate's expense

Relationships would be perfect if everyone was in their Adult as they were participating in one. The trouble with its fulfillment is that very few people are able to remain in this mode 24 hours a day, 7 days a week, when they are human and subject to all human frailties. These so-called "human frailties" are normal reactions to life stressors. In them, one is transported through the process of his mind, and forced to make an instantaneous decision with limited knowledge or missing data. By now, you know what the results are, as one reacts from his ego states:

The Child - Reacts from fear, can become helpless and hopeless, and think everyone is going to abandon him. The Child part of someone is also needy and can easily overtax his partner's resources with his VORACIOUS inadequacy and the energy it takes to triumph over him.

The Adolescent - Reacts to cover up the fear from the Child. What they learn is: the best defense is a good offence and can become highly aggressive to the person who frightens them. This side is what most people call their "evil twin" or their "dark side." It's really the part that sets boundaries and executes most defensive behavior.

The Critical Adult - This part is the one who judges, criticizes, or belittles, themselves or others, to cover up their own inadequacies. They are also the internal re-creation of one or both of their parents or primary caregivers (remember the socialization process). In fairness to the parents, the intention of the message was constructive criticism: how it was received was highly negative, implied the receiver was inadequate and spawned great shame: quite the opposite to its intent. These messages today, when given to a partner, are extremely self-defeating to both parties.

The terminology has to be reframed to match its intent and generate a positive message.

These human frailties are not a problem unless one is in denial or hasn't the skill to facilitate their reaction. When it occurs, the outcomes are highly problematic at best, and volatile or toxic at its worst. In any case, the reaction is mainly dysfunctional....not adaptive....usually ineffective....except when used as a defense mechanism in which it becomes a skillful negative response that's highly polished.

The main distinction between the two strategies used to facilitate the potential self defeating behavior is:

FUNCTIONAL — Generates Living Skills   **(Response)**
DYSFUNCTIONAL — Perpetuates Survival Skills   **(Reaction)**

Dysfunctional Reactions to the Domination

ADULT TO CHILD   The reaction in this mode is the same when the states are reversed; only at this point, the Adult is critical toward the Child and the Child is giving itself up to them. This is a highly inequitable relationship: when one partner is usually dominant over the other and feels inferior in the process.

This relationship is doomed to fail when the Adult is no longer able to function for the needy Child or the Adult wants the Child to grow up. The underlying issues that reside when this mode is in operation are control and abandonment: If the Adult controls the Child....does it good enough....the Child won't leave.

When this process occurs within a relationship....one part of the couple is like a teacher and the other part the student: the teacher is always higher than the student, knows more, and usually leaves the Child playing catch up with the Adult. They are never equals in the relationship.

ADULT TO ADOLESCENT   This condition occurs when the Adult wants more action in their relationship and still wants to control. Like the Adult to Child, this Adult is not able to have a mature relationship with another Adult and usually exercises control in another way. The Child is usually controlled with criticism that invokes shame, to which they shut down and become docile. The Adolescent is controlled through taunting, in which they over-react, and get set up to acquire consequences they wouldn't have incurred if left alone.

This type of relationship is seen in chemical dependence quite frequently. Its matrix is formed as the non-using Adult treats their using partner as a bad little boy or girl when they continue to use or relapse. Both ego states have a vested interest to remain in this relationship configuration in order to perpetuate their false images about themselves and their partner. In this mutual delusion....the Adult becomes drawn into the Problem Loop of the user's Adolescent and begins the following dysfunctional dance between them: the Adolescent sets up their partner's Critical Adult to shame them as an excuse to use: their partner's Critical Adult is in waiting, ready to pounce on their wayward charge, and validate that nothing positive can be sustained in the Adolescent's life. This self-fulfilling prophecy is the heart of the defense mechanism that produced it. Within it one can:

- Form unions with emotionally unavailable people
- Maintain inequitable relationships
- Validate their childhood belief system that all men or women are the same and they will eventually leave you
- Play out their childhood scripts with their current mate
- Maintain their self-esteem through "managing" their user
- Create an illusion of being grown up when their insides don't agree
- Hide from:
  1)Past emotional pain
  2)The consequences of their reaction to it
  3)The pain they are currently experiencing in their unfulfilling relationships with self and others

The above is a huge payoff and to some — a way of life. To overcome the benefits of this dysfunctional strategy, one has to reframe their survival skills to living skills. In the changing process, they will come face to face to their most formidable opponent — THEMSELVES! For in order to change, they will have to identify, expose, process, and feel, most of the following that occurred in their lives:

- What abuse (mental, physical spiritual, sexual, etc.) was done to them
- What needs were not filled by their primary caregivers (parents)
- What they did as a reaction to the above
- How they hurt others because of what was done or not done for them

- How they hurt themselves

When this awareness (out of denial) and process has begun, both will no longer have a need to use the "Action" or "Problem Loop" of a dysfunctional relationship as a survival skill. Instead, both will develop the emotional maturity to transcend their past and present pain by acquiring new living skills in order to learn and grow from their past mistakes. In the process, they will no longer use a problem loop to keep the focus off themselves. The reframing will restore them to sanity as they no longer repeat the same dysfunctional behavior over and over and expecting something different to occur in their present lives.

TO OVERCOME THE BENEFITS OF A DYSFUNCTIONAL LIFESTYLE — ONE MUST REFRAME HIS CURRENT SURVIVAL STRATEGIES TO MORE ADAPTIVE LIVING SKILLS

It's a difficult process to change a way of life that one has used to survive with. There are many loyalties to the system. In their minds, it didn't fail them until now. It's also like a new pair of shoes....tight in the beginning and more comfortable later after they're broken in. The changing is much the same way:

- At first not easy, strange, and almost forced
- As the new strategies are practiced at a greater level — the new responses come more easily and naturally
- Doesn't become comfortable until the new response is internalized and becomes the automatic behavior in the situation or event

ADULT TO ADULT   We infrequently observe this configuration in relationships. If it's in place, there is little need for therapy except in a current situation that's overwhelming and taxes their present coping strategies. When this happens, the therapy is brief; situation oriented, and stops when the overwhelming crisis is over. Examples would be loss of a child, spouse, or sibling; premature death due to illness or war; acquiring a major debilitating disease; losing an important job; a major transition in the Family Life Cycle; losing all of one's possessions in a major natural catastrophe; aging issues.

All of these issues are enough to tax anyone's stress reduction system. When two of these occurrences happen simultaneously or right after one another....the average person has to shut down to avoid the shock (remember the Grief Process) or go into an emotional tail spin. They usually seek help in therapy when they come out of denial and recognize there is something wrong with the current way they are handling their stress.

ASSIGNMENT 29: Which part of your Adult dominates the Executive System in your conflicts with your love object? If it's the Critical Adult….how does he act when your partner is in their Child and Adolescent? Does he belittle the Child or antagonize the Adolescent? Does he second guess the Nurturing Adult with every decision made? Can your Nurturing Adult work with your partner to help them attain their highest good? Is your Nurturing Adult the conduit for spirituality in your relationships with others? Is your Nurturing Adult available sexually to your mate?

CASE STUDY: A good example of a couple remaining in their Adults while they were having a problem with each other is the one that Brent and Sandy worked on when they came into therapy.

When they started to explore some of the sensitive areas between them, it was revealed that several factors were influencing their married environment: Several deaths had occurred over the past couple of years including the death of one of her parents; the children were in adolescence; they were in their 40's; vocational changes were occurring for both; there were changes occurring in the culture that were against their values and frightening to them as parents.

All of the factors raised fear in them. Both adjusted to the fear — talking about it and validating it in one another. All went well until just before a major holiday. Sandy became impatient for some potential changes to happen, and set the changes in motion, by forcing them to happen prematurely without talking it over with Brent — which she usually did. Brent reacted badly to the changes occurring prematurely. He felt betrayed because he wasn't part of the decision-making process with his wife, and suspected there were deeper issues involved when she eliminated him from the process and the outcome was not his choice. This was out of character for her.

Even with his understanding of his wife, his reaction came from his Adolescent, was highly offensive in nature, and emotionally cut himself off from her. Her reaction was to retreat into her Child Ego State and wanted back the love and support she experienced from him since they were married. She was highly confused, lost, did not intend to hurt him, felt the action was well thought out on her part, and didn't understand why Brent was acting this way.

In the first part of the work it took to resolve the issue: Brent could take responsibility for his reaction, knew some of it was his "core" issues that were tapped through Sandy's action, although he felt that the feelings also came from today and he needed to keep Sandy out so she couldn't hurt him again. Sandy felt her action was appropriate to the situation, no "issue" was attached to it, and she never meant to hurt Brent. In fact, it was the last thing in her mind and just wanted her husband back.

Brent would not move on his decision. Stated that Sandy had some issues to look at and if she didn't — would hurt him again. This he would not allow. Sandy sat up and took notice when Brent stated the boundary and said she would look at whatever she had to in order to get the love and support back from her husband that she was used to. All of the factors that were outlined in the beginning of this study were talked about between the couple. Some of them were dismissed by Sandy as being irrelevant — Brent insisted they were major issues and if she didn't look at them he was keeping his distance from her. Brent was confronted by the therapist for using "emotional blackmail" and Brent retorted to the therapist, "Bull — I know my wife — I know me — It's a boundary! She has to do her own inventory. I won't be a target for her unresolved issues! We've come too far in our marriage to do that to each other!" Brent was adamant and Sandy confused when they left this session. They agreed to continue to work on it at home and to come back the following week.

The second session went the same way as the first: Brent maintaining his boundaries unless Sandy worked on her issues and Sandy confused because she didn't mean to hurt him and still didn't see what she had to look at.

During this session, we brought in the model to ascertain where they were with each other: Brent was in his Adolescent with his boundaries, his Child was hidden when he couldn't access the soft feelings he had for Sandy, his Critical Adult was quiet, and his Nurturing Adult was present in his ability to state that he didn't like his reaction, didn't want to hurt her, knew his core issues had been touched by her action, and wanted this episode to be over: Sandy was in her Child, wanted her husband back and at the same time her Adolescent dug in her heels and refused to budge on looking at anything that might resemble her issues. They left the session the same way as the last, except Brent's attitude was a little softer and Sandy was given a written assignment to help her sort things out and included the model as a framework.

Both came in the next session ready to work and the session lasted two and a half hours. In it, Sandy was able to do her own inventory and looked at her issues. She responded.... as Brent and she talked during the week . . . she wrote on what came up for her and the picture of what was occurring became clear.

At first in session, it was surface level only, and about how she reacted to what she thought Brent said to her. When she interpreted Brent as non-supportive....her Adolescent reacted with "I'll show him"....and she made the decision without consulting with him first. When Sandy and Brent talked about her interpretation of his words, how she reacted prior to making a decision for herself which impacted him, she realized she had projected one of her parent's traits on to him, and she reacted to the projection.

Some precipitating factors to the transference were: the recent death of one of her parents, invalidating behavior by her surviving parent just prior to a major holiday, some disturbing events occurring in the culture, her oldest daughter becoming the same age Sandy had experienced major differences with her parents, and while all of these negative factors were occurring....the rest of her life with Brent and the children was wonderful and special. These were an abundance of considerations to struggle with even though they were both positive and negative.

In processing her action in relationship to all of the above described factors, Sandy began to see her issues, and how they affected her behavior. As Brent watched her working in therapy, he softened, started to cry, hugged his wife, and said it was good to feel her love again. What had happened to Brent was as soon as Sandy recognized what she was doing and where it came from: he knew she wouldn't hurt him; he could let down the boundary, take in her love, and was safe again.

This was a good process for each. Both stayed in the Adult with not wanting to cause any more damage than was inadvertently done. Both took care of themselves during the conflict. Each was able to own what was theirs, remained whole within themselves, and wanted the highest good for the other. Both know they still have issues to work on. Both are willing to do the work to keep their marriage intact and viable.

SUMMARY

A "Hidden Agenda" or unknown motives about why someone acts in a specific way to certain stimuli....is contained in any Human Being who has unresolved past issues that were spawned in childhood and adolescence....when their needs were not met in a consistent manner by their primary caregivers.

Each developmental age-stage generates its own issues: the Child's is usually abandonment; the Adolescent's is usually the revenge; the Adult's is their inability to be available to their mates the games they have to play in order to get their needs met, which are usually egocentric and at the expense of their partner. These are covert issues. Overtly, both partners want to be happy and are glad they are in love.

In order to change the toxic process dysfunctional relationships usually engender, one has to know themselves. With increased self-awareness: they will identify their wants, needs, and desires; decide what price they will pay (if any) to get them met; learn how they can self-actualize and complete their spiritual task without another human being ....especially their love object....impeding their progress. When they have completed these tasks, they will be ready to participate in an intimate relationship without the fear of losing themselves; thereby remaining an Adult and maturely handling any conflict that arises between the couple instead of acting like a lost child or an angry adolescent.

The communication that occurs during any interaction between couples can include 18 different configurations, depending on which ego state is verbally communicating, and how it's interpreted by the listener. Ideally, the Adult's domination is preferred. In this way, two full-grown adults....possessing self-awareness and proficient at conflict resolution....based in self-love and the highest good for their partner and couple-ship....complete the transaction between them in an equitable manner.

Emotional maturity between couples was not modeled by the participants' primary caregivers if they were raised in a dysfunctional home. Instead, the parental unit usually consisted of a wounded Child and a revengeful Adolescent, attempting to meet their past unfulfilled needs, in their present relationship. Following the strategies modeled by wounded caregivers does not promote healthy relationships and spawns an environment that creates hostages. Becoming a hostage sets up one partner to be the controller and the other to be controlled (who is the controller during this scenario....the controller or the one being controlled)? In it, both get their sick needs met, avoid facing the fear of abandonment (so they think), and think they are in control. During this dysfunctional strategy, the spiritual energy between partners is expended trying to control, break free of the control, or wonder why there is control....instead of the energy being utilized to self-actualize and create an environment....conducive to both partners.... attaining their highest good within the couple ship.

When the Child is dominated, they are usually "the victim," taken advantage of and used mentally, physically, and sexually for their partner's self-seeking motives. The Child has a vested interest in remaining in the victim role, for all the mental gymnastics of being a hostage allows them not to feel the pain of past or present trauma. In its process, they reduce their shame by rationalizing that it was their fault their primary caregivers either didn't meet their needs or abused them. In this way they won't feel the shame that rises when their needs are met by an emotionally available partner and they can no longer deny any loses which occurred or the deprivation they suffered at the hands of their primary caregivers during their upbringing when their needs did not get met.

When the person is in their Child and used for sexual gratification by their partner, they are being sexually abused, for the Child's need is for love and protection — NOT EXPLOITATION! Anyone who has been sexually abused during their childhood becomes re-traumatized by the sexual inappropriateness of the encounter, as it recreates the same conditions they experienced in childhood: when they went to who they thought were safe adults, for love and protection, and were sexually abused by them.

When the Adolescent dominates the relationship, it is usually permeated with anger, control and revenge. All of the various configurations the ego states can interact from….work their issues out on each other. There is little harmony between the participants: the action of the negativity is used as foreplay, breaks any spiritual connection between the partners, usually signifies deep issues, and is generally combined with substance abuse, addiction, or mental illness. This is the most highly volatile configuration a couple can remain in and is an extremely dangerous way to keep the focus of them. Used as an assessing tool in therapy, the combination signifies major events occurred in the past and possibly great damage was done to them by their abuser. In order to break the toxic pattern one of the Adolescents has to end the war going on between them. The battle will end if their partner slips into their Child and their Adolescent doesn't brutalize their mate, or they move into their Adult, and their partner's Adolescent does the same. It would take a Twelve-Step Program or therapy to make it happen.

When the domination occurs through the Critical Adult, the issue is usually fear, control, and lack of maturity. This ego state lacks the ability to have an adult relationship with another adult and seeks to dominate a partner who operates from their Child Ego State or shame one who operates from their Adolescent. While playing the game of one-ups-man-ship; the Critical Adult will usually remain aloof over a fearful Child.

CHAPTER NINETEEN

Couples grow together or go apart

OVERVIEW

When you have completed Chapter Nineteen, you will be able to:

1. Understand how the Adult will dominate your Executive System
2. What process is needed for the Adult to be in charge
3. How cognitive reframing sets the stage for Adult changes
   a) How to change a survival skill to a living skill
   b) Why it's important to maintain a positive framework with survival skills
   c) How to quiet the Critical Adult who wants to judge the process
   d) How to rebalance a character trait
   e) What the process of reframing looks like
4. Recognize the components of cognitive restructuring
   a) What role the Grief Process takes in the construct
   b) How an ethical system impacts one's thinking and behaving
   c) What role integrity plays in the process when one is trying to interact with another in a confusing situation
   d) How intimacy challenges one's thoughts about personal safety
   e) What contribution one's spirituality makes to their thought process
5. Identify the components of behavioral change in relationships:
   a) To recognize First Order Change (Compliance)
   b) To observe Second Order Change (Internalized response)
   c) How to learn from mistakes instead of repeating them
   d) How to look at change as a process and recognize its structure and determinants
6. Help one acquire the tools to keep them from enmeshing with their love object:
   a) By remaining focused, centered, and grounded
   b) Keep their issues separate from their mates
   c) To stay in their day when a present situation triggers the memories from a past trauma

7. Identify when the workplace is a microcosm of their family of origin:
   a)Understand why one reacts to his boss and co-workers in ways that are greater than the situations call for

RELATIONSHIPS - PART III
THE SOLUTION : ADULT DOMINATION

ADULT DOMINATION OF THE EXECUTIVE SYSTEM

When the Adult dominates one's internal structure: effective, functional, adaptive, non-problematic, and creative decisions are generated for problems that arise out of life's hardships. This allows choices in the process and guarantees the positive outcomes needed to maintain a forward movement in their life: instead of entering a "Problem Loop" to "Do what they did to get what they got," which is only a repeat of the old self-defeating behavior. The next section is an example of an adult process.

Adult Process
The following fires off internally and is generally how the person feels after he has been victimized by someone else's fear:

1. The Child Ego State is hurt and feels sad
2. The Adolescent Ego State feels betrayed, becomes angry, and wants retribution from the offending party
3. The Adult Ego State tries to mediate the conflicting feelings and generates a mature adult solution. As the Adult Ego State travels through its process and tries to order, sort out, identify and devise a solution to the current conflict....its responses separate into two voices:
   a)Critical Voice — This voice is condemning and tries to shame the Adult because of their feelings. No solution is offered when it remains in the problem by mentally rehashing over and over, the events of the situation, and what the Adult did wrong.

b)Nurturing Voice — This voice is validating and affirming....tries to soothe the Child and use logic with the Adolescent....and attempts to come out of the problem and go into the solution by devising mature adaptive strategies to ego reducing situations. Depending on the development of the Adult ego stage, two different responses can be generated:

1)Maximum Development: Creative solutions are developed and utilized. The Child is affirmed and the Adolescent validated. All parts are in harmony and feel safe with the Adult.

2)Minimal Development: The nurturing voice is small, soon overcome by the critical voice, and wanders off confused, helpless and hopeless. The critical voice continues to berate the Child and Adolescent for what they feel, and condemns the Nurturing Adult for its inability to create effective solutions. Within this internal dissension comes fragmentation of the person's ego structure. The Child runs away, shuts down, and hides because it is not safe. This signifies that the Adult will have minimal feelings because they emanate from the Child Ego State. The Adolescent will continue to become angry and it will manifest as acting out behavior or shift internally toward self-destructive behavior. The Adult has previously abandoned itself by wandering off when it was needed to fend off the assault of the Critical Adult.

How this translates into behavior can best be described as a reaction by each ego state: depending on its interpretation of the situation and what it attaches to if the situation becomes a trigger to a past event. We can use the example of someone in a relationship being controlled by their partner's fear over a long period of time to illustrate this concept. The problem is usually common among couples who have difficulty being intimate. In it, they seem to suspend common sense and acquire tunnel vision when the usual strategies fail as the following occurs:

1. **Various solutions are attempted and fail**
2. **Failure leads to more frustration**
3. **Frustration drives the partners further away**

This is the opposite outcome the couple is trying to accomplish.

There are two ways the above can be facilitated by the individual's ego states. The first is predicated on an adult driven executive system and includes the following:

1. No major issues attaching themselves to the current situation (the issue comes up clean).
2. No serious deprivation was caused by the control
3. Most, if not all, developmental goals were met by each partner
4. The relationship was limiting and not toxic
5. Nobody's person-hood was violated
6. There wasn't any substance abuse or addiction involved
7. Nobody was mentally ill
8. Both partners loved one another

The second outcome would be produced by an executive system, fear driven by the Adolescent or the Child, in which issues would not come up clean, and the opposite outcomes to the above would prevail.

The following dialogue and behavior will manifest as the couple begins to confront the control, take responsibility for their part in it, and change. From this point on I'll use the abbreviated name for each ego state and call them Child, Adolescent, or Adult.

FIRST REACTION

The Child Its first reaction when confronted by the facts that they are being controlled is usually shock and denial. The surprise is verbalized in the following statements: "Oh my God!" or "No! That's not true."

The Adolescent Its reaction is one of anger and wants to retaliate after the Child is hurt. Its dialogue consists of ways to get them back for what they did without doing permanent damage.

The Adult (Nurturing) The Adult at this time is trying to rationalize the situation through logic and sort it out for an adaptive resolution. Its dialogue extends in several directions at the same time.

TO THE CHILD: "I don't blame you for not wanting to see it."

TO THE ADOLESCENT: Let's find another way to work this out."

The Adult (Critical) The Critical Adult at this time directly fires off at its adult counterpart and ignores the other states. If it's successful, it will confuse the Nurturing Adult. Its comments are: "You should know better! When are you going to learn? Fool! Idiot!"

SECOND REACTION

The Child   Begins to feel sad and makes statements like: "I wish it didn't happen." "It should have been different. If only . . . "

The Adolescent   Remains in anger, starts to escalate to rage, and offers many different plans to hurt the person. All of its verbalizations are hostile.

The Adult (Nurturing)   Begins to soothe the Child and de-escalates the Adolescent.

TO THE CHILD: "It's not your fault. You did nothing wrong."

TO THE ADOLESCENT: "Sorry you're so angry. I don't blame you for being so mad. I didn't pay attention to the warning signs."

TO THE CRITICAL ADULT: "Thank you for pointing out what I did. I know you love me and want the best for me. Can't you say things a little less critical?"

The Adult (Critical)   Remains negative and highly critical. Continues to reiterate the problem over and over just like a broken record and challenges everything.

TO THE CHILD: "Shut up you wimp! Can't you take it?"

TO THE ADOLESCENT: "Scumbag! All you do is talk. You're afraid to do anything."

TO THE NURTURING ADULT: "Everything you do is bad! Nothing is good. You'll always be taken advantage of. You shouldn't trust anyone. You will always be alone. I told you so!"

THIRD REACTION

The Child   The Child at this point begins to feel the sadness and starts to cry. The crying at first will be deep and painful. Over the coming weeks it will diminish and end. After the crying stops, the child feels safe with the adult and will exhibit a full range of feelings when emotions are aroused in any situation.

The Adolescent   Is quiet at this time. Gently reminds the Adult that they haven't gone away.

The Adult (Nurturing)   The Adult at this time is taking full responsibility for allowing itself to be controlled and is developing and implementing adaptive responses to its prior deficiencies. At this stage it is allowing the Child to feel its full range of feelings and at the same time harnessing the energy of the Adolescent to set new boundaries and limits. There is no dialogue with the Critical Adult because it will only deflect the energy expended toward remaining in the solution. Watch what happens later on in this section when the Critical Adult is given energy.

The Adult (Critical) The Critical Adult is quiet, although makes small negative comments about each strategy weighed. Its comments do not confuse the Nurturing Adult. When small, sly, derogatory comments are made toward the Child and the Adolescent, the Nurturing Adult gently but firmly steps in and redirects its critical counterpart.

Adult Outcomes

"Wow," you exclaim. "What a wonderful process." But, how do you go *from* dysfunctional relationships in which the Child and Adolescent are in charge, *to* an adaptive one guided by an emotionally mature, responsible adult? Good question! First we have to ascertain the prerequisites for the change, which are:

1. The behavior is no longer useful to them
2. There isn't a payoff to maintain the behavior
3. One "wants" the change
4. One is "willing" to work toward the change
5. One has the capacity for honesty
6. One is open-minded enough to take in new data
7. One is not cognitively impaired
8. One can assimilate the new material
9. The pain they are experiencing in their current situation is greater than the pain they are hiding

With all these conditions met, one is on their *journey of self-discovery and change*. In it they will:

- Clean up the wreckage to their past
- Challenge their own problematic behavior
- Learn new adaptive coping skills
- Make amends to themselves and others they have harmed
- Begin a life in which problems are solved and not sidetracked with dysfunctional behavior in "Problem Loops"
- Develop a spiritual life, path, and connection to a Higher Power
- Reclaim their humanity and become part of the Human Race
- Become whole within themselves and not need another person, place, or thing to complete them
- Be able to live in Faith instead of fear
- Attain their worldly goals

- Complete the spiritual task they entered this plane to attain
- Become content in their present life while following a spiritual path
- Will be able to welcome the future as it unfolds

AWARENESS

"OUT OF THE DENIAL" becomes one's new mantra and way of life. It is also the first stage of the Grief Process and the natural way to begin. Remember, before you start, that you won't be able to take in anymore than you can handle. Your body's (cognitive system) natural defense system will keep out most overwhelming material. The unofficial rule is....if you can feel it....you're probably OK. This may not always feel that way. It's OK. You can always ask for it (the new information) to be taken away. It will. You can go back into the protective cover of denial if you become overwhelmed and not come back out until you are ready. It's OK!

Reframing

The easiest way to conceptualize the process of reframing is to look at it as:

- **Coming out of the problem and into the solution**
- **Bringing the Executive System of the Internal Structure into balance**
- **Attaching a spiritual component to the behavioral change which guides and directs them through the process**

In order to complete the process, one will follow the path laid out in the "Three A's" of a twelve-step program: Awareness, Acceptance, and Action....that will reinforce the "Three C's": You didn't Cause it, can't Control it, and can't Cure it, although you can Contribute to it (Fourth "C")....which will (hopefully) help you avoid "The Many "D's"; Drinking, drugging, drag (cigarettes or cross-dressing), donuts (food), daily double (gambling), douche bags (sex), dysfunctional dating (Double "D"), etc, etc, etc, ad nauseum. These are just some of the problem loops one can enter, to avoid looking at themselves, and taking responsibility for their behavior.

SURVIVING TO LIVING The first element we'll explore is the adaptive process that helped to retain one's equilibrium, during extremely discombobulated life events, which affected the environment and one's internal structure. When one is impacted to this degree....the reactions have to be just as profound. In the process, the impacted person took natural attributes (living skills) and turned them into character defects (survival skills). These traits were either enlarged to an over-reaction (too much of the trait) or, diminished in quality in order to nullify its contribution to the personality (too little of the trait). Either way, the attribute is out of balance, and ceases to be a living skill.

We have to use caution about how an attribute is labeled in a functional or dysfunctional environment because rules change as the playing field changes. The strategy is actually a paradox and occurs as one tries to be sane in an insane environment. (Oh God! Shades of "One Flew Over the Cuckoo's Nest" are appearing!) It's true! If you act sane in a crazy environment....you are crazy! You have to act crazy in order to be considered normal in an insane environment and play the roles survival skills dictate in these highly skewed dysfunctional situations. These roles enabled one to function, according to the changing rules in the dysfunctional environment of a maladaptive family structure, by allowing one to: *shift their attributes according to the situation in order to counteract the present confusion being experienced in the dysfunction.*

Whatever was done to maintain personal safety was the appropriate response. We can't judge today....what was done yesterday to survive. It's like making a decision today....about what a soldier did to survive during the middle of a combat situation....he experienced in a past life event. You can't! Hold on to this metaphor because that's what it's like growing up in a highly dysfunctional family.

ONE'S POSITIVE CHARACTER TRAITS, SHIFT TO NEGATIVE DEFECTS, IN ORDER TO DEFEND AGAINST THE ANXIETY AND CONFUSION EXPERIENCED INTERACTING IN A DYSFUNCTIONAL FAMILY SYSTEM

In recovery, the process changes: in order to effect the behavior changes and begin to heal....one has to bring their attributes back into balance. Figure 19.1 is a graphic representation of its results.

TOO LITTLE ←—BALANCE —→TOO MUCH		
ATTRIBUTE		
Giving Up	Determination	Immature Stubbornness
Giving Up or Not Trying	Perseverance	Allowing Abuse by Not Leaving
Trust No One	Trust	Trust Everyone
No Faith	Faith	Faith in Falsehoods
Doesn't Love	Love	Gives Love To Undeserving People

FIGURE 19.1 – RE-BALANCING A CHARACTER ASSET

PROCESS TO REFRAME   Reframing is a process. It takes time, new information, and diligence. To me, it was a relief to know that all I did in the past was not bad or in vain. In fact, it could be added to. For if I could do one thing in adversity….what could I do in recovery?

The work can begin once this concept is recognized as a survival skill. It's not easy to release these shields when they have been such good friends….helping you out of difficulty, and asking nothing in return but their continued usage. The keys to overcoming the resistance to change will be:

1.   **Accept them as they are**
2.   **Continue to recognize them as skills**
3.   **DON'T JUDGE THEM!**
4.   **Work toward shifting them to living skills** *as the need to use them in their extreme form diminishes in your life style.* **(If you still need them . . . the shift will not occur.)**

I don't know of any other way it can be done. Brain or willpower does not work to accomplish secondary change (permanent change instead of compliance). You can get temporary relief on the will alone, but it won't last. The extreme behavior has to stop working for you before change can begin. What I'm attempting to do is to give you a gentle way to:

1.   **Acknowledge your defects**
2.   **Lower your resistance to working on deeper issues**
3.   **Become open enough to learn new adaptive skills**

This is also another avenue in which the Nurturing Adult can address the Adolescent's behavior without incurring its wrath, by not invalidating the very action, which kept the Adolescent alive during some very scary times. Figure 19.2 is a graphic description of the direction the process takes to attain the change.

IDENTIFY THE DEFECT (Out of Denial)
↓
ACKNOWLEDGE THE DEFECT AS A SURVIVAL SKILL
↓
ACCEPT ITS IMPORTANCE IN YOUR LIFE
↓
VALIDATE THAT PART OF YOU THAT DEVELOPED IT
↓
RECOGNIZE THE LIFE CIRCUMSTANCES THAT TRIGGER ITS USE
↓
CONNECT THE ENERGY NEEDED IN ORDER
TO CHANGE THE DEFECT TO AN ASSET
↓
BEGIN THE SHIFT TO:
— CHANGE OR DISCONTINUE INTERACTING IN AN
  ENVIRONMENT THAT REQUIRES SURVIVAL SKILLS
— THE DEFECT RETURNING TO BALANCE, AS AN
  ATTRIBUTE THAT FOSTERS ADAPTIVE BEHAVIOR,
  IN DIFFICULT LIFE SITUATIONS

FIGURE 19.2 – PROCESSING OF RE-BALANCING A CHARACTER TRAIT

ASSIGNMENT 30: Identify the character traits you feel are assets to you. Make a list and check any that are out of balance. Be honest. Don't judge. All behavior works. Do the same for your deficits.

Next, try to identify when and why they shifted. If their use is attached to the past, why do you still use them today? There are no wrong answers — only awareness. Do you see any patterns in your behavioral responses toward stress? If yes — what can you do to change them — if you want to? Do you have the ability to commit the energy needed to change them? If you are spiritual — what role can your Higher Power or God play in the changing? How will you recognize when you're Higher Power or God is helping you to change that character defect?

ACCEPTANCE

After reading the last section you exclaim; "that's cool and I accept what you say ....now let's get to work!" Great! I got your attention. Let's add some more factors to the equation in order to bring the process into focus and "Rock & Roll!"

Cognitive Restructuring

The beginning of the cognitive changes is to label the old behavior as survival skills. Don't judge them. Now, begin to modify them into living skills, while one's environment is being cleaned up, and they're no longer required. This process is cognitive restructuring and operationalizes when the survival skill is reframed to a desired living skill as the trait is brought back into balance. There are three phases to these changes, and my overall strategy to facilitate them is:

Cognition —	Use their thinking process. Cognitive reframing is the main tool
Application —	Apply the knowledge to their current problematic behavior
Behavior —	The changes come in two stages:

1st Order Change — Deliberate practice of new behavior
2nd Order Change — Develops into an internalized response

This change is also a process:
1. **Its structure is the Grief Process**
2. **Its determinants are the three components of the Internal Structure**
3. **The path it meanders toward acceptance is influenced by unresolved issues that occurred over the life span**

All of these issues have to be explored in order to gain a full understanding of the forces that will influence its change. The process, to me, is a clear one — *once someone wants to change.* Without this desire, one has a vested interest to maintain his present behavior, because it is working for him for an unknown reason, and usually doesn't change under these circumstances.

In the process, one is motivated to change as they become aware of their dysfunctional behavior (out of denial). During this time, they need a cognitive process (thinking process) to mediate the feelings that color one's world and add depth to an issue (feelings process). It's the individual's feelings that determine the behavioral set (behavior process) needed to reduce the impact of any incoming data that upsets the organism's equilibrium, integrity, or mental well-being. Most of this chapter is designed to help one identify their problematic solutions in dysfunctional relationships or situations. We can now examine how a Human Being's problem-solving matrix is determined and why it incorporates the following:

- Using drastic solutions
- Giving up
- Using the same strategy over and over, thinking it will yield different results

We will also explore new ways to bring the system back into balance. As one traverses his cognitive process and tries to apply the new thinking, he will need a new framework to guide him through the various obstacles encountered along his journey. This construct is called the Grief Process and will be explored next.

The Grief Process

By now, you have an understanding of the Grief Process, how the various ego states impact it, and what choices you have in either reacting (dysfunctional behavior) or responding (adaptive choices). At this point in time, your little boy or girl (Child Ego State) may be still driving the bus in your life (influencing your decisions) *"OR "* you may be becoming "an emotionally mature, responsible adult" who makes his own daily decisions based on his *present* needs and not the "fear from his inner child (Child Ego State). Either way....making a positive change or remaining there....is a process.

Through the process, the Child will "kick and scream," fearful of pain or abandonment. Soothe them. Tell them they will be OK and help them mature by bringing them through their feelings. The Adolescent will also balk at the changes by acting out and wants to remain in charge because the Adult abrogated his rights for so long. It's OK. Talk to them. Thank both for all they have done and then set healthy boundaries and limits on them. Let them know that you will listen and allow them to help when needed.

Each one of the ego states will go through the different stages of the Grief Process — WHEN THEY ARE READY! This is why we have mixed feelings and how some hang on longer than others. Once you get used to the process, know how to dialogue with your various ego states, the confusion dies down and the clarity increases. *If any state gets stuck in the process, it's usually a deeper issue that has attached itself to the current problem and may take therapy to break the gauntlet it has created, "if" your process stops because of the impasse.* If it doesn't, just catalog the resistance or issue to be worked on at a later time. I don't attempt any unnecessary therapy if I don't have to. If something isn't broken....I DON'T FIX IT! It's an unnecessary side trip and can impede or sabotage the client's recovery. There is such a thing as too much work. The general guideline is; leave them alone if they are progressing along consistent lines. To those of you in self-help.... *do the same!* Listen to your support system. One person can be wrong. Not the entire system.

There will be some persistent resistance to the changes that may mire you in "The Emotional Twilight Zone": bouncing back and forth between Denial, Anger, Bargaining, and Depression (see Ch. 12, Fig. 12.5, p.272). The confusion occurs as feelings rise over the success of the new strategies and reveal the depth of pain one endured, sometimes needlessly, during previous life situations. They will need to be *and can be* , transcended by information, time, process, and perseverance. The following four issues will greatly impact the process in changing relationship outcomes with self, others, and a Higher Power (God): 1. Ethics, 2. Integrity, 3. Intimacy, and 4. Spirituality.

Ethics

There seems to be a general lack of ethics in relationships. It's more: "caveat emptor — Let the buyer beware!" When this philosophy is used — anything goes. While at the same time, the offender wants to be understood without the insight about how their current reactive behavior usually impacts their partner. This egocentric thinking has to be expanded. Applying ethics to the paradigm begins to broaden one's awareness.

Ethics is defined by Webster (1995) as "the science of ideal human character." Within this discipline, something is considered ethical when another human being is treated in a moral way (Webster). Moral is further defined (Webster 1945) "Practice or conduct; right and proper . . . Establishing principles of right and wrong in behavior."

This infers that one has to have a system to evaluate themselves to determine: if the present conduct, in their current relationship, treats their partner in a fair and just way.

"Hold on," you say, "What about the time they did that wrong to me! Am I supposed to turn the other cheek and get slapped again?" "Good question," I reply. "Do you?" "Here you go with that therapist crap again Lou," you exclaim frustrated! "You bounce it back to me and I'm supposed to know the answer!"

This stuff is hard. If one keeps going round and round in the "problem loop" — when do they get off the merry-go-round? Now! It has to start with you. This is the time you decide if your present behavior is moral (based on principles of right and wrong) and if you want to stop it or not. If you are currently "sick and tired" of your current self-defeating behavior; doing the same thing over and over expecting the results to be different....you will answer yes! If you are not and your present dysfunctional behavioral "problem loops" are working for you....throw the book away (not too far because you will have to buy another when your present behavior stops working and you are on your knees again)....and do some more research and development (R&D) until you are willing to try another approach. (This honesty stuff is really hard.)

ETHICAL BEHAVIOR   Cognitive changes began in a previous section of this chapter: when one" current self-defeating behavior became relabeled to a survival skill in which; character assets were unbalanced to overcome the emotional roller coaster of being in a dysfunctional family or situation. In order for them to change back into a balanced asset, they had to be reframed as living skills. This could occur if the individual no longer had a need for the old behavior.

The beginning of the transformation is to develop a system that will allow you to determine if the behavior in your relationship:

- Follows ethical principles of interacting with other human beings
- Treats your partner with dignity and respect
- Is consistent with how you wish to be treated
- Is consistent with established principles of right and wrong
- Is consistent over time and doesn't change drastically
- Is consistent with the way one treats their friends, co-workers, family members, authority figures, and institutions in the larger culture

EXAMPLES   The following questions, if answered truthfully, will allow you to determine if the exhibited behavior in your current relationship follows ethical principles:

1. If you are in a profession which follows ethical principles — can you apply those principles to your relationship? A basic principle in the counseling profession is to "do no harm." Can you follow that ethical principle in your relationship or do you strike back automatically when a hurt is perceived?
2. Can you let go or forgive your current partner as easily as a co-worker or a boss?
3. Can you allow your mate the right to have an opinion, different from yours, as you allow friends, co-workers, bosses, authority figures, institutions, or family members, without breaking up with them or placing sanctions on your relationship?
4. Can you allow your love the dignity of their own choices without threatening or leaving them?
5. Can you love and accept them just where they are and try not to change them?
6. Can you follow "The Golden Rule"?
7. Can you love your partner with the same unconditional regard as you do a child?
8. Are you willing to change the part you played in any situation with your partner regardless of what responsibility they choose to acknowledge?
9. Can you feel the hurt from the wound you inflicted on another human being or do you close them off?
10. If you close them off — how long does it take to allow yourself to feel empathy for them?
11. Are your lovers your friends or do you keep the two separate?
12. If you are in self-help, do you treat your sponsor and support system differently than your partner?
13. Do you have multiple standards when dealing with your partner?

Integrity

Integrity is the substance one is made of. Its internal value to the human being is so important that when it's jeopardized….people have killed to preserve their ideals or to keep it intact. Externally, in relationships, like ethics…. *ANYTHING GOES WHEN A WRONG IS PERCEIVED.* Notice I said perceived and not committed. When one partner senses a wrong, it triggers an issue, and all personal integrity goes out the window as one commits offenses against their partner in retaliation or defense of the perceived hurt. Unless they are shut down….most are guilty of it. If not, you must have a halo or arrived at a place in your recovery that I and most humans I've observed over the past half a century, haven't reached yet.

Once again, we are reframing survival skills to living skills. In the shifting, one modifies the old defensive behavior, designed to keep them in balance, as their world is being turned inside out by partners, parents, bosses, or institutions when they shift gears drastically, change the rules without notice, or become toxic.

In the change, one will transition: *from*, reacting and losing themselves in the process when the reactive behavior is not congruent with their self-image: *to*, responding with behavior appropriate to the situation and true to their current self concepts.

When one responds as "an emotionally mature responsible adult," both internal (one's self-image) and external (one's self-image in regard to someone else) integrity is maintained.

When one has integrity, they think, feel, and behave in a like manner. They are congruent within themselves and demonstrate appropriate behavior. Most times, "the inside matches the outside." When the opposite is true, personal integrity is minimal. *If one lacks it within themselves, they cannot have it in a relationship with another person, because they REALLY DON'T KNOW THEMSELVES!* If one doesn't know themselves….how can they maintain their self concepts in regard to others….when they're challenged by changing everyday life situations. Life can become difficult during these times and even challenges the most competent people.

Webster (1954) defines integrity as: "State or quality of being complete….moral soundness; honesty; uprightness…." How many out there in "Never Never Land" are whole within themselves or complete *"WITHOUT"* a love relationship? I see some glazed looks out there. I wonder what that's all about. How many out there in "dream world" can be honest enough with themselves and share that honesty with their partner without the fear of being abandoned. It raises a lot of fear once someone else finds out about the "real you." There's no integrity in that fear — only insecurity.

ONE HAS TO BE SOLID WITHIN HIMSELF
(COMPLETE), IN ORDER TO MAINTAIN
PERSONAL INTEGRITY, WHILE CONDUCTING
AN INTIMATE RELATIONSHIP WITH ANOTHER.

The following are observable traits when one has integrity:
- Their self concepts are clearly defined
- Their behavior is consistent
- They treat others fairly
- They allow others to be themselves without being threatened
- They are open-minded and teachable
- They are transparent and allow others to see their real self
- They have empathy for others
- They don't participate in emotional cutoffs with others
- They have firm boundaries
- They set healthy limits on self and others
- They are solution oriented and try to stay out of the problem
- Their thoughts, feelings and behaviors are congruent

Intimacy

Intimacy can best be described as: "IN TO ME SEE." When one allows their partner to "see into them" there are no masks, pretenses, or games. All that the person is....is there to see. This is difficult as one wants to look their best at all times and that's impossible. We are human beings....subject to all its frailties....and do not always act in the highest standards. Yes, that's a fact of life. To anyone who doesn't know that....I've just given you the secret to living:

- **YOU ARE NOT PERFECT**
- **I AM NOT PERFECT**
- **THEY ARE NOT PERFECT**
- **WE ARE ALL PERFECT IN OUR IMPERFECTIONS**

A paradox you say? Not so. We do ourselves perfectly each day. Life is a journey. This is our schoolroom. We learn our lessons. Then, in spirit, travel back to the light, in order to bring back the knowledge gained. We are part of the whole. We always were. When we are in communion with others, we are connected to the whole. This is why relationships are so important because in them we connect with God. This is a spiritual principle. One already explored earlier. It will be revisited further on in this chapter.

When two, allow each other, to see into themselves....they have an intimate relationship. When only one participates in being transparent to the other....there is a relationship *"WITHOUT "* INTIMACY OCCUR-

RING. It is shallow at best; doomed to destruction after the original attraction, excitement and sex have diminished.

CHALLENGE TO GROW Intimate relationships provide the arena for one to grow beyond their expectations or to bring to fruition all they thought could be. It's in the relationship that one is forced to grow. A program adage that applies under these circumstances is: "one grows or goes," and it's certainly true in relationships. When the couple-ship doesn't grow....it doesn't last. How many out there gave up and left someone because the relationship became difficult? Maybe there were too many challenges, which forced you to look at yourself when your partner refused to do a "two-step problem loop," and you were left alone with yourself? To some, this is a "fate worse than death." There is no personal integrity or ethical behavior being displayed when a "problem loop" is being deployed instead of coming into the solution and working on you.

An intimate relationship forces both to work hard on themselves (intra-personal) and with each other (interpersonal). Without this effort, when there is a breach of trust (real or imagined), a rift begins between them. It begins as a narrow opening that spreads wider each time a negative event occurs. With work, the breach can be repaired. If it's allowed to remain open for too long without resolution, a wall begins to separate the couple.

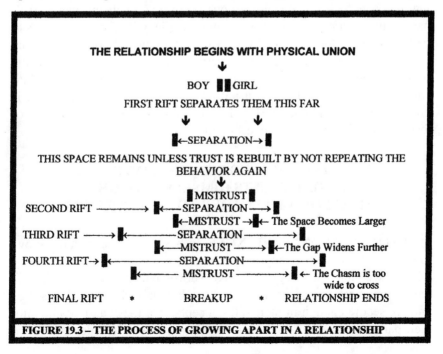

THE RELATIONSHIP BEGINS WITH PHYSICAL UNION

BOY ▌▌ GIRL

FIRST RIFT SEPARATES THEM THIS FAR

▌←–SEPARATION→▌

THIS SPACE REMAINS UNLESS TRUST IS REBUILT BY NOT REPEATING THE BEHAVIOR AGAIN

▌MISTRUST▌

SECOND RIFT ⟶ ▌←—SEPARATION—→▌

▌←–MISTRUST→▌← The Space Becomes Larger

THIRD RIFT ⟶▌←————— SEPARATION —————→▌

▌←—MISTRUST ——→ ▌←–The Gap Widens Further

FOURTH RIFT→▌←—————SEPARATION—————→▌

▌←——— MISTRUST ———→ ▌ ← The Chasm is too wide to cross

FINAL RIFT   *   BREAKUP   *   RELATIONSHIP ENDS

FIGURE 19.3 – THE PROCESS OF GROWING APART IN A RELATIONSHIP

The wall grows as the rift between them becomes wider with each subsequent event. Figure 19.3 is a graphic example of the process.

According to the above process, it's easy to identify how couples grow apart when the trust between them is consistently violated. Most do not want to see this process because it's painful. They want to put the last rift "behind them" and get on with the couple-ship thinking, "It will be better this time." It doesn't! The gap between them only becomes wider. What they don't realize is….unless they complete the work to heal the wound or re-establish the trust that was lost in the rift…. *the mistrust will only be left behind as another brick in the wall, erected to protect themselves from the emotional onslaught experienced, as their trust was being violated by their love object.*

There is really a two-stage process occurring as the couple is "going apart" instead of "growing together": The first stage is depicted in Figure 19.3 and occurs as the distance between them widens because of the mistrust: The second stage occurs while they build a wall around themselves for protection that won't allow their partner to "see into them." When this occurs, there is no intimacy in the relationship. One who allows themselves to remain in this type of relationship possesses very little personal integrity (internal), or integrity within their couple-ship (external). Violating trust is not ethical behavior for one is not treating themselves or their partner in a moral way. Too many times, people will allow themselves to be brutalized in the name of love, in ways they would not tolerate from friends. Other times, they can be the perpetrator and do absolutely horrible things to their lovers, spouses, partners, that they wouldn't do to their friends. When asked why, they usually justify why they retaliated. This is not a loving intimate relationship. It's only a war zone in which two Adolescents can take turns hurting each other.

LOVE IS DISPLAYED THROUGH INTIMACY, AS ONE TRUSTS HIMSELF ENOUGH AND ALLOWS THE OTHER TO "SEE INTO HIM"

INTRA-PERSONAL CHANGES In order for a relationship to grow, there must be honesty, integrity, an ethical value system, and intimacy within the couple-ship. For these traits to develop there needs to be consistent communication on a regular basis, by individuals who know themselves and are secure enough in their self concepts, that they can risk allowing their partners to get to know them on the same level. In order to achieve this self-knowledge....deep intra-personal work has to be accomplished in the following way:

First: *One has to now himself and find out:*
- What their wants, needs, and desires are
- Feel confident in their self concepts (roles one takes in life)
- What their personal issues are and how they are affected by them
- How to identify, label, sort out and process their feelings
- Separate out yesterday from today

Second: *They have to know themselves in relation to anaother person and:*
- Determine what they want, need and desire from their love object: ASK TO GET THOSE DESIRES MET AND BE WITH SOME-ONE WHO WANTS TO MEET THEM
- Maintain their self concepts by daring to be themselves with others who are important to them (Internal Integrity)
- Maintain External Integrity by knowing the effect others have on their personal issues, not blame them for being triggers because they are in a couple-ship, and in so doing allow them the power to be a trigger.
- Know when they are over-reacting to a current event and stop the reaction before it does damage to their partner (Personal Ethics)
- Separate yesterday from today with your partner's behavior by not accusing them of someone else's antics (Projection)
- Keep themselves separate mentally, emotionally, and spiritually while coming together in physical and sexual union. (No matter how close we feel to someone — we are still individuals within ourselves. *It is the Human Condition!*).

Facilitating the Changes Anyone can have a relationship with themselves. It's when another comes into their life that the challenge begins. Some of the questions that arise are:
- Who am I in relation to this other person?
- Is your thinking sound when in conflict?
- Is what you ask of them appropriate when they balk at it?
- Is your value system well grounded when conflict arises?
- What happens when changes occur in the other person that you don't like or vice versa?
- What happens if your goals are discounted or ignored?
- How do you handle differences of opinion?
- What occurs when you both feel differently over the same situa-

tion and it's important to either one that feelings should be mutual?

- What conflict arises when either is challenged in an important area?
- What happens when a major decision is made and both have different strategies?

Most of these questions don't come up when there is only one. One is usually in agreement with oneself after the initial thinking or soul searching has been performed. None of the above is right or wrong....it's only a fact. People are different. It's OK. As long as there are similar values, love, respect, admiration, ethics, integrity and spirituality....the relationship will grow along with those in it. People grow as individuals. To me, it's finite. When they grow as a couple....it's infinite!

The main theme that prevails in a relationship dominated by personal ethics and integrity is: *YOU CAN'T GET BETTER AT SOMEONE ELSE'S EXPENSE!* This creates an environment that is fair to both partners. The intra-personal work required to achieve this goal makes possible the added growth one experiences. Neither would have received it if they remained by themselves and not entered into the relationship. This concept is also very spiritual in nature and will be expanded further on in this chapter.

Spirituality

The spiritual principle in all relationships is a simple one: *YOU CAN'T GROW AT SOMEONE ELSE'S EXPENSE.* We are all travelers on a journey. Your current partner has to be viewed in this way. When this occurs, a new realm is opened. The pettiness of everyday trivia (persons, places, or things) is no longer important and the larger vision of why someone is on this plane comes into view.

When a struggle ensues between the couple, all energy is diverted to facilitate its carnage or aftermath, instead of continuing along their spiritual Journey. When both are in harmony, the couple-ship, and individuals within it grow!

As two individuals travel together in a couple-ship and work in harmony, the roadblocks of everyday life are usually handled more easily or lifted more quickly when two work together....accomplishing more than with one working alone. In this efficiency, one attains their lower order needs more quickly (safety, security, food, shelter, affiliation), as Mazlow (1954) states, and is able to spend more time and energy to explore and discover what their spiritual purpose is (higher order needs).

This book is part of my spiritual purpose. Everything that has happened to me in my life has added substance to my current profession, and subsequently this book. I could have told you when I was a little boy that I was going to do something important that would benefit man, and it would be my individual contribution to the culture. In the undertaking, I would become the person that I thought I could be (Self-Actualization) and complete the job I was sent here to do. The first half of my life was spent fighting to survive, struggling with the internal battle that raged in me: to stop what I was doing in survival and start to live by changing my life and finishing my spiritual goals. This is what I've done today. Many things have changed in my life and the universe is currently rewarding me in ways that I originally dared not imagine.

My spiritual path opened up to me as the world around me quieted down when I wouldn't allow anyone in my life that was "a vexation to my spirit," take me off my course. As I continued along this quiet path, my purpose became clearer. The help the universe (God) was sending to me became more profound as I became less fearful of not having what I used to think was important (money, property, prestige, etc). Subsequently, my spiritual path opened before me in a way that eliminated any questions about the road I was to travel.

I remember when I first began reading about others who were connected and could commune with a higher power or spirit guide....I was jealous. I wanted what they had. I was alone and had everything in my life that I worked for. I was still unhappy and asking myself why.

Today, I'm still not able to see God, although I feel His presence and certainly see Him working in my life. What I am able to do because the noise level in my head and distractions in my life have been quieted down or eliminated....is to see the events occurring in my life at a deeper level, gain the spiritual knowledge it provides, and grow in the process. Another spiritual benefit occurred: as I helped myself....I also helped others to heal. It's no longer a self-centered act designed just to help me. It helps by the nature of its being.

When I am on my spiritual path today....I know it because my fear is gone and I totally trust the universe will send me what I need. My present job is a good example. Prior to it, I was looking in an area I thought was my path. Nothing opened up. No matter how hard I tried, I couldn't use in my life what was offered to me. Then a friend told me about several jobs that opened up at once. We talked about which would be the most appropriate for me. In the next two, days every job was gone except the one we termed the least beneficial. This was on a Thursday, I couldn't interview until the following Tuesday because of prior commitments, and had no fear about how the job would go. Over the weekend, my friend had a "choice" run-in at the supermarket, in a store she usually doesn't shop in, with the person I was to interview with. Coincidence? Who knows! Nobody else applied for the job. Another coincidence? Maybe. I interviewed and got the job and it has turned out very well for me. Does it give me everything I want? No. Did it give me everything I need? Yes, and then some. The job fits into my life perfectly and is where I'm supposed to be.

This is not the first time this has happened. My first job in counseling came much the same way when a friend of mine who was an LCSW in private practice, said that I would make a good counselor, made a recommendation of where to start, and then paved the way for me to begin in much the same way I have my present job. In fact, every job I've had in the counseling field has been given to me in the same fashion. All the ones I actively sought never came to fruition. Is all this a coincidence? I think not! There is a plan and a purpose to my life and the experience I received during this time. My job is to stay open and receptive to it. If this is all very mysterious to you, I don't blame you for being skeptical. It's no mystery to me....just very spiritual.

My life today progresses spiritually. I'm married and have a partner who is my soul mate. She is not afraid of my success and encourages it; she doesn't work her issues out on me; is my friend; loves, respects, and admires me; wants to be with me; supports my choices; sticks to her principles; is not afraid to challenge my thinking or appreciate my knowledge; is a good mother; works on herself constantly; and is not afraid of our succeeding as a couple. These are wonderful attributes and ones that I didn't draw in a partner until I learned about myself and changed. I feel strongly about this. I know that my wife would have passed me by if I didn't change, for I would have been a "vexation to her spirit if the old me was still around. Our meeting and getting together is another story full of coincidences. If I didn't follow my spiritual path, I would have lost out on all the pleasure I experience today in having a wonderful, fulfilling adult relationship.

ACTION

Negative relationships don't just happen. People are set up to have them from early childhood. The relationship our parents had, models our ideal or opposite ideal of what we think one should be. It's not our fault it happens. It's not their (parents) fault. They modeled what was modeled to them by their parents, with personal modifications determined by what they liked (continued), or disliked (stopped) and changed. Sound familiar? It should. This is how we learn. It's called social modeling and its part of the socialization process we are given by our parents to get us ready for society in order interact along prescribed paths with other human beings in various cultural relationships.

The only problem is, the information is usually a generation behind because we're being raised with parents who have modified the previous generation's cultural transmissions. The human potential movement of the "60's" greatly excelled the changes within intrapersonal and interpersonal roles. We have come a long way over the last two millennia. We have moved from hunters to gatherers; from an agrarian society to industrialization; from farms to cities; from extended families to nuclear families, to one-parent families; from single families to blended families; from involvement with our fellow man in neighborhoods to isolation in the suburbs; from rigid stereotypical sex role expectations to more flexible roles men and women can play in the culture; from women and children being chattel to self-determining human beings; from women being barefoot and pregnant to the bread winners of many families. We couldn't deal with this kind of changes today with yesterday's information. We need succinct ideas, which will bring us through the changes, and maintain the culture at the same time. I don't have any answers for societal changes. I only know if we do the best we can as individuals, we remain in the solution by contributing to the whole, and won't reduce the culture. Believe it or not, *everyting rises or falls of its own weight*, and it happens in its own time. Our job is to do the best we can with what we got. Nobody can ask more of us....not even God.

Where do we go with all this new information: we practice; try it on; see if it fits; take what you like and leave the rest; and learn and grow from your past mistakes instead of repeating them and thinking something will be different this time. Sound too simple to be true? It is simple. The following are ways to put it into action.

CHANGE

Change occurs only after something has changed. If one does the same old behavior over and over: they will get the same outcome each time, as nothing changed. Simple concept? Yes. Hard to put into effect? Yes. Then how do you change? A little at a time and usually when the old behavior is no longer working for you. Behavior changes happen in two stages: First and second order change. In the process one will learn:

- What their current self-defeating behavior is (Problem Loops)
- New strategies to stop the behavior and illicit desired outcomes
- To work on blocks to attaining their desired goals
- How to internalize the new behavior

First Order Change

First order change is usually demonstrated in compliance. It's the first uncomfortable changes one makes. Everything is an effort. One has to remember what the new response is and *then do it.* This is the place in program when people "talk the talk" and "act as if." They don't trust it will work. They will try out the behavior because "those who came before them"suggested it.

First order change occurs along a continuum. First, the change is presented. Second, it's tried out. At first it's hard to remember the change and old behavior (the internalized response to the stimuli) will prevail through most of the situation. The new strategy will usually come into cognition as the event is ending.

In a backward process, as one continues to "talk the talk" (remind themselves of the new behavior and acting as if they already do it well), they will become more cognizant of the time the behavior actually occurs. At this time they will laboriously practice the new behavior, insecure of its outcome, and too fearful of returning to their old strategy.

At this point, they will practice the behavior, and become increasingly skillful at the adaptation. The whole process is highly cognitive because it takes a conscientious effort to remember the strategy and place it into action. During this strategy, awareness is a backward process; each time one remembers, they are closer to the activating event of the behavior. It's at this time that one actually has a choice over their behavior. See Figure 19.4.

Another way to look at behavior is as a sequence of events that complete the range of the response. Once the steps are identified, it makes it easier to identify when the maladaptive response will begin and the new behavior should intervene.

CASE STUDY: Our real estate broker, Joe, was trying to change the established patterns of behavior with his wife, which grew over the time they were married. One of his major goals was to step arguing with her. No matter how hard he tried to break the pattern….the more he seemed to fight. He didn't know if she was "setting him up" or he was just too hot headed. To me, it seemed a little of both. She would set him up and off he would go. Usually this happened when he was trying to get his needs met, or to negotiate a more equitable situation.

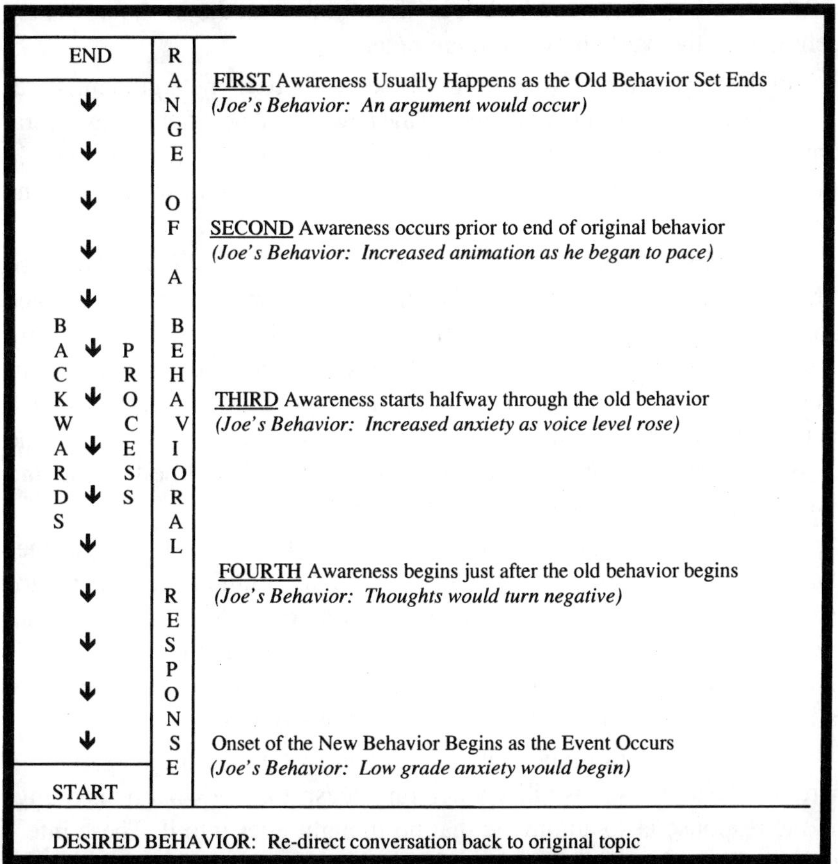

END	R A N G E	FIRST Awareness Usually Happens as the Old Behavior Set Ends *(Joe's Behavior: An argument would occur)*
⬇ ⬇ ⬇ ⬇ ⬇	O F A	SECOND Awareness occurs prior to end of original behavior *(Joe's Behavior: Increased animation as he began to pace)*
B P A ⬇ R C O K ⬇ C W E A ⬇ S R S D ⬇ S S ⬇	B E H A V I O R A L	THIRD Awareness starts halfway through the old behavior *(Joe's Behavior: Increased anxiety as voice level rose)*
⬇ ⬇ ⬇	R E S P O N S E	FOURTH Awareness begins just after the old behavior begins *(Joe's Behavior: Thoughts would turn negative)*
⬇		Onset of the New Behavior Begins as the Event Occurs *(Joe's Behavior: Low grade anxiety would begin)*
START		

DESIRED BEHAVIOR: Re-direct conversation back to original topic

FIGURE 19.4 – BACKWARDS PROCESS OF AWARENESS

We explored the obvious setups, worked on anger management skills, did some intra-perspective work, identified the feelings, and still to no avail until we broke his behavior down into a clear sequence in which he could identify at what stage he was at when his behavior began to escalate. As we broke it down, it occurred in this order (also see Figure 19.4):

1st Low level anxiety would begin

2nd Thoughts would turn negative

3rd Anxiety would rise with increased voice level

4th Animation would begin as he began to pace

5th The argument would begin

Once this sequence was identified; awareness during any stage becomes the stimulus to implement the desired behavior. Remember....this is a backward process and had to be done in the middle of the unwanted behavior as the battle between them raged.

In the beginning, he found himself somewhere in the argument, (usually at the end), before he remembered the new behavior. After trying several times, he finally remembered during the argument (Stage Five), would simply state, "I'm sorry. I don't want to fight" and would walk out of the room.

As his awareness increased, he began to remember the new behavior when his animation began (Stage Four). Further along, his increased voice level (Stage Three) and negative thinking (Stage Two) would remind him that he was escalating. During all of these stages, he would stop the argument, apologize, and leave the room. This process was not easy, for each step of the way his Adolescent wanted to go in and show her who "The Boss" was. His Nurturing Adult knew the victory would be fleeting and that it was insane to remain in the old "Problem Loop."

It was when he recognized the onset of low-level anxiety (Stage One) that he started to make personal gains. At first, he continued to stop, apologize, and leave because that was all he was capable of doing. As he progressed, the anxiety was detected at its onset, he was able to facilitate it internally, and then he could redirect the focus back to what they were talking about before the anxiety rose and diverted him.

It's at this point in time that couples "grow together or go apart." It's hard to take self-responsibility when one doesn't know what he is doing, or, the response is so automatic that no thought goes into it. These internalized responses are so ingrained that it's almost a part of a person's soul because his self-concepts are tied into continuing the behavior. They become their behavior for without it, they are incomplete. This is heavy duty stuff and not to be toyed with lightly.

Joe's wife did what she knew best: exhibited the behavior that was modeled in her parents' relationship. Her mom would do the same to her dad: antagonize him to divert his attention each time he would bring up something that wasn't equitable in their relationship or marriage.

In couples' counseling, Joe's wife was able to see her behavior and it appeared that she had a vested interest in maintaining it, for it didn't change. I believe this is one of the main reasons Joe finally divorced her.

Joe stated over and over that he was tired of constantly being set up, that he would rather use the energy to solve the problems between them, and if nothing changed, he would not remain married. Each time she was confronted, she would agree to stop the behavior, and later just repeat it again. She also refused to do any additional work with it, other than to try and change it, as it began. This never happened in the marriage. What she has done since the divorce is unknown because Joe left the area after he completed therapy.

LEARNING FROM OUR MISTAKES Joe's experience shows us that behavior doesn't occur in a vacuum. What it does teach us is "that all behavior is useful" and unless it stops working….that it will not change. Joe needed a cognitive process to change his undesired behavior. While he was working on the cognitive/behavioral strategies, feelings and issues of self concepts arose. HE HAD TO WORK THROUGH THE FEELINGS OR BECOME MIRED IN HIS FORWARD PROGRESS. He also had to redefine some of his self concepts, especially the ones having to do with being a husband and having a healthy relationship with his love object, without losing himself as a man or a human being.

In order to complete the work, he had to find a way to stop the self-defeating behavior (arguing), apply the new strategy (stop, apologize, and leave), learn what he was doing wrong in the interaction (being diverted from the present topic), apply the new learning (redirect the conversation back to where it was side tracked), *and eventually get his needs met through remaining on task, or realize that they weren't gong to be met.* Either way, he had a choice to do "the same old — same old" or change things. The choice was his to do with as he pleased. He chose to do things differently, thereby learning from his past mistakes. This was the prime goal of his therapy.

ASSIGNMENT 31: Identify behaviors you want to change and can't. Write down the desired behavior you want to replace it with. Break down the behavior into a sequence that leads up to it just like Joe did with arguing. It doesn't matter how much awareness you have at this point. Whatever you have is more than adequate. The rest will come.

Devise a response to extract you out of the self-defeating behavior when you realize you are doing it. *Most people are there before they real-*

ize they left. Don't judge yourself. Like Joe, stop, apologize, and leave if that's all you're able to do. After awhile, you will be aware of all the stages to your escalation process and your behavior changes will happen sooner. When you are aware of the beginning of your escalation process, you will have choices in your behavioral responses.

**ONE CAN'T CHANGE SELF-DEFEATING BEHAVIOR
UNTIL HE KNOWS WHAT IT LOOKS LIKE!**

Second Order Change

Second order change occurs when the new behavior becomes the internalized response to the situation. It doesn't come easily, takes practice and perseverance, and is subject to regression under massive stress to which one has no control.

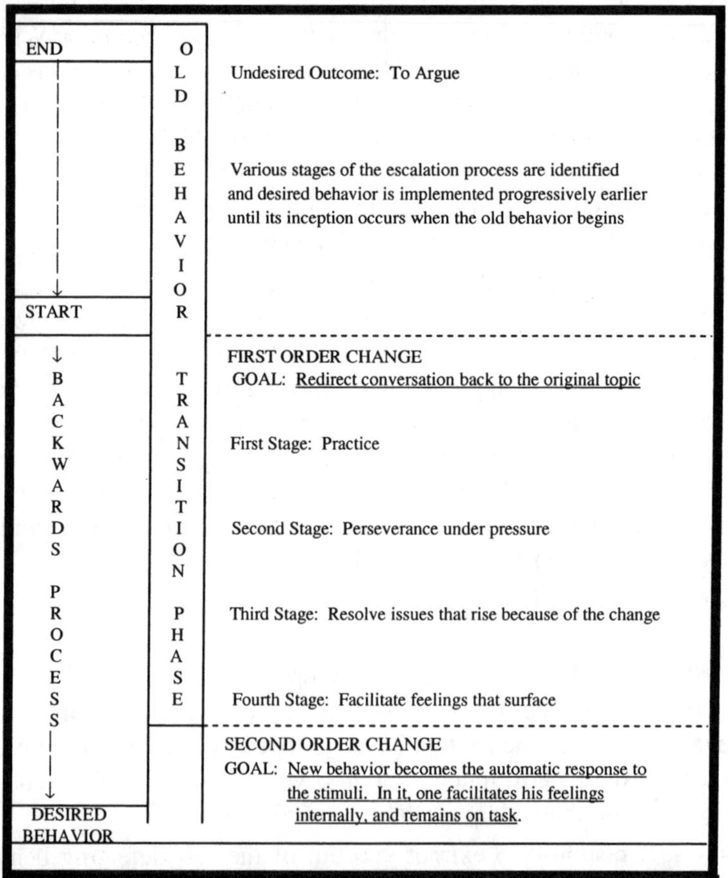

```
END          O
 |           L    Undesired Outcome:  To Argue
 |           D
 |
 |           B
 |           E    Various stages of the escalation process are identified
 |           H    and desired behavior is implemented progressively earlier
 |           A    until its inception occurs when the old behavior begins
 |           V
 |           I
 |           O
START        R
------------------------------------------------------------
 ↓                FIRST ORDER CHANGE
 B           T      GOAL: Redirect conversation back to the original topic
 A           R
 C           A
 K           N    First Stage:  Practice
 W           S
 A           I
 R           T
 D           I    Second Stage:  Perseverance under pressure
 S           O
             N
 P
 R           P    Third Stage:  Resolve issues that rise because of the change
 O           H
 C           A
 E           S
 S           E    Fourth Stage:  Facilitate feelings that surface
 S         ------------------------------------------------------------
 |                SECOND ORDER CHANGE
 |                  GOAL: New behavior becomes the automatic response to
 |                        the stimuli.  In it, one facilitates his feelings
 ↓                        internally, and remains on task.
DESIRED
BEHAVIOR
```

FIGURE 19.5   PROCESS OF BEHAVIOR CHANGE

TRANSITION PHASE Prior to the new behavior becoming the automatic response, one experiences a transition phase that is highly cognitive; as they have to remember the behavior, apply it, fine-tune it, and ultimately learn from it.

It's during this phase that the work is the hardest, raises the most feelings and objections, and is subject to failure when the rewards of the behavior change *appears* to be less than the payoff for maintaining the old behavior. It's at this time that one "either grows or goes" individually, and in a couple-ship "grows together or goes apart." See Figure 19.5 for the complete process to change.

CASE STUDY: We will continue with Joe. As Joe progressed through first order change and stopped arguing with his wife, he was able to stay focused on the topic by redirecting the conversation back to the original topic. As he stayed on task, practicing the new behavior, he would find himself digressing at various times. At this time he would just bring himself back into focused conversation.

Remaining on task became difficult as his wife shifted gears, became more subtle in her behavior, and challenged the outcome of his present boundaries. Joe stayed firm because he liked what he saw in himself AND no more was he "tied to the apron strings." He could be his own man, still love her, and want the best for both, without giving himself up in the process.

As the behavioral change became more pronounced, Joe's issues of insecurity with women began to surface. Most were attached to his lack of having an affectionate mother. Through his adult relationships today, Joe was trying to fix his "little boy" (Child Ego State) when he could "fix" emotionally disengaged women.

Joe was able to identify that he learned to have female relationships today based on the relationship he had with his mom as a little boy. This was painful for Joe because he began to see why he lasted so long in his current marriage and why he sabotaged or broke off more self-fulfilling relationships with healthier women. As these feelings emerged, Joe was covered with great shame, and he slipped into a depression that lasted several months. During this time he continued to come to therapy, was involved in a twelve-step program and increased his meetings, worked on going through his feelings, and maintained the boundaries with his wife.

When the new behavior was internalized, Joe was able to remain on task, facilitate his own feelings internally, not "take the bait" or "go there" when his wife pressed his buttons, and redirect the conversation back to the original topic. He accomplished this most of the time, except, when several stressors would hit him at once, and he didn't have the energy to field the attempted diversion his wife would create. At this time he would close off the encounter by saying that he didn't want "to go there" and leave the room.

Joe learned some serious lesson about his agenda during therapy. He realized that if he didn't take charge as the Adult, his "little boy" (Child Ego State) would be in charge of dating women and all the Child knew was how to have relationships with emotionally unavailable women. What his "little boy" thought: if he could fix those women (his mother in disguise)....they would be restored to wholeness....and take care of him. What he didn't know....they were not going to change and the energy was wasted on them. Joe had to learn to take care of himself, and at this time, didn't have a clue of what his needs were, for he spent so much time trying to fix them that he ignored himself.

The spiritual underpinning of this process is enabling.... *doing for someone, something they would not have been able to do, without your help*....which is in direct violation of God's plan for them. Out of this process comes resentment;

1. **RESENTMENT BY YOU** toward your partner for draining your energy, and
2. **RESENTMENT FROM YOUR PARTNER** toward you for the harm done to their spiritual potential by your enabling

This is a lose-lose situation. One that doesn't improve until the enabling stops and defined boundaries exist between the couple.

For Joe, his wife's Adolescent hated him because she knew he was only trying to fix her, and his own Adolescent had no respect for him because he wouldn't get his real needs met as long as he was locked in his obsession with his wife. It was both their Adolescents that fought it out. The battle would not have ended if Joe hadn't become "sick and tired" and decided to get some help in the form of professional therapy. The process of healing, effective counseling engenders, revealed the internal strife that precipitated his external behavior.

Process of Change

Change is a process and has three major components to its matrix: structure, determinants, and path. In this paradigm, one traverses each phase to complete the change cycle. In their journey, they gain self awareness, intra-personal skills, higher self-esteem, and solidify their self concepts. A major residual benefit occurs as they learn and maintain the change process. The added benefit happens as thoughts, feelings, and behaviors become congruent once their self concepts are solidified.

STRUCTURE   The formal structure of change is the Grief Process. In it, one goes through five distinct phases, each time a change is made: Denial, Anger, Bargaining, Depression, and Acceptance. It doesn't make any difference whether the change is positive or negative....the process is the same for both.

In it one will experience a myriad of feelings. When the feelings can be identified and applied to the Grief Process....the individual will have an idea of where they are in their process of going through them. This is a prime tool of self-awareness, for most people enter into fear when they become lost. Identifying and using the stages for mile markers along your road; will tell you approximately where you are, how far you came, and how long you have to go. It will also tell you if you are stuck. This information should release any fear that surfaces along its path.

DETERMINENTS   What determines how the change is handled....depends on the maturity level of the Ego States. If we have immature states, each phase of the internalization process will be hindered or impossible to achieve. If you ever wondered why your clients or self-help people, become and/or remain stuck, the answer is in the maturation level of the ego states.

It's easy to identify how one gets jammed up in the Grief Process, and once they are aware of their position, they can move on. Understanding how the ego states move through the process, is more complicated.

The Child - The Child gets hung up easily if the Adult hasn't worked on their feelings. Every new situation raises fear, to which the Child shuts down, or begins a problem loop to mask the feelings from the event. The correct intervention is to take the Child through their fear. In therapy, the clinician can do this easily. In self-help, the group, a sponsor, or one's support system can be there for them. To those of you without either — a long-time trusted friend can aid you through your process.

A word of caution at this point: If you can't do it on your own— GET HELP—IT'S OK—THIS IS NOT A MORAL ISSUE —IT'S HUMAN TO NEED HELP IN ONE'S HOUR OF NEED!

Feelings during this process are extremely important because the system of changing is an internal process and if thoughts and feelings are not aligned, neither will the behavior. When not congruent, would be to change (the Adult),   will be fearful (the Child), and instead of a   change occurring, a problem loop will begin (the Adolescent).

The Adolescent - An immature Adolescent will use a problem loop to cover up the fear from the Child, instead of lending his energy to the Adult in order to develop a creative and adaptive solution to the problem. During this time of change, all energy is needed to keep them on the strategy of the desired behavior change. As energy is diverted to a "Problem Loop" or just inattention, the change process becomes sabotaged, and the old behavior is perpetuated.

The correct intervention at this time is to make the Adolescent aware of the negative consequences, give them insight into why they do it, and let them know what the appropriate behavior is. If this fails, the next action would have to be negotiated through a mature adult state.

The Adult - When there is no heavy-duty issues or pathology getting in the way….the Adult Ego State usually responds to new information well. It's usually a case of "they didn't know" and lacked the necessary information for an adaptive solution. When they have it, they are usually able to apply it immediately and enjoy successful outcomes. These people are very grateful because they had a dilemma and didn't have the necessary tools for its successful facilitation. New information (this book, self-help, or therapy) gave it to them.

When there are deep issues; one may need therapy or a twelve-step program to get them out of the abyss life build around them. The Adult during this time has to be empowered, given parenting skills, and taught about their internal process. With these skills, they will learn to feel their feelings (let their Child live) and demonstrate effective strategies in stressful situations, instead of entering a "Problem Loop" (set boundaries and limits on their Adolescent). At this point, they will become an emotionally mature, responsible adult who can successfully facilitate stress with creative, adaptive solutions and maintain internal integrity when thoughts (Adult), feelings (Child) and behavior (Adolescent), remain in harmony.

AN EMOTIONALLY MATURE RESPONSIBLE ADULT
IS ABLE TO SUCCESSFULLY FACILITATE STRESS
WITH CREATIVE AND ADAPTIVE SOLUTIONS
THAT MAINTAIN INTERNAL INTEGRITY
AS THOUGHTS, FEELINGS AND
BEHAVIOR ARE IN HARMONY

PATH   The path in life, the change process meanders is determined by what issues are invoked by the change. In rule of thumb, if it's highly emotional, it's usually the Child Ego State, and invariably will emanate from an incomplete relationship with their primary caregivers who are usually their parents. This is a highly charged issue and difficult to break the established pattern of behavior because it's ties into the core of the human psyche.

When the reaction involves manipulation, inappropriate behavior, abusing ANY SUBSTANCE, or creating a problem loop, it's usually the Adolescent. These issues generally require a fully empowered Adult Ego State to set firm boundaries and limits on their Adolescent if appropriate information is not enough. The behavior experienced when these issues are paramount will be acting out (addiction or aggressive behavior), or acting in (depression, self-mutilation, or suicide). Both of these reactions may require professional help because the behavior is self destructive and generally indicates the issues are deep. If we follow the concept of "least restrictive environment," we can take the following course before professional help is followed:

1st Make a mental commitment to stop the behavior
2nd Commit to someone else that you will stop
3rd Complete a written contract you will change
4th Try changing some "things" in your life that precipitate or trigger the unwanted behavior
5th Go to a Twelve-Step Program
6th Start therapy
7th Detox
8th Enter a residential treatment program. These programs can be seven to twenty-eight days, one to three months, a year or better, inpatient, out-patient, or partial hospitalization program. All work under various circumstances.

The Adult is easiest to work with once the new information and skills are shown to them via:

- Feelings work with their Child (how to handle feelings)
- Appropriate boundaries and limits on their Adolescent
- New stress-reduction strategies
- Identification of major issues which can impede their progress

Armed with this arsenal of new parenting skills, the Adult learns quickly, becomes empowered, and demonstrates mature behavior. It is very heart-warming to watch these changes occur as one makes progress in therapy.

Psychodrama is usually the treatment modality of choice. The interventions become extremely powerful when the individual can observe their internal process working: when their ego states are personified as a role in the drama. The awareness is profound. The ramifications of the behavior changes, implemented because of the insight, are just as far reaching.

The whole process of therapy is designed to create new positive parenting skills in which the client will learn to:

- Nurture themselves, instead of giving it away to emotionally unavailable people, or, waiting for someone else to nurture them
- Set parameters on their behavior to increase positive choices
- Increase their self-awareness
- Identify their major issues
- Learn new stress reduction strategies
- Develop more adaptive decision-making skills
- Increase their current interpersonal skills while maintaining Adult relationships with family, friends, co-workers, love objects, or the larger culture and its various institutions
- Decrease problematic behavior
- Reframe and change survival skills to living skills

Application

The whole process to change is application. Everything that's applied in the process will change the undesired behavior. This occurs as the new knowledge is applied to current situations and a new strategy, one that had not been previously perceived, is devised and applied. This is learning.

TOOLS — The following are tools for self-balance and help to keep you:

1. Separate from your love object (mental, physical, emotional, spiritual boundaries)
2. Focused, centered, grounded and in your day

3. Help you to separate your "stuff" from theirs
4. Know when you are over-reaching
5. Keep you from getting into more trouble

FOCUSED — CENTERED — GROUNDED   I'm constantly amazed how our thoughts and feelings can project us out of our day. What we feel and how we think, can seem like reality when it's not, and we are convinced that it is. Thoughts are merely what our brain does twenty-four hours a day and feelings are just visitors. They both come and go. The following are simple exercises to keep one intact while all cylinders are cranking.

First   One does a 360 degree scan of their position to determine if there is any reality to what they are feeling. When it's completed, they are *CENTERED.*

Second   They look down at their shoes which are standing on the ground. At this point, they validate they are standing in the room and not at the place their thoughts have propelled them to. They are now *GROUNDED.*

Third   They take the palm of one of their hands and bring it to their face. As they concentrate on the palm coming toward them, they become *FOCUSED.*

SEPARATE THEIR STUFF OUT FROM YOURS   **This is usually very hard, for one generally desires to be appropriate in their relationship, and want to keep their love object in their best light. Each partner's "stuff" or issues can cloud the reality. What did she say? How did he say it? What did he mean by that? Questions, confusion, suspicion, mistrust, anger, and blow up. Sometimes, it's that simple. How do you change the process and short-circuit the negative energy that's going to be released? Don't know? Hard answer to find, you say? Right. The following is an effective beginning:**

First   If they come at you "from left field," blaming you for something you didn't do…. *IT'S THEIR STUFF.* This is projection ….what they project on you is someone else's behavior that effected them in the past.

Second   If you have a large emotional response to something another person has done….*IT'S PROBABLY YOUR STUFF.* The only exception is, when its anger, can be identified quickly, and diminished by setting a boundary. IN THIS CASE, IT'S PROBABLY A BOUNDARY VIOLATION WHICH YOU DIDN'T REALIZE OR WANT TO CONFRONT. (Your Adolescent takes care of it when your Adult doesn't).

Third   When something is asked of you and your response was not
appropriate to the situation….ask yourself if the request could be
considered an *ACCOMODATION OR WAS THERE A PRIN-
CIPLE INVOLVED*. If it's an *accomodation,* the reaction was
your stuff. If there was a *principle* involved, the reaction usually
involves a boundary, and would be their stuff.

The misunderstanding of one partner's principles usually signifies that
their mate doesn't know them intimately. You own the inappropriate reaction and owe your partner the proper information about yourself to prevent
them from making the same mistake twice. Intimacy develops when one is
willing to give personal information about them to their love object, instead of becoming defensive and pointing fingers (blaming) at their partner
for their ignorance in the violation of their boundary.

HOW TO KNOW WHEN YOU ARE OUT OF YOUR DAY   **It's
especially difficult in early recovery to recognize if feelings are current or emerging from unresolved issues triggered by their love object.
One's objectivity diminishes as they are bombarded by a plethora of
emotions that bounces them off walls, jumbles up their ability to reality test, and suspends their reasoning power. It's at this time that frozen
feelings are becoming thawed; new awareness is occurring continuously, confusion is the current state of mind, and defense mechanisms
are poised to engage at the least sign of trouble.**

Not an easy place to be. It's overwhelming when one is expected to
keep their side of the street clean, in any relationship, to avoid adding any
more unresolved issues onto their agenda. The issues (baggage) they came
with are enough.

The strategies I use on myself are simple, effective, and teachable. I
use them in practice, as an intervention, to teach others how to stay in their
day. A by-product of the process is it further enhances boundaries between the members of the relationship. The purpose of the construct is to
stop the downward spiral into shame (clinical depression), so many fall
into, when they can't sort out the incoming data. It's at this time that   (Intellect over Emotion), or, cognition (thinking) over feelings (affect), can
stop the building up of self-depreciating emotions. The strategy is this:

YOU ARE OUT OF YOUR DAY if the conflict is not resolved quickly.
Any major situation you encounter with your love object seems to linger
and doesn't get resolved: is probably dragging up old issues and attached
them to it. This makes the circumstance bigger than it is. What you are
probably reacting to is an unresolved issue and not the current event.

IF YOU ARE IN YOUR DAY the conflict gets resolved easily. It may take work, but it will come to right size in a reasonable amount of time. In doing so, will not damage the relationship, as prolonging it usually does.

These strategies may seem simplistic to you — don't be fooled! They are very sophisticated. On surface level issues they are very simple. As one digs deeper into their behavior and uncovers their "Hidden Agenda" or identifies the subtler nuances of their behavior; these tools become highly valuable because as far down as you wish to go, these tools will keep you focused, centered, and grounded in your relations with others.

THE WORKPLACE

All of the insight, awareness and application learned or gleaned out of the three chapters on relationships can be applied to the workplace.

Most vocational environments are a microcosm of what was modeled in our family of origin: how we allow others to treat us; what our boundaries are or are not; how we treat others; what we strive for or conversely settle for. The way we play these scripts in our work lives today is usually determined by how we were socialized in our family of origin. If we were raised in a loving, supportive environment, our ideals, self-esteem, and aspirations are high; our personal identity is rock solid, for we know what our self concepts are and we are willing to maintain them. We usually stand on a firm foundation in life, and small issues cannot knock us off course. The opposite is true for those raised in a cold and unsupportive environment with primary caregivers (usually parents) who were disengaged.

How this translates in a work environment is....we usually seek out what we know! If we are use to a positive environment, we will not remain in a negative one. The same is true in a negative one. Ever wonder why you seem to draw the same kind of jobs, settle for less, seem to be overworked, underpaid, and can't break the mold? That's because you aren't use to being in a positive work environment. In fact, if you chose one, your words would be: it's uninteresting; the pace is too slow; it's not enough of a challenge; things are too quiet; all your talents are not being used; there's no growth; and a plethora of other statements that would turn you away from the job.

WE RE-CREATE IN THE VOCATIONAL SETTING
THE SAME ENVIRONMENT WE WERE SOCIALIZED IN
WHEN RAISED IN OUR FAMILY OF ORIGIN

Your Boss is Not Your Parents

How many times did you feel like you were talking to one of your parents when you had to see your supervisor or owners to: get a raise, bring up an issue, or talk about improving your work environment? Most do not know what the workplace triggers inside of them, let along facilitate the stress that is generated. It seems to come out of nowhere; mouth gets dry, stomach queasy, hands sweating, knees knocking, and anxiety rising.

Most of the time these are signals that one has not fully disengaged emotionally from the family of origin (cut the apron strings); still carry unresolved issues from their family of origin; are projecting these unresolved issues onto their bosses and supervisors, and giving them emotional power over them in the process. It's also an indication that one's self concepts are not fully developed. One may have to work very hard to identify where the deficiency lies, build it up and develop it more.

The process encompasses more than self-esteem issues. It's working with the very core of what someone is as a human being. I don't feel that our culture values this type of self-analysis because it's too individualistic, and it's not production-oriented. It's too bad because the benefits to the culture are great; as one knows themselves to a greater degree....they will instinctively choose professions they can grow in....and be fully productive in the highest sense for themselves and the culture.

If this section inspires one to look deeper into themselves about their vocational choices and out of it comes a happier and thereby a more productive worker ....I am pleased.

This part will not be very long. It is designed only to make you aware that there is more going on in the workplace than meets the eye. All of the concepts in this book can be applied to situations that happen in work which confuse you. Once you begin to use them for filters in how to interpret a situation that occurs in your work environment . . . the confusion will end.

THE CHILD   The Child Ego State is the part of you that gets scared when having to face or confront an authority figure in work. It's the part of you that feels helpless about changing anything in your current vocational environment, and is insecure about losing a position that's well below your capability or qualifications. When one does not understand their internal structure, this ego state can reduce their self concepts in work because it's constantly in fear and doesn't want to risk. The Child at this point has projected their childhood fears of their parents, onto the boss, who now receives undeserved emotional power over the Adult. This is mainly due to lack of differentiation between the Adult and their parents and emotional immaturity because the Adult is still emotionally enmeshed with their parents.

The initial work for the Adult is to soothe the Child's fear when they make decisions in work, as a fully empowered person, instead of a fearful Child. The emotions will mature (the Child will have less fear) as the Adult makes more adaptive decisions for themselves on the job. During the process, they will have to confront any fear that surfaces. Any place they become stuck may indicate a need for therapy or a twelve-step program to overcome the blockage.

Being raised in a dysfunctional family is a prime example of people who carry the kind of baggage that impacts their vocational choices and makes them overqualified for self-help. Any issue that can't be worked on in a twelve-step program would be a candidate for professional individual or group therapy. Adult Children of Alcoholics, and Codependents Anonymous, are two examples of a twelve-step program that can help you to work on unfinished business from your family or origin.

When you are a member of a twelve-step program and work "the steps" in AA, NA, OA, AL-ANON, etc. you can always touch upon the issues, although most frown upon working them in depth because it "takes the focus off themselves and diverts the energy from their "primary purpose," which is to remain clean, sober, or abstinent. Some AL-ANON meetings will allow it. In ACOA and CODA — it is their "primary purpose."

THE ADOLESCENT The easiest way to describe the Adolescent on the job is to look at Johnny Paycheck's song entitled, "Take This Job and Shove it!" Who do you think wrote it? You got it....the Adolescent!

The Adolescent on the job is the energy one puts into it. It's the part of the worker that helps him to "keep on — keepin' on" and finish the job. It's also the part that tells the boss, "screw you," and to "take this job and shove it!" How many times on the job have you "had it up to here," didn't want to hear another promise, and only wanted to see the fruits of your labor to begin? When it didn't—you exploded, and/or quit!

Once again, this is the Adolescent saying hear me....look at what I've done....give me what you promised....if you don't, you have to pay. Sometimes, on the job, they are only trying to set boundaries. If you are not solid in your self concepts, the reaction will go internal into depression or external into anger or rage. These issues also stem from the family of origin when needs did not get met on a consistent basis. A strategy had to be devised to attain them. Unless someone matures, develops adaptive strategies, they will refine and perpetuate what was learned being raised in their family of origin.

The Adult at this time has their hands full trying to place healthy boundaries and limits on their Adolescent. The Adolescent usually balks at this time because the Adult has abrogated their rights for so long that it's foreign for them not to be in charge.

Additional work that may have to be done during this time is to either, better define their present boundaries, or to set up new ones. Once this is done, the Adolescent usually backs off. If you have trouble with what needs to be defined, expanded, or changed; there is probably work that needs to be done to determine why you continue to let yourself be exploited when you don't receive fair compensation for your work efforts or don't feel you deserve an emotionally safe environment to work in. Some of these issues can be traced back to your family of origin, others can be poorly-defined self concepts, or may be mired in emotional immaturity where one has not out-grown manipulation and doesn't use negotiation to get their needs met.

THE ADULT   Any problems the Adult has in developing adaptive negotiation skills in the workplace has its roots in the lack of maturity, being developmentally stuck, or having debilitating issues that block adaptive strategies from being formulated. In these blocks, the Adult's positive traits have either not been developed fully, or are out of the picture completely. If it's the latter: the Child will be fully present and the Adult will present as being helpless and hopeless. If the Adolescent's dominant, the Adult will present as an arrogant adolescent. When the Adolescent remains dominant, the individual may require therapy to break the impasse, because there's usually a co-morbid condition of depression or anxiety along with a food disorder, substance abuse, or another obsessive-compulsive behavior.

If the Adult is partially present, it's usually appropriate information; mainly awareness, insight, and parenting skills they need to become fully functioning in an adaptive manner. Most of the time, they will lack the basic skills, because they were never taught or modeled in their family of origin. Once they know "what they didn't know," the progress is amazing and they recover quickly.

What this translates into is having a highly skilled and productive worker who is not afraid to negotiate for what they deserve; change jobs, or starts their own companies to attain the goals they deserve. Not a bad payoff for getting to know yourself.

Peers and Subordinates

I've used boss, owner, and supervisor throughout this section because authority figures usually invoke the strongest reactions. Others take place with peers and subordinates as well. The main difference between the boss and peers on your level or below, and how you react to them is: the boss is generally your parent and a co-worker is usually a sibling — or you at a vulnerable time in your life. Either way, unless the Adult is in charge of negotiating problems that arise because of them, you will give yourself up, or get lost in yourself trying to fix them. This is codependency at best.

The reaction to the situation has to be identified first; the ego state attached to the reaction queried; and the boundary in question restated, re-evaluated, or established. It's a simple process that raises many issues at the beginning, which later becomes merely routine, as one's self concepts mature in the workplace.

I could write an entire book on relationships in the workplace. This section was only written to make you aware of: the problem, some generalized antecedents, and some possible solutions when used in conjunction with the rest of this book. Any deeper explanation is beyond the scope of this book. Maybe it's a topic to a sequel? If the need is there I'll write it.

SUMMARY

In order for the Adult to dominate the Executive System, one needs insight into themselves: how, what and why they feel (Child); be aware of what precipitates their behavior and acquire choices in their behavioral responses (Adolescent); and be able to facilitate stress without constantly second guessing themselves (Critical Adult). Instead, intuitively handle stress reduction in a manner that considers their entire ego states, where thoughts, feelings, and behavior are congruent, and the final outcome is adaptive (Nurturing Adult).

In the process of learning to make adaptive decisions during stressful situations, instead of continuing in the old "Problem Loops," one has to reframe the old dysfunctional behavior to a skill that went out of balance. In this strategy, one does not have to invalidate any of their parts (Child & Adolescent) because they found a non-conventional way to survive the traumatic or non-child centered living environment in which they were raised.

In the change process, the survival skill is viewed as an attribute that was needed in a time of great childhood stress. As we examine the survival skill today, it's determined if it's needed presently and if not, what behavior could replace it that could generate adaptive solutions instead of "Problem Loops." The new behavior becomes a "living skill" as it modifies its use of the targeted attribute and brings it back into balance. Remember....an attribute is a behavior or a character trait....that is exhibited in a mid range of a scale....not too much or too little....and doesn't enter the extreme ends of the scale. (See Figure 19.1, p.434, for an illustration).

There is a process to the change. It encompasses the following format, as part of the cognitive restructuring in changing a character or behavior trait today, that was thought to be negative because its need was not previously understood: understanding the Grief Process as a road to identify where you are in your change process and using grief's stages as mile markers; having ethics in your relationships in order to guide and direct the type of behavior you will exhibit when interacting with others and being consistent with your morals, values, goals, and self concepts. In order for the new behavior to materialize, one has to maintain personal integrity in the relationship....for if they lose themselves in another....they no longer exist....and any type of reactive behavior can and usually prevails. Intimacy is a challenge in a relationship: it's goal is to be honest, open, and to help each other attain their highest good in life; creating spirituality in which both connect to a Higher Power who will guide and direct them; and to attain their "Birth Vision," whether it be singular as an individual or together as a couple. All of the above factors have a process in order for the couple to complete their journey. Through the insight the factors give, as the couple assimilates the knowledge learned in the process; they learn and grow to become mentally, emotionally, and spiritually fit in order to complete the spiritual task they were born to accomplish.

There are some problems inherent in the system. The individual has to overcome them in order to continue their growth. In an intimate relationship with others....one has to know themselves first....before they can know themselves in relation to another. Without knowing themselves first, it's like stumbling in the dark....each time a problem arises, they will not know themselves....and thereby....guess at their need or capitulate to their partner's demands. Either way they lose. When they know themselves first, the dilemma ceases to exist, for they understand their own need....and when a problem arises with their mate....can negotiate to get their needs met. This is a real challenge to grow because the fulfillment of the process will trigger all the past pain from situations in which they were used to fill someone else's needs as theirs were ignored. This is also a spiritual problem, blocks the free flow of guidance from God, as one tries to get their needs met at someone else's expense.

Changing one's behavior is a two-step process: First he will expend all energy trying to remember the behavior and applying it in the targeted situations....this is compliance and "First Order Change." The second will happen when the new behavior becomes the automatic response to the situation....this is permanent and "Second Order Change."

In the process of changing, he has to see what behavior is no longer acceptable, identify the situations it happens, how the behavior escalates into an unacceptable practice, and change it to a new response as he is doing the behavior....at the point he will recognize it as it occurs. Recognition is usually a backward process because the response of the behavior is so automatic....that it's produced unconsciously *before* the individual even realizes they are using it (One is there before they knew they left).

The process of change has a definitive structure and is found in the Grief Process as he uses its stages as mile markers. The markers will indicate where their ego states are in resolving, either what's attached to the change or acceptance of the change. Determinants to the change are the issues each ego state brings to the equation and how the change is internally facilitated. One's path of how the changes are made is usually determined by the depth of the issue which necessitated and/or perpetuated the behavior. Behavior precipitated by simple issues can be changed through awareness of them only. Ones that are deeper or have been used for a long period of time may need some therapy or a twelve-step program to help assist him to change. If the wounding is deep....the resulting behavior toxic to self and others, and occurred over a long period of time....may need a residential treatment program lasting from 28 days to two years.

The entire process of change is designed to have the individual apply the new behavior to present situations and attain more adaptive results. In relationships one spends time in self-reflection, when they have a problem with their love objects, and try to devise solutions that will enhance the relationship instead of destroying it. Having new tools will allow one to maintain personal integrity during conflict with their mate, remain focused, centered and grounded by staying in the day instead of playing old tapes and reacting exponentially because a present hurt attaches itself to a past trauma. Other tools will help you to separate out their issues from yours when: a conflict occurs, creates a reaction in them or you, and is greater than the present situation would usually invoke.

THE WORKPLACE — The work environment generally mirrors some of the same problems we encounter in the family of origin when, unresolved family issues, are triggered by a supervisor or co-worker within their vocational environment. This phenomenon generally occurs because of how one is socialized and takes these concepts with them when they are seeking employment. In the workplace the boss becomes the parent and co-workers become various members of their family. Some take on the significance of siblings, others aunts or uncles, still others become grand-parents or cousins. This can be positive or negative: positive when the transference creates good relationships; and negative when it creates per-sonality clashes. The next time you have a problem with the boss or a co-worker....see whom they resemble in your family of origin....and the problem may end quicker than you thought.

As in any relationship....don't be surprised by the reaction you re-ceive from a supervisor or co-worker....when you define or restate a professional boundary. If they are not mature enough to handle the change, their Child will get bruised and their Adolescent will attempt retribution. If this happens....remain in your Adult . . . negotiate the change....for you are now becoming an emotionally mature responsible adult who is learn-ing in the workplace how to teach people how to treat you and others, by having healthy boundaries and limits. We teach others how to treat us by what we allow them to do to us when we disallow our own boundaries and limits as we interact with them.

Feels good . . . doesn't it. After doing this, you may like the response you were given....and keep the job. You may not, and seek another one. Either way, it's OK. You stuck to your principles and remained intact. Usually, something good follows this type of action: the boss has greater understanding and engenders value being placed on you, or it's clear that your needs will not be met and you seek other employment that will. It's a win-win situation for you: you get your vocational needs met and no longer enable employers who don't place a value on you.

CHAPTER TWENTY

Remember where you've been
So you know how far you've come

OVERVIEW

When you complete this chapter, you will be able to put together the new systems and concepts this book introduces, into an integrated stress-reduction system which will allow you to create adaptive solutions to life's problems without giving up your self concepts, values, morals, ethics, or sacrificing your spiritual goals.

Throughout the chapter you will recognize the transformation process: In it you will know:

1. When you view life as a problem instead of a solution
2. What a Problem Loop is, its process, and path
3. How to avoid Problem Loops
4. How your internal structure impacts a Problem Loop.
5. How to deal with life on life's terms as a growing experience
6. How a catastrophic event can alter your life's plans
7. How multiple stressors can overwhelm one's usual coping strategies
8. What an adaptive stress-reduction system is
9. How we can learn the language of the brain and use the information it provides to:
   a)Facilitate overwhelming situations
   b)Know one's self with more confidence
   c)Respond to crisis with equanimity
   d)Exhibit appropriate behavior in times of stress
   e)Better maintain one's dignity and integrity in the face of adversity
   f)Understand one's feelings better
   g)Set boundaries on self and others
   h)Understand one's reactions to others
   i)Maintain one's spiritual course

TRANSFORMATION

The road has been long, sometimes very difficult, and at this point you may or may not be sure that the effort is worth it. When you come out the other side of your pain — like going through a dark tunnel to emerge into the sunlight and a breath-taking landscape — you will have your answer. For me it was!

What's happened to you over the course of this book and what do you have to look forward to? It's as if one is reborn - reborn to a world you've never known. In it, when you have a problem, your path out of it is clearer: You now work The Steps, know The Traditions, may have had some therapy (if you read this book you certainly have), learned some lessons, removed yourself from the Problem Loop and come into the solution.

Your life is now opening up. Free from bondage to the past, which took the form of self-centered fear. Free from past obsessions that kept you mired in problematic behavior. It doesn't matter if the addiction was alcohol, drugs, relationships, food, sex, and work, gambling, over achieving, criminality, or any other behavior that consumes you mentally, physically or spiritually, and takes you out of balance. *ALL ARE NOT THE SAME! WHILE YOU'RE CONSUMED WITH THEM —YOU'RE NOT TAKING CARE OF YOURSELF IN A FUNCTIONALLY ADAPTIVE WAY!*

ANY BEHAVIOR THAT CONSUMES A PERSON'S ENERGY AND THROWS HIM OFF BALANCE — DIMINISHES THE REMAINDER OF HIS LIFE!

Free from The Problem Loop, life on life's terms, opens up to you. No longer are you like a ship during a storm without a rudder, being tossed around by a turbulent sea - nor are you a victim being persecuted by an angry and capricious God when something bad happens in your life.

You now become fully empowered, able to assess a situation, determine a course of action, and apply the strategy, 1) gleaned from previous experience or, 2) generated from creative solutions, in an adaptive, non-problematic manner.

Isn't it refreshing being an emotionally mature, responsible adult, instead of a pouting child who becomes the victim, or, the acting-out adolescent who hurts those around him and gets victimized in the process.

Life is not always easy. Sometimes it goes smoothly, other times it can be a very bumpy road and full of many pitfalls. Either way, we have to learn to facilitate a stressful event, maintain our self concepts, not alienate our fellow travelers, continue to self actualize, and remain on our spiritual path in order to complete our life's goals.

This book has been about the ways we can be sidetracked off our spiritual path, what happens internally to us in the process, and how we can regain our original course. During the journey, we can view the external events as opportunities to expand our knowledge about ourselves and others, creating effective solutions to an adversarial event and thereby *growing in the solution*; or, we can *wane in the problem* by creating a series of Problem Loops to divert the discomfort of the situation instead of going through the pain and growing.

IN LIFE, ONE:
GROWS BY CREATING ADAPTIVE SOLUTIONS OR *DIMINISHES* WHEN HE DIVERTS THE PAINFUL OPPORTUNITIES WITH PROBLEM LOOPS!

The overall lessons that have been learned in the maturation process are:

1. How to maintain balance between one's thoughts, feelings, and behavior
2. How to make decisions based on internal agreement
3. How to generate an adaptive process
4. How to come out of the problem and go into the solution

LIFE AS A PROBLEM

Life can be viewed in many ways: As various opportunities to grow when one goes through the challenge and his life is enriched by the experience — or, as problems to be avoided by diverting the potential growing experience through a Problem Loop, and seeing life as an enigma that continuously keeps him down.

The Problem Loop

The Problem Loop is simply a behavioral sequence used as a survival strategy and designed to allow a human being to transform psychic pain, by diverting the internal originating pain, into an external event.

In these Problem Loops: the individual repeats the same behavior over and over as the conditioned response to the actuating event, just like Pavlov's dogs did when they salivated to the bell whether the food was present or not.

In this behavioral response, the human being, subconsciously, expects relief from the pain generated by the activating event. He does receive temporary relief, at a high price, for all he receives is a sabbatical from the inevitable. He will have to eventually face whatever he is trying to avoid. A negative side bar to this survival skill is that he is:

- Placing another layer of grief on top of the original event, that will have to be worked through
- Doing the same thing over and over, expecting things to change
- Hindering the development of living skills which engender creative solutions
- Blocking emotional maturation

THE PATH OF THE LOOP   The path of the Loop is a consistent one:

1. Problems are experienced in life
2. Feelings are generated during the situation which can go as high as anxiety or as low as depression
3. A behavioral loop is formulated in which the rising feelings are transformed into a behavioral sequence *to divert its energy and focus from an internal experience to an extrernal reaction*
4. The Problem Loop cycle is broken in recovery or treatment
5. In recovery, The Loop is avoided by experiencing the emerging feelings and resolving them through the Grief Process
6. Figure 20.1 is a graphic representation of the process

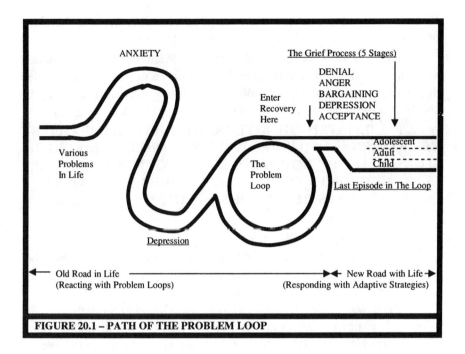

FIGURE 20.1 – PATH OF THE PROBLEM LOOP

CASE STUDY: Our executive, Joan, is a perfect example of some- one who doesn't want to face the pain from her past, and uses the Problem Loop to facilitate the feelings each time they begin to surface.

In therapy, Joan was able to identify that she came from a "looking good" family. On the surface they appeared to be the "perfect" family. Living with them was another experience. Both parents worked hard at holding full-time positions in prestigious firms. Along with the jobs came much socializing, late-night meetings, golf on weekends and business trips. The only problem was that, as parents, they had very little left over for her.

Joan grew up with lots of amenities, very little love, lonely, and won- dering what was wrong with her that Mommy and Daddy did not have any time for her. These being her role models, she sought the same type for companions - ones that looked good on the outside, were emotionally dis- tant, and appeared to have much potential. Joan attracted what she knew and received from her new love objects what she got from her parents - emotional unavailability! (You do what you did — you get what you got! Sound familiar?)

Instead of Joan owning the pain from her childhood, she continued to seek emotionally unavailable mates. Each time she applied the usual strat- egy, the pain from the disappointment would propel her into another Problem Loop as she broke up the unsatisfactory relationship and immedi- ately became involved with another "looking good" man — instead of looking at her to see what went wrong and changing the self-defeating behavior. During this process, the following "benefits" were attained:

1. REMAINED IN A PROBLEM LOOP and through a behavioral sequence (break up the old relationship and start a new one), she avoided the feelings of her unhappy childhood when they started to surface. She also didn't have to feel the consequences to her redundant behavior.

2. FACILITATED THE INTERNAL CONFLICT, CREATED BY HER EXTERNAL BEHAVIOR, WHEN SHE AVOIDED TAKING RESPONSIBILITY BY NOT BECOMING ACCOUNTABLE FOR HER CURRENT CHOICES WHEN SHE CONTINUED IN SELF-DEFEATING BEHAVIOR: AS SHE DID THE SAME THING (avoid responsibility) **OVER AND OVER!**

3. HER PROCESS WAS:

> *THE CHILD EGO STATE:* Maintained the Child's belief that she was not good enough. If she was, the new love object would be there for her, and be emotionally available.
>
> *THE ADOLESCENT EGO STATE:* Continued to think that all love objects are the same: they use you, abuse you, and leave.
>
> *THE ADULT EGO STATE* : Knows she is good enough to have a special   relationship, but doesn't know how to do it. If the Critical Adult Ego State is activated, it says, "I told you so!" to all three ego states, and the current disastrous relationship is the evidence that reinforces her belief system. If the relationships are many — life becomes nothing more than a series of Problem Loops.

LIFE AS A SERIES OF PROBLEM LOOPS — When one's life becomes a series of Problem Loops, the same kind of behaviors are exhibited over and over, with the expectation that something will change. Nothing changes, except in the resulting activity. The problem seems to blow over until the next time one encounters it. Nothing has been learned about what to do when the problem rises again. The only thing accomplished is; the person survives through the episode by diverting the emerging pain via an external event. Another facet to these Problem Loops is that they intensify over time because the pain they hide increases with each dysfunctional strategy the person tries. It's like being in a high-stakes poker game as the ante is increased with each bet. Except this time one is playing against oneself. Look at Figure 20.2 and observe how the consequences increase with each Problem Loop. Note how the preceding reaction becomes the trigger for

the next Problem Loop, and how the consequences to each proceeding loop are intensified.

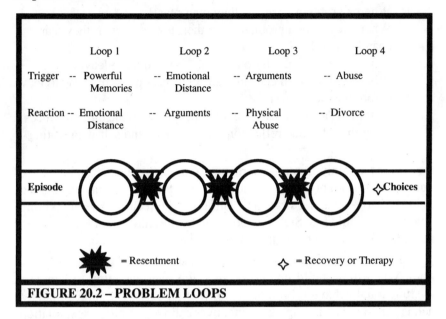

FIGURE 20.2 – PROBLEM LOOPS

THE INTERNAL STRUCTURE

The Internal Structure of the Human Being evaluates and acts upon any external stimulus which is taken in through the senses. In the process, each ego state becomes a filter in which meaning is added to the material. At this time, thoughts are induced, feelings provoked, and issues stirred. It's up to the Executive System to sift through the preponderance of data and determine an appropriate response. Hopefully, the decision-making process (Executive System) will be guided by an emotionally-mature, responsible Adult Ego State, which can generate adaptive strategies, and use creative solutions, in an effective way— based on self-love, self-actualization, and spiritual goals, instead of fear from the Child Ego State or anger from the Adolescent Ego State.

When the Adult Ego State is not present — logic can't prevail. Emotions run high, mostly fear-based, and at this time, the Child is in charge. All material taken in is filtered through the Child, and a skewed sense of perception is developed. In it — fear is the primary feeling and protection the most pressing goal. In this distortion, persons, places, things, events, and situations are deemed harmful by the Child — when in reality — they are not!

The following are examples of how someone lives in a dysfunctional world:

1. When a problem arises — they over react!
2. When they have a problem with their love object — they fear abandonment!
3. When there is difficulty on the job — it's time to leave!
4. When they misread cues in their relationships — it's time to leave before they leave *you*
5. Nothing is as it seems — reality changes with the circumstances
6. Most thoughts and reflections are negative and self-deprecating

This is a highly immature structure. One that makes decisions based out of fear. It is highly reactive and generally does not display any balance in its decision—making strategies. This type of Executive System is dominated by the Child Ego State and powered by the Adolescent Ego State, for the Adolescent is the strength that drives the system.

In a juvenile internal structure, problems are buried, masked, or put on hold. When these build up and become too overwhelming to handle, a dysfunctional behavioral set, in the form of an obsessive and compulsive act, is generated (drinking, drugging, over eating, gambling, sex, relationships, criminality, etc.). This addictive behavior further covers up the pain, when the problem wasn't attended to sooner in a more adaptive fashion.

This skewed perceptual system within the fearful human being, is what creates and maintains the need for the Problem Loops that are experienced in a dysfunctional lifestyle.

CASE STUDY: Joan, our earlier case study, is a good example to use to isolate the emotional immaturity in an otherwise mature adult.

In the non-love-relationship parts of her life, Joan is fully grown-up, capable, and a highly polished businesswoman. She makes business decisions with care, thought, and the precision of a high-level executive. She is admired by many, including her ex-loves, who can't figure out why this upstanding business woman seems to come apart in love relationships.

When they were asked what drew them to her and how they felt in the beginning of the relationship: each felt she was a strong person, solid in her self-identity, confident of her path in life, secure in her relationships with others, and a person with whom they could learn, grow, and have a successful relationship. A couple of them even described her as their soul mate. None could project the negative ending of their relationship, nor suspected it.

What happened? What changed a positive beginning into a disastrous ending? The filters of the Internal Structure did it. In their interpretation of the daily data entered about their love object, their filters skewed the data and made highly subjective assessments based on tainted information. This further led to biased decisions that released reactive behavior, which didn't fit the event. SOMETIMES THE DATA WAS SO SKEWED THAT A PSYCHOTIC (non-reality-based) REACTION OCCURRED!

To say that this process created major confusion in Joan's life is an understatement. Here she was a full-grown woman, successful in most major areas of her life, acting like a jealous child, by exhibiting juvenile behavior in life situations with her love object, instead of using these challenges as an opportunity to grow by going through them, and coming closer to her mate in the process.

Internally, Joan's Child Ego State was extremely fearful in love situations. In business, Joan had a powerful Adult Ego State— this was not the case in love. When in love with someone, Joan's Executive System would become dominated by the Child Ego State. It was as if she went brain dead, all logic would leave, and she would become a big bundle of emotion.

When this happened, all events occurring between her and the love object would be scrutinized by the Child Ego State, who was searching for any indication the person was going to leave her. This could be a gesture, inflection in the voice, an expression on the face, or GOD FORBID — HE ACTUALLY MADE A MISTAKE! With this filter in place, the other person had to exhibit perfect behavior — according to whatever Joan's Child Ego State determined it to be in the moment — using raw emotion as the only guideline — or, he had to be a mind reader. This included *both* being mind readers: Joan to know what was going on inside her mate internally as she was interpreting the external cues, and her love object as he had to do the same and additionally guess at how she was perceiving him.

Nobody really has the tools to accomplish this. And even though I excel at reading and interpreting others, I ASK WHAT IS GOING ON WITH SOMEONE ELSE INSTEAD OF GUESSING!

GUESSING IS A PROBLEM LOOP!
THE ANSWERS YOU RECEIVE —
VALIDATE YOUR THINKING ONLY,
AND DON'T ACCURATELY CONVEY THE
CORRECT INFORMATION ABOUT *WHAT*
YOU ARE TRYING TO DETERMINE!

Following Joan's childlike assessment of the potential abandonment of her love object, came the behavioral response of the Adolescent Ego State, in which all energy is expended toward establishing "the truth"! The Adolescent picks, badgers, blames, and ultimately pushes away the love object.

During this time, the Nurturing Adult is virtually non-existent, except in a few moments of clarity between battles when Joan realized that she had done this before and didn't know how to stop its ultimate conclusion. At this realization, the Nurturing Adult fades out when it doesn't have the necessary information to alter the ending, or shuts down when the Critical Adult begins to demean it.

Joan's Critical Adult comes alive at this time to: shame the Child, taunt the Adolescent into action, and drive away its nurturing counterpart. This is the time Joan's Committee becomes energized and creates a negative hell in her mind. This is also called a spiritual battle that occurs as Joan remains in the negativity of egocentric fear from the Child instead of entering the hope of the Nurturing Adult and creating an adaptive solution to the problem.

At this point, you have to remember the Internal Structure's system of hiding past pain, or, preventing the current situations of today from becoming a valid learning experience. In it, feelings and emotions are transformed into a behavioral set, in which the human repeats learned behavior patterns, which creates an external diversion from one's internal confusion. The system's final purpose is to divert the energy from the feelings into a behavior, which acts as a pressure release valve within the human psyche, and keeps it from becoming overloaded. Figure 20.3 is a modified version of Figure 2.3 and designed to illustrate what influence the various ego states have in the process.

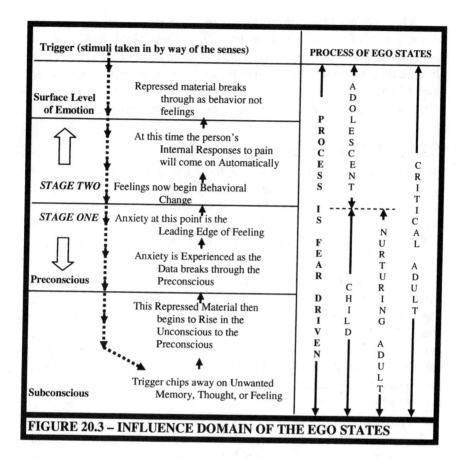

FIGURE 20.3 – INFLUENCE DOMAIN OF THE EGO STATES

LIFE IN THE SOLUTION

Life can be viewed in many ways: Some see it through the eyes of the victim — as a continuing problem that keeps them down; others see it as different events that present them with opportunities to grow. Both are true for the individual who interprets life's vicissitudes as a problem or a solution.

It's only an attitude. How do you view it? As a glass half empty or one that is half full. The contents of the glass don't change — the level remains the same — it's only what we do with it that changes. When the glass is half empty, the connotation is that it's going to dry up and there will not be any more. With this attitude there is no hope and faith that things will change and get better. If the glass is half full, a new world opens up, and that's where we want to go.

What changes? Everything. One comes out of remaining in the problem as a way of life, in which his living is nothing more than a series of Problem Loops — and goes into living life in the solution. It's at this point that creative solutions are gleaned through previous experience, as one learns from his past mistakes and applies the new strategies as an emotionally mature, responsible adult, without entering into Problem Loops.

Life on Life's Terms

To experience life as it unfolds, without trying to manipulate others or the environment, is a formidable task. Many stressors can foul up the works and sidetrack even the most dedicated student, especially if multiple events happen simultaneously or one after another. The impact of these situations can overwhelm anyone's stress-reduction strategies.

LIFE HAPPENS AS WE MAKE OUR PLANS — How many times have you heard that? The first time it came to my attention was on a tea bag. I laughed. The philosophical tidbit was correct; I thought about how many plans I had made over the years that family, money, circumstances or events within the culture, prevented from coming to fruition. Most probably they happened the way they were supposed to so that I could be where I am today. If I could have controlled it — I would have orchestrated the events in a different way.

My visualization of "Life on Life's Terms" — experiencing the events as they unfold in my life — is depicted in the following illustration. In it, life can be viewed as a series of predictable storms, in which we learn and grow through the event. As we learn the lessons we need in order to develop and grow, the storms become shorter in duration, less intense, and further spaced. Notice I didn't say they went away. They don't. We just get better at facilitating them.

Is this a negative statement? No. It's a positive one! Those who think otherwise are not fully prepared for life and will be taken aback with every turn in the road life offers them.

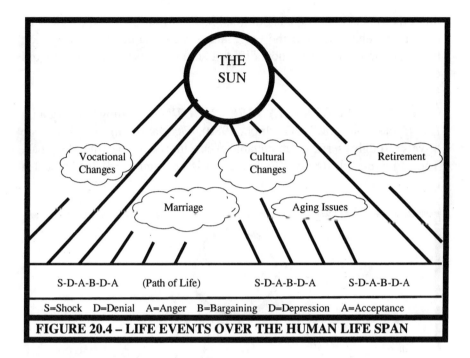

FIGURE 20.4 – LIFE EVENTS OVER THE HUMAN LIFE SPAN

In Figure 20.4, normal or predictable life events are illustrated as clouds. These block the sun from shining on our lives, as the impact of a serious event takes away the joy and happiness we experience when all is going well. To remain functional, one has to feel and traverse the event via The Grief Process.

The letters S, D, A, B, D, A, located on the path one chooses or gets exposed to in life, are the stages to The Grief Process: Shock, Denial, Anger, Bargaining, Depression, and Acceptance. Each one of these stages is like a door: one has to open them and proceed through each one in order to get on with their life.

If the doors are not opened and the process not completed — a Problem Loop will be created in order to generate a diversion from dealing with the situation. The Problem Loop dissipates when the feelings from the situation have passed or become adequately buried with an additional layer of confusion generated by the energy of the Loop.

In an immature emotional system, the feelings are stuffed, denied, or buried. (In a mature system, the activated behavior response has to have greater influence than the rising dislodged feelings in order to prevent the Problem Loop from occurring). As these behavior strategies are usually dysfunctional, the current crisis created by the Problem Loop becomes another issue the human has to resolve or work on, before he can heal from the activating event. Add an additional layer of issues created by the self-defeating behavior, onto the original pain each time the feelings are triggered, and you can see how difficult some of these issues are to work on.

LIFE IN "THE FAMILY LIFE CYCLE"   According to the Family Life Cycle (Carter & McGoldrick, 1980), each family in today's culture travels through a series of predictable events that occur over their life span. The following illustration (Figure 20.5) is an example of the impact it creates.

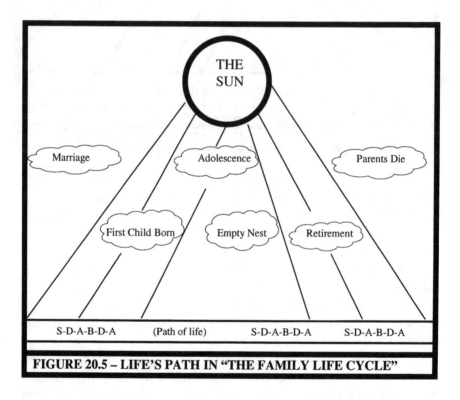

THE
SUN

Marriage   Adolescence   Parents Die

First Child Born   Empty Nest   Retirement

S-D-A-B-D-A   (Path of life)   S-D-A-B-D-A   S-D-A-B-D-A

FIGURE 20.5 – LIFE'S PATH IN "THE FAMILY LIFE CYCLE"

During the path of "The Family Life Cycle," individual members are bound to, and influenced by, their family of origin. In the process: they either adapt to its developmental challenges of creating a family, raising and launching its children, retirement and death — or — become mired in a process of maladaptation when its members either enmesh or disengage from one another instead of accomplishing individualization and healthy separation.

Unlike the personal life events an individual experiences alone, the above are traversed with the family, and resolved through the stages of the Grief Process.

IMPACT OF A CATASTROPHIC EVENT — The impact of a fatal event or natural disaster can overwhelm the individual's or family's ability to facilitate stress. Add this to the predictable events of one's life span, and the system can break down and may require outside help (therapy or support) to overcome the impact of the event(s).

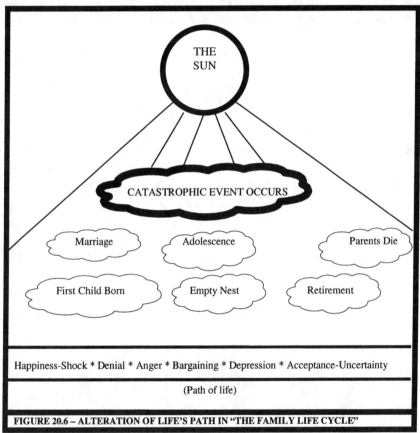

THE
SUN

CATASTROPHIC EVENT OCCURS

Marriage   Adolescence   Parents Die

First Child Born   Empty Nest   Retirement

Happiness-Shock * Denial * Anger * Bargaining * Depression * Acceptance-Uncertainty

(Path of life)

FIGURE 20.6 – ALTERATION OF LIFE'S PATH IN "THE FAMILY LIFE CYCLE"

These events can include: death of a child, premature death of a parent or grandparent, war, loss of a home, or a serious cultural change. When one of these occurs along with: the natural losses and events of the individual over his life span and the family through their cycle, there is a synergistic effect created as the loss from one event magnifies the pain from the next one that occurs. Figure 20.6 demonstrates its impact on the individual's life path.

In this process, it is as if another layer of clouds - these ones dark and impenetrable — has been added to the existing cluster that materializes over the average person's life span. These are natural breaks or thinning sections in the clouds that occur from the expected events. That is why one can see a ray of hope shimmer through the blackness of depression. With an unexpected event, as described previously, there are no such breaks. The darkness continues for more prolonged amounts of time, which gives one a sense that he is not going to pull out of the spiraling dive he is experiencing.

THE DYSFUNCTIONAL FAMILY - In the dysfunctional family life span, trauma never ends, as new events continuously occur, to keep the family out of balance. This cycle is never ending, for each new episode, is designed to cover or medicate the carnage of its predecessor.

On and on it goes adnauseum, until something happens to change the pattern. Maybe it's a family member who gets into therapy or comes in recovery. It could be an unexpected death or major illness that will no longer support the energy drain of the continuous Problem Loops. It might be as simple as age, in which one has tried enough to change the old way, and cannot continue to support the loss of energy due to the new limitations.

As you can see in Figure 20.7, the clouds are so thick and expansive that it prevents the light of hope from penetrating and illuminating one's life.

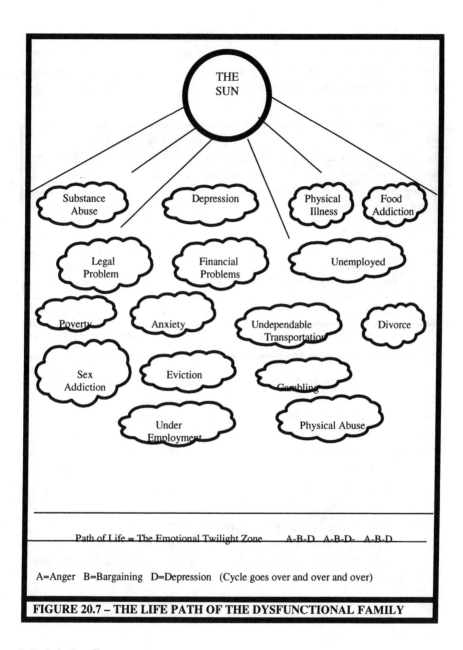

FIGURE 20.7 – THE LIFE PATH OF THE DYSFUNCTIONAL FAMILY

Multiple Stressors

When major issues prevail throughout one's life, or occur simultaneously, no time can be allotted to resolve any of the existing events, and
it leaves the individual stranded in The Emotional Twilight Zone of his
internal process. During this time, he bounces between the stages of anger,

bargaining, and depression in The Grief Process. Sometimes a person slips as far back as denial. During this phase, a new situation occurs — stops the processing of the event it interrupted — and the individual remains stuck at the level reached with that issue. Figure 20.8 is a visual presentation of the concept.

NUMBER ISSUE	STAGES OF THE GRIEF PROCESS				
	Denial	Anger	Bargaining	Depression	Acceptance
1ˢᵗ Issue : Depression	√	√	√	√	
2ⁿᵈ Issue : Substance Abuse	√				
3ʳᵈ Issue : Legal Encounters	√	√	√		
4ᵗʰ Problems Issue : Financial	√	√			
5ᵗʰ Issue : Unemployment	√	√	√		
6ᵗʰ Issue : Physical Abuse	√				
7ᵗʰ Issue : Gambling	√				
8ᵗʰ Issue : Eviction	√	√			
9ᵗʰ Issue : Poverty	√	√	√		
10ᵗʰ Issue : Divorce	√	√			

FIGURE 20.8 – IMPACT OF MULTIPLE STRESSORS ON RESOLVING EVENTS

During the chaos that prevails as multiple stressors breed, each issue is in flux, and rarely remains at rest. Their movement is usually influenced by the ebb and flow of the emotional impact of the issues or events that surround them. If some of the trauma abates — they can move forward; if it increases — they can regress. The forward progress indicated in Figure 20.8 is the highest gain they were able to achieve when the next one hit.

You now understand why some issues never seem to get resolved and the only way to change this process is to:

1ˢᵗ **Stop adding any new Jackpots to your life's path**
2ⁿ **Stop any addictive or compulsive/obsessive behavior**
3ʳᵈ **Focus on cleaning up one issue at a time. (As you free up one — others will naturally move forward.)**

In the issues illustrated in Figure 20.8, the order of importance is as follows:

1ˢᵗ Don't add any more issues. Sex, food, or toxic relationships are usually the next road one goes down if he experiences multiple stressors. They are natural, usually free (except food), and readily available.

2ⁿᵈ Stop the current obsessive/compulsive behaviors of substance abuse, gambling, and physical abuse.

3ʳᵈ Address the depression if it's major. Some depression will abate by itself as self-defeating behavior has ended. Medication may be needed if the current events are too overwhelming. Look at it (medication) as handrails to help you over a bumpy road. If the depression is physiological, the medication may be required for life. Some depression is normal (part of the Grief Process) and one may have to learn new ways of going through it. This is where therapy or a twelve-step program can help.

4ᵗʰ Look for a job. Some problems will dissipate once a person is working (financial problems, poverty, and unsafe domicile).

5ᵗʰ Take care of legal problems. If they were more urgent, they would take a higher priority on this scale. Example: if one had a court date in one week and didn't have representation, one would have to take immediate action and would move this to first place.

6ᵗʰ Clean up the residue of any issue that impedes one's current forward momentum in life.

A by-product of this process is maturity. It occurs as the individual stops acting out of his Child or Adolescent Ego State, takes responsibility for the part he played in his current self-defeating circumstances, and starts to take corrective action instead of wallowing in self-pity or blame.

ADAPTIVE PROCESS

In order for Mankind to continue, it has to adapt to the following changing conditions that occur over each generation's life span: individual health, family changes, cultural modifications, global conditions, vocational changes, one's own maturation, financial changes, self-image, roles, and expectations.

Without the flexibility to change in uncontrollable life-span situations, the individual will wither and die.

The Perceptual System

The human being's Perceptual System includes two processes:

1. **Physical Process** which takes in the external data
2. **Psychological Process** which orders it and gives it meaning

PHYSICAL PROCESS — The Physical Process includes all the senses: visual, auditory, tactile, olfactory (smell), and gustatory (taste), and includes the sections of the brain to which the senses connect.

COGNITIVE PROCESS — The raw data that is taken in through the senses is ordered into concepts by the psyche and given meaning. At this point, the process is rudimentary. The process becomes more complicated as the need to take action on the data becomes necessary. During this time, the material has to be filtered to determine what kind of response, if any, should be taken. It's here that the process becomes complicated, as previous experience becomes the colors that paint and weave our life's tapestry. It's also here that unresolved issues impact the decision-making process which determines the appropriate behavioral response to the processing data.

Figure 20.9 is a graphic illustration of both processes and in it we will look at The Psyche as a system:

1. **INTAKE** is through the senses
2. **FILTERS** come on line through the Child, Adolescent, and Adult
3. **THE DECISION MAKING PROCESS** happens in the Executive System
4. **DEPTH OF THE PROCESS** is the Conscious, Preconscious and Subconscious

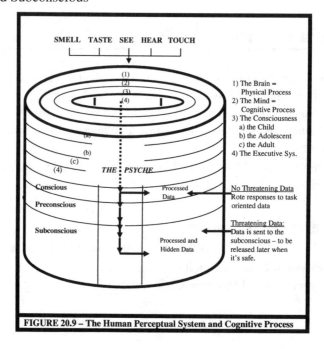

FIGURE 20.9 – The Human Perceptual System and Cognitive Process

REACT OR RESPOND This is the decision the Cognitive Process has to make on all data taken in that doesn't just require a rote response. When its task oriented, the behavioral response is an internalized motor sequence, which is performed automatically, and takes very little cognition.

When it is not task oriented, the entire psyche comes on line to interpret, give meaning, and respond to the incoming data. It's at this time that feelings and emotions come alive and bring the colors and texture to the event. It's in this tapestry that insight becomes complicated as life becomes richer. It's in this richness that living....consisting of physical survival and procreation....transcends the ordinary and becomes life. As one's immersion in life becomes deeper, his colors become brighter, his life's tapestry more beautiful, and his ability to interpret and respond to internal dialogue, feelings, and emotions becomes extremely complex. The complexity of the process and the fear it generates is less fearful when the individual has grown with the process, understands himself, and can work with his internal structure.

What makes this process so fascinating is the myriad of responses one situation can evoke. As you begin to explore the possibilities, you can see them occurring at several sublevels, depending on which Issue became triggered. At the beginning, it's enough to drive you crazy — so much happening, trying to get a handle on it, and feeling overwhelmed when the desired insight is not accomplished. Don't despair! It takes time.

The Language Path of the Human Brain

The following illustrations are an example of the process a triggered reaction travels when it meanders through the filters of the ego states, as the consciousness tries to determine a course of action after the Psyche has:

1. **Ordered the data into concepts**
2. **Determined the data warranted attention**

```
TRIGGER

AN AUTHORITY FIGURE MAKES AN UNCOMPLIMENTARY REMARK
WITH A SARCASTIC VOICE AND AN INDIFFERENT ATTITUDE.

SURFACE LEVEL RESPONSE:    1) Shut down and listen
                           2) Come back at him and defend
                           3) Speak up to ground him with facts
                              and set a boundary.

INTERNAL RESPONSE:         1) The Child becomes scared
                           2) The Adolescent becomes angry
                           3) The Critical Adult is activated
                           4) The Adult becomes confused about:
                              a) Which course to take with the
                                 authority figure
                              b) Why it happened
                              c) How to take care of himself
                                 internally while attending to an
                                 external situation
```

FIGURE 20.10 – INITIAL RESPONSE TO NEGATIVE EXTERNAL STIMULI

The first illustration, Figure 20.10, is the initial surface and internal responses of the trigger. In it, are the basic external behaviors usually displayed by the ego states, and the internal reactions usually observed or reported by the recipient. All of these generally coincide with an ego state.

```
INTERNAL SUBLEVEL ISSUES

                          THE CHILD
SUBLEVEL ONE:    First - plays old tapes from his primary caregivers
SUBLEVEL TWO:    Second - transfers all of this power to authority figures for
                 they are the cultural counterparts of the parents

                       THE ADOLESCENT
SUBLEVEL ONE:    First – plays old tapes from his primary caregivers
SUBLEVEL TWO:    Then – transfers the power to authority figures
SUBLEVEL THREE:  Then – rebels against the cultural parental icons
SUBLEVEL FOUR:    He also rebels as a normal developmental process

                     THE CRITICAL ADULT
SUBLEVEL ONE:    When activated berates all the ego states:  Ridicules the Child –
                 Taunts the Adolescent – Reprimands the Nurturing Adult
                     THE NURTURING ADULT
SUBLEVEL ONE :   Soothes the Child
                 Redirects the Adolescent
                 Addresses the Critical Adult and tries to set boundaries
                 Assures himself that he can handle it
SUBLEVEL TWO:    Helps the Child to sort out what he is feeling
                 Encourages the Adolescent to work in conjunction with him
                 Validates the intention of the Critical Adult's message
SUBLEVEL THREE:  Helps the Child to go through his feelings
                 Informs the Adolescent about why he reacts, and teaches
                 options
                 Quiets the Critical Adult by not engaging, uses the message as
                 input, and says thank you for caring
```

FIGURE 20.11 INTERNAL RESPONSES TO THREATENING EXTERNAL STIMULI

The second illustration, Figure 20.11, depicts the various sublevels the triggered issue can affect within the individual. If you have two or more issues stirred up by the stimuli, the results can lead to overload as too much comes up at the same time, and overwhelms the person's usual coping strategies.

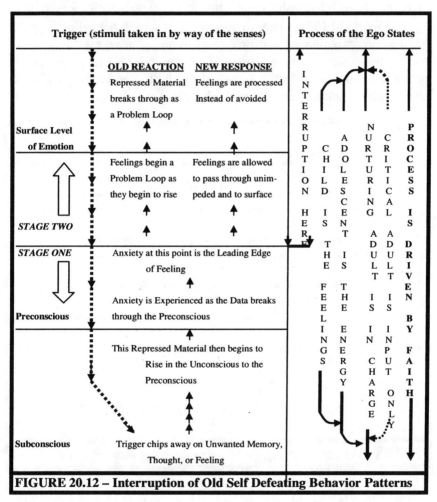

FIGURE 20.12 – Interruption of Old Self Defeating Behavior Patterns

The third illustration, Figure 20.12, demonstrates how the adaptive process becomes the predominant coping strategy when Stage Two is interrupted and:

1. **A behavior loop is *not* created to block the emerging feelings**
2. **Feelings are allowed to surface at the conscious level and become processed**

It's at this point that the individual has grown up, "cut the apron strings," become a separate person from his family of origin, and is able to facilitate life's uncertainties as an "emotionally mature responsible adult." He is also able to identify and secure his wants, needs, and desires in an adaptive fashion, and to have healthy boundaries with the ability to maintain them in various relationships, including intimate ones with a love object.

In Figure 20.13, the stress is not masked with a behavior loop; the feelings are experienced and processed in an adaptive fashion and the human grows through the experience as it enriches his life. At this point, he is a fully empowered adult, on task through life's endeavors, self-actualizing and accomplishing his spiritual goals.

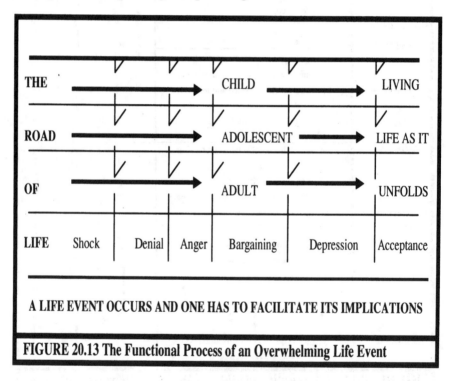

A LIFE EVENT OCCURS AND ONE HAS TO FACILITATE ITS IMPLICATIONS

FIGURE 20.13 The Functional Process of an Overwhelming Life Event

ASSIGNMENT 32: Where are you on the road of transformation? Are you free from Problem Loops? Know adaptive solutions to life's problems? Write a list of your issues, problems or stressors, and dilemmas or problem loops. With each; 1) dialogue with your Child, Adolescent, and Adult to see how they think, feel, and want to act, then, 2) identify where your Child, Adolescent, and Adult are, in resolving the issue or problem using the stages of the grief process as indicators. Next write a list of successful strategies you used in the past in similar situations, another list of problem loops you got into in order to avoid the situation, and a final list of ways you tried over and over in order to fix things and they never seemed to work no matter how hard you tried. When you finish the assignment you will have a definitive assessment of how far along you are to becoming an **emotionally mature responsible adult** who can respond to life's problems with appropriate strategies instead of reacting with problem loops or inappropriate behavior.

REMEMBER IN THE PROCESS THAT LIFE IS A JOURNEY AND NOT A DESTINATION, THAT YOU DO THE BEST YOU CAN WITH WHAT YOU GOT, AND ALL YOU HAVE TO DO IS TO LEARN FROM YOUR MISTAKES IN ORDER TO GROW. *BE GENTLE WITH YOURSELF—YOU DESERVE IT!*

Life In The Problem: Are you still doing the "same old — same old" and can't understand why things don't change in your life? Do you view life as a problem? If yes....why? Do you know what path your Problem Loop takes? Why you create them? How they are beneficial to you? Can you put your Problem Loop on paper? Is your life a series of Problem Loops? Do you know how the internal structure affects the Problem Loop, Child, Adolescent, and Adult? Do you know what triggers the Loop, how it rises, and what behavior comes from it?

Life In The Solution: Do you view life experiences as opportunities to grow? Can you handle life as it unfolds or do you try to control it? Can you make adjustments to your plans when life situations mandate it? Do you understand that there are anticipated problems that can happen to you and your family over your life span? If yes....how do you handle them? Be Specific. What have you done in the past to go through traumatic events and remain functional? What do you do to take care of yourself when hit with multiple stressors? Do you understand what goes on inside of you when massive stress occurs? Do you react or respond? Do you have an adaptive process? Do you understand the language of the brain and how it impacts your behavior? Are you an emotionally mature, responsible adult?

SUMMARY

Chapter Twenty is an exacting chapter. In it, one will be able to succinctly review the transformation process. In the process, one views life as an opportunity to grow, doesn't create Problem Loops to hide behind, and develops adaptive solutions to life's problems that will normally occur over the human being's life span.

When one traverses life problems as an emotionally mature, responsible adult who can create non-problematic solutions in a functional manner, one remains true to his self concepts. He maintains his values, morals and ethics, and will not give up his honesty and integrity. He won't violate his or others' boundaries, and will maintain high standards of acceptable behavior. He will follow all these principles when dealing with his family, interacting in a relationship, or negotiating with the culture and its designated institutions. He will not violate his spiritual principles nor allow another person, place, or thing (including himself) to divert him from his primary spiritual goals.

CASE STUDY

Bill is the 29-year-old recovering addict who relapsed after two years of good clean time, and came into therapy to find out why. At the initial session, Bill disclosed that his dad was a chronic alcoholic who physically abused his wife and children on a daily basis. When questioned about being an ACOA (Adult Child of an Alcoholic), Bill replied, "I know I have those ACOA issues, and every time I tried to work through them in the past, it was too painful and all I wanted to do was use."

Further along in session, Bill revealed that he had a difficult time putting clean time together his first two years of becoming abstinent. He would put 30, 60, or 90 days together and then use. No matter how hard he tried to stay clean — he couldn't.

Then he met his current wife, and all that changed. He remained clean, earned raises when his production increased as he stopped using in the afternoon, and was just promoted to foreman. During this time, they were able to purchase a modest home. And just two weeks ago his wife told him that she was pregnant.

Bill was immediately placed in group therapy because of his involvement with NA, and the kind of work I wanted to do with him would be most effective and economical in a group setting.

Bill was placed in a psycho-dynamic open-ended group, which included experiential therapy, and was comprised of members in each state of the group process. The average length of stay for the members was three months, in which they met once per week for two and a half hours. Most of them had individual therapy with me.

In the first month of group, Bill was given education of the model we use in therapy and allowed to participate in other members' psychodramas. During this time, Bill became aware of his own internal structure and began to identify and separate its major components. It was also mandatory to complete the first five steps and was an essential requirement to join the group. Part of this assignment included a professional Fourth Step that was comprised of a 500-question inventory which included major areas from his childhood to the present and encompassed important issues that ranged from his using to his sexuality. His Fifth Step had to be done with his sponsor and any unresolved issues brought back to group.

Bill completed all his assignments, actively participated in group, and retained his commitment with his primary twelve-step program, during the first four weeks of group. In group, he began to do some work with his internal structure in order to identify some of the dynamics of his using. He was fascinated at the process, although progressed very cautiously. It was during this time that he began to recall lost memories and feelings. The first time it happened it was like an electric shock to his body and he shut down. In processing the event with the group, he was able to verbalize that something "bad" happened to him, his little kid (Child) was terrified, and his Adolescent was angry as hell, but didn't know why.

This was the first time an issue surfaced that didn't directly attach itself to his substance abuse or the usual ACOA issues that rise in recovery or treatment.

It was now month two, and as a result of the above disclosure, he was asked to write a letter to his Child about the fear, and to use his non-dominate hand to have the Child reply. While he was working in group the following week, he blurted out that he was sexually abused by an uncle when he was nine.

Bill did a lot of work healing his Inner Child from the abuse he endured. It was during this time the effects of his dad's alcoholism and Mom's emotional distance surfaced. He remembered how lost and alone he felt when Dad drank, fought with Mom, and would then begin to physically abuse her. The memories came back rapidly once they began, and he was flooded with feelings as they opened. Between the support Bill was given by the group, his sponsor, and his wife, he did not relapse or leave therapy.

During this process, Bill recognized the underlying pain which his addiction medicated, how he had to shut down, stuff, deny, and minimize his feelings in order not to become overwhelmed and die (the Child feels this), because of being raised in the war-zone-like environment of an alcoholic home and being sexually abused.

He also discovered how he shut down or manipulated his feelings when he had a problem with himself, the job, his wife, or a life event. This dysfunctional stress-reduction system was halted as Bill went through his feelings with the group instead of running away, and he began to develop emotional maturity. In this maturation, Bill was able to identify, label, express, and process his feelings instead of being a scared and lost little boy who just avoided them because he thought they were going to kill him.

As Bill went through this painful part of his recovery, he was also entering month three of therapy, and began to get angry. This came as a surprise to Bill, and he disclosed that his cravings were beginning to increase. It was at this point that we began to work with the Adolescent. Bill essentially did the same work with his Adolescent that he did with his Child: wrote him a letter with the Adolescent responding with his dominant hand, worked on the results in group, and processed — until it was further revealed that he had also been sexually abused by other males because of the places his increased drug use had taken him. During the time we were working on his Adolescent, it was revealed he had also questioned his sexuality because of the pleasure he experienced during the acts.

Bill was able to relieve the obsession with his sexuality through the Sexual Development Model I use with sexually abused people. It's simple, effective, answers many questions, and quiets the mind. Once the mind is quiet and it comes up at another level, it can be revisited at a higher level of awareness.

My main task during early recovery is to ground my clients in today's reality, work on any issue that takes them out of their day, identify their internal structure and begin to work with it, teach them how to use the results of therapy and integrate the new concepts in program to their everyday life. In this process they will acquire the rudiments of remaining abstinent from all forms of mood-altering substances and have choices in their decision-making process. The reason I offer this explanation is be-

cause some issues do not become resolved quickly. They can be temporarily satisfied — not important in the moment — and open up at a later
date. The important part of the unfolding is that they know themselves
enough and acquire the skills to facilitate them in an adaptive manner
when they open up again. This is what was done for Bill.

Month three of therapy was used to work on his Adolescent. During
this time, he discovered the true impact that using had on him, when,
during psychodrama, his Child Ego State was dialoguing with his Adolescent Ego State and revealed how afraid he was of him when he used. The
Adolescent confessed that it was the only way he knew how to protect the
Child and was appalled how the results impacted him. When I pulled him
out of the drama, placed him as an observer, and had the original alters of
the Child and Adolescent repeat their dialogue, Bill could see what damage his using had really done to him, and stepped in to dialogue with his
alters. With direction, he was able to determine their needs and made a
promise to fulfill them in an appropriate way.

In month four of group, we applied the gains made in therapy as insight into any self-defeating behavior that arose. It was during this time
that the Critical Adult was quieted and the Nurturing Adult bloomed.

What we had done for Bill was to fill in the void left by his family of
origin:

1. We provided an emotionally safe environment in which to be and
   work
2. We validated his feelings and affirmed his right to be alive
3. We taught him about himself and gave him a model to work with
4. We helped him to not only reclaim his lost feelings, but to
   identify, label, express, and process his present ones
5. We taught and modeled new adaptive stress-reduction skills
6. We gave him insight on how to identify where he was with his
   issues by teaching him the Grief Process
7. We helped him increase his spirituality and connectivity to God
   by the faith he received through watching others grow in the
   group
8. We loved and accepted him unconditionally

We didn't do anything for Bill that he couldn't do for himself. We
only taught him new skills which he had to work in order to progress in
group. He did it all — we merely supported him through it. The group
stood in for his parents who were not able to be there for him because of
their enmeshment with alcoholism. If they could be in therapy, gain the

same skills, identify and resolve some of their issues, be there for themselves, THEY COULD HAVE BEEN THERE FOR BILL THE WAY HE WANTED, NEEDED, AND WAS ENTITLED TO! They weren't. That's sad. The good news is that Bill can now do it for himself. A by-product of no longer being needy is that he can now go back and claim the love they gave him. During his time of need as a child, the love was inadequate. In adulthood it's healing.

As of this year, Bill has been clean and sober for over five years, has a stable marriage, is doing well on his job, and is going back to school to pursue the education that was interrupted by his drug addiction.

WHERE ARE THEY NOW

If you're wondering what's happened to the subjects I used in my case studies . . . remember . . . they were composites. The following are composites as well. Most have positive endings because they stuck it out in therapy of a twelve-step program. None are perfect because life is not perfect — nor do they have to be perfect. Most did not have serious abuse. If they had, the process would be longer, and the prognosis guarded as it was for the few that couldn't adjust their present behavioral strategies and didn't make it. All were cognitively intact and other than a little bipolar behavior, did not have any serious psychiatric problems like acute schizophrenia, severe paranoia, delusions, or hallucinations. Some had a behavioral psychiatric diagnosis, although the behavior was not viewed as pathology. The presenting behavior was reframed to a survival skill and when it was brought into balance — the psychiatric symptoms disappeared.

The work each accomplished in therapy — Jump-started them in a twelve-step program. Each was ahead of most who only attended a program because they had the benefit of *a fully trained, highly credentialed, well knowledgeable therapist who could skillfully help identify their issues and process, possessed a model of treatment which facilitated healing and skill building, and imparted the necessary inter and intra personal skills in order to insure success in relationships with self, others and the larger culture.* Treatment that doesn't cover these basics is ineffective at best.

The professional process usually saves several years of struggling in early recovery when one is only in a twelve-step program because newcomers are novices who lack the skills of a professional or a "long timer" in program. It takes a lot of knowledge to ferret out the necessary information or glean the appropriate strategies to identify and change self-defeating behavior.

Change is a process. It takes time, diligence, and skill. The beginner only has faith and hope. The rest is missing. I've been at meetings, heard someone's struggle, and gave him his answer. Even with the answer, the newcomer lacks the skill base to apply the answer. One of the prime reasons for writing this book is to help him get the skill base early and be able to apply the answers.

DARLENE is doing well today. She attends a sexual abuse survivors group in a twelve-step program, has sought some specialized therapy for the intrusive thoughts that began to surface after the sexual abuse was disclosed, and checks-in once every three months for a "recharge." During this time, Darlene presents as having a sense of humor, can laugh at herself when she gets "crazy" (confused and doesn't know what to do about it) as she starts to exhibit old behavior and doesn't know she's doing it. Her group gives her plenty of reality checks, love and acceptance. She does well with her daughter, doesn't get too restrictive, maintains her male relationships, and remains internally congruent. On a bad day, she has the skills to mediate any internal confusion without hurting herself or others.

Darlene is healing. In time, she will be healed from the wounds that were inflicted on her while being sexually abused. She is blessed, for if she had reacted to the sexual abuse in a more destructive way other than dissociation — she would have created another layer of guilt and shame to work through. If this had happened, she would have had to create another problem loop to cover up the pain of her reaction, which would have given her two layers to work through instead of one. I suspect that this has happened to most substance abusers, food addicts, compulsive gamblers, sexaholics and career criminals.

JOAN remains an executive in a large city firm, loves her job, and is working on remaining a competent woman in a love relationship — the same person she is when she works. Joan did a lot of work in therapy, attended a twelve-step program, and is trying to apply all she has learned in each, not to "go down the same roads" she did before with men.

Joan is now taking her time with relationships. She is not letting her Child or Adolescent pick out her men, although, she will take their input. Joan has discovered that she lacks self-knowledge because she spent so much time worrying about the man in her life that she totally ignored her own.

She is currently going slowly with men, getting to know them as friends, before she decides if she wants a deeper relationship with them . . . based on her needs and not just what he wants. She has experimented sexually, doesn't like the residue feelings of the encounter, and has decided to abstain for now.

BILL is a good example of the person who enters a twelve-step program for relief from his compulsions, finds initial success (abstinence), and then relapses after a period of time. People like Bill gain a rudimentary understanding of the program, work it to their ability, and don't get to the underlying reasons for their addictions. During the period of abstinence, life becomes manageable, good things begin to happen and positive feelings are experienced. At this time, their feelings level is increased, they become more vulnerable because their feelings are closer to the surface, and they become susceptible to the rising pain from unresolved feelings. Most of this is an unconscious process and because the trauma was never addressed, they are not even aware of what's going on internally. Like the others, Bill was there (relapsed) before he knew he left. With therapy or a good Fourth Step, one can change the outcome.

Bill is now clean and sober for seven years, attends three twelve-step programs, is actively involved in service, doing well on his job, attending college and happily married. He is working through his ACOA issues, resolved any questions about his sexuality, and enjoys good insight into himself and others.

JOHN is typical of those who come into therapy without life-threatening issues. People like John usually have a current event that has taxed their usual repertoire of coping strategies, lack the ability to facilitate it in an adaptive manner, and it has happened before under other circumstances that they have been able to handle. This is different from a sudden trauma (death, war, divorce, loss of a highly valued job, etc.) which the individual has no control over. Usually the trauma is attached to unresolved issues from their family of origin which can include: emotional disengagement or enmeshment, abandonment, over-involvement or under-involvement, failure to complete healthy separation (cut the apron strings) or the individualization process in which they become separate from their family of origin and still belong.

John's problems were overwhelming to him because he was old enough to be a grownup, but in his parents' eyes he was just a child, and when in the presence of authority figures, he felt like one.

In therapy, John discovered that his lack of advocating for himself with his parents or authority figures left him vulnerable to weight gain, sickness, shame and low self-esteem. As he gained insight and acquired new skills he began to complete developmental tasks he missed in childhood. It was during this time that he was able to acquire healthy separation from his parents and his self-esteem increased.

Since treatment, John's life has improved. He feels better about himself; his parents are less intrusive, and still able to press his buttons when he loosens up his boundaries. John is still not satisfied completely with his life, although states that it's the best it's ever been. He still "resists" joining a twelve-step program and promises when the time is right he will "check it out."

DENNIS was like Bill, had the rudiments of a program, limited self awareness, and relaxed when the feelings of past trauma began to be released because his ability to be vulnerable was increasing.

In therapy, Dennis was able to transcend these limitations, gained insight into himself and others, increased his emotional maturity and stress-reduction strategies, and became able to facilitate the increased pain he was experiencing due to his increased authenticity.

Because of his increased knowledge, Dennis is clean and sober today, is actively involved in service, and attends ACOA (Adult Child Of Alcoholics) and ALANON meetings, in addition to AA & NA. He states that although AA is his "Primary Program," drugs will trigger his compulsion to drink so he attends NA. If he doesn't attend ACOA, his issues will drive him to drink. He goes to ALANON because he still carries resentment toward his alcoholic father. Dennis also checks-in every six months.

VALERIE is a successful businesswoman today. She was able to use the ego strength of being a successful wife and mother to launch her second career. In the process, she facilitated "The Empty Nest Syndrome," renegotiated her relationship with her husband, reframed her self concepts, and is moving on to self-actualize in the business world.

Valerie was fun to work with. She had many good qualities and was a valuable asset to the group. Once she recognized her fear, she was able to face it and move on.

In treatment, Valerie was considered developmentally stuck, because of the cultural changes toward stay-at-home moms that were common through the Sixties, and now due to precarious economic times, is getting to be rare. Once the cultural shock was faced, and the feelings of the sense of betrayal she felt toward the culture were resolved, she was able to redefine herself according to her self concepts and not the expectation of the culture, and was able to get on with her life.

JOE is no longer married to his emotionally unavailable wife. He reports in a phone call to me about six months ago that he was still in therapy, actively involved in a twelve-step program, and engaged to a woman who has the capacity to be there for him. Joe also reports that it's not always easy and sometimes he reacts to old tapes instead of the actual event. The good part is that the reactions are less, he doesn't feel crazy anymore, and is working hard on eliminating them. He sounded terrific and all I could offer was to check out the reaction being a boundary by The Adolescent if the reactions persisted.

MARY is currently living in an ALF (Assisted Living Facility) which is common in Florida due to the transient nature of the population. She is leading an active life, no longer in depression, was able to overcome some mild physical set-backs to her health, maintains a good relationship with her children, and is still taking trips up North to see her family.

CONSTANCE refused to work in the program and was discharged. When she returned home, she continued to remain in a deep depression and died. It was almost like she lost her ability to live, gave up, and died: how tragic and certainly not necessary. There were three ways women like this ended up 1) as described above 2) died in an accident, and 3) died of a physical disease (cancer or heart disease).

STAN also refused to work in the program and was discharged. When he returned home he also remained in depression by watching TV, having a "few" drinks at nighttime, and becoming mean when someone tried to change his routine. Stan died shortly after some minor surgery that had no mortality rate. It was as if he lost the ability to live, gave up, and died.

POLLY is married today to her "Soul Mate," checks-in every now and then, and is a faithful member of a twelve-step program. Her family still struggles. Polly reports that she is very comfortable in a twelve-step meeting, and her group has taken on the significance of a surrogate family when her biological family becomes too disruptive to interact with. Polly further states that her group has given her much support and understanding. Their unconditional love has also helped her to be more empathetic and available to her family without losing herself. She also exclaims that her twelve-step program reinforces all that she learned about herself in therapy. They use different words but the meaning is the same.

BRENT & SANDY are still married, continue to work on the problems life sends them, are happy with themselves and each other, maintain involvement in a twelve-step program, and check-in with me every now and then on an "as needed" basis. They are able to work on and resolve their problems in an amiable fashion, keep the lines of communication open between them, and enjoy a high degree of intimacy in their couple ship. Both respect the other's boundaries. Neither blames the other for the problems that life sent them (both enjoy life as it unfolds and feel that problems are in life's natural order). Neither is a vexation to the other's spirit and thereby maintains a high degree of spirituality between them in order for God to guide them in their individual quests.

TANYA is symbolic of the teens I've treated. Their success was high because it was a one-year program with high family involvement as all were mandated to treatment by the Juvenile Court System. If families balked or withdrew, we went back to the judge, who held them in contempt if they did not comply. The only exceptions were the 16½ or 17-year-olds whose families were so dysfunctional that they would actually impede treatment and those residents were given independent living skills instead of working on family reunion.

Most of the teens who graduated the program are doing well today, did not receive any more criminal charges (some had minor scrapes with the law) and are attempting to have a normal life like you and me in that they have started vocational careers, educational pursuits, and families. One has died due to gang related activities. None are perfect. All struggle with the same life problems that we all do. Most are using socially prescribed ways to solve those problems without the use and abuse of mood altering substances.

EPILOGUE

How do you feel? Sad because of the things that happened to you; Happy because your questions were answered; Hopeful because there is a light at the end of the tunnel; Angry for being violated; Relieved to know it wasn't your fault; Frustrated because of lost time; Invigorated because it's never too late to heal; Inadequate because it's hard implementing the changes; Confident you can persevere through the change process; Intimidated by the changes that have to occur; Empowered to make the necessary changes? All your feelings are wonderful. They are the tapestry of life. Without them, there would be no color in our lives. Remember . . . there is no right or wrong feelings . . . THEY JUST ARE.

How is your relationship with yourself? Do you understand your internal structure and its process after reading this book? Is your Child fearful, cautious, or excited? Is your Adolescent angry, suspicious, or open to change? Where is your Adult with each? Is your Critical Adult shaming The Child, taunting The Adolescent and berating The Adult, or is he quiet? Is your Nurturing Adult affirming The Child, validating The Adolescent, setting healthy boundaries and limits on each, taking in new data to supplement the skewed information they received from less than perfect caregivers, and redirecting the Critical Adult? It's important to know who is dominant because they are leading you down life's path. Success is when an emotionally mature, responsible adult is in charge and can negotiate life's vicissitudes in a functional and adaptive manner without the use of Problem Loops.

How is your self-knowledge? Can you identify your issues? Can you use The Grief Process to identify/determine where you are toward resolving them? Can you recognize where each of your ego states are in this process? Are you stuck in the Emotional Twilight Zone? I know you are not totally lost in the darkness anymore. This book and its concepts illuminate many dark corners.

How is your relationship with your love object? Are you now a fully empowered adult, or does your Child or Adolescent pick your mate? Can your relationship deepen because of the information given in this book? When the concept of spirituality in relationships between partners was presented — did it change the way you view your past or present relationships? Do you enjoy honesty and integrity within your couple ship, or does anything go?

How is your relationship with God? Has it improved? Do you feel different or more connected? Is God more personal to you? Are you more empowered with God knowing you are a part of Him and not just a helpless and hopeless Child?

How are your relationships on the job? Do you see differently or have additional filters due to what you read in this book? Did you recreate your family of origin or are you "drawn" to a particular work environment because of a dysfunctional background? How can you change or make your vocational life more pleasant based on what you learned from this book about yourself or others?

Some questions from the author to the reader: Has this book helped you? How? What would you wish to see added to this book? What would you like to see expanded (I have my own ideas)? What kind of book would you want me to write next? Do you have any questions you want me to answer? Do you disagree with anything I wrote and why? Do you see any of my concepts more clearly than I do? Explain. Have you done anything

My last word (thank God). This book is not the "end all." It's only a beginning. Some will need professional help, some will do it in a twelve-step program, some will do it on faith or in combination with self-help or therapy. This book was designed to help you to help yourself, and to enhance the professional helper's skill base in order to be a more effective clinician when they are treating you. I feel that I have done my job well in writing this book. I know that I abuse Standard Written English, but feel I am a good communicator. God has validated that for me. You, the reader, are the final judge of that. I hope I've lived up to your expectations and pray your journey has unfolded in front of you as mine has for me. If this has occurred . . . like my life . . . your life is now open, bright and warm.

MAY THE FORCE BE WITH YOU!

REQUEST FOR INFORMATION

As part of my next book I need to solicit information from you in order to validate what I see as a societal trend – grandparents raising their grown children's – children. I deliberately wrote it this way because according to the family systems theory I follow in my practice, the cultural values I was raised with by my parents, and how I raised my own children; *PARENTS ARE SUPPOSED TO RAISE THEIR OWN CHILDREN* with grandparents being a support system to their grown children. *At no time does a grandparent try to gain control of the upbringing of their grandchildren because they disagree with the religion, life style, or the parenting style . . . their grown children decide to raise their children with. Nor should they use their grandchildren as pawns in a game of self-seeking because they need a purpose in life, have unresolved childhood and marital issues, deficiencies in their past parenting styles of how they raised their children, are lonely, need or have too much money.*

The trend is disturbing to me and to have healthy families, *who raise healthy children and launch functional adults who have good morals, healthy respect for themselves, others, and the culture; are civic-minded – thereby responsible to their community and the country in general; and vocationally competent with a healthy work ethic . . . WE HAVE TO REVERSE THE TREND BECAUSE THE DAMAGE I SEE OCCURING TO THE CHILDREN, THE PARENTS AND THE FAMILY AS A UNIT . . . IS DEVESTATING TO ALL . . . AND WILL TAKE ANOTHER GENERATION TO HEAL FROM THE DEVESTATION IT CAUSED . . . PROVIDING THE TREND IS REVERSED IN THIS GENERATION!*

I would like to address the observation in my next book because the issue is part of its theme. The information I'm soliciting from you, is about the role your parents play in raising your children and maybe you can cover the following questions in your reply:

1. Are your parents supportive of the ways you raise your children or do they disagree with your methods.
2. Are you in a power struggle with your parents on how to raise your children?
3. Do they support your position with your children when your children disagree with you, or do they openly disagree, undermine your authority, and come in between you and your children?
4. Do your parents tell you they know what's best for your children?
5. If you were raised in a dysfunctional home, does your parent(s) have euphoric recall, and forget the damage they did to you and

your siblings when you were being raised?

6. Do they *now* "walk on water" and know what's best for you and/ or your children because they have some recovery, therapy, finally got divorced, or their acting out spouse died or left, and the "good" parent is remarried and currently enjoying a healthy lifestyle?

7. Do you pay a price for help with child care and take an emotional battering or lose control of your children, or is help with child care given in a loving way, with your values, limits, and boundaries respected when they help you?

8. Did your parents have a good relationship with their parents or are they :

   a) Working out their childhood issues on you by blaming you for what you are *doing "to" you children* **OR** *what you are not doing "for" them,* when in reality it's their issues surfacing because it didn't occur in their childhood and they still haven't resolved the issue with their parents or within themselves?

   b) Are they mixing up, you as a child with your children, because your children mirror you when you were your children's ages, and are they reacting in an irrational way because of it? This happens when they blame you for something they failed to do for you, or failed to protect you from, when you were a child . . . demand you do it now for your children even though you disagree with it . . . and then call you a bad parent when you won't comply with their wishes. This can make you crazy if you don't know where it comes from.

9. Did one of your parents call a child abuse agency and accuse you of doing to your children, what they did to you or your siblings when you were growing up. This can also happen if they accuse you of "failing to protect", when in reality they failed to protect you, and in a further reality, their parents failed to protect them.

10. Are you like one of your parents when they were your present age (looks, mannerisms, habits, speech) and does your other parent blame you for their faults because you are similar to them? Mom would say you are acting like dad! Dad would say you are just like mom! Either could accuse you of being like grandma or grandpa. This would present as being blamed for being emotionally or physically abusive because one of your parents was like that. Sometimes it's the emotionally abusive parent, who was a rage-a-holic, now sees you raise your voice when you talk to you children, and accuses you of emotional abuse.

11. If child protective services was involved did they:
    a)Investigate the complaint impartially?
    b)Did they listen to you and take action on what you said?
    c)Did they violate your civil and legal rights?
    d)Did they abuse you?
    e)Did you loose your children?
    f)If you parents called the agency – did they get custody?
    g)Did your parents break up your family or your marriage?
    h)Did the custody process give them financial gain or did it allow
       them to over- indulge their grandchildren in a way that would
       never be possible without custody and the subsequent financial
       gain, or, the threat of going to a child abuse agency.

PLEASE SEND THE REQUESTED INFORMATION TO:

Lou Block

P.O. Box 6405

Spring Hill, FL 34611

Or

http://www/formorethanwords.com

I'll try to answer as many questions as my schedule permits. A written reply will require an SASE. Any questions I give will be generalized only, according to what I usually see in therapy, and may not be specific to your circumstances.

This statement would be Informed Consent in Florida and any other answer, more specific to your situation, would require a therapeutic relationship, which is considerably more in depth than an author-to-reader one.

REFERENCES

Abbott, D.W., & Mitchell, J.E. (1993). Antidepressants vs. psychotherapy in the treatment of bulimia nervosa. *Psychopharmacology Bulletin, 29,* 115-119.

Abramson, L.Y., Seligman, M.E., & Teasdale, J. (1978). Learned helplessness in humans: Critique and reformulation. *Journal of Abnormal Psychology, 87,* 49-79.

Ackerman, N. (1956). Interlocking pathologies in family relationships. In Rado & G. Daniels (Eds.), *Changing Concepts in psychoanalytic medicine* New York: Grune & Stratton.

_____ (1958). *The Psychodynamics of Family Life.* New York: Basic Books.

_____(1966). *Treating the Troubled Family.* New York: Basic Books.

Ackerman, N.W. (1970). *Family Therapy in Transition.* Boston: Little Brown.

Ackerman, R.J. (1987). *Children of Alcoholics: A guidebook for educators, the rapists, and parents. (3rd edition).* Homes Beach, Florida: Learning Publications.

Al-Anon Family Groups (1985). *Alateen- Hope for children of alcoholics.* New York: World Service.

_____ (1993). *Al-Anon's twelve steps and traditions.* New York: World Service.

_____ (1995). *How Al-Anon works for families and friends of alcoholics.* Virginia Beach, VA: World Services.

_____ (1996). *Courage to be me - Alateen - Living with Alcoholics.* New York: World Service.

Alcoholics Anonymous (1987). *The Big Book: The Basic text of Alcoholics Anonymous.* New York: World Services Inc..

_____ (1987). *Twelve steps and twelve traditions.* New York: World Services.

Alder, A. (1949). *Understanding human nature.* New York: Permabooks. (Originally published in 1918)

_____ (1964). *A Social Interest: A challenge to mankind.* New York: Capricorn Books.

Alexander, M.J., Craig, J.J., MacDonald, J., Haugland, G. (1994). Dual diagnosis in a state psychiatric facility: Risk factors, correlates, and phenomenology of use. *The American Journal on addictions, 3 (4),* 314-324.

American College Testing Foundation (1984). *Discover: A computer based career development and counselor support system.* Iowa City, IA: American College Testing Foundation.

American Psychiatric Association. (1994). *Diagnostic and Statistical Manual of Mental Disorders, 4th ed.* Washington, D.C.: American Association Press.

Baer, L., Jenike, M.A., Ricciardi, J., Holland, A.D., Seymour, R.J., Minichiello, W.E., & Buttolph, M.L. (1990). Personality disorders in patients with obsessive-compulsive disorders. *Archives of General Psychiatry, 47,* 826-832.

Bandler, R. & Grinder , J. (1979). *Frogs into Princes.* Moab, UT: Real People Press.

Bandura, A. (1977). *Social learning theory.* Englewood Cliffs, NJ: Prentice-Hall.

Bauer, L.O., Yehuda, R., Meyer, R.E., Giller, Jr., E.G. (1992). Effects of a family history of alcoholism an autonomic, neuroendocrine, and subjective reactions to alcohol. *The American journal on addictions, 1 (2),* 168-176.

Beattie, M. (1992). *Codependent no more -How to stop controlling others and start caring for yourself.* New York: Harper Collins.

Beck, A.T., Rush, A.J., Shaw, B.F., & Emery, G. (1979). *Cognitive therapy of depression: A treatment manual.* New York: Guilford.

Beck, A. & Emery, G. (1985). *Anxiety disorders and phobias.* New York: Basic Books.

Belsky, J., Steinburg, L. & Draper, P. (1991). Childhood experience, interpersonal development, and reproductive strategy: An evolutionary theory of socialization. *Child Development, 62,* 647-670.

Benjamin, J. (1974). Structural Analysis of Social Behavior. *Psychological Review, 81,* 392-425.

Berglund, M. (1984). Suicide in alcoholism: A prospective study of 88 suicides. *Archives of General Psychiatry, 41,* 888-891.

Berne, E. (1961). *Transactional analysis in psychotherapy.* New York: Grove Press.

_____ (1963). *Structure and dynamics of groups and organizations.* Philadelphia: Lippincott.

_____ (1964). *Games people play.* New York: Grove Press.

_____ (1966). *Principles of group treatment.* New York: Oxford University Press.

_____ (1972). *What do you say after you say hello?* New York: Grove Press.

Black, C. (1981). *It will never happen to me.* Denver, CO: M.A.C. Printing.

Blackson, T.C., Tarter, R.E., Martin, C.S., Moss, H.B. (1994). Temperament mediates the effects of family history of substance abuse on externalizing and internalizing child behavior. *The American journal on addictions, 3 (1),* 58-66.

Blatner, H.A. (1973). *Acting in: Practical applications of psychodramatic methods.* New York: Springer.

Blau, P.M. & Duncan, P.D. (1967). *The American occupation structure.* New York: Wiley.

Bowen, M. (1976). Therapy in the practice of psychotherapy. In P.J. Goverin, Jr. (ed.) *Family therapy: theory and practice.* New York: Gardner Press.

_____ (1978). *Family therapy in clinical practice.* New York: Aronson.

Boszormenyi-Naggy, I., & Spark, G. (1973). *Invisible loyalties.* New York: Harper and Row.

Breier, A., & Strauss, J.S. (1984). The Role of social relationships in the recovery from psychotic disorders. *American Journal of Psychiatry, 141,* 949-955.

S. Brockway. (1987). Group Treatment of Combat Nightmares in Post-traumatic Stress Disorder. *Journal of Contemporary Psychotherapy 17 (4),* 270-284.

Brown F.(1961). Depression and childhood bereavement. *Journal of Mental Science, 107,* 754-777.

Brown, R.W. & Kottler, J.A. (1992). *Introduction to therapeutic counseling (2nd ed.).* Pacific Grove, CA: Brooks/Cole Publishing Company.

Brown, S. & Yalom, I. (1977). Interactional Group Therapy with Alcoholics. *Journal of Studies on Alcohol 38,* 426-456.

Bradley, B.P., Gossop,M., et al (1992). Attributions and relapse in opiate addicts. *Journal of consulting and clinical psychology, 60 (3),* 470-472.

Buchanan, R.O. (1984). Morenos social atom: A diagnostic and treatment tool for exploring interpersonal relationships. *The arts in psychotherapy, 11,* 115-164.

Butheil, T. & Gabbard, G. (1993). The Concepts of Boundaries in Clinical Practice: Theoretical and Risk-Management Dimensions. *American Journal of Psychiatry 150,* 188-196.

Carter, E.A. & McGoldrick, M. (eds.), (1988). *The Changing family life cycle (2nd ed.).* New York: Gardner Press.

Certification Board for Addiction Professionals of Florida (1990). *Code of ethics and conduct.* Tallahassee, FL: Author.

Charatan, F. (1985). Depression and the elderly: Diagnosis and treatment. *Psychiatric Annals, 15,* 313-316.

Ciraulo, D.A., Barnhill, J.G., A.M., Greenblatt, D.J., & Shader, R.I. (1989). Parental alcoholism as a risk factor in benzodiazepine abuse: A pilot study. *American Journal of Psychiatry, 146 (10),* 1333-1335.

Clarke, J.L. (1993). *The sexual functioning of adult women molested as children: A review of empirical studies.* Biola University: Doctoral research paper.

Cohn, L.D. (1991). Sex differences in the course of personality development: A meta-analysis. *Psychological Bulletin. 2, (109)* 252-226.

Compernolle, T. (1981). J.L. Moreno: An unrecognized pioneer of family therapy. *Family process, 20,* 331-335.

Cormier, L. & Bernard, J. (1982). Ethical and legal responsibilities of clinical supervisors. *Personnel and guidance journal, 60 (8),* 486-490.

Corsini, R. J., Freud, Rogers & Moreno (1956). *Group Psychotherapy, 9,* 274-281.

Corsini, R. J. (Eds.). (1981). *Handbook of innovative psychotherapies.* New York: Wiley.

Cory, G. (1985). *Theory and practice of group counseling (2nd ed.).* Monerey, CA: Brooks/Cole Publishing Company.

Craig, G.J. (1992). *Human Development (6th ed.).* Englewood Cliffs: Prentice-Hall.

Daley, D.C. (1987). Prevention with substance abusers: clinical issues and myths. *Social work, 32 (2),* 138-142.

Doherty, W.T., (1981). Cognitive processes in initmate conflict; I. Extending attribution theory. *American journal of family therapy, 9 (1),* 3-13.

Dowd, T.E. & Seibel, C.A. (1990). A cognitive theory of resistance: Implications for treatment. *Journal of mental health counseling, 12 (4),* 458-469.

Doyle, R.E. (1992). *Essential skills and strategies in the helping process.* Pacific Grove, CA: Brooks/Cole.

Dupree, L.W. & Schonfeld, L. (1986). *Assessment and treating planning for alcohol abusers A curriculum manual.* Tampa FL: Florida Mental Health Institute.

Durant, W., Durant, A. (1975). *The Story of Civilization Vol. 1-13.* New York: Simon and Schuster.

Dusay, J. (1977). Four phrases of TA, In G. Barnes (Eds.), *Transactional analysis after Eric Berne.* New York: Harpers College Press.

Dusay, J. (1977). *Egograms: HowI see you and you see me.* New York: Harper and Row.

Ellis, A. & Grieger, R. (1977). *Handbook of Rational-emotive therapy.* New York: Springer.

Ellis, A. (1982). *Rational-emotive therapy and cognitive behavior therapy.* New York: Springer.

Egan, G. (1990). *The skilled helper.* (4th ed.). Pacific Grove, CA: Brooks/Cole Publishing Company.

Ensel, W.M. (1982). The role of age in the relationship of gender and marital status to depression. *Journal of Nervous and Mental Diseases, 170,* 536-543.

Erfurt, J.C., Foote, A. (1992). Who is following the recovering alcoholic? Examining the role of follow-up in employee assistance programs. *Alcohol health and research world, 16* (2). 154-159.

Erikson, E.H. (1963). *Childhood and society.* (2nd ed.). New York: Norton.

_____(1968). *Identify: Youth and Crises.* New York: Norton.

Ettin, M. (1988). By the Crowd They Have Been Broken, By the Crowd They Shall Be Healed: The Advent of Group Psychotherapy. *International Journal of Group Psychotherapy 38* 139-167.

Farkas, G. et al. (1990). Culture Resources and School Success: Gender, Ethnicity, and Poverty Groups within Urban School District. *American Sociological Review 55.* 127-142.

Finkel, J. (1992). Development tasks of the long-lived marriage. *Journal of adult development, 12,* 36-51.

Flanders, N. (1965). *Teacher Influence - Pupil Attitudes and Achievement.* Washington, D.C.: H.E.W. Monograph 12.

Framo, J.L. (1981). The interaction of marital therapy with sessions of family of origin. *Handbook of family therapy.*

Frankl, V. (1960). Paradoxical intention: A logotherapeutic technique. *American Journal of Psychotherapy , 14,* 520-535.

Freud, S. (1919). Lines of advance in psycho-analytic therapy. *The Complete psychological works, the standard edition, 17* 157-168.

_____ (1960). *Group Psychology and Analysis of the Ego.* New York: Bantam Books.

Freud, A. (1936). *The ego and mechanisms of defense.* New York: International Universities Press.

Fromm, E. (1941). *Escape from Freedom.* New York: Farrar & Rinehart.

_____ (1947). *Man for Himself.* New York: Rinehart.

_____ (1956). *The Art of Loving.* New: Bantam Books.

Gabel, S. & Shindledecker, R. (1993). Parental substance abuse and its relationship to severe aggression and antisocial behavior in youth. *The American journal on addictions, 2,* 48-58.

Galanter, M. (1988). Zealous Self-Help Groups to Psychiatric Treatment: A Study of Recovery, Inc. *American Journal of Psychiatric, 145,* 1248-1253.

Gans, J. (1989). Hostility in Group Therapy. *International Journal of Group Psychotherapy, 39,* 499-517.

_____ (1991). The Leader's Use of Metaphor in Group Therapy. *International Journal of Psychotherapy, 41,* 127-145.

Ganzarain, R. (1992). Introduction to Object Relations Group Psychotherapy. *International Journal of Psychotherapy, 42,* 205-223.

Gleuck, S., & Glueck, E. (1959). *Predicting delinquency and crime.* Cambridge, Mass.: Harvard University Press.

Gold, M.S. (1984). *800-Cocaine.* New York: Bantam Books.

Goldenburg, I. & Goldenburg, H. (1991). *Family Therapy: An overview* (3rd ed.) Pacific Grove, CA: Brooks/Cole Publishing Company.

Gorski, T.T. (1986). *Staying Sober- a guide for relapse prevention.* Independence, MO: Independence Press.

Greenburg, J. & Mitchell, S. (1983). *Object- relations in psychoanalytic theory.* Cambridge, MA: Harvard University Press.

Haley, J. (1963). *Strategies of psychotherapy.* New York: Grune & Stratton.

_____ (1976). *Problem solving therapy.* San Francisco, CA: Jossey-Bass.

_____ (1980). *Leaving Home.* New York: McGraw-Hill.

Harris, T. (1969). *I'm OK, you're OK.* New York: Harper and Row.

Havighurst, R.J. (1972). *Development tasks and education (3rd ed.)* New York: McKay.

_____ (1962). *Growing up in River City.* New York: Wiley and Sons.

Hawton, K., Salkovskis, P.M., Kirk, J., & Clarke, D.M. (Eds.). (1989). *Cognitive behavior therapy for psychiatric problems- a partial guide.* New York: Oxford University Press.

Herr, E.L. & Cramer, S.H. (1992). *Career guidance through the life span.* (4th ed.) Boston: Little Brown.

Hoffman, L. (1981). *Foundations of family therapy.* New York: Basic Books.

Holland, J.L. (1985). *Making vocational choices: A theory of careers.* Englewood Cliffs, NJ: Prentice-Hall.

Honig, A.S. (1986). Stress in coping with young children. *Young Children, 5,* 50-63.

Horney, K. (1942). *Self-analysis.* New York: W. W. Norton.

_____ (1950). *Neurosis and Human Growth.* New York: Norton.

Horowitz, M.J. (1985). Disasters and psychological responses to stress. *Psychiatric Annals, 15,* 161-167.

Hsu, L.K.G. (1980). Outcome of anorexia nervosa: A review of the literature. *Archives of General Psychiatric, 37,* 1041-1046.

James, M. (1978). Self-reparenting. *Transactional Analysis Journal, 4,* 3.

Janoff-Bulman, R. (1985). The aftermath of victimization: Rebuilding shattered assumptions. *Trauma and its wake.*

Jellinek, E.M. (1960). *The disease concept of alcoholism.* Highland Park, NJ: Hillhouse.

Johnston, L.D., Bachman, J.G., & O'Malley, P.M. (1981). Drugs and the nation's high school students. *Drug abuse in the modern world: A perspective for the eighties.* 87-98.

Jones, M. (1953). *The Therapeutic Community.* New York: Basic Books.

Jung, C.G. (1934). *The archetypes and the collective unconscious.* Collecting Works. Vol. 9, Part 1. Bollingen Series XX. Princeton, NJ: Princeton University Press.

530   *More Than Words*

Kahler, T (1975). Scripts: Process and content. *Transactional Analysis Journal, 5,* 277-279.

Katon, W., Egan, K., & Miller, D. (1985). Chronic pain: Lifetime psychiatric diagnoses and family history. *American Journal of Psychiatric, 142,* 1156-1160.

Kellerman, P.F. (1979). Transference, countertransference and tele. *Psychodrama and sociometry, 32,* 38-55.

Kendra, J. (1977). Research presentation at ITAA Conference in 1973. *Egograms: How I see you and you see me.* San Francisco: Harper and Row.

Kinney, J. & Leaton, G. (1987). *Loosening the Grip (3rd ed.).* St.Louis, MO: Times Mirror/Mosby College Publishing.

Kitchener, K. (1984). Intuition, critical evaluation and ethical principles: the foundation for ethical decisions in counseling psychology. *The Counseling Psychologist, 12 (3),* 43-45.

Klerman, G.L., Weissman, M.M., Rounsaville, B.J., & Cheveon, R.S. (1984). *Interpersonal psychotherapy of depression.* New York: Basic Books.

Kohlberg, L. (1984). *Essays on moral development: The psychology of moral development.* (vol. 2) New York: Harper and Row.

Kolodny, R.C. (1983). *Sexual issues in id-adulthood.* Las Vegas, NV: Presented at the Las Vegas Symposium.

Kopp, R.R. & Kivel, C. (1990). Traps and escapes: An Adlerian approach to understanding resistance and resolving impasses in psychotherapy. *Individual psychology, 46 (2),* 139-147.

Kubler-Ross, E. (1969). *On Death and Dying.* New York: Macmillan.Kushner, M.G., Sher, K.J., & Bertman, B.D. (1990). The relation between alcohol problems and the anxiety disorders. *American Journal of Psychiatric, 147(6),* 685-695.

Lahey, B.B., Piacentini, J., McBurnett, K., Stone, P., Hartdagen, S., & Hynd, G. (1988). Psychopathology in the parents of children with conduct disorder and hyperactivity. *Journal of the American Academy of Child and Adolescent Psychiatry, 25* (2). 163-170.

Lazarus, A.A (1989). *The practice of multimodal therapy.* Baltimore, MD: Johns Hopkins University Press.

Levenson, E. (1972). *The fallacy of understanding.* New York: Basic Books.

Lieberman, M., Yalom, I., & Miles, M. (1973). *Encounter Groups: First Facts.* New York: Basic Books.

Lieberman, M., & Borman, L. (1979). *Self-Help Groups for Coping with Crisis.* San Francisco, CA: Jossey-Bass.

Lieberman, M. (1993). Self-Help Groups. *Group Psychotherapy,* 300-301.

Linehan, M.M. (1993). *Cognitive-behavioral treatment of borderline personality disorder.* New York: Guilford Press.

Mabe. A. & Rollins, S. (1986). The role of a code of ethical standards in counseling. *Journal of counseling and development, 64* (5), 295-297.

Macionis, J.J. (1989). *Sociology.* (2nd ed.). Englewod Cliffs, N.J.: Prentice-Hall.

Marmar, C.R., Foy, D., Kagan, B., & Pynoos, R.S. (1993). An integrated approach for treating posttraumatic stress. *Review of psychiatry, vol. 12.* 239-272.

Marlett, G.A. (1983). The controlled drinking controversy. *American psychologist, 38,* 1097-1110.

Maslow, A. (1954). *Motivation and personality.* New York: Harper and Brothers.

_____ (1963). The need to know and the fear of knowing. *Journal of general psychology 68,* 111-125.

_____ (1972). *The farther reaches of human nature.* New York: Viking Press.

Masters, W.H., Johnson, V.E., & Kolodny, R.C. (1988). *Human sexuality* (3rd ed.). Glenview, IL: Scott, Forescman and Company.

May, R. (Ed.). (1961). *Existential psychology.* New York: Random House.

Maziade, M., Caron, C., Cote, R., Merette, C., Bernier, H., Laplante, B., Boutin, P., & Thivierge, J. (1990). Psychiatric status of adolescents who had extreme temperaments at age 7. *American Journal of Psychiatry, 147,* 1531-1536.

McGoldrick, M., Gerson, r. (1985). *Genograms in family assessment.* New York: Norton.

McGoldrick, M., Pearce, J., & Giordano, J. (1982). *Ethnicity and family therapy.* New York: Guilford Press.

Minuchin, S., et al. (1967). *Families of the slum.* New York: Basic Books.

_____ (1984). *Family kaleidoscope.* Cambridge, MA: Harvard University Press.

Moreno, J. (1934). *Who shall survive?* New York: Beacon House.

_____ (1937). Interpersonal therapy and psychopathology of interpersonal relations. *Sociometry* Vol.1, No. 1.

_____ (1939). Psychodramatic shock therapy. *Sociometry 2.* 1-30.

_____ (1940). Psychodramatic treatment of psychoses. *Sociometry,* Vol. 3, No.2.

_____ (1940). Mental catharsis and the psychodrama. *Sociometry,* Vol. 3, No.3.

_____ (1944). *A case of paranoia treated through psychodrama, proceedings of the second brief Psychotherapy Council.* Chicago: The Institute for Psychoanalysis.

_____ (1944). Psychodramatic approach to performance neurosis. *Psychodrama Monograph,* No.2.

_____ (1964). *Psychodrama.* (Vol. 1), (Rev. ed.). Beacon, NY: Beacon House.

Murphy, D.L., & Pigott, T.A. (1990). A comparative examination of a role for serotonin in obsessive-compulsive disorder, panic disorder, and anxiety. *Journal of clinical psychiatry, 51,* 53-60.

Nace, E.P. & Davis, C.W. (1993). Treatment outcome in substance-abusing patients with a personality disorder. *The American journal on addictions, 2 (1),* 26-33.

Narcotics Anonymous (1988). *Narcotics Anonymous (Basic Text).* Van Nuys, CA: World Services.

_____ (1993). *Narcotics Anonymous - It works. How and why.* Van Nuys, CA: World Services.

Nuckols, C.C., Mowery, J., & Toff, D. (1992). *Affirming the adolescent in you: A new approach to working with anger, depression, and addiction.* Manuscript submitted for publication.

Papajohn, J., & Spiegel, J. (1975). *Transactions families.* San Francisco: Jossey-Bass.

Paul, J., & Paul, M. (1983). *Do I have to give up me to be loved by you.* Minneapolis, MH: CompCare Publications.

Perls, F.S. (1973). *The Gestalt Approach.* Palo Alto, CA: Science and Behavior Books.

Perry, J., & Cooper, S.H. (1989). An empirical study of defense mechanisms. *Archives of general psychiatry, 46,* 444-452.

Piaget, J. (1954). *The construction of reality in the child.* New York: Basic Books.

Redfield, J. (1993). *The celestine prophecy.* New York: Warner Books.

_____ (1996). *The tenth insight: Holding the vision.* New York: Warner Books.

_____ (1999). *The Secret of Shambhala: In search of the Eleventh In sight.* New York: Warner Books.

Redmond, D.E., Jr. (1979). New and old evidence for the involvement of a brain norepinephrine system on anxiety. *Phenomenology and treatment of anxiety.* 153-203.

Rittenhouse, J.D. (1982). Drugs in the school: The shape of rug abuse among American youth in the seventies. *Drug abuse in the modern world: A perspective for the eighties.* 99-105.

Robins L.N. (1966). *Deviant children grown up.* Baltimore: Williams and Wilkens.

Roe, A. (1956). *The psychology of occupations.* New York: Wiley.

_____ (1957). Early determinants of vocational choice. *Journal of Counseling Psychology, 4,* 212-214.

Rogers, C.R. (1961). *On becoming a person.* Boston: Houghton Mifflin.

_____ (1970). *Carl Rogers on encounter groups.* New York: Harper and Row.

_____ (1972). *On becoming partners: Marriage and its alternatives.* New York: Delacourte.

Rosenthal. R & Jacobson, L. (1968). *Pygmalion in the classroom.* New York: Holt, Rinehart & Winston.

Rosenthal, R.N., Hellerstein, D.J., & Miner, C.R. (1992). A model of integrated services for outpatient treatment of patients with co-morbid schizophrenia and addictive disorders. *The American journal on addictions.*

Roy, A. (1985). Early parental separation and adult depression. *Archives of General Psychiatry, 42,* 987-991.

Roy, A., Adinoff, B., Roehich, L., Lamparski, D., Custer, R., Lorenz, V., Barbaccia, M., Guidotti, A., Costa, E., & Linnoila, M. (1988). Pathological gamblers. *Archives of General Psychiatry, 45,* 369-373.

Roy, A., DeJong, J., & Linnoila, M. (1989). Extraversion in pathological gamblers. *Archives of General Psychiatry, 46,* 679-681.

Rychtorik, R.G., Prue, D.H. et al. (1992). Self-efficacy, aftercare and relapse in a treatment program for alcoholics. *Journal of studies on alcohol, 53,* (5), 435-440.

Salvendy, J. (1989). Brief group therapy at retirement. *Group, 13,* 43-57.

Santrock, J.W. (1992). *Adolescence.* (4th ed.) Dallas, Texas: Wm. C. Brown Publishers.

Sarason, I.G. & Sarason, B.R. (1993). *Abnormal psychology: the problem of maladptive behavior* (7th ed.). Englewood Cliffs, NJ: Prentice-Hall.

Satir, V.M. & Baldwin, M. (1983). *Satir step by step: A guide to creating change in families.* Palo Alto, CA: Science and Behavior Books.

Scheidt, D.M. & Windle, M. (1994). Axis 1 and Axis 2 co-mobidity among alcohol-disordered men in a sample of Vietnam-era veterans. *The American Journal on addictions, 3* (2), 151-159.

Schonefeld, L. & Morosko, T.E. (1988). Joining forces rather than "waging war": A commentary on alcoholism treatment. *Journal of mental health counseling, 10,* (3), 171-178.

Shapiro, D. (1979), *Neurotic styles.* New York: Basic Books.

Sheeley, V. & Herlihy, B. (1986). The ethics of confidentiality and privileged communication. *Journal of counseling and human services professionals, 1* (1), 141-148.

Silberman, C. (1970). *Crisis in the classroom.* New York: Random House.

Small, S.A., Luster, T. (1994). Adolescent sexual activity: An ecological risk-factor approach. *Journal of marriage and the family, 56,* 181-192.

Solomon, S.D., Gerrity, G.E., & Muff, A.M. (1992). Efficacy of treatment for posttraumatic stress disorder. *Journal of the American Medical Association, 268,* 633-638.

Starr, A. (1977). *Psychodrama: Rehearsal for living.* Chicago: Nelson-Hall.

Steiner, C. (1964). A script checklist. *Transactional Analysis Bulletin, 6,* 38-39.

_____ (1970). *Games alcoholics play.* New York: Grove Press.

_____ (1971). *Scripts people play.* New York: Grove Press.

Stevens, M.J.. Pfost, K.S., & Potts, M.K. (1990). Sex-role orientation and the willingness to confront existential issues. *Journal of counseling and development, 68,* 414-416.

Sullivan, W.P., Wolk, J.L., & Hartman, D. (1992). Case management in alcohol and drug treatment: Improving client outcomes. *Families in society: The journal of contemporary human services, 73* (4), 195-204.

Super, D.E. (1957). *The psychology of careers.* New York: Harper & Brothers.

_____ (1970). *Work values inventory.* Boston: Houghton Mifflin.

_____ (1977). Vocational maturity in mid-career. *Vocational Guidance Quarterly, 25,* 297.

_____ (1980). A life-span, life-space approach to career development. *Journal of Vocational Behavior, 16,* 282-298.

Tater RE

Telner, J.I., & Singhal, R.L. (1984). Psychiatric progress: The learned helplessness model of depression. *Journal of psychiatric research, 18* (3), 207-215.

Tennyson, W. & Strom, S. (1986). Beyond professional standards: Developing responsibilities. *Journal of counseling and development, 64* (5), 298-302.

Terr, L. (1991). Childhood traumas: An outline and overview. *American Journal of Psychiatric, 148,* 10-20.

Thompson G. (1972). The identification of ego states. *Transactional Analysis Journal, 2,* 196-211.

Toseland, R. & Hacker, L. (1982). Self-help groups and professional involvement. *Social Work, 27,* 341-347.

Travers, R.M. (1972). *Essentials of learning* (3rd ed.). New York: The MacMillan Company.

United States Department of Human Services (1987) *Confidentiality of alcohol and drug abuse records.* Federal Register 42CFR Part 11: 21796-21814.

United States Department of Labor (1992-1993). *Occupational outlook handbook.* Washington, D.C.: U.S. Government Printing Office.

Ursano, R.J., & Hales, R.E. (1986). A review of brief individual psychotheralpies. *American Journal of Psychiatry, 143,* 1507-1517.

Vaillant, G.E. (1971). Theoretical hierarchy of adaptive ego mechanisms. *Archives of General Psychiatry, 24,* 107-118.

Vernon, J., et al. (1961). The effect of human isolation upon some perceptual and motor skills. *Sensory deprivation.*

Victor, M., & Adams, R.D. (1953). The effect of alcohol on the nervous system. *Proceedings of the Association for Research in Nervous and Mental Diseases.*

Victor, M., Adams, R.D., & Collins, G.H. (1989). *The Wernicke-Kosakoff syndrome.* (2nd ed.). Philadelphia: F.A. Davis.

Warnat, C.F. (1975). Vocational theories: Directions to nowhere. *Personnel and Guidance Journal, 53,* (6), 422-428.

Weiss, R.D., Griffin, M.L., Hufford, C. (1992). Severity of cocaine dependence as a predictor of relapse to cocaine use. *American Journal of Psychiatry, 149* (11), 1595-1596.

Weiss, R.D, & Collins, D.A. (1992). Substance abuse and psychiatric illness: The dually diagnosed patient. *The American Journal on addictions, 1* (2), 93-99.

Wegschedier, S. (1987). *Another chance: Hope and behavior for the alcoholic family* (2nd ed.). Palo Alto, CA: Science and Behavior Books.

Wehr, T.A., & Rosenthal, N.E. (1989). Seasonality and affective illness. *American Journal of Psychiatry, 146,* 829-839.

Wells, K.C. & Egan, J. (1988). Social learning and systems family therapy for childhood oppositional disorder: Comparative treatment outcome. *Comprehensive Psychiatry, 29,* 138-146.

Whelen, C. & Teddlie, C. (1989). Self-fulfilling prophecy and attribution for responsibility: Is there a casual link to achievement? *ERIC Ed. 323211.*

White, K. & Strange, C. (1993). Effects of unwanted childhood sexual experiences of psychosocial development of college women. *Journal of college student development, 4,* (34), 289-294.

Wilens, T.E., O'Keefe, J.O., O'Connell, J.J., Springer, R., Spencer, T. (1993). A public dual diagnosis detoxification unit: Part 2: Observations of 70 dually diagnosed patients. *The American Journal on addictions, 2* (3), 181-193.

Wilkins, W. (1973). Client's expectancy of therapeutic gain: Evidence for the active role of the therapist. *Psychiatry, 36,* 184-190.

Woititz, J. (1983). *Adult children of alcoholics.* Deerfield Beach, FL: Health Communications, Inc.

_____ (1990). *Adult children of alcoholics* (Expanded version). Deerfield Beach, FL: Health Communications Inc.

Woody, J.D. (1990). Resolving ethical concerns in clinical practice: Toward a pragmatic model. *Journal of marital and family therapy, 16* (2), 133-150.

Yablonsky, L. (1976). *Psychodrama.* New York: Basic Books.

Yalom, I. (1966). A study of group therapy dropouts. *Archives of General Psychiatry, 14,* 393-414.

_____ (1967). Prediction of improvement in group therapy. *Archives of General Psychiatry, 17,* 159-168.

Yalom,I. & Greaves, C. (1977). Group therapy for the terminally ill. *American Journal of Psychiatry, 134,* 396-400.

Yalom, I. (1980). *Existential psychotherapy.* New York: Basic Books.

_____ (1983). *Impatient group Psychotherapy.* New York: Basic Books.

_____ (1992). *When Nietzsche wept.* New York: Basic Books.

_____ (1995). *The theory and practice of group psychotherapy.* (4th ed.). New York: Basic Books.